ADDITIONAL PRAISE

"In high school, R. H. Blyth's four-volume *Haiku* was the first book on Japan I read. Together with his books on senryū and his translation/commentary on *Mumonkan*, I have continually reread them for inspiration and pleasure and relied on them as valuable references. I knew little about the man himself—nobody did in those days. Fortunately, *Poetry and Zen* finally fleshes out the life of this eccentric scholar. The book also provides the background for the remarkable internationalization of Zen in the second half of the twentieth century. On all fronts, *Poetry and Zen* is an enjoyable read."
—John Stevens, translator of *The Art of Peace*

"Blyth's previously unpublished writings are reason enough to purchase this book. A second reason its quality of the writing. One aspect that Blyth found vital in haiku and senryū is humor, which he called 'the dance of life.' His essays back up this claim, making reading them a pleasure. Along the way, Blyth compares haiku to senryū, to mysticism, to Zen, to Western literature, to Christian texts, to Buddhism, and to Western humor, to name a few. He also writes about Suzuki and Aitken, bringing new light to their notable Zen lives and teachings. For anyone who has not read Blyth, a treat awaits you. And for those who have, there is much more still to enjoy."
—Stephen Addiss, author of *The Art of Zen*

POETRY

AND

ZEN

*Letters and Uncollected
Writings of R. H. Blyth*

EDITED WITH AN INTRODUCTION BY
NORMAN WADDELL

SHAMBHALA

Shambhala Publications, Inc.
2129 13th Street
Boulder, Colorado 80302
www.shambhala.com

Cover Art: "Cherry Blossoms" The Harry G. C. Packard Collection of Asian Art, Gift
of Harry G. C. Packard, and Purchase, Fletcher, Rogers, Harris Brisbane Dick, and
Louis V. Bell Funds, Joseph Pulitzer Bequest, and The Annenberg Fund Inc. Gift, 1975
Cover Design: Erin Seaward-Hiatt
Interior design: Katrina Noble

9 8 7 6 5 4 3 2 1

First Edition
Printed in the United States of America

⊗ This edition is printed on acid-free paper that meets the
American National Standards Institute Z39.48 Standard.
♻ This book is printed on 30% postconsumer recycled paper.
For more information please visit www.shambhala.com.
Shambhala Publications is distributed worldwide by
Penguin Random House, Inc., and its subsidiaries.

LIBRARY OF CONGRESS CATALOGING-IN-PUBLICATION DATA
Names: Blyth, Reginald Horace author. | Waddell, Norman, editor.
Title: Poetry and Zen: letters and uncollected writings of R. H. Blyth /
edited with an introduction by Norman Waddell.
Description: First edition. | Boulder: Shambhala, 2022.
Identifiers: LCCN 2021026481 | ISBN 9781611809985 (trade paperback)
Subjects: LCSH: Blyth, Reginald Horace—Correspondence. |
Critics—Japan—Correspondence. | Critics—England—Correspondence. |
Buddhist scholars—Japan—Correspondence. | Buddhist
scholars—England—Correspondence. | Haiku—Translating into English. |
Haiku—History and criticism.
Classification: LCC PL713.B69 A25 2022 | DDC 828/.91209—dc23
LC record available at https://lccn.loc.gov/2021026481

CONTENTS

EDITOR'S PREFACE

MOST OF THE MATERIAL IN THIS BOOK WAS ORIGINALLY ASSEM-
bled over fifty years ago when I was compiling a volume of R. H. Blyth's
miscellaneous writings—articles and essays that had appeared in magazines
and journals, book reviews, introductions written for student textbooks—
for his publisher Hokuseido Press in Tokyo. I was working with Nakatsuchi
Jumpei, president of Hokuseido Press, contemplating something along the
lines of D. H. Lawrence's *Phoenix* (1936), although I wanted it to include a
selection of letters as well. In the course of the project, I made the acquain-
tance of two of Blyth's closest friends, his cousin Dora Lord (Dora Orr after
her marriage in the 1950s) and Robert Aitken. They both readily agreed to
help, kindly providing encouragement and numerous insights into Blyth's
personal life and copies of the letters they had received from him. Dora
even included a group of letters to Blyth's parents that his mother, Hetty,
had entrusted to her. The letters to Dora were of special importance since
they provided virtually the only record of Blyth and his daily life during the
prewar period (1929–1940) when he was teaching in Korea, a period that
has hitherto been virtually a blank.

When I began the project in the late 1960s, his books—almost all of
them published by Hokuseido Press—had very poor distribution in the
West. Blyth himself was perfectly happy with that arrangement. In a letter
to Nakatsuchi Jumpei, Blyth wrote that having him as a publisher "was one
of the (few) luckiest things in my life. . . . I don't want to make any money.
I only want to write books and eat. To write excellent books is my greatest
pleasure. The second is to have you as my publisher." He often stated that
one good reader was enough for him.

Nonetheless, one of my aims in compiling the original miscellany was
to make Blyth better known overseas, in America and continental Europe.

It seemed to me that the best way to draw attention to the book would be to induce one of his well-known admirers in the American artistic community to contribute a foreword. I knew from Blyth's letters that he had corresponded with the novelist J. D. Salinger, so I wrote Salinger, told him about the proposed book, and asked if he would consider writing an introduction.

I felt fairly sure that Salinger had never written such a foreword before and had no great hopes of even receiving an answer. But answer he did, quite promptly, and in a kind, warmhearted manner. "I can't tell you what his books have meant to me," he wrote. "The idea of a miscellany interests me very much . . . For a first posthumous book . . . it seems to me right to show Blyth first, away from his beloved haiku, at his miscellaneous best." His readiness to agree to write the foreword was, of course, extremely encouraging, but, as the Chinese say, "Many things have good beginnings; few reach a successful end."

It was over a year later, August 1968, when Salinger's next letter arrived. He apologized for failing to write earlier, saying that the past year had been "an unquiet one" for him: "I'm very sorry. Blyth surely deserves something or someone better and zennier." But as he also said in ending the letter that he would "no doubt be pulling [himself] together within the year," and I was as convinced as ever that he was the right person for the job. I decided to wait a bit longer and give things a chance to work themselves out.

There was, however, no word for another year or more. By this time, though still harboring hopes for an introduction, I began to get caught up in other priorities, teaching and translating. The project fell by the wayside, and I had no further contact with Salinger for more than twenty years.

Although I had packed the material away, the idea of the miscellany was never completely out of mind. I mulled over one other piece of advice Salinger had given, against including Blyth's letters in the book. He objected as a matter of principle to publishing a writer's letters unless the writer himself had authorized it. Later, in the 1990s, when I got to know him personally, he was even more adamant on this point, perhaps as a result of the widely reported troubles he had recently gone through concerning the publication of his own letters. In any case, there was no reason to press the point any further, and that is how the matter ended.

The boxes were still on a back shelf in 2011, forty years later, when I was invited to give lectures on the Suzuki-Blyth relationship at a memorial library dedicated to Blyth's mentor Daisetz Suzuki. I brought the boxes out and combed through the material once again, thinking it would jog my memory. In reading through the letters, it didn't take long for me to see, with much greater clarity than before, the importance of getting them published, if only for the valuable firsthand information they contained about the role Blyth played in the immediate postwar period, when the Imperial system, the Japanese government, and society itself were undergoing drastic and fundamental change.

Today, Blyth's books are mostly out of print and hard to come by. If he is remembered at all, it is probably as the "father" of the international haiku movement. It is my hope that this miscellany, though long overdue, will help to spur new interest in Blyth, perhaps inspiring a new generation of readers to turn to his major works and be afforded their first glimpse of the storehouse of treasures that Blyth opened for readers of my generation.

The number of works on haiku, both translations and commentary, has of course grown enormously in the fifty-odd years since Blyth's books appeared, but I believe that many of today's readers would agree that his marvelous translations, and his enlightening comments on them, remain unsurpassed. His translations of classical Zen texts may in some cases have been superseded—that is only to be expected, given the great advances in scholarship that have taken place. As for "Blyth's Zen," whatever it may be, and it is certainly not of the orthodox variety—not Beat, nor Square, nor garden variety either, far from it—I would still contend that so far no one has spoken or written so freely and eloquently about "Zen" in English as R. H. Blyth has.

I would like to thank Ian Hamilton for his assistance, sound counsel, and word processing skills that have been invaluable in the preparation of this volume. I apologize for failing to thank or even worse (alas) to remember all the many friends who have kindly and generously responded over the half-century that has elapsed since this work first began to an endless variety of questions about correct dates and clarification of other points of fact. But I am deeply grateful to them.

POETRY
AND
ZEN

INTRODUCTION

THIS VOLUME CONTAINS A SELECTION OF THE LETTERS, UNCOL-
lected articles and reviews, and posthumous papers of Reginald Horace
Blyth (1898–1964), a man whose books on Zen, Japanese culture, and the
Japanese verse forms of haiku and senryū (the satirical cousin of haiku)
captured the imagination of a great many readers in the English-speaking
world in the decades following World War II. His inimitable style and illu-
minating wit struck a particularly sensitive chord in the artistic community,
providing inspiration to many poets, writers, and artists and playing a sig-
nificant role in kindling Western interest in Zen and haiku. Blyth's pene-
trating insights on these and related topics in a series of over a dozen major
works published between 1942 and 1970 helped lay the foundation for the
remarkable expansion of Zen in the West and the global popularization of
haiku as an international verse form, which took place after his death.

Blyth, who expressed reservations about composing haiku in English,
also wrote that "haiku should be the chief subject in primary and secondary
schools in every country in the world . . . but it should be prohibited in the
universities."[1] He could hardly have imagined how prescient this tongue-
in-cheek comment would turn out to be. A decade or two after his death,
haiku would appear in school curriculums around the world and become an
influential part of world culture. His translations and writings on haiku and
senryū were so seminal to the global spread of these verse forms that with-
out Blyth, it seems unlikely it would have happened and certain it would
not have happened as it did.

I first discovered Blyth's works over sixty years ago. A friend showed me
a copy of *Zen in English Literature and Oriental Classics*. "I think you might
like this," he said. I did indeed, so much so that I was moved for the first and
only time in my life to sit down and write the author. I received a beautiful

handwritten letter from Blyth in return, thanking me for my comments and saying that he would send me any of his other books I didn't have. This led to a brief correspondence and eventually to my decision to go to Japan to meet him. He died shortly before I was able to make the trip, but I went anyway. A trip that pretty much decided the future course of my life.

Zen in English Literature and Oriental Classics, his first and perhaps still most influential book, was published in Tokyo in 1942, a few months after the attack on Pearl Harbor. Although Blyth was interned for the duration of the war as an enemy alien, as soon as hostilities ended, he moved to Tokyo and busily set to work finishing up further volumes on his chosen subjects, publishing superb translations of Japanese haiku and senryū accompanied by inspired commentary that revealed, as no one before him had done, their significance as poetry and their intimate kinship with religion and the larger scheme of life and art. He was at the same time writing books on another of his favorite themes: humor—Japanese and Asian humor, humor in English literature, world humor. From then on until his death, he never ceased writing assiduously, publishing the series *Zen and Zen Classics* (1960–1970) dealing with traditional Zen history and the classic texts of China and Japan, though two of the originally proposed five volumes appeared posthumously.

These achievements, I don't think it is too much to say, opened Western eyes for the first time to the inherent character and spirit of Japanese poetry and culture. It should perhaps be added in passing that the essential message of one of Blyth's central themes—the oneness of Zen with the artistic and social genius of traditional Japanese arts—was in no way inconsistent with what a long line of distinguished Zen figures and artists in the Far East had been transmitting for more than a thousand years.

Blyth expressed his thoughts on Zen, Japanese poetry, English literature, humor and culture East and West, and other subjects simply and directly in what he called his "neutral style," infusing the pages of his works with great wit and humor, apt aphorisms, and quotations that enchant the reader. In the end, what makes Blyth's works such a constant delight is not just his marvelously sensitive translations of haiku and senryū and the deep and inimitable reflections on life, poetry, and human character, but the presence of Blyth himself, shining radiantly through all his writings.

While assuming a heavy teaching load in the immediate postwar years, writing books that would reveal the unknown riches of Japanese culture to Westerners and attempting at the same time in his public lectures and

Blyth, circa 1960.

writings to point out to the defeated and demoralized Japanese themselves what he called their "true nonmilitary glory," he was also actively engaged in momentous (nonliterary) extracurricular activities for his adopted country as an unofficial liaison between General MacArthur's GHQ, the Imperial Household Agency, and high officials in the Japanese government such as Yoshida Shigeru.

He is, for example, credited with suggesting and even drafting Emperor Hirohito's *ningen sengen*, the famous speech he delivered after the war to renounce his "divinity." Another notable policy shift, the decision made by the emperor to "go out among the people"—that is, make trips throughout the country as an ordinary person—also seems to have been suggested by Blyth. Prior to this decision, Blyth had presented the emperor with a book of photographs, *The British Royal Family in Wartime*, showing King George VI's wartime visits to comfort and encourage his subjects. Nor was that the extent of Blyth's influence on the Imperial Household. Beginning in 1946 and continuing until his death eighteen years later, he served as personal tutor to Crown Prince Akihito.

BLYTH'S INFLUENCE

I will return to his liaison role in the biographical sketch that follows. First, I believe it may be helpful in introducing Blyth to a new generation of readers to present, by way of background, some of the assessments admiring contemporaries made of his life and work, prefacing them with this thumbnail sketch that Blyth wrote, at the age of sixty, for the foreword to *Japanese Life and Character in Senryū*:

> When I look back at my one and only life I find that I was led by my inner destiny to pass through certain phases, which however were not mutually exclusive, and indeed have all persisted strongly to the present time. I began with an inborn animism, the original of all Wordsworth's poetry, and then passed rather naturally to vegetarianism, which was or should have been one of the bases of Buddhism. By a fortunate chance I then came across haiku, or to speak more exactly Haiku no Michi, the Way of Haiku, which is the purely poetical (non-emotional, non-intellectual, non-moral, non-aesthetic) life in relation to nature. Next, the biggest bit of luck of all, Zen, through the books of Suzuki Daisetz. Zen is what we hear in the music of Bach, which tells us that all things, including pain and death, that is, annihilation, come from the loving hands of God. Last but not least there appeared senryū, which might well be dignified by the term Senryū no Michi, the Way of Senryū, for it is an understanding of all things by laughing or smiling at them, and this means forgiving all things, ourselves and God included. It is strange that animism, vegetarianism, haiku, Zen and senryū should blend so easily and comfortably, and there seems to be something oddly right too about their chronological order.[2]

Blyth's discovery of Suzuki was a defining event in his life. Suzuki had published a series of books in English in the decades leading up to World War II in an attempt to introduce Zen and Mahayana Buddhist teachings to Western audiences. Although at the time their distribution was limited, when they were republished after the war, they, and the works of his student, collaborator, and friend Blyth, played an important role in awakening the remarkable interest in Zen Buddhism that emerged during that period.

Blyth's great esteem for Suzuki's writings is conveyed throughout his works. Although he dedicated his first book, *Zen in English Literature and Oriental Classics*, to his Zen teacher Kayama Taigi (also given as Daigi) Rōshi and his four-volume *Haiku* to Prime Minister Yoshida Shigeru, who had financed its publication, his other books all bore tributes to Suzuki:

> Dedicated (as all my books should have been) to Daisetz Suzuki.
> Dedicated to Daisetz Suzuki who taught me that I knew.
> Dedicated as all my books shall be to Daisetz Suzuki, who taught me all that I don't know.
> Dedicated to Daisetz Suzuki, the only one who can write about Zen without making me loathe it.
> Dedicated to Daisetz Suzuki, who taught me not to teach.
> Dedicated to Daisetz Suzuki, the greatest Japanese of this century.
> Dedicated to Daisetz Suzuki, who can read what I can't write.

Suzuki was in his sixties at the time of Blyth's first visit. He was not a man who was easily impressed, but he seemed to form a genuine and deep regard for Blyth and his work. In a note inscribed in a daybook that has recently been published in his *Complete Works*, Suzuki states,

> Blyth San is a rare person. A great man. . . . Since he is a poet, one who has had the benefit of Zen training, we might regard him as a latter-day Koizumi Yakumo [Lafcadio Hearn].[3]

He expanded on this in an obituary of Blyth in the *Eastern Buddhist*:

> With the death of Dr. Reginald Horace Blyth on October 28, 1964, the world lost one of the most eminent exponents of Japanese culture. . . . His studies on haiku and the Japanese sense of humor as well as Zen were unique contributions towards East-West understanding. . . . *Zen and Zen Classics* were to have been in eight volumes and promised to be the most complete work on Zen so far to be presented to the English-speaking public. . . . It is regrettable, indeed, that only three volumes could see the light while he lived. Perhaps to those of us who knew him, he was first and foremost a poet with a wonderfully keen and sensitive perception.[4]

The American novelist J. D. Salinger did not know Blyth personally. They never actually met, but I believe he grasped the essence of the man as surely as Suzuki did. Falling under Blyth's spell in the 1950s after discovering *Zen in English Literature and Oriental Classics* and the four-volume *Haiku*, Salinger sent Blyth a letter of appreciation along with a gift of his recently published *Catcher in the Rye*. This led to a correspondence that continued sporadically into the early 1960s. When I wrote to Salinger in the mid-sixties informing him of Blyth's death, he replied,

> The news of Dr. Blyth's death hadn't reached me. . . . I used to send him hellos through the mail, and he was always kind enough to respond, but I never had the pleasure and honor of actually meeting him. It's very sad to lose him. An irreplaceable writer, understander, person. I can't tell you what his books have meant to me. I think he was a great artist. Possibly only Bashō and Issa and Buson and Shiki would know how fine and great an artist he was, in his unique way.

Other prominent writers were equally enthusiastic. Aldous Huxley, a close contemporary of Blyth, named one of Blyth's works as the book he would take to the proverbial desert island. Blyth's writings came as a revelation to Lawrence Durrell, who learned of them from his friend Henry Miller, another ardent Blyth admirer, and became a devotee: "Suzuki's works on Zen, Paracelsus, Boehme, Meister Eckhart—and, finally, R. H. Blyth, bless the name."[5]

The composer John Cage was a great admirer of Blyth's works. E. E. Cummings, Richard Wright, Gary Snyder, Jack Kerouac, Allen Ginsberg and other Beat Generation writers, Alan Watts, and the critic Donald Richie were all deeply in Blyth's debt. Many of them have left glowing tributes to his work. Of Blyth's book on senryū, Richie wrote, "Dr. Blyth has translated hundreds of them [senryū verses] in a manner it would underestimate to call brilliant."[6]

During a 1976 class at Naropa Institute in Boulder, Colorado, Allen Ginsberg expatiated on the importance of Blyth's four-volume anthology of haiku:

> He [Ginsberg] stressed to his class how fundamental those texts had been for the young poets [Snyder, Whalen, himself]—a bible, an ency-

clopedia, a primer in direct perception and use of concrete details, as well as in the mind that was still enough to catch these and the hand that was confident enough to set them down on paper.[7]

It soon became apparent that his students knew nothing of Blyth or his work, however, so in a somewhat exasperated response, Ginsberg went through the whole thing a second time:

> This time he told how the volumes were divided one per season, how the texts were bilingual [etc.] . . . He extemporized a rather passionate advertisement of Blythe [sic], linking him to the previous eighty years of American poetry, from the Imagists down to the Beats. Ginsberg then recounted how he and his shackmates [Kerouac, Snyder, Whalen] had treasured the books, shared them, pored over them, incorporated them into a kind of internal mutual vocabulary, eventually writing haikus of their own.

The English poet Edmund Blunden, who became friends with Blyth while teaching in Japan, felt impelled on rereading Blyth's first book to send him a postcard: "My dear Blyth. I do not think I shall ever cease to wonder with delight at this marvelously perceptive writing *Zen in English Literature and Oriental Classics.*" Christmas Humphreys, the founder of the London Buddhist Society, who met Blyth after the war when he was serving as a prosecutor in the war crimes trials in Tokyo, wrote after hearing of Blyth's death, "I found him the most utterly 'Zen man' I have ever met in a Western body." The well-known ethnomycologist Gordon Wasson, an avid reader of Blyth's haiku books, corresponded with him in final years; he no doubt spoke for many others when he wrote to Blyth, "You, and you alone, have succeeded in making the West grasp the spirit of the haiku."

Film critic Donald Richie felicitously conveyed his enthusiasm for Blyth's books in reviewing them for the *Japan Times* and other English-language newspapers. He commented on the senryū books that "to read his books is to learn and to learn is to live; to own all Dr. Blyth's senryū books is to hold a world in your hands."[8] He went on,

> Unlike most scholars, he has succumbed to none of the occupational disease of that profession, unlike most dilettantes he has produced a

most impressive body of absolutely first-rate work. To know the book is to know the man: completely learned yet completely enthusiastic; a complete sense of humor coupled with a complete subtlety when dealing with subtle matters; and completely eccentric in that precious way now fast disappearing wherein a man dares to be himself.

And again

Reginald Blyth remains the single writer to successfully weld the aesthetics of the two island nations—Great Britain and Japan. In his four volumes of haiku translations and commentary (1949–50), his two-volume haiku history (1964), and his three books on senryū, he gave the West its first full explication of these poetic forms. And in his volumes of cultural comparison, *Zen in English Literature and Oriental Classics*, *Buddhist Sermons on Christian Texts*, and his five-volume *Zen and Zen Classics*, he gave a wealth of parallels that defined religion and poetry, East and West, as alike and equal.

The artist and writer Frederick Franck was another admirer convinced of the importance of Blyth's works, writing in his introduction to an edition of Blyth's *Zen and Zen Classics*:

To my mind, R. H. Blyth is destined to become the indispensable interpreter of, and initiator into, Zen for the Western mind. His writings . . . seem to me the catalyst needed for a profound integration of Eastern and Western spirituality . . . as far as I am concerned, Blyth's openness, sanity, faith and fearlessness, his inimitable style, remain a constant delight even if it sometimes becomes appropriately uncomfortable . . . I owe him unbounded gratitude.[9]

BLYTH'S LIFE

Reginald Horace Blyth was born December 3, 1898, the only child of Horace Blyth and Henrietta (Hetty) Blyth (formerly Williams). His birth certificate records the place of birth as 93 Trumpington Road, Cann Hall, Leyton, a city located in the county of Essex northeast of London. His father

Young Blyth with harmonica.

was employed as a ticket collector for the Great Eastern Railway; the birth certificate gives his occupation as railway clerk. The family soon moved to nearby Ilford, where at the age of five, Blyth was enrolled in the Cleveland Road School. He was raised in circumstances that somehow recall the childhood and early life of his near contemporary D. H. Lawrence.

Margaret Rawlinson, a neighbor and close friend of Hetty Blyth who took care of her for many years, described Hetty in a letter to me as "a very unusual person, completely unconventional, like her son." She also wrote, "I think they must have been very close to each other—both mentally and emotionally. . . . Mrs. Blyth's husband was a gentle, retiring man." Mrs. Rawlinson reported that when Hetty learned of her son's death, she burnt all the letters he had sent her. She added that in the ones Hetty had shown her, Reggie didn't say much at all about his life in Japan.

Other glimpses of these early years appear in scattered remarks in Blyth's writings and the testimony of his first cousin and close friend Dora Lord, the recipient of many of the letters in this book. She stayed with the Blyth family for some time in her youth when Blyth was attending London

Hetty Blyth, circa 1950s.

University (1919–23). She married in 1952, and it was with Mrs. Robert Orr, then living in Canterbury, that I corresponded in the 1960s. She wrote me that Blyth was an inattentive student in his grammar school days, and it was only after entering high school that his great thirst for knowledge, which remained with him to the end, emerged. She also said, "He was a brilliant pupil at school, but not a rebel." At the age of thirteen he entered Ilford's County High School for Boys for five years of secondary education.

Blyth recalled earning pocket money by running along the station platform where his father worked, hawking chocolate to train passengers. He further reminisced about his schoolboy years in a sketch he wrote for a Japanese university newspaper:

In the primary school I was always at the bottom of the class. This was partly because I was completely unable to do any kind of sums; even now I cannot add up a row of figures without making a mistake. Partly it was because I found nothing interesting in what the teacher was saying. The only good thing about school was the ending of the day's lessons.

Dora Lord at twenty-one, 1919. Photo courtesy of Takeda Yuji.

However I was always a very "good" boy. I sat up straight, looked at the teacher's face all the time—but never listened to anything he said. When he found this out, he became very angry with me; I suppose he felt insulted.

I should mention here that my mother and father never said anything to me about being at the bottom of the class. This was very wise and kind of them. . . .

When I went to the secondary school, I began to find certain subjects interesting, English literature, and French, and a few things in geometry. . . . I now worked very hard, and strangely enough the chief reason for this was to please my parents, who would never have reproached me for poor marks. (From "'Bloodknot' Was Very Fond of Teasing Boys," on p. 247)

From 1914 or 1915 to 1916, while still a student at County High School, Blyth taught French, Spanish, and English at Highbury Park School, a preparatory school in the Islington district of north-central London. He also

Blyth at seventeen.

taught at the Cleveland Road School. "I recall him saying that he was only one lesson ahead of the pupils," recalled Dora, "mugging up from lesson to lesson" (in a letter to Oka Kuniomi, one of Blyth's students at the Preparatory School in Keijō).[10] It was during these years, if not earlier, that he was teaching himself to play a variety of musical instruments and to read German, Russian, and other European languages.

He engaged in sports, in particular football (soccer in the United States). Japanese friends told of Blyth showing them purplish marks on his lower legs, claiming they were the result of having been kicked in the shins so often as a young boy. His continuing keen interest in the sport is seen in a letter he wrote Dora from Korea, apparently dating from the early 1930s, in which he mentions tuning in to the BBC overseas late-night service to hear the English football scores.

By 1916, when Blyth graduated from secondary school in his eighteenth year, the war in Europe had reached a stalemate. The British government, faced with massive casualties on the battlefield, was forced to introduce conscription for the first time in its history. Under the Military Service Act of January 1916, all single men between the ages of eighteen and forty-one were eligible to be called up.

Blyth acted by registering as a conscientious objector before receiving his induction notice. He refused to contribute to the war effort in any way, even in a noncombatant role. He did so, he said, "not because of any fear of death, but because of a horror at the thought of having to kill another human being." As a result, he was incarcerated at Wormwood Scrubs Prison in London, doing heavy labor, and later at Dartmoor Prison in Princetown, Devon, where he worked at the prison's Work Centre for the duration of the war. Although he rarely referred to these years either to friends or in his writings, it is likely that he was subjected to harsh treatment from prison guards. Dora Orr wrote in a letter to me, "Feeling ran very high in this country in the war against men who refused to fight . . . in fact there was a threat at one point by the government to have them shot. This would have made no difference to R. H. B., so strong was his conviction."

It was during his incarceration that Blyth realized—in addition to being a pacifist and teetotaler—he was a vegetarian as well:

> When I was eighteen years old, one day a man [a fellow inmate] said to me, "Do you eat meat?" "Yes, of course," I replied. "Don't you know that you can live quite healthily without having animals killed for you to eat?" he asked. "Why, yes, I suppose so . . ." I mumbled—and from that day to this I have never eaten any meat or fish. It is quite clear from this anecdote that I was a vegetarian before the man asked me these two simple questions, that I was a born vegetarian, or to express it in the language of Zen, in a transcendental way, I was a vegetarian before I was born, beyond time. ("Buddhism and Haiku," on p. 280)

He took to vegetarianism, he said, "like a duck takes to water"—the idea being that a duck is from the first a *water bird*. He explained his decision in this way: "The universe tells us to eat and/or be eaten, to kill and/or be killed. Also it tells me to cause no pain or death while I am alive . . . between my two deaths, that of birth and that of annihilation. Being sufficiently greedy of life, I make a compromise and kill only things that don't run away from me, like cabbages and cocoanuts, onions and eggs." And, "My love of animals is like Wordsworth's love of mountains, Bashō's love of the moon and cherry blossoms, but above all like Christ's love for men, for it embraces without effort or self-consciousness the most snaggle-toothed dogs, slit-eared cats, snakes, lice and bedbugs, stopping short unfortunately at the intestinal worms."[11] His love of animals was all-inclusive. He would startle companions by stealing a kiss from a llama on trips to the zoo or by taking large, hairy spiders in the palm of his hand and petting them.

Following his release from Dartmoor Prison in 1919, he taught for six months at Cleveland Road Primary School and then enrolled at University College, London University. He majored in English literature and contin-ued his study of classical and modern languages. At this time, his favorite poet was Matthew Arnold, "whose Anglo-Saxon gloom, combined with the Celtic sadness, spoke to [my] condition in many of his lines,"[12] although this fondness for Arnold, he would later often say, came about only because he had not been taught how to read Wordsworth properly.

At London University, Blyth was fortunate in having as a teacher the bril-liant Scottish literary scholar and essayist William Paton Ker (1855–1923). In the one-page preface to *A Chronological Anthology of Nature in English Literature*, Blyth expressed his gratitude to Ker as someone "unique in the strength and depth of his self-immersion in literature."[13] J. R. R. Tolkien and W. H. Auden were also admirers of Professor Ker. Auden described his dis-covery of Ker's writings as a turning point in his career: "No other critic whom I have subsequently read could have granted me the same vision of a kind of literary All Souls Night in which the dead, the living and the unborn writers of every age and tongue were seen as engaged upon a common, noble and civilizing task."[14]

In 1923, at the age of twenty-five, Blyth graduated from London University with a Bachelor of Arts with First Class Honors. In a letter to Oka Kuniomi, Dora Orr wrote, "I believe he wanted to get a job in India, but there was nothing suitable, so he took the appointment to Seoul University."[15]

In his final years at London University, he became friends with Fujii Akio, a young Japanese scholar who was in London on a two-year govern-ment scholarship to study English literature and language. A graduate of Tokyo Imperial University, Fujii was a pupil of Saitō Takeshi (1887–1982), a Japanese scholar who would later aid Blyth's teaching career in Japan.

Fujii was scheduled to take up a teaching position on his return to Japan in the English department of Keijō Teikoku Daigaku, a new impe-rial university being established in Keijō in Chōsen (Korea), then a colony of Japan (Keijō is the Japanese reading for Gyeongseong, the old name for the city of Seoul). Fujii had been charged with the task of finding an Englishman to teach at the new university during his stay in London and decided to ask Blyth. The following exchange was recounted many years later by Fujii's wife, Motoko. It is said to have taken place at a vegetarian restaurant in London:

> One day, my husband broached the matter, asking Blyth, "Would you like to come to Japan and teach at Keijō University?" "Why not?" Blyth immediately replied. "Let's go."[16]

It is not known just how much Blyth knew about Japan at this time. He once remarked that his fascination with Japan began when he saw the wonderful *maki-e* (Japanese lacquerware decorated with gold and silver brushwork) collection at the Victoria and Albert Museum. He felt drawn, he said, to a country that could produce such marvelously beautiful objects.

In 1924, in preparation for his new position, Blyth acquired a teaching certificate from the London Day Training College. That same year he married Anna (Annie) Bercovitch, an Englishwoman of Jewish heritage who had studied philosophy at London University. Anna graduated with honors in 1924 and, like Blyth, took a teaching certificate from the London Day Training College. Beyond that, and the references Blyth makes to her in his letters, not much is known of her. Shinki Masanosuke, Blyth's friend in Keijō and colleague at the Peers School after the Second World War, described her as being small, with Eastern European or Middle Eastern features. According to the chronology of Blyth's life that Shinki compiled in 1984 (*Kaisō no Buraisu*), the couple left England in July 1924 by ship, proceeding by way of the Suez Canal, India, and Singapore. Fujii Akio and his wife had already returned to Japan and were on hand to welcome them at the port of Kobe. Unfortunately, Mrs. Fujii's recollections of their subsequent travels omit any further reference to Anna:

> On our way to Keijō, we stopped for one day in Kyoto. The next day we continued on to Hiroshima, where we showed him around Miyajima (Itsukushima) Shrine. You can imagine how delighted Blyth San was to find himself surrounded by the herds of sacred deer. We gave quite some thought to the Japanese food our vegetarian friend might like and ended up offering him vegetarian sushi—Inari and kanpyo-maki—with

unseasoned rice. We were relieved to see him eat the sushi with great gusto. My husband later introduced Blyth San to a sushi restaurant in Keijō. Blyth and the owner of the restaurant took to each other immediately and from then on, I believe, he ate there almost daily.[17]

The two couples arrived in Keijō in September 1924, and Blyth soon began teaching at the Preparatory School of the soon-to-be-opened Keijō University. According to Shinki's account in *Kaisō no Buraisu*, Blyth started lecturing in the department of English Language and Literature at Keijō Imperial University when that faculty was launched in 1926. Four years later, in 1930, he also began teaching classes at the Commercial School of the Fourth Higher School of Keijō, a professional school that offered a three-year program.

As a foreign lecturer at Keijō University, hand-picked and invited by the Japanese government, he received a very generous salary, amounting to more than twice that of the president of the university. Reg and Anna built a two-story Japanese-style house on a hill on the opposite side of the railroad tracks from the school, living on tatami mats. According to Oka Kuniomi, the hill continued to be known as "Blyth's Hill" even after he departed in 1937.[18]

The letters and reminiscences of friends and associates provide glimpses into Blyth's private life during his years in Keijō. We know, for example, that his house was always filled with a variety of dogs and cats, the garden and yard with other animals, including horses and goats. Music was, as always, central to his life. He played alone but also enjoyed performing chamber music—Mozart was a favorite—with others, holding musical evenings at his home and occasionally organizing public recitals in the school auditorium as well. He frequently had difficulty in locating performers to take part, so he was always keenly on the lookout for anyone he thought could be taught to play an instrument and enlisted in his musical endeavors, including those who lacked any knowledge whatever of Western music.

His own early letters are filled with references to a variety of classical composers. He assembled what he later referred to as "an enormous library of classical orchestral and chamber music." But from the late 1930s on, the single-minded devotion to the music of Bach that we see throughout his postwar writings becomes increasingly evident, as Dora Orr explained in one of her letters to me:

Blyth teaching, 1950s.

He had this great feeling for music especially for that of Bach; life would have been almost nothing for him without Bach, in the days when I was closest to him. . . . He taught himself to play the piano, organ, flute, clarinet, oboe, viola, violin, and cello. . . . His musical intuition was so strong that he could pick up any instrument and play it, having, of course, knowledge of the construction of the thing and what you did to make it speak, so to say.

In two letters to me (in late 1962), Blyth wrote,

I play the organ (I have six) every day, Bach only, or pre-Bach, and almost all the other instruments except the bassoon and the French horn. The most difficult is the recorder.

There is no music but the music of Bach. All the rest, even that of Mozart, cannot wring a tear from me.

Blyth restored several pipe organs and even seems to have built one using reclaimed organ parts. He bought and repaired old violins and cellos, gave them to students, and then helped them learn to play the instruments. When they gained sufficient proficiency, he would recruit them to perform chamber music with him. Violins went to cooks and housemaids, fresh from the country and totally unfamiliar with Western music, who in time, thanks to Blyth's tutoring, were able to take part in the musical programs held at his home.

When Blyth learned of the difficulties that poor but especially qualified students had paying for their education, he arranged with the university to apportion among them twenty yen from his salary as grants each month. He and Anna, having no children of their own, unofficially adopted a bright young Korean student named Li Insoo. Nicknamed Jimmy, Insoo had studied under Blyth at the Commercial School attached to Keijō University.

On summer vacations, Blyth would avoid the stifling heat and humidity of Keijō by taking a small boat and drifting slowly down the Han River, which flows through some of the country's most magnificent mountain scenery:

I'm about to embark on another journey up the Han River, alone this time. I'm taking a little dog, Dante's Paradiso, an oboe with Bach's organ trios, a camera, paints and paper & feel myself to be a real highbrow, but I'm a low brow at bottom, & I expect I shall spend the whole time rushing up the river at 100 yards an hour & get as far as I can before I get tired of it. (Letter #14 on p. 70)

He must have picked up a fairly good working knowledge of spoken Korean and Japanese during the early years in Keijō, well before his focus was turned to the written languages. During an interview on the NHK[19] after the war, when asked how he first began to study written Japanese, he answered,

I didn't begin until about five or six years after I arrived in Korea. The reason was because I had the idea that Japanese literature wasn't all that admirable. I began learning Japanese by reading Miyamori Asatarō's English translations of haiku [ed. *An Anthology of Haiku, Ancient and Modern*, 1932]. Then when I read Suzuki Daisetz's English works on Zen, I felt that I had to read the Zen texts in the original, so I began studying the Chinese written language. It was all done on my own, without teachers.[20]

He also quickly acquired a taste for the art of Korea and Japan, and the letters show him occasionally sending his mother and Dora Japanese prints and paintings. He evinced a strong dislike for the colorful Kutani wares of Kanazawa, telling people after the war, "All those pottery stores along the roadsides would better have been destroyed by air raids during the war."[21] His preference was for the rough simplicity of Korean and Japanese wares such as Iga and Karatsu, a taste he shared with his friend Yanagi Sōetsu, founder of the Mingei movement. In Korea, and also later when he lived in Tokyo, Blyth bicycled everywhere he could, and his modest habits extended to all areas of his life. As he ate no meat or fish and did not consume any alcohol, his own staples of vegetarian sushi and carbonated Japanese cider were provided whenever he attended the obligatory parties held periodically by teachers and other university groups; even when invited to attend dinners at the imperial palace, special vegetarian meals were always provided.

Poetry was always a consuming passion for Blyth. He wrote poems as a young man in England and continued doing so during the first years in Keijō. In 1927, two of his poems were published in the August issue of *The London Mercury*. As *The London Mercury*, edited at the time by the poet

J. C. Squire, was one of England's leading literary journals, it was an impressive debut, made even more auspicious by the distinguished company he shared in this issue. Following Blyth's poems in the poetry section was W. B. Yeats's "Among School Children," its first appearance in print. In the prose section was "The Man Who Loved Islands," a story by D. H. Lawrence, a writer for whom Blyth would come to have the highest regard.

Two more of his poems appeared in the late twenties in *Kaikon Jidai*, a student periodical published at Keijō University.[22] Dora Orr sent me a copy of a manuscript containing a few more verses. The fish poem in *Zen in English Literature and Oriental Classics* (p. 303), published in 1941, is also his own, though it was probably written during the same period as the *London Mercury* poems. That same year (1927), Blyth's first known prose publication appeared, an article titled "Natura Resurgens," in a quarterly review issued by the English Seminar of Tokyo Imperial University.[23]

Given the central importance poetry of all kinds had for Blyth, even before he left England he was no doubt aware of Chinese and Japanese verse in translation. Arthur Waley's *A Hundred and Seventy Chinese Poems* had appeared in 1918, followed by *More Translations from the Chinese* (1919), and *Japanese Poetry: The Uta* (1919), and *The Nō Plays of Japan* (1921). References to Chinese and Japanese literature, generally poetry, begin to appear in earnest in the surviving letters in the early 1930s. He is extolling the glories of Japanese haiku to Dora, asking her to send him some translations of Chinese poetry, and even making his first attempts at translating Chinese verse himself.

Having in his student days been inspired to learn German in order to read *Faust* in the original language, Spanish to read *Don Quixote*, and Italian to read the *Divine Comedy*, Blyth now set about the more formidable task of learning written Japanese and Chinese in order to read the words of their great poets as well. He also, it is clear, felt an impulse to translate them into English. Blyth seems to have ceased writing his own poetry by the early 1930s, perhaps realizing, like Waley and other distinguished translators, that he could put his poetic gifts to best use in translating the works of others—the great poets of the past.

The only hint I have found of Blyth's own assessment of his early poetic efforts, and it is open to question, appears in a story Robert Aitken told me: "On one of our rare trips to the dentist when we were in the [Kobe] camp,

I ran across a British literary journal of the middle thirties which featured two of his poems. I bought the magazine, and though B. scorned the poems, he 'borrowed' the magazine, and I never got it back" (personal letter, July 1967). The journal is most likely *The London Mercury* referred to earlier, although the year of publication was 1927, not the mid-thirties.

His student Oka Kuniomi wrote that in the mid-thirties when Blyth was teaching in Keijō students were sometimes made to translate haiku in the classroom. The earliest reference to his own translating activity that can be clearly dated is March 1934, in a letter to his parents:

> Just lately I have started reading some Chinese poetry, of course in Japanese pronunciation. I have succeeded in managing one, so I will write it out and translate it. (Letter #21 on page 79; he then gives a literal word-for-word translation of a poem by Li Po.)

Most such references, however, appear in letters to Dora like these, the first two dating from the mid-thirties and the last from 1940:

> Recently I have gone barmy on Chinese poetry & sit up half the night ruining my eyes on Chinese dictionaries. (Letter #19 on page 77)

> I have been reading Chinese poetry until 2 o'clock every night for the ·last month or two. (Letter #37 on page 96)

> To translate and translate and then discover some sentence which makes worthwhile the hours of dictionary-thumbing is really exhilarating and satisfying. There is something almost religious in this communion with the dead, ourselves so near death that the difference and distance are seen as nothing. (Letter #45 on page 102)

Other letters mention reading *The Tale of Genji* in Japanese and learning to write Japanese with a brush. One includes a translation he had made of a haiku by Buson, a poet who would become one of his favorites. It is interesting to note that he includes a commentary to the translation, and read together they have a marked similarity to the translation and commentary style of the haiku books he would go on to write in the 1940s:

Horace Blyth, 1930s.

I am sitting here still translating and explaining Japanese poetry, listening to the Brahms Second Symphony. . . . The verse I am now doing I will throw at you without comment—

Water birds;
Among the withered trees,
Two palanquins.   Buson

(Perhaps after all that is a little cruel.) On a lonely winter path stand two empty palanquins. Beside the narrow road there is a marshy pool, on which a few water birds are seen. The sky is low and grey, but it is too cold to rain.

These two palanquins,—where are the carriers, where are the passengers? What is it like to be a water bird? These questions do not arise as we stare at the colourless picture; but we know the answers, answers that are wordless. (Letter #37 on page 95)

In April 1934, Anna left for England, taking Insoo with her. No mention is made in the letters of her reason for going. Blyth writes that she and Insoo intended to stay in England for "at least eighteen months," which indicates they intended to return. But Anna never went back. She is described as teaching in the London school system, and Insoo, after enrolling at London University and graduating with honors, lived in England until after the war, when he returned to teach in Seoul.[24]

In July, three months after Anna left, Blyth returned to London as well.[25] He tells Dora that he gave a Keijō friend his piano before he left, an expensive item in Korea at the time, indicating that he did not intend to go back. This is further substantiated by the description Blyth's colleague Shinki Masanosuke gives of his state of mind when he went to say goodbye to Shinki prior to setting out:

> He stood outside the doorway, as he always did, but there was a downcast, haggard look about him. "I'm going back to England in two or three days," he said. On my asking if he would be coming back, Blyth replied, almost inaudibly, "I don't know."[26]

We know that while he was in London Blyth did not stay with Anna and that from this point on the two of them lived separate lives, so it seems fair to assume that their decisions to return were both connected in some way to the breakdown of the marriage. It is not known if divorce was contemplated or what action, if any, was taken in that regard during Blyth's stay in London.

He spent the next few months at his parents' home, during which time he was seeing a great deal of Dora Lord. Indeed, seeing her may have been one of his primary reasons for returning to England. A romantic involvement of some kind, hinted at in earlier letters, becomes evident from those he sent her while he was in London. His feelings toward her may explain an enigmatic remark he makes in the first volume of *Zen and Zen Classics* that he was led to Zen owing to a disappointed love. While the indications are clear that Dora reciprocated his feelings, there is nothing in the letters to clarify why either of them ended up holding back from a deeper relationship. It may simply have been that they were first cousins at a time when many considered a marriage between first cousins to be inappropriate.

After less than three months in London, during which time he had apparently sought employment without success, Blyth received an urgent letter from Fujii Akio in Keijō begging him to return. In a letter to Dora postmarked October 6, 1934, Blyth writes,

> I'm very very sorry to have to tell you that I am going back to Korea in a few days. I received such an urgent, almost frantic, letter from Mr. Fujii that I decided I must go back.
>
> I hope you will be angry and cry and do all the rest of it before you come. I am very, very sorry, but it seems the only thing to do. . . . I sent a telegram yesterday to say I was going back. I am sorry that I came at all to upset you, but as I grieve at it so much, you may bear me the less malice & resentment.
>
> Love, Reg (Letter #32 on page 91)

The following year Blyth, now thirty-seven years old, was back at his teaching posts at Keijō University and its Preparatory (Daigaku Yoka) and Commercial Schools (Kōtō Shōgyō Gakkō), living in a two-story house in the north-central area of the city near the university.

Two years later, in 1937, he married Kurushima Tomiko, the twenty-two-year-old daughter of a Japanese family living in Keijō. References appear in letters written over the next few years to a threat of some kind that Anna seems to have made in letters to Blyth. Although its precise nature is unstated, one assumes it was connected somehow to the breakup of the marriage. Blyth appears to have responded to these occasional provocations—they never seem to have gone beyond that—with a sympathetic forbearance.

It was during his return to Japan on the Trans-Siberian Railway in the autumn of 1934 that Blyth first read Arthur Waley's recently published *The Way and Its Power: A Study of the Tao Te Ching and Its Place in Chinese Thought*, and Daisetz Suzuki's *Essays in Zen Buddhism*.[27] He was soon urging Dora to buy and read them, and references to them, especially to Suzuki's work, are frequent from the mid-thirties on. Their discovery was a turning point in Blyth's life. He had struck ore.

In 1938, at the age of forty, Blyth visited Kayama Taigi Rōshi (1891–1945), head priest of the local Myōshin-ji Betsu-in temple in Keijō, and began practicing Zen under him. The temple was a branch of the Myōshin-ji

Blyth doing zazen, Keijō, circa 1937.

monastery in Kyoto, which since the seventeenth century had been the most influential branch of Japanese Rinzai Zen. Taigi Rōshi was somewhat unusual for his time in having studied Indian philosophy at Tokyo Imperial University before entering the Nanzen-ji training hall in Kyoto under Kōno Mukai (Nanshinken Rōshi). After receiving Nanshinken's Dharma transmission in 1929, Taigi Rōshi was sent to the Keijō Betsu-in; his predecessor there, Gotō Zuigan, later became known for the role he played in the transmission of Zen to America. Taigi Rōshi served at the Betsu-in until 1945, when, shortly after the war ended, the ship taking him back to Japan struck a mine and sank with all on board.

Blyth devoted himself assiduously to Zen practice under Taigi Rōshi, going to the temple to do zazen every night and, when his teaching duties allowed him to, living in the temple with the monks. One of his few references to this period occurs in an essay he wrote after the war, in which he describes winter in Keijō, where "the temperature often falls below −20":

When we entered the temple, we often had to step over the bodies of beggars sleeping under the Great Gate of the temple.

Sometimes, as we came out, full of Zen and satori and transcendental bliss, one of the beggars would be really asleep, frozen to death. ("In Praise of Suzuki Daisetz and Zen," on p. 326)

Blyth dedicated his first book, *Zen in English Literature and Oriental Classics*, to Taigi Rōshi, with the words, "but for him I should have known nothing of Zen." He reminisced about his study under Taigi Rōshi in an interview published two years before his own death:

My interest in Zen came from reading Suzuki Daisetz's *Essays in Zen Buddhism*. However I was led to practice Zen for the first time when one of my students suggested that I go to the temple with him and do zazen. Zazen, he explained, was a matter of sitting quietly and experiencing some kind of realization, so I decided to give it a try. Besides the two of us there were twenty or thirty others, both Koreans and Japanese, sitting at the temple. After two or three months I was the only one left. . . . I lived at the Myōshin-ji Betsu-in for quite a long time. My Zen teacher was Kayama Taigi Rōshi.

Taigi Rōshi died after the war when the ship carrying him back to Japan struck a floating mine. Some years ago a funeral was held for him at Nanzen-ji in Kyoto. As for my *sanzen* with Taigi Rōshi, I remember that when I asked him strange questions, he would give me a look of contempt and scratch his bald head.

You asked about the Rōshi's formal Zen lectures (*teishō*). He gave them on the *Mumonkan* [*Gateless Gate*], *Zenkai-ichiran* [*One Wave in the Zen Ocean*], and other texts. I found them completely different from any Christian sermon I had ever heard. One thing I remember when I took *sanzen* with him. He told me not to smoke while I was taking a pee. This next teaching is a bit indelicate. He spoke about how you feel when after relieving your bowels your finger breaks through the toilet paper as you're wiping yourself—and he said that when that happens you must focus with great intensity on that feeling. . . . I suppose he meant getting intimately in touch with your own essential filth. Having your fingers touching your own shit puts you in touch with the fundamental self.[28]

Japan, whose hostilities in China had started in July 1937, was now converting its forces in Korea to a war footing. Amid rampant xenophobia, anti-British feeling ran high. There is only one allusion to this restrictive social climate in Blyth's letters, when he remarked that "nobody comes to see us, partly because they might be suspected by the police, partly because I don't want anybody to come."

In March 1939, the Commercial School at Keijō terminated Blyth's teaching contract. In September, Germany invaded Poland, and World War II in Europe began with Great Britain and France declaring war on Germany. In March 1940, Fujii Akio, still one of Blyth's closest friends, died of a heart attack. The following month Blyth and his wife Tomiko left Keijō, crossing over to Yamaguchi prefecture on the main Japanese island of Honshu. They took a house in her hometown of Hagi, an old castle town on the Sea of Japan.

During his three-month stay in Hagi, Blyth was able to focus on finishing *Zen in English Literature and Oriental Classics*. He made several trips to Tokyo to seek friends' help in finding some employment, apparently knowing that his contract at Keijō University would probably not be renewed. A letter to his parents dated September 1940 shows that his Zen training was another matter weighing heavily on him at this time:

This summer I have moved to Hagi, Tomiko's native place. . . . The rent of the house in Keijō was 50 yen. For this house, which is larger and has an extensive garden with orange trees etc., is 7 yen. I shall go back to Keijō on about the 21st of this month. In Keijō I shall live at the temple Myoshinji (rise at 4:30, sweep up, do zazen, gruel and soup for breakfast and the leavings for dinner), for which board and lodgings I pay 12 yen a month. (Letter #48 on p. 104)

In November, he received news of the cancellation of his main teaching contract at Keijō Imperial University. Fortunately, it seems that by this time he had been offered employment at the Daiyon Kōtō Gakkō, Fourth Higher School, in Kanazawa, Ishikawa prefecture, a preparatory school with a three-year course designed to prepare students for one of the seven imperial universities. He was obliged to scrub the plan to return to Korea and leave for Kanazawa almost immediately. The alien registration (*gaijin tōroku*) form Blyth submitted at Kanazawa on November 20, 1940, sheds valuable light on his biography: it records his original arrival in Japan as September 1924 at the port of Kobe and lists his previous *gaijin tōroku* address as the Myōshin-ji Betsu-in Keijō, the temple where he had lived and practiced before leaving for the Japanese homeland.

In Kanazawa, Blyth would no longer be teaching at the university level, but he was offered the same monthly salary—forty yen—that he had received at Keijō. Considering the strength of anti-foreign feeling at the time, it is surprising to learn of this Kanazawa appointment. Influential friends and acquaintances in the Japanese academic community were working privately on Blyth's behalf. Among them were Saitō Takeshi, a prominent professor of English literature in Tokyo Imperial University, and probably also Yamanashi Katsunoshin, president of the Peers School in Tokyo, who operated in close connection with the Imperial Household and also the highest levels of government.

Blyth and his wife arrived in Kanazawa toward the end of November 1940, moving into a house the university had provided just outside the walls of Kanazawa Castle. The beautiful old city of Kanazawa was much to Blyth's liking, even though its leaden skies apparently reminded him of his native London. For the citizens themselves, he had nothing but praise:

> The people of Kanazawa, as I think I told you, are extremely good, in the sense that they have no malice in their hearts, have a real love of peace and quietness, with no hypocrisy or false politeness. The shopkeepers show no special wish to sell anything in the shop; the love of money has few of its roots here. (Letter #49 on p. 105)

By the time Blyth began his teaching duties toward the end of 1940, the British Embassy was strongly urging all British subjects to return to England. He made tentative plans to follow this advice, acquiring from foreign embassies the necessary transit visas for traveling to London via the Trans-Siberian Railway. But rapidly deteriorating conditions in Europe—Germany's occupation of Poland and much of Western Europe, fears in England of impending invasion, the Battle of Britain in full swing—soon made an overland journey unthinkable.

In the spring of 1941, Blyth's father, Horace, died. In a letter to his mother dated April 18, 1941, acknowledging the news of his father's death, he wrote, "I receive Dad's letters after he is dead like a voice from the tomb—but no that is a very false way of expressing it. As you know he had something good, something charming, something pathetic about him that touches the heart when greater virtues or power would not affect it." He goes on to tell her of the progress of "the book"—*Zen in English Literature and Oriental Classics*:

> I have just finished the chapters of the book *Children, Old Men & Idiots, Death, and Poverty*. The last [chapter] is on Animals all in relation to Zen and English Poetry, with a very great many quotations from both, and from Japanese literature and Chinese. The only trouble is that no one will be able to understand it: I myself must read it twice when I look over some of the earlier parts. However, there are some easy bits here and there, and the quotations are all worth the money. (Letter #49 on p. 106)

In April, Blyth applied for Japanese citizenship, furnishing the government with letters of endorsement by prominent Japanese figures. For some reason, however, no action was taken on his application. He did not reapply after the war and would remain a British subject until his death.

Toward the end of April, he completed *Zen in English Literature and Oriental Classics*, his first book, and submitted it to Hokuseido Press in Tokyo. In a May 25 letter to his mother, he mentions the book once again, appraising it in words noteworthy for both their objectivity and their prescience:

> I have finished my book. It contains a vast amount of quotations, mostly from English literature, but also from Chinese, Japanese, Italian, and Spanish (translated) and French and German (untranslated). Dora always said I would do something. Well, I have done it; it is a book of national and international importance. All that's wrong with it is that it's too good, too rich, like a Christmas pudding or a trifle—no easy or flat bits, all purple patches. (Letter #50 on p. 106)

On October 17, 1941, Blyth met Daisetz Suzuki, the great Zen layman and scholar, for the first time. He had been reading Suzuki's works avidly for a number of years now. In his first known letter to Suzuki, dated May 1940, he asks Suzuki's help in obtaining his *The Training of the Zen Buddhist Monk* (published in Kyoto in 1934) and "any other books on Zen and Japanese poetry he might recommend."[29]

Suzuki's recently published notebooks show that he was in Kanazawa from October 14 to 18 to visit his parents' gravesite. He also notes, "Went to see Mr. Blyth of Daishi [Daiyon] Koto Gakko." Blyth's description of the meeting, written after the war, has him going to visit Suzuki at this time:

The first time I met Suzuki Daisetz was in Kanazawa, his native place, just before the beginning of the Pacific War [1940]. I had read his books and done zazen. . . . I was in the middle of [my first book] *Zen in English Literature*, and my mind was full of the question, "What is Zen?"

When Dr. Suzuki asked me to go and see him at the inn where he was staying, I was of course most excited. I pictured him as a very fierce-looking person, something like Daitō Kokushi, who would rap me over the knuckles and ask me that most unanswerable of questions, "What is Zen?"

Anyway, I prepared my answer and went to the inn. I found him to be a very gentle, sympathetic person, more interested in me and my life than in philosophizing. He reminded me of the minister, Mr. Hayhoe, in T. F. Powys's story *The Only Penitent*:

He never spoke to any for the purpose of teaching them, for God chooses His own time for that, but was always ready to speak of the most trifling matters, for who can tell through what little corners the joy of religion may enter the soul?

Dr. Suzuki asked me how I came to be interested in Zen. I answered eagerly that it was through his *Essays in Zen Buddhism*. He bowed his head, and I cannot say how much that action impressed me. It was not modesty, hardly gratitude, rather a kind of expression of the inevitable. At last, I said to him, "Dr. Suzuki, I thought you would ask me what Zen was, and I see I was mistaken, but as I have prepared the answer, I will tell you anyway. The answer is 'There is no such thing as Zen.'" "Yes," he said, smiling, "that is true; there is no such thing as Zen." ("In Praise of Suzuki Daisetz and Zen," on p. 323)

Not long after this meeting, on December 7, 1941 (December 8 in Japan), war in the Pacific began with Japanese air and naval attacks on Pearl Harbor, Wake Island, Guam, the Philippines, and British installations in Malaya, Singapore, and Hong Kong. Blyth and Tomiko were taken into custody the same day by the Ishikawa Prefectural Police. They were examined by governmental officials, and Blyth, as an enemy alien, was confined at police headquarters. He was still confined there in February of the following year when his daughter Harumi was born. On February 29, *Zen in English Literature and Oriental Classics* was published in Tokyo in a print run of one thousand copies.

It is something of a mystery how a book written by an Englishman, in English, which was (to say the least) frowned upon as an "enemy language," came to be published in wartime Japan. Nakatsuchi Jumpei, who became president of Hokuseido Press in the postwar period, said that Hokuseido published it simply because they had contracted to do so. While that is no doubt true, it doesn't explain why government censors allowed it to appear. Could it just have escaped their notice? Or was it passed because of the central theme of the book, epitomized in its opening words, "Zen is the most priceless possession of Asia," and of the love and respect for traditional Japanese culture that is so apparent throughout the text?

In March 1942, Blyth's contract with the Fourth Higher School in Kanazawa was officially terminated. He was taken from Kanazawa under police escort to a temporary detention center for noncombatant enemy civilians at the Hotel Eastern Lodge in Kobe, a facility housed in a two-story, semi-Japanese-style building located about a ten minutes' walk up a hill from the Sannomiya railway station that had been run by, and mainly catered to, Indian nationals. The only contemporary account I have found—an American Department of State memorandum dated July 10, 1942—describes "rooms with two European beds . . . running water . . . two good Japanese cooks who prepare three meals a day . . . tea and coffee every day . . . unrestricted supplementary rations, vegetable garden . . . hygiene and health good . . . daily baths, billiards, ping pong, cards, checkers, newspapers, books, walks . . . permission is given for visits to or from the outside."[30] After a few months, Blyth was moved to a detainment center set up at Gloucester House, the dormitory of the Canadian Academy in Kobe, in the hills behind the city of Kobe. The same memorandum, which lists R. H. Blyth among the twenty British nationals interned at the Canadian Academy, states that the four civilian internment camps in Hyogo prefecture (where Kobe is located) are among "the best Japanese camps with an excellent camp commandant. Discipline and morale very good, no complaints." Red Cross parcels and supplies were allowed to the internees beginning in November and after that distributed on a more or less regular basis. Still, accounts of the Kobe camps' internees published after the war speak of hunger, cold, inadequate clothing, and malnutrition that resulted in a prevalence of skin disease. The austere diet probably explains the eruptions of unsightly boils on his face and neck that Blyth experienced at one point during his internment. There was no heating except for occasional charcoal briquets, which were in short supply.

As a noncombatant internee, Blyth was not required to do manual labor and was able to pass his two years and more at the Canadian Academy studying and writing. He had the use of its library as well as books that his wife, now relocated to Kobe with their young daughter, was allowed to bring him from home. As noncombatant civilians, internees in the Kobe camps received relatively lenient treatment, a circumstance no doubt also owing to prewar Kobe's history of foreign intercourse and large European population. In an interview he gave a few years before his death, Blyth remarked that life in the Kobe camps was much easier than the treatment he encountered during the First World War at Wormwood Scrubs and Dartmoor Prison.

During Blyth's internment, his wife and daughter moved to Kobe together with all the family belongings and his large library of books, locating in the central Motomachi area of the city. This was not far from the internment camp, where she was allowed weekly visits. She would bring Blyth sushi and other vegetarian food to supplement the rations he received, which sometimes included small bits of meat or fish.

On May 23, 1944, Japanese authorities transferred internees from all four Kobe camps to Rinkangaku, a former reform school in the hills of Futatabi (also described as Chikuba Gakuen School for the Handicapped). It was located four or five miles north of Kobe, beyond the range of expected Allied bombing raids. A representative of the Swiss Legation at Tokyo who visited this new camp that summer in 1944 described it as "situated in a healthful and picturesque region at an altitude of 1200 feet . . . with the main two-floor school building housing all the internees (157) in crowded circumstances."

It was at the Futatabi camp that Blyth met Robert Aitken (1917–2010), who later founded the Diamond Sangha Zen group in Honolulu and went on to become a leading American Zen teacher. Aitken, nineteen years Blyth's junior, had been engaged in construction work on the island of Guam when

Marks House, 1942; one of the early Kobe internment camps. Robert Aitken is behind the man with the puppy on the right. Photo courtesy of Tom Haar.

the Japanese attacked the island. He and his fellow workers were sent to Japan and spent over two years in several Kobe internment camps before being transferred to Futatabi in 1944. While there Aitken fell under Blyth's guidance, inspiring an interest in Zen and haiku, not to mention English poetry and classical music, that pretty much determined the future course of his life. In reminiscences that Aitken wrote in his later years of meeting Blyth, he describes him working on drafts of the haiku books that would appear after the war, a senryū book, and translations of various Zen texts:

> [When I was interned in the previous camp] a guard came into my room, quite drunk, waving a book in the air and saying in English, "This book, my English teacher. . . ." He had been a student of R. H. Blyth at Kanazawa, and the book was *Zen in English Literature and Oriental Classics*, then just published. . . . I suppose I read the book ten or eleven times straight through. . . .
>
> In May 1944 all the camps were combined [at Rinkangaku], and it was there that I met him for the first time. . . . Our camp consisted of three

large, connected buildings, containing dormitories, commons rooms, and classrooms. One hundred seventy-five men completely filled this complex, and Mr. Blyth lived with six others in what had apparently been the commons room for the teachers. He had his bed in the *tokonoma*, the alcove usually reserved for scroll and flower arrangement in Japanese homes and offices. His books teetered on shelves he himself had installed above his bed. All day long he sat on his bed, sometimes cross-legged and sometimes with his feet on the floor, writing on a lectern placed on a bed-side table, with his reference books and notebooks among the bedcovers. It was during this time that he was working on his four-volume *Haiku* and his *Senryū*, as well as *Buddhist Sermons on Christian Texts* and other works. I recall that he wrote rapidly, with his words connected, using two sets of pen and ink, black for his text and red for his quotations.[31]

Conditions in the Rinkangaku camp that Aitken personally described to me are a far cry from those that prisoners of war experienced in Japanese prison camps elsewhere. He said that when inmates were allowed to receive Red Cross parcels, they had better food than their guards or the Japanese civilians outside the camp, and that prisoners would sometimes share their rations with them. He also said that at one point some of the internees who had girlfriends in Kobe were even able to slip out of the camp to visit them.

Two months before the Japanese surrender, on July 5, 1945, an Allied bombing raid destroyed the house where Blyth's wife Tomiko was living, along with most of their belongings. After the war, to receive compensation for the losses, Blyth submitted to the Japanese government a two-page inventory of the items that had been lost, concluding the list with the words, "The above represents the whole of my worldly possessions at the time—with the exception of some clothes and bedding at Futatabi Internment Camp, Kobe."

This list of personal losses, which is among Blyth's posthumous papers, includes furniture, kitchen equipment, and flower arrangement utensils among the household items as well as:

a gramophone, records (over 300), musical instruments including a German cello, a piano, five German violins, a German viola, [his beloved English] silver flute, and an English oboe . . . about 30 hanging scrolls, a library of more than 10,000 volumes in Japanese and Western languages, and an enormous library of Orchestral and Chamber Music—only

Classical—complete works of J.S. Bach . . . all the chamber music of
Handel, Mozart, Haydn, Beethoven, etc. Orchestral works of Haydn,
Mozart, Beethoven, Handel, etc. etc. an incalculable amount of music.

It was only because Blyth was now imprisoned at a rather safe distance from
the downtown area that the manuscripts of his books on haiku and Zen
were not destroyed as well.

On August 15, the emperor announced Japan's surrender, and on Sep-
tember 2, the Instrument of Surrender was signed. Released from custody,
Blyth spent the next several weeks with his family at the Kobe home of
Kaneko Bush, the Japanese wife of Lewis Bush (1907–1987), an English-
man and longtime resident of Japan. A lieutenant in the Royal Navy, Bush
had been captured in Hong Kong at the outset of hostilities and survived
brutal concentration camps in China and later Yokohama. Mrs. Bush may
have taken in Tomiko and Harumi after they were bombed out, and the
offering of temporary shelter Blyth and his family received at this time was
probably owing to the friendship the two Japanese women formed during
their husbands' incarceration. Blyth's most pressing need now was finding
a job. He made one or two trips to Tokyo, visiting former friends he hoped
could help him secure another teaching position.

Daisetz Suzuki was one of the people Blyth most wanted to meet. In
one of Suzuki's recently published notebooks, his entry for October 3, 1945,
reads: "Letter from Blyth, who came out safely from imprisonment for four
years. Answered at once."[32] In his reply, Suzuki expresses his great relief on
learning that Blyth survived the war. He goes on to say that he thinks he
should be able to help him find a teaching job at a university. The letter
also reveals that Suzuki had made considerable effort to communicate with
Blyth after hearing of his arrest in Kanazawa, but that during the four years
of Blyth's internment, there had been no contact at all between the two men.

Blyth visited Suzuki in mid-October at the Shōden-a subtemple of the
Engaku-ji in Kita-Kamakura, south of Tokyo, where the latter had lived
out the war. It was the first of many meetings they would have in the post-
war years. Suzuki availed himself of Blyth's help in editing his English-
language manuscripts. The two men also collaborated on *The Cultural East*
(1946–47), a journal dedicated to Buddhism and Japanese culture with the
avowed aim of "constructing a cultural bridge between East and West"—a
mission whose time both men felt had come. This mission can perhaps

From left: Jack Brinkley, Christmas Humphreys, Daisetz Suzuki,
Lewis Bush, Blyth. Shoden-an, Engaku-ji, Kamakura, 1946.

best be explained as cautioning the Japanese, who in the wake of crushing
defeat were turning their backs on their traditional culture, of the danger of
throwing out the baby with the bathwater, while also opening the eyes of
Westerners, most of whom were ignorant or misinformed about Japanese
culture, to its priceless, time-honored virtues.

Suzuki had in mind a post for Blyth at Ōtani University in Kyoto, where
Suzuki had taught before the war. But Blyth had already received overtures
from several universities in Tokyo. In late November 1945, he accepted an
offer from the Peers School (Gakushūin), whose president, Yamanashi
Katsunoshin, had offered to furnish him with an on-campus residence.
Gakushūin was an elite institution originally established in the nineteenth
century for educating children of the nobility. Daisetz Suzuki had formerly
taught English there. His notebooks record meetings at this time with both
Yamanashi and Foreign Minister Yoshida Shigeru, suggesting the possi-
bility that Suzuki as well as Yoshida may also have played a role in Blyth's
appointment.

The five or six years following Blyth's move to Tokyo are, in many ways, the most remarkable period of his life. While many of the details of the activities he engaged in are not clearly known, two letters he wrote not long after his release from prison—one to Dora, the other to his mother—provide important information about his activities and thinking during this time.

The letter to Dora, dated January 21, 1946, reads,

What the western world needs is just what the east has got, not a solution to its problems, but a restatement of them in such a form that we are satisfied that the questions should remain as such, their own answers. As I said to my mother, my duty is here in Japan, to make the Japanese proud of being Japanese, to make them proud of their faithful guardianship of the open secret of Zen, so that they may not be Americanized or Anglicized, but may Japonize the Americans and the British.

. . . As for MacArthur approving of my appointment, I didn't ask him. In any case I have been so useful to MacArthur in quite uneducational affairs, that the thought never entered my head. . . . MacArthur is all right. Just leave everything to him and it will go fine. There is of course a section of the American command that wants to Americanize Japan, but they are just nit-wits, assisted by Japanese nit-wits, who want Japan to turn into another Philippines. . . . In the past six months I have given a great deal of advice, had it acted upon, and always with success, but this was because, although the matters concerned the destiny of Japan, or things I was imperfectly acquainted with, I myself was not concerned with or in it, and so my judgement was good. (Letter #52 on p. 108)

The letter to his mother, dated June 21, 1946, is of particular interest because of its references to Blyth's contact with the Imperial Household Agency and the imperial family:

After I was released from internment, we went to live, as you know, at Mrs. Bush's house in Kobe and stayed there until December last year. I went up to Tokyo several times and found a position in the Peers School. This has a primary, secondary and high school department. The Crown Prince was in a primary school at this time. I was also made a professor of the Nihon University. We came up to Tokyo in December and live in an official residence in the school grounds, which are very "extensive," and full of trees, so it is the best, perhaps the only good place in Tokyo to live in. I was appointed to teach the Crown Prince early this year, and every week also I teach seven princes separately in this house. Then I was asked by the Foreign Minister, Yoshida [Shigeru], who is now Prime Minister, to teach anything I liked in the School for Diplomats, in which young diplomats in the Foreign Office are preparing themselves for the time when Japan is allowed to have relations with foreign countries. Last of all, I have to lecture in Tokyo Imperial University on a Comparative Study of English and Japanese poetry. In addition to this Dr. Suzuki (the Zen fellow) and I are publishing a magazine called *The Cultural East*, the first number of which should appear at the end of this month. I am also a Counsellor of the Imperial Household, and in the last six months I have gone to and fro between the American Army and the Imperial Household, and engaged in all kinds of secret business which I cannot tell you about. I had an interview with the Emperor the other day, and spoke to him in Japanese for an hour and a half, a thing no foreigner has ever done. The Crown Prince himself is a plump and rather charming boy, and it is of course my idea to humanize him as much as possible, rather than teach him English. As I said, I am a Counsellor to the Imperial Household, and they have taken all the ideas I have given them so far. About two months ago I suggested that it would be a good idea if the Crown Prince could have the run of an American household with children of his own age in it. Of course that is impossible, but I proposed that they should have a young and charming American lady to teach him, because it is of the utmost national and international importance that he should *like* English. This suggestion got a little twisted in transition and they arranged to ask for an American lady of between 50 and 60 to come. However this is being modified but I don't know what will come of it. (Letter #54 on p. 38)

Here Blyth, otherwise mute about his activity as a counselor for the Imperial Household and his work as a liaison between the Imperial Household and Douglas MacArthur's General Headquarters (GHQ), reveals to his mother an unprecedented one-on-one interview with the emperor, the news that he had been made a "Counselor of the Imperial Household," and the fact that in that capacity he was offering advice relating to Emperor

Hirohito's role in the new postwar Japan. Not to mention that he was engaging in "secret business" of "all kinds."

The casual reference to a proposal he made to the Imperial Household to invite a "young and charming American lady" to join him in tutoring Crown Prince Akihito sheds some interesting new light on the circumstances surrounding Elizabeth Vining's selection to teach the Crown Prince.

Blyth suggested that the Crown Prince would benefit from being taught by a woman tutor, "preferably an American Quaker and pacifist." Ōgane Masujirō, a court officer of the Imperial Household who was charged with overseeing the Crown Prince's education (he would soon become Jijū-chō, or Grand Chamberlain), disclosed in later years that when Blyth came to him after his interview with the emperor and told him that he would be serving as the Crown Prince's English tutor beginning in April 1946, Blyth added that it would be a good idea to invite an American lady to act as his tutor as well. Blyth's suggestion apparently set in motion a train of events that resulted in Emperor Hirohito's decision to invite the Quaker schoolteacher Elizabeth Vining to be his son's English tutor. Vining served in this position from 1947 to 1950. Blyth's own tutoring sessions, every Thursday for three hours, began in 1946 and continued until shortly before his death.

At this time, Blyth was also giving advice to General MacArthur, high-ranking members of his staff, and Japanese government officials such as Foreign Minister Yoshida Shigeru. Unfortunately, nowhere does Blyth explain how and why—so soon after his release from incarceration, having no previous political links or interests whatever—he was chosen for such an extremely sensitive role. In his excellent profile of Blyth, Adrian Pinnington says it was Yoshida Shigeru who asked Blyth to act as a channel between the two sides.[33] Yoshida had become foreign minister in the first general election following Japan's defeat, but a few months later, in May 1946, he was appointed prime minister. Pinnington's statement is entirely plausible, though I strongly suspect that the good offices of Yamanashi Katsunoshin, and perhaps Daisetz Suzuki, were somehow involved as well, perhaps by introducing or recommending Blyth to Yoshida.

Yamanashi Katsunoshin had served as president of the Peers School since the mid-1930s and was a close confidant of the emperor. He and Blyth were very close in the postwar period, and perhaps long before that as we shall see in a letter Yamanashi wrote Blyth in 1964 (quoted in the following paragraph). Yamanashi had invited Blyth to teach at the Peers School, and I believe that he had a leading role in the decision to use Blyth as a liaison between the Imperial Household and MacArthur's GHQ. Two years before his death, Blyth revealed his feelings toward Yamanashi in an essay in a Japanese newspaper, calling him "his best friend" and the "most perfectly rounded personality of anyone [he had] ever met." In a dinner speech after the war, Blyth is said to have declared that Yamanashi Katsunoshin and Daisetz Suzuki were the two men he respected above all others: "If Yamanashi became Prime Minister and Suzuki the leading Buddhist cleric, Japan would surely become an ideal country."

In a letter dated August 1964, Yamanashi wrote Blyth of his "profound respect for your many previous scholastic accomplishments, which it had been my most agreeable personal pleasure to help in many ways since we first met at Mejiro [the Peers School] about 40 years ago." This, if Yamanashi's recollection is correct, would take their acquaintance back to the time Blyth arrived in Korea in 1925. Or could they have met in London even before Blyth left?

Yamanashi had been an admiral in the prewar Imperial Japanese Navy. He was one of the leaders of the so-called Treaty Faction that in the 1920s and 1930s advocated lessening tensions with the Western powers. When this faction lost out in the mid-1930s to the increasingly hawkish military establishment, Yamanashi was "systematically retired" along with other moderates. In 1939, however, the emperor appointed him to the important post of president of the Peers School, which charged him with the education of Crown Prince Akihito, a position he held until 1946.

In his youth, Yamanashi lived for several years with an American family in Sendai, where he attended a Christian school. He also studied the Chinese classics and developed a deep interest in Zen Buddhism. As a young naval officer, he spent a number of years in England and seems to have acquired a love of English poetry. Blyth tells the story of mentioning with sadness the sudden death of a friend and colleague to Yamanashi, and Yamanashi replying simply, with words of Tennysonian, and Buddhist, resonance, "Mister Blyth, life is tears."

Although Yamanashi seems to have been as tight-lipped as Blyth about the liaison activity in which they were both deeply involved, he did refer to a meeting Blyth had with General MacArthur:

MacArthur discussed with Blyth the question of making the Emperor change his Shinto religion. But Blyth answered that a man's religion is a sensitive personal matter, and its impulse must come from within. Therefore the Emperor should not be approached on this matter. However, Blyth said he would try to explain Christianity to members of the Imperial Family and to encourage their understanding of the Christian point of view.[34]

It was at this meeting, according to Yamanashi, that Blyth suggested the Crown Prince would benefit from instruction from another Westerner in addition to himself and then floated the idea that the teacher might be an American, a Quaker, and a pacifist—the exact profile that Elizabeth Vining provided.

In *Windows for the Crown Prince*, Vining quotes what she heard about Blyth from Yamanashi:

Mr. Blyth is in an entirely different category, he has become almost more Japanese than English. . . . [H]e had been recommended by Mr. Yamanashi, who had great respect and admiration for him both as a man and as a scholar, to tutor the Crown Prince . . . though of course actually he brought far more to the Prince than that.[35]

Among older generations at the Peers School, Blyth is known as the person who stepped in and saved the school in 1946 when Allied military headquarters was formulating plans for abolishing Gakushūin and Gakushūin High School. Blyth discussed the matter with MacArthur and apparently was able to convince him to turn the schools, which had been the property of the Imperial Household, into private institutions open to the public. They were reestablished in 1947 under different administration, and in 1949 Gakushūin University officially opened its doors. An interesting sidelight that has not been known, but which Blyth's letters reveal, is that Blyth was asked to become president of Gakushūin, succeeding his friend Yamanashi. The idea had probably emanated from Yamanashi himself in recognition of the valuable service Blyth had contributed to the school. In reporting this offer to Dora Lord (Letter #53 on p. 112), Blyth underscored his lack of interest in the idea, although he did add that circumstances might force him to accept. Few people could have been less suited than R. H. Blyth for administrative duties, so it is no doubt fortunate that nothing came of the plan.

Another of Blyth's proposals set the wheels in motion to save the beautiful Japan Folk Crafts Museum (Mingei-kan) in Komaba, Meguro, Tokyo, which had been built before the war to the design of its founder Yanagi Sōetsu, one of Suzuki's leading students. Yanagi was notified in late 1946 that occupation authorities had decided to requisition both the museum building and Yanagi's adjacent house for use by the Dutch military attaché. Protests from various quarters ensued, generated not only by fear for the buildings themselves—it was said they were to be painted in European style—but by concerns that the loss of the museum would greatly impact the Mingei movement that Yanagi had launched before the war. Despite the protests, the decision remained unchanged until, as Yanagi himself explained it, the "three B's"—Blyth and his friends Colonel Laurence Bunker[36] and Beth Blake—intervened to save the day. Elizabeth Blake, the wife of Colonel Frank Blake, worked for the Red Cross in Tokyo. Colonel Bunker, who had helped Blyth implement other ideas involved in his liaison work, was aide-de-camp to MacArthur, so the matter was rather quickly resolved.

A much more momentous event in Blyth's liaison work had occurred the previous year when he drafted, perhaps even conceived, the famous *ningen sengen* or "Declaration of Humanity" that Emperor Hirohito issued on January 1, 1946, denying that he was a "living god" above the rule of manmade law.

It was a perilous time for the emperor and the imperial system itself. The occupation staff of U.S. civil servants and military personnel—dubbed SCAP for MacArthur's title of Supreme Commander for the Allied Powers—had been engaged in deliberations on the imperial system even before they set up shop in Tokyo. Many among them felt strongly that the emperor should be removed, the imperial system and the peerage abolished, and the emperor's assets transferred to the nation. General MacArthur, however, was not convinced that this should be done. When the idea was put forward that the emperor should make a public statement to the nation, proclaiming he was not a "living god," MacArthur is said to have been delighted. On New Year's Day 1946, an Imperial Rescript was published to that effect, which is credited with securing the survival of the imperial system.

There has been much speculation about the provenance and evolution of this document, but I find the narrative Adrian Pinnington sets forth in his essay on Blyth to be the most plausible one. He prefaces it with the observation that "much about the precise generation of this declaration remains a mystery or a matter of hearsay, partly for the obvious (and very Japanese) reason that it was important that it not be identified too closely with any one person or group, and yet had the backing of all concerned."[37]

Blyth was meeting several times a week with Lieutenant Colonel Harold Henderson (1889–1974), a Columbia University professor and haiku scholar who had published *The Bamboo Broom* (1933), a haiku primer of which Blyth had spoken highly. Henderson was attached to the Monuments, Fine Arts, and Archives (MFAA) section of MacArthur's staff at the time. According to Pinnington's account, one day early in December 1945, Blyth came to Henderson's office saying that he had heard from Imperial Household Minister Ishiwata that the emperor wished to renounce his divinity to ensure that his position could never be misused again. As Ishiwata himself recalled it, however, the whole idea began with a hint from Blyth. According to historian Takemae Eiji, Blyth pressed Henderson for suggestions, and Henderson jotted down a few thoughts that Blyth took to Yamanashi, who "sounded out the Emperor's advisors, who seized on the idea as a 'heaven-sent door.'"[38] The following day, a draft rescript of the Declaration of Humanity that Blyth had drawn up was agreed upon by the emperor's advisors. It was shown to MacArthur, who pronounced himself delighted and returned it to Blyth. Blyth then had Henderson burn the original draft in his presence, a condition stipulated by the Imperial Household.

Yamanashi later maintained that it was important the Declaration be seen as the emperor's own words while at the same time gaining the approval of GHQ. It is sometimes claimed that others proposed similar ideas as well, yet even if that were true, the fact remains that only someone in Blyth's unique position could have successfully brought it all together in this way.

Surprisingly, Blyth's contribution to this crucial pronouncement, though now acknowledged by most historians, still has not received widespread notice, even in Japan. As Harold Henderson remarked after Blyth's death,

He and I were once very close—outside the world of haiku. We were the "sub rosa" liaison channel between the imperial household and MacArthur. Blyth was in a great degree responsible for the Emperor's giving up his "divinity." And for that—as for many other things—he never received proper recognition.[39]

While Blyth was engaging in all these activities, he was also trying to get a grip on a busy teaching schedule as a member of the Gakushūin faculty and tutoring the Crown Prince once a week at the Imperial Palace. He took on weekly teaching assignments at the Diplomat's College where he instructed young Foreign Office officials, at Tokyo University, and at Nihon University, and a few years later at Tokyo University of Education, Jissen Women's University, and Waseda University as well.

Blyth's second daughter, Nana, was born in July 1947. He described for Dora the extraordinary life he was now engaged in:

It might interest you to know my time-table for the week.

Monday 9–4 Lecturing at Nihon University

Tuesday morning lecturing at the [Tokyo] Imperial University; afternoon teaching the Crown Prince

Wednesday morning teaching at the Peers School, afternoon lecturing at the Diplomat's College

Thursday teaching at the Peers School and a private lesson for Prince Rikyu

Friday lecturing at Imperial University 8–10; lecturing at Nihon University 10:30–4

Saturday morning, lecturing at Diplomat's School 9–12; afternoon, lecturing at University of Literature and Science [Tokyo Bunrika Daigaku] 12:30–4:30

In addition to this I have to give special lectures, and write articles for magazines in English and Japanese. This brings me about 4000 yen a month, of which I save about 1500.

. . . As I suppose you have seen from the papers, Mrs. Vining has arrived here, and we are going to do our best to use her for the demoralization of the Crown Prince, and indeed Court circles generally. She is like all American women, a little on the hard side, but very capable and tactful and will be a great success, I think. In her own words, she is "keeping her eye on the ball." (Letter #57 on p. 119)

Blyth used a bicycle to commute between these widely separated institutions, which required him to pedal long distances in the vast metropolitan

From left: daughter Nana, Tomiko, Blyth, and daughter Harumi, circa 1950s.

area. In what may have been a throwback to his boyhood days in London, he would sometimes hitch a ride by grabbing on to the side of a truck or car.

Robert Schinzinger, who lectured on German philosophy at Gakushūin, explained his colleague's unique method of teaching in a tribute he wrote after Blyth's death:

> His clothing was extremely simple. He joined no association whatever, because he was a very independent man. . . . It was his great purpose in teaching to make the students think for themselves and express their thoughts in English. . . . He compelled students to do this by making radical and provoking remarks. The students got angry and spoke. This ironical method was similar to that of Socrates. And as in the case of Socrates, so in the case of Blyth—not many understood his ironical and provoking method. Indeed, his provocations were sometimes shocking—like the beatings by an old Zen master. . . . For himself he needed very little. He did not drink or smoke, he did not eat meat, and he went to no place of amusement. His clothing was extremely simple, and he

moved from one university to another on his bicycle. When he came home, he would sit over his books and manuscripts until late at night.[40]

Blyth gave his own tongue-in-cheek description of his teaching style in a letter to Robert Aitken:

> I teach my students by insulting them; they don't mind it, because I look as if I don't care if they do. They feel I am giving more than I take away. (Letter #108 on p. 175)

Now that he had an income once again, Blyth lost no time in replenishing his library, and before too many years had passed, it would rival in size the one he lost in the war. He complained to Dora about the high price of books, but there are stories of him bicycling back and forth to the famous Kanda bookselling district, ferrying heavy loads of used volumes to fill his bookshelves at home. After Blyth's death his secretary Kobayashi Akiko donated his very considerable library—close to eight thousand volumes—to Daisetz Suzuki's Matsugaoka Library in Kita-Kamakura and his enormous collection of Bach musical scores to the Tokyo Bach Society.

In 1945, soon after finding a position at Gakushūin and moving to Tokyo, Blyth began trying to find a publisher for his book on haiku, not an easy task at a time of severe paper shortage and an almost total lack of English-language publishers in Japan. It ended up taking over three years to begin the publishing process, and another three to complete it—thanks, as we shall see, to help arriving from an unexpected source.

The haiku book, which Blyth had been working on during his internment, by now had "assumed such enormous dimensions" that he decided to publish the introduction as a separate volume. This finally appeared in 1949 as *Haiku, Eastern Culture*, published by Kamakura Bunko (Kamakura Books), a new firm specializing in Japanese literature that had been founded in 1945 by the Kamakura novelists Kume Masao, Kawabata Yasunari, and Takami Jun. As he explained to Dora early in 1949, probably during the spring,

> Mr. Yoshida [Shigeru], the Prime Minister, kindly found me a rich and patriotic chap who is willing to put up a million yen (!) to publish my four volumes of haiku translations (500 pages each) so they will be out this year. (Letter #69 on p. 135)

Soon after Blyth's book appeared, however, Kamakura Bunko declared bankruptcy, and Hokuseido Press, which had earlier published Blyth's *Zen in English Literature and Oriental Classics*, stepped in and agreed to publish the additional volumes. *Haiku, Spring* appeared in 1950, and *Summer-Autumn* and *Autumn-Winter* followed in 1952.

The first two of the four-volume set bear dedications to someone named Sakuo Hashimoto, "whose patriotic generosity made the publication of these volumes possible." The final two volumes, with similar wording, were dedicated to Naoto Ichimada, the governor of the Bank of Japan. Blyth confided to close friends some years later that Prime Minister Yoshida himself, who had earlier helped finance the publication of *The Cultural East*, had put up the funds—perhaps, it has been conjectured, in recognition of the contribution Blyth had made to preserving the imperial system.

Senryū, Japanese Satirical Verses, another work he seems to have begun in the internment camp, appeared in 1949, followed by two slim volumes, *Thoughts on Culture—Or, How to Be a Human Being* (1950) and *Buddhist Sermons on Christian Texts* (1952). He compiled student editions of favorite authors such as Henry David Thoreau, Robert Louis Stevenson, and Dorothy Wordsworth with short introductory essays for use in his lecture courses, and he contributed numerous articles and essays in both English and Japanese in answer to requests from Japanese newspapers and periodicals, most of which have never been reprinted.

In 1953 he was awarded a Bungaku Hakase (Doctor of Literature) degree from Tokyo University for *Zen in English Literature and Oriental Classics* and the four *Haiku* volumes.

Japanese Humour (1957) was the first of Blyth's books devoted exclusively to humor, which was directly linked in his mind to poetry and Zen. *Oriental Humour* and *Humour in English Literature* followed in 1959. Humor is also an essential theme of *Senryū, Japanese Satirical Verses* (1949) as well as two further works on senryū published in 1961—*Japanese Life and Character in Senryū* and *Edo Satirical Verse Anthologies*. Blyth spoke of humor as "the joyful, unsentimental pathos that arises from the paradox inherent in the nature of things," pointing out that "poetry and humour are thus very close; we may say that they are two different aspects of the same thing." Elsewhere he explained it more simply as "laughing at all things . . . seeing that 'all things are empty in their self-nature,' and rejoicing in this truth."[41]

In 1958, with retirement age approaching, Blyth purchased a house in Ōiso, a small town facing Sagami Bay, an hour-and-twenty-minute train ride southwest of Tokyo. With its splendid location and distant views of Mount Fuji, Ōiso had been favored since the Meiji period as a place of retirement by politicians and literary figures. Prime Minister Yoshida Shigeru spent his retirement in Ōiso in a spacious villa overlooking the sea.

Blyth is said to have taken the step at the urging of Yamanashi Katsunoshin, who facilitated the transaction in other ways as well. Blyth seemed to have been delighted with his new home situated in the hills behind the town. His final years were spent there in a small, two-story dwelling he built with his own hands behind the main house, together with his secretary, Kobayashi Akiko, a former student at the Jissen Women's College in Tokyo. In her he said he had found a kindred spirit, "a secretary, real wife, nurse, and comforter" (Letter #126 on p. 192). They took walks into the hills with their wirehair fox terrier, Guppy, viewing and sometimes sketching the Shōnan shoreline below. Blyth even put the long hours commuting to and from Tokyo to good use by reading or writing his books, many of which were composed in part on the train. He was readying for a divorce from Tomiko, from whom he was now separated, so that he could remarry. Stricken with a sudden illness, these plans were never realized.

In the spring of 1964, Blyth began to experience severe headaches that caused a loss of appetite, nausea, vomiting, and difficulty sleeping. In mid-May he gave what turned out to be his final lecture at Gakushūin. At the beginning of June, he requested sick leave from the university and entered a hospital in Hiratsuka, a large city next to Ōiso. He returned to his home at the end of June when no physical cause was found for his sickness, but the recurring headaches continued, greatly debilitating him. His physicians advised a change of surroundings.

Robert Aitken suggested a move to Hawaii and seems to have made preliminary inquiries about a position for Blyth at the East-West Center in Honolulu, an educational institution recently established at the University of Hawaii. It is unclear whether Blyth ever seriously contemplated such a move, but he finally wrote Aitken, "I will never, never, never go to Hawaii" (Letter #119 on p. 185) and in mid-September entered Saint Luke's (Seroka) Hospital in Tokyo. Again, no physical cause for the headaches could be found, and the following month he transferred to the Seiwa Neurological Hospital in Shinjuku, Tokyo. His condition grew steadily worse, and there,

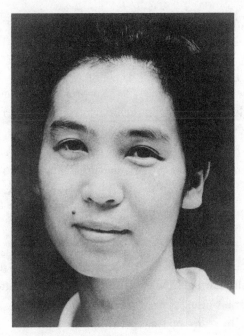

Kobayashi Akiko, circa 1970.

on October 28, he died from "complications of pneumonia." An obituary in the *Mainichi Evening News*, October 30, 1964, "based on Gakushūin sources," reported "he had lost his appetite and it is believed that general prostration was the cause of death"—which is perhaps as good an explanation as any that has been offered.

He was cremated and his ashes interred at Tōkei-ji, a subtemple of Engaku-ji in Kita-Kamakura, a few steps from where his friend and mentor Daisetz Suzuki's ashes would be laid to rest two years later.

I should perhaps add a word about the so-called "death verse," a haiku in English that Blyth is said to have written in his final days. It would have been totally out of character for him to write such a verse, even if he had not been plagued at the time by what he called "sick headaches" that rendered him so feeble that even his beloved Bach had lost all its flavor. But those who were with Blyth during his final illness have stated that no such verse was written. The English haiku usually cited as Blyth's was, in fact, by an elderly Japanese lady, an immigrant to the United States who was suffering from a terminal illness; his secretary had told Blyth about the verse after hearing the woman's story on the radio.

BLYTH'S LITERARY LEGACY

Considering that his first book did not appear until he was in his mid-forties, Blyth left behind a surprisingly large body of work, more than forty volumes between 1942 and 1964. He also produced miscellaneous prose writings in English and Japanese, including essays for journals and articles for newspapers, most of which have yet to be collected. Two works were published after his death: Volume Four of the *Zen and Zen Classics* series containing his translation of the *Mumonkan* koan collection, a text he had been working on since before the war, in April 1966, and Volume Three, entitled *History of Zen, Nangaku Branch*, in February 1970.

Blyth began to experience his sick headaches just as he was keenly looking forward to retirement and the opportunity of stepping up his already formidable literary efforts. He had recently confided to his secretary that he felt he had "finally learned how to write a book." A 1962 letter addressed to Mihoko Okamura, Daisetz Suzuki's secretary, lists four books he was working on or had in the planning stage:[42]

> *Zen Sermons on Christian Texts*, 200 pages, ⅓ finished. [It is not known whether this was to be an expanded version of his *Buddhist Sermons on Christian Texts* or a totally new work.]
>
> *A Zen Catechism*, 200 pages, not begun (translations from *Zenmon Kōan Taisei*). [ed. The *Zenmon Kōan Taisei* is a large classified compendium of Zen koans compiled by Otobe Kaihō and published in 1918.]
>
> *The Humour of the Japanese*, 400 pages, 1/2 finished.
>
> *Postulations and Expostulations* (quotations with commentary on religion, poetry etc.) 400 pages of materials already collected. [ed. The "materials" consisted of passages he had marked off in books during his reading, which his secretary had copied into notebooks, one to a page, leaving space below the excerpts for Blyth to add his "postulations."]

Blyth was often asked why he didn't leave Hokuseido Press and accept one of the offers several larger Western publishers had made to him that would ensure his works would reach a much wider audience. But he was perfectly satisfied with Hokuseido, which had published most of his books, and its president Nakatsuchi Jumpei, so he never showed any concern with selling his books in large numbers. A customary reply to such questioners would be something along the lines of "One true reader is enough."

It is nonetheless true that with their limited worldwide distribution, his books were never easy to find. Most American and European readers, me included, came to them by word of mouth. We have seen how Blyth's reputation among the Western artistic community, which had caught on early, had risen to enviable heights. By the 1960s, signs that he was being read by those in the literary establishment were appearing as well. *The New Yorker* was considering Blyth for its well-known Profile series. Scholarly British journals and the influential bimonthly American magazine *Horizon* were soliciting articles. Had he lived even another ten years, such channels would no doubt have made him and his writings much more widely known among the Western intelligentsia at large.

Today, over fifty years after his death, Blyth is probably best known for the haiku books and as the father of "world haiku." But we must not forget the extraordinary influence his writings on Zen and Zen culture exerted during his lifetime and in the decades after his death in helping to create the great interest in Zen that arose in America and Europe during these years. Indeed, their influence was so pervasive that some suggest that in spreading this enthusiasm for Zen in the West, Blyth's writings surpassed even those of his great mentor, Daisetz Suzuki.

Although today many of Blyth's books have become fairly rare items, the relevance of their message remains undiminished. I have no doubt that new generations of readers who have yet to discover them will experience the same excitement and receive the same inspiration from them that those of my generation did in the fifties and sixties. One farsighted member of that older generation wrote, "Long after his death, Blyth, like the best of Bodhisattvas, will go on refreshing our spirits, laughing away our conceits and evasions."[43] The well-known tribute of Blyth's friend J. D. Salinger, *Seymour: An Introduction*, struck a similar note:

> The best short Japanese poems—particularly haiku, but senryū, too—can be read with special satisfaction when R. H. Blyth has been at them. Blyth is sometimes perilous, naturally, since he's a high-handed old poem himself, but he's also sublime—and who goes to poetry for safety anyway?[44]

EDITORIAL NOTE: In order to preserve authenticity, Blyth's original writings have been mainly preserved in this book, including punctuation and, at times, wording idiosyncrasies.

LETTERS

As writers go, Reginald Blyth does not seem to have left behind a particularly large body of correspondence. This is no doubt due in part to the relative anonymity he enjoyed during the first forty-five years of his life: until he was known as a writer, recipients of his letters probably would not have been as likely to save them. There are no letters at all prior to 1924, the year he left England to assume his post at the Imperial University in Korea. I believe the present collection contains the great majority of the letters, and perhaps even all, that survive from the period of his long residence in Korea and continuing up until his release from internment in Kobe in 1945. No letters from the four-year internment are known. A U.S. State Department memorandum dated August 26, 1943, records that civilian internees at the civilian camps in Kobe were allowed one letter of 100 words each month.[1] I have found no evidence Blyth had this privilege; even if he did, his letters would probably have gone to his mother and thus would have been lost along with the others in her possession when she burned them after learning of his death.

With the letters from the postwar period—those written during the twenty years of Blyth's growing literary fame—the situation is different. I succeeded in tracking down a fairly large number of them. But there were two groups, one of letters to Robert Aitken, the other to Daisetz Suzuki—which were of an extraordinary interest that gave them a special priority. On that account, and in consideration of limitations of space perhaps inherent in a miscellany of this kind, I decided in the end to allocate virtually the entire postwar section to them.

Letters to Dora Lord and Parents

1929–49

As the British passport Blyth used during these first years in Korea does not seem to have survived, it is difficult to know how many trips back to England, if any, he made during these first years in Korea. He and his wife Anna apparently returned via the Trans-Siberian Railway during the summer recess of 1929. In 1934, he went back again, this time alone.

The 1929 trip is known only from references in Blyth's letters to his cousin Dora Lord, but it no doubt followed the same itinerary as the 1934 trip, which can be traced from the stamps in his new passport: he crossed over to Hagi in Yamaguchi prefecture in mid-July 1934, then sailed over the Japan Sea to Vladivostok, the railway's Asian terminus. In October, he renewed his Japanese visa in London and set out on the return trip to Korea, reaching Keijō at the beginning of November 1934, in time for the beginning of the fall semester.

8 Oct 1934	*Japanese Consulate-General London visa*
11 Oct 1934	*Calais passport stamp*
12 Oct 1934	*Aachen passport stamp*
13 Oct 1934	*Polish passport stamp*
21 Oct 1934	*Russian passport stamp*
24 Oct 1934	*Polish passport stamp*
30 Oct 1934	*Manchurian passport stamp (Japan had taken control of Manchuria, Manchukuo as they called it, in 1932.)*
31 Oct 1934	*Manchurian passport stamp*

When Blyth left Korea, and after arriving in London as well, he seems to have been more or less decided on not returning to Korea. Various circumstances, including meager prospects for a job in

England and a "desperate letter" from his friend Professor Fujii
begging him to return, made him change his mind.

1

August 17, 1929. Letter to Dora Lord during a trip home to London
with his wife Anna. I should probably point out that although my
own correspondence with Dora was addressed to Dora Orr, which
she adopted on her marriage in 1952, after that, her correspondence
with Blyth seems to have ended. In this book she is usually referred
to as Dora Lord.

Dear [Dora],
I have thought of several other things besides you since last night. (This is a figure of speech which might be called inverted understatement).

Will you meet me at the same time and place this Monday? If you can't come, don't bother about it, I will write and suggest another time. I don't give you the address because I don't want this letter returned to me by any chance. By a touch of genius on my part, Anna is under the impression that we formed and shall form on Monday, a party of three. I have to draw on my imagination for the appearance and conversation of the other gent.

I felt yesterday that you must think me fast (not in the vulgar, but in the ordinary sense of the word), but it was due entirely, as I fumbling tried to explain, not to an impetuous nature or a momentary mood, but to a sense of harmony both physical and mental, between us, existent then and potentially existent always.

You feared too, and rightly from a shortsighted view of the matter, the physical side rising up as a disturbing factor in our suddenly matured relations. In spite of all the Huxleys, we feel a desire, in our most elevated and discerning moments, to live as disembodied spirits, pure bright flames of thought. But this fear is lack of vitality, lack of self-respect. I cannot compress my thoughts into a single letter, however long. Thoughts of you spread and grow until they touch or embrace everything, involve all the past with its poorly assimilated experiences, until I despair of plucking and offering to you even one leaf of the forest of thoughts which encompasses me.

This may and perhaps must seem to you little more than an inedible and incredible mushroom but serenity comes rarely to me. I have many other things to say to you but on paper they seem to have the wrong tone and to have the additional disadvantage of sounding like a selection from popular sentimental ballads.

2

August 1929. Written to Dora during the same London trip as the previous letter.

Dearest,

As you know, the smaller the mistake, the greater its significance, and the slip of the pen on the envelop of the letter I sent you was an excellent though somewhat obvious example of this universal law. It might and should, however, be taken as absolute and direct evidence of what must otherwise be inferred only circumstantially, namely, that I think as highly of you as I say I do, and that the sentiments I feel for you spring from the deeper layers of personality.

I felt the letter to be pompous in tone and insincere in manner though not in content. This one is a little better, though terribly stiff and on its highest horse (so far).

To love trees and to love Bach and to have an unlimited sense of humour, to possess these with health of mind and without gush or insincerity,—that is what draws me to you. "Health of mind" is an overworn phrase but by it I imply the air, the aroma, the light and the shadow, without which nothing is really beautiful. It is, essentially, the style of the mental life, the way it runs and skips and pauses and runs on again, informing and softening every act of thought with grace.

To love Bach, is not merely to like the best music; it is to be religious in the profoundest, the most joyful and most agonized sense of the word.

To love trees is to feel the deep meaning of Nature not so much for its picturesque, as for its physical, vital, primitive value; we feel their abounding life so fully that we could burst into bud and leaf ourselves.

"An unlimited sense of humour": I wish I could end my little sonatina with a scherzo; a Coda must suffice, and that pianissimo.

3

Written either in 1929 or 1934, when he was in London and contemplating prospects for a job that would enable him to return to England.

Dear Dora,

Thank you very much for the booklet. After such kindness, it is a dismal thing to have to say I won't go with you. The reasons are various, chiefly these—I have little money, no immediate prospect of a job; if I go somewhere with you, I would rather go to a concert or something. In addition, I feel I must look economical as well as be it.

Going back to pleasanter things, I haven't looked at the booklet yet, but even the sight of it is stimulating and the feeling that somebody cares for me-and-the-things-I-care-for is perhaps what I am most in need of. The book of animal pictures is so good it is only with a slight effort that I begin to look at it—with me an invariable sign of goodness in the object.

I have no time to write anymore as I am going out with my mother. Yesterday I went to a dog show by myself. I felt very melancholy there—none of the dogs cared tuppence for me.

Love, Reg

4

Written while in England; the salutation and opening lines suggest a 1929 date, before he and Anna left to return to Korea.

Dearest,

I have had time but no opportunity to write to you before. I am at Brighton alone; this Saturday or Sunday we start on our return journey. I cannot see you before I go; I can only ask you to write as often as you feel inspired. It was very fortunate that Anna was so well impressed by you. She said, "When we come back I would like her to become part of the family circle." As I am much the most likely to be the first deceased (of Anna and me), I cannot help strongly recommending you (though it is a form of autodentistry) to get married as quickly as you can to the other gent. If you don't

I feel that you will live to regret it. I have found that life, in the form of the mere passage of time, effects more reconciliations than breaches, and unites more often than it divides. This can occur, however, only when two reasonable and amiable persons are forcibly held together during the early trying periods. This formal and artificial connexion is provided by churches and registry offices.

Love, RHB

5

Possibly written in the early 1930s. The music references suggest
an earlier date, and "two mouths to feed" to the responsibility of
educating the young Korean boy Li Insoo, who, according to Shinki
Masanosuke's biographical sketch of Blyth, began to live with Blyth
and Anna around 1929.

Dear Dora,

Not writing to you is only laziness. The summer holiday is about to begin, and I am making my plans for it. They are almost entirely musical ones except for a few days on the boat up the river. This year there has been plenty of rain, so now Korea looks a little more Formosan than usual.

You say in your letter to my mother that I probably have longings for England, especially for some people in it. I do not deny it but would put it a little more paradoxically & say I would like to be [in] England on account of the people who are not in it.

I would return to England today (I think) if it were not for the money. Consumption here means consumption of money also & I have nothing (literally) in the Bank at present. The cost of living here is about 3 times normal also.

War conditions & half-witted patriots make things here very disagreeable. But there are two mouths to feed & I must stop here indefinitely at present. The students are extremely charming & amiable & make life tolerable for me. All my spare time & some of the rest, is spent in playing.

I have found a farmer who is also a pianist. He comes from his fields in Jinsen once a week to play.[2] His touch is a blow of the fist but he reads well enough. He does not seem to distinguish the minor & major scales very clearly. However, Corelli is supposed to have done the same thing at times. For light reading Grove's dictionary of music is always a pleasure. I haven't read a novel for a couple of years, nor been to the cinema for six months. On Wednesday we play Mozart; concertino for Violin & Viola (the viola part is not easy); Mozart Trio no. 1 (cello very easy except when not); & Trio for Violin & Viola of Buxtehude.

Then after the violinist has departed, I shall play a Purcell Sonata for Violin, Weber Clarinet Concertino, Marcello cello sonata, Telemann oboe sonata & Schumann's 3 Fantasiestücke for oboe & if any breath or strength is left, Matheson's flute sonatas. All this. All this is really only practice of fingers & brain, one can't really get any musical satisfaction unless all parties are playing musically. One day we shall play them together, I trust.

This summer I intend to study the sonata & symphony form so that I can *hear* the exposition & development & so on, & *hear* where they begin to leave off. Mozart's sonatas (piano) & symphonies are the best for such a purpose, I suppose.

Love, Reg

———

6

Undated; from the content, I would date this 1930–32, perhaps even a bit earlier.

Dear Dora,

Thank you for the French, but it was surprisingly easy to read. After that insult you will be glad to hear that the other teachers thought from the photo that you were under 20.

You ask me about Blake's philosophy. Well, as you probably know, he hadn't one, if by philosophy you mean system of metaphysics. But putting things in a practical way—there are two worlds, the visible and the invisible. The world of eating drinking marrying banking and so on, & the world of music religion & so on. In this latter world most of us, even the best, live momentarily, by fits and starts, and sometimes for long stretches, not at all. Blake, like St. Francis, was not a great thinker but was consistent, believed what poets only say, took spiritual things at first hand, not predigested, & of course paid the penalty: he was a bit off his chump.

To see forms and not blots of matters, to hear music and not merely noises, to see the spiritual world like Bunyan—*all the time*—this is more than human nature can bear. Something must bust. To create a world of Grace in this world of Nature is the collective task of human beings, but what a see-saw, what a tug of war it is.

I myself (& almost everybody is the same) have a great dislike of symbolism that is not simple and direct & based on common & natural facts of life. So the symbolic books of Blake are merely irritating.

As an artist, the strangeness of his symbols is an advantage for they may be neglected with ease & pictures may present intellectual difficulties which to lyrical poetry at least, is forbidden.

I don't know whether you read much poetry: probably not: it is hard work and has little social value. Recently, I bought the *Oxford Book of English Verse* (I had never looked at it before) and have begun reading it through backwards. I would be glad if you would do the same & tell me what you like & what you don't. Quiller-Couch has unfortunately a penchant for the wordy and sentimental which is deplorable but a lot of poetry has also crept in. I am very fond of pictures in poetry but how rare they are in spite of the long descriptions. As in painting it is not the scene or the objects of it which matter, but the lighting and juxtaposition of masses and colors which only the *eye* can give that make a poem alive.

I cannot have any prejudice against programme music. The three best examples I know (from records, of course) are "In the Steppes of Central Asia" by Borodin, which is perhaps the best, "March to the Scaffold" of Berlioz, and "Siegfried Idyll" of Wagner (*not* Forest Murmurs or something like that).

The first & the last are two aspects of nature or of men in relation to them, the "wide open spaces" and German Fairy Tale mountains valleys & forests.

The second is man as I see him, myself being the cor anglais at the end, the poor bloke they murdered so artistically (death in a frock coat, so to speak).

The servant has a radio & I hear it only too often. The other day they relayed the 9th Symphony from Berlin. I thought someone was learning the concertina. Last night a Tchaikovsky piano concerto very well played from Tokyo. I don't like Tch. a bit. His slow movements are sentimental & the fast just scrambling about without any inner severity.

I hope you will write a long letter next time about music & poetry. Nothing else matters. You will say, "What about myself." "Yourself?" They are unknowns & unknowables. They are "subjects." Poetry & music are "objects," always the same, without mood or passion pure & perfect, very different from you and

Reg.

7

This seems to have been written soon after the previous letter in which he asks Dora to buy the Oxford Book of English Verse *(1931–32). The content and tone of this letter suggest the earlier Keijō period when Blyth's chief priorities were European poetry and music.*

Dear Dora,

Here is another begging letter. As you probably know, there is a series called "The Hundred Best Lyrics" in various languages. I have the French and the German, and don't want the English, but I would be glad if you would send me all the rest of the series.[3] The publishers are Gowans and Gray and they used to be 6d books but must be more expensive now. It seems you didn't do as I suggested, buy the *Oxford Book of English Verse* and tell me what you liked in it. I keep two notebooks, one for English and one for foreign poetry and copy the bits I like into them. Without some kind of self-competition or collection, it is difficult to keep on pegging away at poetry. In music it's different; Bach is enough, or rather too much.

I will send the colour prints via Siberia so you will get them at about the same time as the letter. Send me the bill for the Bach.

Love, Reg

8

The mention of Italian poetry and predominance of musical references suggests a 1930–33 date.

Dear Dora,

I was really pleased that great minds think alike and that you have not been forced to hide the *Daily Mirror* in the city every day.

Wood made the 1st Symphony sound like the 10th or at least the 4 ½th.[4] When Easton sang the machine fortunately went wrong.

While wiggling the nob about last night I accidentally knocked into the Passacaglia on the organ and I am sorry to have to inform you that it was much much better on the organ than on the orchestra. It was of course splendidly played (in France, where they have the best organists in the world) and with the unified solemnity that it was written for. The fugue was much slower than the record so the parts were very clear.

From what I can hear of it Harriet Cohen seems to be playing very well but I would rather listen to the 5th Symphony—it has the *con moto*, the lack of which I think puts Brahms in the second class as you say.

This letter is all about music; it ought to be about It.[alian] poetry but we must temper the mind to the shorn lamb or rather the unfledged eagle.

Love, Reg

———

9

1932–34?

Dear Ma & Pa,

I have started Russian again and I am quite surprised to find how much I haven't forgotten. The reason for restarting is rather remote. Recently, I find I have a better understanding of poetry, particularly of the simply pictorial unsophisticated kind. English poetry is, by contrast with German and Russian, very gushing and flamboyant and so the content of German and Russian poetry especially deprived of a proper feeling of the sound, seems prosaic and uninspired—Chinese poetry is the same.

Ma speaks rather slightingly of a life spent apart from others; after all, it is relative in two ways. What is solitude in one is oppressive in another and it is better to be at peace and peaceful alone than to be boorish and uncomfortable in company. So with myself. I study best in a crowd of people as long as they are people I know well and who have no emotional, financial or other designs on me. In the presence of others I smile falsely or become controversial.

Everything in life is receiving something from others, the highest form being the reception of pleasure by giving. What I have to give, others do not wish to receive. What I wish to receive others cannot give. So I must take from the dead or absent their best and live like Robinson Crusoe in the middle of the city.

In reading the compositions by the students on "my character" I could not help being struck by the thought that they found it difficult to distinguish their bad and good points because so many of them are both good and bad in different combinations.

So for example, my best point is perhaps that I never get angry and never sulk but it is also my worst, because I give way to the madder, lack emotion, lack the power to persevere once begun, am in fact a weak character.[5]

Love, Reg.

10

1932–34?

Dear Dora,

I have lost your letter so I can't reply to it but I don't suppose you mind that.

I have begun several letters to you but never finished or sent any of them. The reason is of course that I would not insult you by sending anything other than a personal letter. In my shallow cold nature there are three deep warm places: they are (not in order) the opposite sex (plural only consecutively) animals and music.

About the first, the less said the worse, no doubt, but its profundities are so simple that even a child could understand them.

Animals are very concrete beings, often too much so as one feels when kicked by a horse, and hardly to be written about in letters. The love of animals is an atavistic affair, like all good things, and the meaning of the hand of a monkey or the tail of a dog is not to be put into words.

But music has the happy quality of perpetual enjoyment; even in the most silent night, or the hardest dentist's chair, it can be tasted and enjoyed.

For us however the difficulty is not to bore each other by gushing about what the other has not heard. Here there are no concerts & no radio. Records & one's own playing keep the standard of taste very high.

I think I remember your saying something rather cool about Bach. Rather than suppose there is anything wrong with yourself I would assume that the playing you hear is bad. All the orchestral playing of Bach is poor. I remember Myra Hess grinning like a Cheshire cat and banging away at a piano concerto. I remember the flute concerto all sentimentalised or played double the speed that Bach intended it. It is strange, but true that Beethoven may be played badly & still emerge here & there but Bach disappears immediately. To play Bach requires two things, a spiritual outlook on life (in the sense of the German Wert-Philosophie[6]) and a concept of the meaning of the form and pattern of notes and phrases.

If Beethoven had not lived it would be a great loss to me: if Bach had not lived then I myself might just as well have not been born. I say this quite simply and unemotionally, but mean exactly what I say & more. I feel alive only when I hear Bach. When I read poetry or look at pictures I have some birth tremors but they come to nothing, they are mere spasms. Of course I have the same experience with Scarlatti and Haydn & Mozart but I cannot give myself freely to them as I can to Bach. Mozart often, in the overtures and Beethoven almost everywhere drops out of the world of music into the world of emotion or vulgarity or mere noise.

Anyway I have written a letter to you & I hope you will write as often as you have anything to say.

I spend my time playing Bach on the piano, Bach on the flute, Bach on the violin, and Marcello on the cello, with Haydn trios as a recreation, thirty-one seems only too few to play again & again.[7]

Love, Reg

———

11

1932–34. The explanation of Wert-Philosophie suggests this was written soon after the previous one.

Dear Dora,

The other day I sent you a few Japanese colour prints, so please tell me when they arrive.

You are right when you say "somewhat inexactly, that music and so on makes life possible." They are life itself. You asked me in another letter to explain Wert-Philosophie & I would like to do so if possible, & see whether, in the process of explanation, I really understand it myself. I am inclined to believe what Croce says, that inability to explain an idea means that you haven't got it: if I can't say what I mean I don't mean anything.

We live two lives, in two entirely different worlds, they may overlap & to our clumsy analysis appear to insensibly gradate into onto another, but fundamentally & in reality they are distinct:—the world of the body and the world of the spirit.

The one is so transitory & ephemeral that we are almost tempted to call it unreal. To the other, the notions of time & space do not apply at all. I draw *a* circle and I erase it, but *the* circle existed before I drew one & will exist when I erase it.

The spiritual life, which we now & then live, is of four different kinds, again, separate and distinct in character:—the worlds of the intellect, of beauty, of morality and of religion.

The difference between the last two, or rather the existence of the last one at all, is very obscure to me, though very clear to many people. But I cannot deny its existence any more than a deaf man should deny the existence of the world of music. I have a glimpse of it when I see that Christ says to the rich man, not, with Bernard Shaw, "Thou thief!" (that is a moral judgment) but "Thou fool!" (a religious one).

There are then four of these values (Western) to be achieved in life. It is the purpose of life to realize them. And here is a point of the greatest practical importance. When you look at a picture you may have one of two entirely different standpoints. You may say, "I like it, I think it to be beautiful"; other people may differ, & they have a right to their own opinions. If we disagree no one knows who is right & who is wrong. It is all a "*matter of opinion, of taste*. What is admired now may be despised a few years hence."

The absolutist says, "The beauty & poetry of this picture exist existed & will exist, before it was painted, after it is destroyed, whether you appreciate or not, when you look at it & when you turn your eyes away from it. It is God, it is the great 'I am.' Here is one of the 'Wert,' realized in time & space for our contemplation. If you cannot see its beauty you are blind. If you deny its worth, you are wrong. 'Get thee behind me, Satan!'"

At first sight by the way, the first seems more humble & and the second intolerably arrogant but upon closer examination, the precise opposite is seen to be the case. After all, which is more conceited, to say, "I believe in God" or "I don't believe in God"? (Agnosticism is impossible, at least in practical life: you must adopt one hypothesis or the other.)

Relativists may be defeated only by analogy but that is perhaps the only way anyone can be persuaded of anything.

Like this:

$2 \times 2 = 4$ An intellectual judgement. No one denies the absoluteness of this. It is relative to no one at any time.

The Samaritan was good. This is a moral judgement; by analogy equally absolute.

The Divine Comedy *is a work of art.* (aesthetic judgement.)

"Blessed are the pure in heart." This is (I suppose) a religious judgement.

It may be that in my dull way I have oversimplified it, but I see it just as simply & no more profoundly than I have expressed it (a very apt illustration of Croce).

Speaking of the boat, no, I don't carry the boat, it's too heavy, but I have to pay two or three men to pull it up, places where the water rushes so fast that you can[not] stand up even in a couple of feet of it. Yes, I would like to go up the river with you, in fact live on the river with you & drown in it too, solo, or accompanied as you wish. I hate the sea: it is so vast & speaks of eternity in every falling wave, but a river carries one away more insensibly, the melancholy is not so frightful. If you wish to get a book on Japanese poetry there is a rather bad one (but the best) for £1, published by Maruzen and Co. in Tokyo, called *An Anthology of Haiku, Ancient and Modern* by Miyamori [1932].

For me, Japanese Haiku are the next best thing in the world after Bach. I don't know whether I mentioned it before but you *must* get HMV Toccata in F, Bach, London Symphony Orchestra.[8]

I only hear it on a small gramophone but I imagine on a modern affair it would be unbearably triumphant & glorious. Bach never wrote anything better. On the second side there is one specially appealing note (after a dim. held on for two bars[9]), near the end, a d, I think on the clarinet which is almost painful; it is so full of (formal) meaning. [I have just put the record on & (am) already blubbering].

Love, Reg

The post cards are my favourite film actors.

12

June 8, 1933. Prior to the return trip in the summer of 1934 and to Anna and Li Insoo's departure for England.

Dear Ma & Pa,

In one of the last letters I included a letter for Dora. It was very stiff I'm afraid but really she is, other than yourselves the only person in England I want to see when I get back. I often wish I were there, especially I would like to let you hear me play. In fact, a great proportion of my playing is to prepare myself to play in trios and quartettes when I get back.

Jimmy plays the violin very well now—much better than I, at least technically.[10] But when we play together I am always at a disadvantage because I must play myself and listen to both. He just goes on playing, right or wrong, he doesn't care. Another advantage for him is that he is left-handed. You can see, I suppose that I am a little jealous of him. I suppose it can't be helped.

Everything now is green and lovely but things are beginning to look too closely planted together. I can't dig anything up because I have nowhere to put them, so they must do their best and fight one another for light and shade.

I haven't heard anything lately about Ma's health; I hope it is because there is nothing to write about.

Love, Reg

13

Early 1930s?

Dear Dora,

This paper is not very inspiring but it's all I could get at the moment. By the way the Japanese teachers always admire your writing when the letter comes.

I can't help thinking how strange our relations have been. Let me write down everything I remember, you will see what a "will to forget" I have.

You used to live with us at 22 Pyrmont Rd. [ed. Chiswick, West London]. I felt attracted to you, only because you were of the opposite sex. I think only two things remain in my head, neither very much to my credit. One is, leaning over your shoulder for half an hour trying to see more than the regulation six inches of neck below the Adam's apple. The other is, hearing Pachmann with you and hating him & the Chopin he played.[11]

I'm still the same; we never change. Of course I hated you for agreeing, as you invariably & sometimes unnecessarily did, with my mother. I feel that even now we might quarrel about that. You see it's not a family question, or a question of emotions, but of judgements. There are four deadly sins, each fatal by itself, sentimentality, vulgarity, snobbery, cruelty. You can arrange them in your own order. My mother has only the first, but in a very chronic & subtle form, as incurable as an ingrowing toenail. It is an exquisite torture to live with, not to love & to be loved by such a person.

After having thought about yourself in regard to the above four, perhaps you will spare a thought for me as well. I may as well tell you that I have none of them but hasten to add that though I have no vices, I am deficient in the virtues, especially of what seems to me the highest, namely depth & tenacity of emotion. However I will not pursue such a painful subject.

Just at the moment there seems nothing more delightful than landscape photography (especially as it is raining heavily just now). Nowadays I walk about glaring like a hungry lion & things appear good or bad merely as they are photographable or not. I have forgotten the number of the road you live in, so instead of waiting for your letter to arrive I will send this to my mother & you will get it quicker.

Love, Reg

14

Circa 1933–34?

Dear Dora

My mother sent me your letter to her as well as that to me. I think the tonsillitis more serious than the other. People never die of a broken heart but always of a broken neck.

In the cinema when the hero & heroine are parted, temporarily or permanently, there is always some vulturish smooth-faced creature standing about to pick her up. I feel like that myself. It's a pity someone won't die & leave you a fortune so that you could take a trip out here. Anyway I felt like a different person already engaging in a correspondence with a lady (& by the way that reminds me, you *are* a lady).

Speaking of music, the expression you use, "emotions surging through at me," is so apt, it so exactly gives the game away.

No one may lay down laws for art, but I think there is no doubt that in art as in life, objectivity is everything. This is the superiority of Buddhism over Christianity, or rather, of Buddha over Christ, or to put it another way, lowness of the subjective element leads to vulgarity, as in Weber and Schubert; in the objective element it can only cause a negative quality, dryness or mere intellectuality. However, it would be a poor argument to suggest that what can fall lowest cannot rise highest. But "through *at me*" seems the hallmark of the transitory & impermanent. If you don't feel that a picture is beautiful whether you are there or not, if you don't feel that its beauty, once discovered (not invented) by the artist is eternal & self existent, then you do not know what art is, you only know a kind of artistic masturbation. So with music, to say that the Jupiter Symphony is heavenly is the right way to feel & express. It belongs to the ideal, the real world, into which we sometimes peep (not "range") and live for a moment out of space and time. You speak of Bach's slow movements. "Slow" is a little suspicious. I think you will find that the best music is always fast. The cloven hoof is most visible in sarabandes and other slow movements. Mozart's slow movements often show him up and Mendelssohn always collapses. You see, a rapid movement whips one out of oneself a little, one hasn't time to think, "Isn't it beautiful," and to blubber, "Isn't it beautiful!" when analysed always resolves itself into a subjective judgement, being equal to "Don't *I* enjoy really *good* music." Or "How sensitive I am to all that is good and noble!"

As to myself, I'm about to embark on another journey up the Han River, alone this time. I'm taking a little dog, Dante's Paradiso, an oboe with Bach's organ trios, a camera, paints and paper & feel myself to be a real highbrow, but I'm a low brow at bottom & I expect I shall spend the whole time rushing up the river at 100 yards an hour & get as far as I can before I get tired of it.

Your handwriting is rather like mine, except that it is a little more manly perhaps. There is nothing more preposterous than the pretence of reading character from handwriting, don't you think?

I have nothing else in my head at the moment so I'll stop, otherwise this will degenerate into a mere letter.

Love (of various kinds)

Reg

15

Circa 1933–34?

Dear Dora,

This week I am sending you a little book on Zen Buddhism. I think you will understand it, especially if you read it in the light of your appreciation of Nature and Music.

In one of your letters to my mother which she sent to me, you said, perhaps only facetiously, that you might travel out to the Far East. If that would be possible, I will give you twenty or thirty pounds; that would almost pay your fare here and you will have no expenses here so you would really only want your fare back.

This morning I crammed eight people into my small room and we played two Brandenburg Concertos, the one with two flutes and violin in G and the one with flute, violin, oboe and trumpet in F. I wrote out the trumpet for another violin. The other day we played No 6, but the second viola broke down in the middle of the last movement and said he would take it home and practice it.

Love, Reg

16

January 19, 1934

Dear Dora,

I have this morning received the pictures you so kindly and wisely sent. I have already asked the school clerk to make frames for them and they will be hung in the English room from the beginning of the next term. Of them all I like the Bronte country best.[12]

When I received your last letter and read that you would probably now not gush about Chopin, in a fit of perversity I went out and bought a Chopin record, a rondo for two pianos; even now I think it's rather good, please hear it if you can.

But when I hear Bach I hear the voice of God; Mozart and Beethoven are the tinkling cymbal and sounding brass, except here and there. The angels might sing the music of Mozart but they would have to listen to Bach.

This is getting perilously near gush and froth but nowadays I speak very little English; if I speak at all, it is Korean or Japanese so I am degenerating somewhat.

I suppose I must be happier than most people, not temperamentally, for I have the monkey's heritage of peevishness and discontent, but in regard to the number of sources of pleasure from which I can and do draw there is only one, I think, which is barren to me, and that is the pleasure of social life. I like to get it at second hand from the cinema, but it is disagreeable in prospect, false and degrading in realisation and loathsome in retrospect. This is, of course, abnormal and morbid, but not therefore uncommon or wicked.

There are one or two books & pieces of music I would like you to get for me, but I will tell you next time (and enclose the money).

By the way, what do you think of animals? What do you think of Socialism? What is your religion? These are among the most unimportant things but you might fill a page or two talking round them.

Love Reg

17

According to the chronology in Shinki Masanosuke's Kaisō no Buraisu, *Anna left for England in April 1934, which would mean this was written March or April 1934. However, the next letter implies she left before late January 1934, probably in 1933 and perhaps as early as the spring of that year. Professor Shinki is the only witness we have. His memory may have been wrong, or perhaps Anna and Insoo did not end up leaving "within a week or so" as Blyth states in this letter.*

Letter to Dora.

Dear Dora,

What I know about human beings, I have learned from animals, especially monkeys and dogs. Monkeys need freedom more than food and love more than freedom. It is not very difficult to distinguish between a dog that is loved by someone, and one that isn't. Of course some people, like some animals, prefer loving to being loved. You will please tell me to which type you think you belong. But as a rule, I suppose, the higher the type the more love there is to give or be given. Now you are certainly of a very high type (after all, we are relatives!) and consequently, or anyway, you have that grinding feeling of not-wantedness from which the unemployed suffer. You will not thank me much for putting you among the

Letter to Dora.

unemployed, animal and human, but there it is. I am self-assured enough to think that if I were in England I could help you out of your emotional slough of despond but I must stick onto the job until they throw me out. It is quite impossible for me to get a job in England and I have to keep one other person besides myself.

You will be interested to hear that Anna and the Korean boy who lives with us and the son of a rich Korean, are setting off for England within a week or so. It is a blessed relief for me but financially it will be a strain. They intend to stop 18 months at least.

My great ambition at present is one day to be able to play through without stopping the 48 Preludes and Fugues.[13] I often think that if Bach had not

Letter to Dora.

been born, life would not have been worth living—pleasant, here and there, but valueless.

This is a very unsatisfactory & unsatisfying letter. I am sorry. But I cannot do anything else except throw up my job and wait for you at 5 or 6 o'clock outside the bank every day.[14]

Love, Reg

18

January 25, 1934. Professor Shinki has stated that Anna departed for England in May 1934; in this letter, however, Blyth says that she has already left.

Dear Dora,
I want you to send me the following books; on the understanding of course that books without a bill will not be accepted. They are

1. *More Translations from the Chinese*—Arthur Waley pub. by Knopf, New York
2. *Chinese Poetry in English Verse*—H. A. Giles, pub. unknown
3. A single-volume unannotated Spanish edition of *Don Quixote*

As far as Anna is concerned we can only let nature take its course (sometimes Nature is rather in the raw).

You tell me not to ask you about love—well, I wasn't going to. I know all about it, how rare, how profound it is always; how embarrassing, inconvenient and unwanted it may be sometimes.

You say you are a bitter disillusioned perplexed creature. It's like finding out that a Brahms symphony, for example, is just a lot of shallow sentiment; or that Wordsworth was just pulling the public's leg. Bitterness, too, implies more activity of nature than I have. My head is always bowed when bloody.

"Perplexed" also is kicking against the pricks of the intellect. It would be more strange that the world were intelligible than that it is the mystery we find it to be. Shaw once said that the only way to be happy is to have no time to wonder if you are happy or not. That is all very well for a cold fish like him.

If you had called yourself "unfortunate" I could have assented (and my letter would have been so much the shorter). You should have been born one of those love-lucky persons who cannot love but are loved, in profusion. Even God seems to share our human weakness of wishing to be loved rather than to love. The saints, boiled in oil or buried alive, were to love Him in spite of it.

Anyway, understanding the nature and causes of our troubles is the only alleviation that is given to us.

At first the enclosed programmes gave me such a pang I didn't know what to do with myself, but afterwards I managed to persuade myself that I would rather listen to my old favourites of the first rank (on the gramophone) than the potpourri of good and indifferent likes and dislikes that even the best concert must offer.

You seem to be mixed in your horns. The horn I know nothing about except that bubbles are inevitable in a man of ordinary salivary glands. The English Horn is always out of tune because the reed is double, like the oboe and bassoon, but the oboe is short in length, and the bassoon seldom has solos using the whole range; the cor anglais differs very much in the upper and lower registers and is used over its entire compass for all sob-stuff solos.

I think of you very often in a very misty kind of way. You will wonder as I do myself, what "misty" means and signifies.

I think it is this. I must stop here and get as much money as I can (which means at the moment, none at all, with Anna gone to England), and England and all the people in it *must* be about as real as Paradise and you as living as the Virgin Mary.

19

On Keijō University paper; mid-1930s? The reference to a Don Quixote book suggests a follow-up to Letter #18.

Dear Dora,

I received your rather badly written letter today & the books as well. I am sending pounds 2 to cover (as they say) the cost of the books & the Chinese Poems which I hope are better than the title. The passage on love which you quote is true but not inspiring: no one is proud of being a polygamist.

Nowadays, I regret the time I spent on the study of English Literature more than that spent on Mathematics. So many beautiful passages hackneyed or associated with weariness or anxiety, not to speak of nausea.

The Don Quixote is just right, the pictures do no harm to the eye of the mind.

Recently I have gone barmy on Chinese poetry & sit up half the night ruining my eyes on Chinese dictionaries. I might say that I love poetry: I feel the same warmth of pure affection that I have for—whom?

Reg

The following passage is apparently a postscript Blyth added to the letter.

What does that impudent Dora mean by calling me an introvert? Do I listen to music as an introvert? Do I see fawns & fairies or dragons & demons? What is there introverted about Zen? Who wants to meditate on his own stinking self? Everything good in the world is made & is to [be] understood objectively. And one may consider oneself an object also of course. This is close to but absolutely different from subjectivity & introversion. Three cheers for Reg the extrovert!　　　　　Love from same

————

20

This letter, lacking the "Dear Dora" salutation, chimes in overall content with the pre-1935 period of the previous letters. The words "about being 45" are difficult to explain if taken literally. If they were forty-five at this time, the letter would date from the period of the Kobe incarceration, improbable since he doesn't seem to have been allowed mailing privileges while in the camp. Or is Blyth alluding to a remark Dora may have made about the future—what it would be like "when we are 45"? The reference to "Rangoon and a C. of E. [Church of England] at Worthing" (a seaside resort in West Sussex) is also not altogether clear, although one explanation may be that around the time of Blyth's 1934 (or possibly 1929) trip home, when he was thinking of returning to England for good and wondering about his job prospects, Dora had sent him a list of applications that included these two strikingly different job options. I tentatively date this letter to the first half of 1934.

I received your letter, with a list of vacancies, this morning: Rangoon and a C. of E. at Worthing. Atheists also suffer for righteousness' sake.

Don't mess about with your ears; go to a doctor if you must.

About Harriet Cohen, you agree with me or I with you that simply playing (as in singing) is difficult to find.[15]

About being 45. I don't consider birds, flowers and so on the small things; there is nothing larger; I read Dante almost entirely to be taught how to look at such things. His poetry, when it is poetry, deals with hardly anything else. He himself was always moping about the country-side though he had many other interests—different from you and me. When I was a boy, I remember the children used to ask the ice cream man for a "taster." It would be a good idea if you could get hold of Dean Church's essay on Dante; it is very short and you would then need no urging to do what you are predestined to do. There is a Greek saying to this effect: I follow destiny joyfully, and if with tears, I still must follow (with tears means unwillingly).

Love, Reg

21

March 1, 1934

Dear Ma & Pa,

Just lately I have started reading some Chinese poetry, of course in Japanese pronunciation. I have succeeded in managing one so I will write it out and translate it; you must read it downward and from right to left, but even then I don't think you will make much sense of it.

Translating it word for word, it is this: (6 lines; 7 words in each line)

1. yellow-cloud-castle-surroundings-crow-desirous-home
2. return-fly-ah-ah-bough-above-croak
3. loom-inside-brocade-weave-Shin-sen-woman
4. blue-cloth -like-smoke-passing-through-window-talk
5. stop-shuttle-melancholy-think-faroff-man
6. Alone-empty-sit-room-tears-resembling-rain

The poet, Li Po, lived about a thousand years ago.

鳥夜啼
黃雲城邊烏欲棲
歸飛亜亜枝上啼
機中織錦泰川女
碧紗如烟隔窓語
停梭悵然憶遠人
独宿空房淚如雨

22

May 24, 1934. Just prior to his trip to London in 1934, which he undertook in mid-July.

Dear Ma and Pa,

The cherry blossoms have fallen, the sports day is over, and it is raining spasmodically. The frogs are croaking and squeaking in the rice fields and the servant and her boy are shouting to each other down in the kitchen. Korean people always seem to shout from a distance of inches. My life flows on in endless song above the earth's lamentation. I can't remember any more, but what an indelible impression the IBSA has on me, more,[16] I suppose, than on you both. I think in some points in their terms and with their minds; it is very odd. I am anxious about the picture but I think you will get it safely. I really must get out and take some more photos but I begrudge the time from the violin and piano. I am very well lately and happy too, I must say. At present I have no troubles of any kind.　　　　　　　　　　　　Love, Reg

---

23

This probably dates from spring 1934. The next letter also refers to Dora's "style."

Dear Dora,

I sent a letter to you yesterday, but I received such a pathetic letter today that I must write another immediately. Your letters are always painful to read, the undercurrent of loneliness, over-estimation of myself, occasional bad style, your beauty of character—all these miserable elements make me feel uneasy when I see your handwriting on the envelope. But 'occasional bad style,' you will say, that's a blow. Like a bad pronunciation or a homely mug, it is the source of more irritation (when criticised) than anything else. And rightly so in the case of style, for criticism of style is a deeper and more fundamental thing than mere psychological criticism or judgement of action. So I know what I am doing and you are (and should be) feeling when I tell you of your personal failings, defects of soul, deformations and callosities of spiritual per- ception, under the disguise of pedantic carping at matters of expression and manner of writing. Croce says that what you cannot express you cannot feel; if you do not believe this it is at least better to act on it (as with the freedom of the will). It makes great men greater, real discoverers and almost *inventors* of great things. As a corollary it follows that secondhand phrases and modes of *ex*pression mean weakness of sensation and vagueness of *im*pression. Now connect with this an amusing psychological law that frowning makes you angry and turning up your nose makes you feel contemptuous;—a correction of style is followed by (its precedent) a correction of feeling. But you must be impatient to know what things I am talking about. Here are some I have 'culled,' as you would say, from your last letter.

delightfully cool
enormous thickness
an entertaining old boy
the soft springy turf
these days of rush and tear
a wonderful peace
a beautiful little poem
especially do I like
you simply must not

Each one is almost nothing but cumulatively they have a stronger effect than the greatest single mistake or judgement. You will notice that the faults are of two kinds, hackneyed phrases and ineffective hyperbole. You said once that I am rather schoolmasterish sometimes, that wasn't an exaggeration, was it?

You apologise for your letters being chatty. They are not. They are entertaining certainly, but much fuller of matter and sweetness than any others I have ever read. (That is some jam after the powder, but equally true though not, I am afraid, very mollifying.)

The back of this is some sentences I wrote for the students. The writing is very bad but it will look good enough to you. I have just read through this letter very anxiously to see if I have given you a chance to say "Physician heal thyself!" I think not, but though displeased I will be grateful if you will do the same for me as I have done (only too willingly and smugly) for you.

Love, Reg

Written on the reverse side of the preceding letter in pencil.

The other day someone came from Tokyo and played Beethoven's "Appassionata". He played it brilliantly, but I found it as I find mere life "A tale told by an idiot, full of sound and fury, signifying nothing." Exhilarating but to no purpose, stimulating but with a sickening reaction. Even the best of Beethoven is only a shower bath, like the Coriolanus overture; Bach is the well that Christ spoke of, "If you drink of this water, you will never thirst." There is only one piece of Bach that I have ever got tired of, and I don't think it is my fault. It is the Aria for the Suite in B, usually ground out on the G string, all throaty and repulsive.

Here is another commission for you; I'm really very impudent but just this once. It is an oboe introduction to a cantata by Bach. I heard it on a record (Columbia) played by Goossens,[17] in a series called the "History of Music," in the second album. I have an idea it is published by Novello (the music, I mean). It goes like this

The time and key are a bit worky, but see if you can get hold of this music for me and I will give you a special reward of some kind. In the same album there was another Bach chorus from a cantata with an oboe obbligato; it begins

Or notes to that effect. The bars seem all wrong. The music and the words are the best I know. The records of that series, by the way, are very poor, though some of the playing is good.

I have sent a picture to my mother; I will try and get one for you if you feel sufficiently jealous and envious of her. The trouble is not the money or the sending but finding a good enough picture. Of course, you understand that the above picture is a compromise of tastes.

24

Spring 1934?

Dear Dora,
You are a very very nice girl and your letter was very charming. The books have not come yet but I will be no more grateful and affectionate when they do.

I am just off to play some string trios. We've not got anyone good enough to play the piano so we play two violins with the cello taking the base; not bad if only the cello would play in time more often.

I am still picking the sores (if you will forgive the disgusting metaphor) on my sonata for violin, oboe, cello, and piano. The trouble is I think so much of the form that it sounds harsh and repellent. What is hard to get is what Beethoven and Bach have so much of, the '*con moto*'—no jerks or pauses, the succession of titbits but a continuous movement. I'm afraid this letter is not written '*con moto*' though it will be read so. Ever since I wrote that letter about your style I have hoped you weren't hurt (or perhaps you will be hurt by my saying this) and also self conscious myself in writing so that I have to stop and tear up page after page in case I should make myself vulnerable.

Love, Reg

25

Postmarked Keijō June 18, 1934, Chosen [Korea]; return address, R. H. Blyth, Tennori Seikyori, Keijō Korea.

Dear Dora,
I didn't know you were so hard up though I might have guessed it. Your letter sounds rather thin, emotionally, I mean, & makes me feel I 'adn't ought 'ave sent that letter about the pains of reading yours. Anyway reassure me one way or another.

I enclose some money. Should there be any over I hope you will do a kindness on that day by using it on yourself; it would give me a great deal of pleasure to think of you making yourself sick on ice cream at my expense.

What you say about "the East" is quite right. No doubt one has here a unique opportunity of choosing to become a Machiavelli or an Oblomov[18] & you are right too to pay more attention to the poems than the ravings in a letter.

I have no time to write any more just now.

I remain your unlovable cousin,

Love, Reg

26

Circa 1934? The content of this letter suggests it may belong to the same general time period as the previous three letters. The request for Tovey's books links it to the next.

Dear Dora,

When I received your last letter I composed a reply in my head and the result was that it never got into print. However here are a few embers of my righteous indignation.

You talk of the "East" in a most idiotic way. Korea, though a sleepy kind of place itself, is part of the Japanese Empire and the Japanese are pushing, militaristic, modern unpoetical, money loving, unintellectual, and blatant as I am not. The temples, that is the prosperous ones, not in ruins, are just places of rest on well traveled roads; the women's clothes are all in bad taste with meaningless designs and bad colours, all the men show two inches of shirt below the waistcoat (I do myself) by not wearing braces; there is not a peaceful, old fashioned place to be found anywhere except in the remote mountains, where, after all, Africa or China, it is all the same—merely trees and rocks. Lafcadio Hearn's Japan, if it ever existed, exists no more. There is less poetry and art here than in England and when, as always, house decorations are insipid in the Orient, it is altogether duller than the most screaming bad taste in England. With regard to living in the past,—it is true that great men seem to have an unfortunate habit of being born in the past.

It is only human love that lives in the temporal present; for art and poetry past and present and future are inapplicable terms. To speak quite frankly I don't care much for Shakespeare, partly perhaps because the form (drama) is repugnant to me. But Bach and Dante I gravitate to naturally. Besides their poetry they have a certain sternness of attitude (audible in the words of Christ so often) which appeals to me. Let me write out a poem I found the other day, which breathes the same air.

THE DAY OF JUDGEMENT

I. Watts

When the fierce north wind with his airy forces
Rears up the Baltic to a foaming fury,
And the red lightning with a storm of hail comes
   Rushing amain down,
How the poor sailors stand amazed and tremble!
Whilst the hoarse thunder like a bloody trumpet,
Roars a loud onset to the gaping waters
   Quick to devour them!
Such shall the noise be, the wild disorder
(If things eternal may be like these earthly,)
Such the dire terror, when the great Archangel
   Shakes the creation;
Tears the strong pillars of the vault of heaven,
Breaks up old marble, the abode of princes;
See the graves open, and the bones arising,
   Flames all around them.
Hark, the shrill outcries of the guilty wretches!
Lively bright horror, and amazing anguish,
Stare through their eye-lids, while the living worm lies
   Gnawing within them.
Thoughts like old vultures prey upon their heart-strings,
And the smart twinges, when the eye beholds the
Lofty Judge frowning, and a flood of vengeance
   Rolling all before him.
Hopeless immortals! How they scream and shiver,
While devils push them to the pit wide-yawning
Hideous and gloomy to receive them headlong
   Down to the centre.
Stop here my fancy (all away, ye horrid

Doleful ideas) come, arise to Jesus,
How he sits God-like, and the saints around him
 Throned, yet adoring!
Oh may I sit there when he comes triumphant
Dooming the nations; then ascend to glory
While our hosannas all along the passage
 Shout the Redeemer.

It is better to read it in print, when the eye can move faster, take in the sweep and rush of the classical metre (as I suppose it to be).

To go from the sublime to the same, will you please send me

1. *Die Kunst der Fuge*, ed. by Donald Tovey (Ox Un Press)
2. *A Companion to the Art of Fugue*, Tovey and a catalogue of the Oxford Press Musical Publications.

 Reg

27

Tovey's Musical Form and Matter *appeared in 1934; in the next letter Blyth offers his review of that book, which he holds back in this one. This letter may have been written shortly after the book's publication when Blyth was in England, in which case, his comments here on work may be related to searching for a local job.*

Dear Dora,

I must say you were very tactless & put me in the awkward position of wanting the medicine but denying the diagnosis in regard to Women. And with regard to Work, what I want is what the French want, security. When I get that, via a job or otherwise, I can get going on music & literature (as long, of course, as there is no money in it).

I have read through *Musical Form & Matter* once.[19] I will tell you what I think of it after you have read it.

By the way, when I say, "like me," or "like a louse," or any such thing, I mean exactly what I say. So when I said you are inactive like me, I mean I am inactive like you. I detest active busy energetic people. I want all that movement transferred entirely to the mind; & it must be a *moto perpetuo*[20] & not a rhapsody, like gravitation, not like a volcanic emotion.

The best thing I have heard lately is a Piano Concerto in B minor of Mozart. It seemed to be the next best thing after the half a dozen great symphonies.

The classical chap read from Vergil today: he has a remarkable power of making the war scenes sound like something on the Somme. I can't decide whether this is a very good or very objectionable thing.

Anyway give me the Past, give me solitude, give me a dog. The past smells of eternity, in solitude only I have dignity, from a dog alone I get unadulterated love.

The present has only a potential value—it may one day be worthy to become the past. Let us leave the present to those to whom it belongs, those who come after us; and calmly & confidently withdraw into the never-dying never-changing past.

On the negative side solitude means the cessation of the struggle for existence, on the positive, it implies the presence of Nature, with its life, beauty & indifference, & a man feels if he cares to do so, his own life beauty & indifference—what is that but dignity?

As to dogs—animals can hardly be classed among the absolutes. I am not speaking of them as they appear in that German book—rather as they feel in the dark, with cold wet noses and hairy backs. Animals and humans are a couple of makeweights that won't fit into the scheme of religio-moral-aesthetic-intellectual values.

I suppose humour is greatly overrated—it is just a survival device, I suppose to prevent us going potty, I suppose.

Love, Reg   I suppose

28

A notation on the letter dates it as October 3, 1934. Blyth was in London at this time.

Dear Dora,
The mildness of tone in your reproach (for not having written) is, as I supposed you intended, very effective.

I think, by the way, I must have mixed up Clive Bell & Roger Fry, but in any case, I shouldn't meddle in such things. In fact it is my forte *not* to know any names except Homer & Wordsworth, etc.

With regard to *Musical Form & Matter*—it seemed to me to get nowhere, as you would say, to lack "helpful thoughts" as my mother would say. For example, I didn't know at the end of it what he meant by form & matter. Is form the intellectual & matter the emotional content? Is form, for example, the ups & downs of the theme of a fugue & if so, what is the matter? Or is it the fugal form as such?

There was a good article in the *Listener*, illustrating the value of abstract formulas, lacking in Tovey, to help one to look at pictures in the right way. He said (of the Rout of San Romano by Uccello) "I like the picture because its remoteness from Nature gives a feeling of security (the aesthetic thrill), a momentary sense (or illusion) of order in the universe."

"Representation is a condition (not an aim) of painting" & so on.

To turn from the subtle to the ridiculous, my mother is gradually getting better & better, and if I don't show her how much I dislike her, in a short while she will be as well as she can be. So perhaps you had better come down the next weekend.

I saw *Viva Villa* & thought nothing of it as a film though Beery never ceases to be a lovable actor.[21]

I would write more but just at this moment, I am off to the dentist.

Love, Reg

29

This letter, bearing the postmark October 3, 1934, Brighton, Sussex, was written while Blyth was visiting London. The comment about Dora's ears suggests this letter was sent after Letter #20, which contains a similar reference. The mention of an unnamed text in Italian may link it to references to Dante in the next two letters.

Dear Dora,

I am so sorry about your ears and the Italian and my nasty letters. I don't know who the doctor you saw was but I wish you would go to a specialist, it would put your mind at rest, because I'm sure you must be worried about them.

As for the Italian, it makes me smile to read how those little bits of words trouble you: it was just the same with me. But doing it in the way you are by yourself, though it is discouraging, means that you are learning it in a way that you couldn't if you had someone to explain everything to you. My Italian edition has no comma after *notte*. Perhaps it is put there because *la notte* has no grammatical connection with the preceding part of the sentence & has to be translated "during the night." You certainly are a lazy blighter but never mind, peg away & you'll soon begin to feel how well worth while it all was and remember me in your will.

As for my letters, they are what you say: what do you think about buying the postcards published by the National Gallery twice and going through them one by one. That might warm things up a little. Listening to music together is as remote at present as playing together. How about going through the Preludes & Fugues together—that's not so impossible—& write about the meaning & execution of them. You have notes on it, so to speak, with the records. We could do the same thing with the *Inferno* but you seem rather short-tempered or at least short-winded about it.

It is very sweet of you to be so (properly) sensitive about your writing.

I suppose you will be coming down this Sunday, but see about your ears first before you spend the money.

Love, Reg

30

Written while he was in London, probably during the 1934 trip,
although it could conceivably date from the earlier trip in 1929.

Dear Dora,

It is a great pleasure to get your letters—they are so short. No, I don't mean that, I mean that you waste no words, say just the right things and show you are a superior person, in the Confucian sense, in every syllable.

With regard to Haydn and Mozart that evening, the fault was chiefly in the composers and the players. That, by the way, is one of the advantages of playing; doing it yourself gets you into the habit of seeing the goodness and shallowness of minor works, whereas listening only puts you more and more into the way of listening for the purple patches of the best bits.

I think you had better do as you say; come as early as possible Sunday morning and let me know when to meet you at the station. Perhaps we'll have tea at home.

You are quite right about Dante though how you separate the religious from the poetical core beats me. And anyway, when you say "religious" are you sure you don't mean "symbolic-moral"? or moral only?

The Hymn of Empedocles is good but it ends in sublimity.[22] It approaches music, not in wordlessness or meaninglessness but in the blending of great themes with simplicity and grandeur.

I am listening now to the chorales sung in the Foundations of Music.[23] They all seem to me perfect. I heard Brahms 4th Symphony this afternoon. You once said that you felt you always know what he was going to say. What you evidently meant was that you wished he was going to say something different, though equally inevitable. I still can't quite make up my mind about it.

Love, Reg

31

English postmark 1934; written while in England.

Dear Dora,

Thank you very much for the book & the opposite of thank you, whatever that may be, for all the letters you have sent. I seem to be no nearer getting a job. I feel like a newly moulted crab. My mother is in a very bad temper the last few days, by which I mean in bad health. I imagine she over eats, especially cream, gets a clogged liver, gets argumentative, sulks, does all kinds of unnecessary & heavy housework & vents her feelings on my poor father who doesn't help her *in* the house because he doesn't want to be flayed. There's the same vicious circle with regard to me. If I eat, I make work, if I don't I insult her as a housewife.

I will need some stimulus of some sort & I see quite plainly now, that the Dante business was a round about way of giving myself one. You are a necessary link in that chain so will you kindly do your bit (or "do your stuff" as the Americans say).

I didn't hear the Brahms last night so I can't say anything about it. There is supposed to be a thing known as "womanly tact." I have never seen any, perhaps because it is by nature invisible & skillfully disguised but if you wished to exercise any yourself, you would pester me about the *Art of Fugue* when it comes, & as a by-product make yourself an indispensable nuisance. Like me, you suffer, let us say, a little, from inactivity, in more philosophical language, half-aliveness. Mere sensitivity may be mistaken for something better: think of a small ant and an elephant. (You understand, I am writing this letter to & for myself.) There is another confession I should make: between 10 & 12 at night I read through one [of] the stupid books that my father gets from the library: couldn't you stop that and get me to read something else?

This letter must sound to you pleasantly like an SOS & see what a delightful example of determinism & Buddhistic "no one can save you but yourself" it is.

This is a very unsatisfactory letter but it faithfully represents some part of me at the moment.

Love, Reg

32

Postmarked London W.C., October 6, 1934.

Dear Dora,

I'm very very sorry to have to tell you that I am going back to Korea in a few days. I received such an urgent, almost frantic, letter from Mr. Fujii that I decided I must go back.

I hope you will be angry and cry and do all the rest of it before you come. I am very very sorry but it seems the only thing to do. My mother has invited Eva and Charley on Sunday afternoon but as long as we are in to tea that will be enough.

I sent a telegram yesterday to say I was going back. I am sorry that I came at all to upset you but as I grieve at it so much you may bear me the less malice & resentment.

Love, Reg

33

Probably written in late October 1934, while Blyth was in London. In another letter from that year he writes, "I must buy a piano too."

Dear Dora,

I was very glad to get a letter from you and to hear about the piano. I don't think much of the installment system but if you paid a very large proportion of the sum down, it wouldn't be such a bad thing. Anyway, you must think you have another fifty years of playing to provide for and you don't want to regret misplaced economy. Don't forget the BBC things; they are rather important really.

I rather regret not getting miniature scores of Mozart's 3 symphonies. Perhaps—I was going to say you get them and send them on a few months later, but of course the piano.

As to going, I feel neither excited nor bored, active nor passive. I just feel I am probably going and that is all.

As I grow older I seem to get lighter, so to speak, not, I hope, more superficial but rather abstracted from this world, getting more religious in a way, at least, loving God more if not my fellows.

I will write to you on the way but it is rather hard to do one's best under train conditions

Love, Reg

34

June 3, 1935.

Dear Dora,

I received your not unjustly reproachful letter together with the BBC book. You say you are always giving and not receiving, well, it is no use my crying over the spilt milk; I must see what I can send you. The difficulty is that I have too high an opinion of your taste to risk sending things that I would send to my mother. Anyway, will you go and see my mother and if you like the imitation Nō masks or the Japanese dolls, tell me, and I will send you them. In the meantime, I am sending you a few more colour prints that I can bear to part with, if only to enable me to ask you to send me the instrumental arrangements of the *Art of Fugue* including the proper piano arrangement as I simply can't manage it as it is in Tovey's edition.

Your writing was rather difficult to read so this letter seems to be a kind of unconscious revenge.

I would like you to read *The Masterpieces of Chikamatsu*, by Miyamori

(Kegan Paul) and *The Nō Plays of Japan* translated by Arthur Waley (Allen and Unwin) and tell me what you think of them.[24] I have no account to give you of lovely musical performances attended. I have just switched on the radio and there is a piano Concerto, rather whistley, relayed from Osaka. I can't guess whose yet, it sounds like Brahms or somebody even more Hungarian. Every week we play Haydn and Beethoven quartets. Haydn is more difficult, strange to say. Then on Sunday Brandenburg Concertos. Last time we did the A minor and E major Violin Concerto with Solo Violin and String Quartette and Piano, but solo violin is a little weak, being female, and the 1st Violin too strong, being male and a Czecho Slovakian. The viola never has enough resin on his bow.

I have a very fine ginger cat with a very fierce face and a very mild disposition.

By the way I am reading the Nō plays and Chikamatsu in Japanese, besides Chinese Classics such as Laotze (recently translated by Waley as "The Way and its Power") and Po Chü-i's poems.

The announcer said the jangling was Liszt, so I wasn't far wrong. Wasn't he one of those chaps with a feather in his hat?

I must buy a piano myself. Before I went to England I gave my piano to my one and only friend and I can't ask for it back. I can get a new one for about 400 x 1/1 15/16,[25] which is not so cheap considering the quality.

You never told me what you thought of the *Tale of Genji*. It is very hard to read in Japanese. The style in the original is very different from Waley's, which is not bad, but in another way. In the Japanese it is flowing and flowery, allusive and vague, the language of people who have nothing else to do but to talk beautifully. It might be better in French.

The students at the school want me to conduct a Chorus for them. Last time at the ceremony on the Emperor's birthday, they sang the National Anthem, the Kimigayo, and got sharper and sharper until they were singing half a tone higher than the piano; not a soul of two or three hundred people noticed anything wrong, least of all the pianist, who was playing with one finger.

The teacher next to me was bawling like mad with his breath smelling of stale tobacco but his total range of notes was not more than three semitones. So you see what a grand time I shall have.

I am learning Japanese writing, I mean with a brush, when I can do a little I will send you some.

I will send the colour prints via Siberia so you will get them at about the same time as the letter. Send me the bill of the Bach.

Love, Reg

35

A spring 1935 date seems probable.

Dear Dora,

I find writing to you very difficult. I don't wish to write about myself. I don't want to say pert things about you. On essential things we are more or less, actually or potentially agreed,—so what is there left to say?

The best thing perhaps is the kind of judgements of relative merits of great works, such as you gave of the 6th Brandenburg Concerto. It has the same lack of smartness and dullness, melancholy and frenzy as Mozart's Trio No 7 for Clarinet, Viola and Piano (Columbia).

I would be glad if you would go through the 48 [Preludes and Fugues] and say something, however irrelevant about each. As Shakespeare says "ripeness is all" and it is impossible to approach that state without the necessary stimulation. Read Renan's *Life of Christ*.[26] Don't read the newspapers. Don't waste any time at all. Play the piano like mad. Ask me for some kind of book. Have a clear idea what your religion is (and tell me). Learn some foreign language (not French).

Love, Reg

36

1935, perhaps 1936; after the preceding letter.

Dear Dora,

I received the *Art of Fugue* yesterday; thank you very much. I practice the piano very irregularly: the violin, viola, oboe, flute and cello take some time.

I am always glad to think of your piano, though I don't understand how you can bear to play anything but the 48 [*Preludes and Fugues*]. Of all the books and monuments of art and wisdom, I rate that the highest.

The best thing in a letter I received the other day was a quotation from one of mine: "Life is disfigured yet transfigured by death." This dilemma is I suppose the meaning of life, the dilemma I mean of wishing away the impermanence from the world which gives (by contrast) to art its death-lessness. Spinoza said that a wise man thinks of nothing less than death. I must be one of the foolishest people in the world.

Your last letter was the best I have received. I suppose getting something warmed you up a bit.

I have heard very little of Dante for the past few letters; I hope you don't waste your time on newspapers anymore.

I hope you believe as I do that your mother and other such people get no real artistic pleasure whatever out of the much they surround themselves with. It is just that they feel at home among things made by people with minds like their own.

No person with bad taste will be found gazing at rubbish for 15 minutes on end and feeling better for it—unless it be for entirely extra-esthetic reasons.

Today I picked up by accident some of Pascal's *Pensées* translated and I was amazed at the power of it.

Love, Reg

37

This letter to Dora lacks a salutation. The remark about owing money for staying at Dora's house during his trip to England seems to date it to 1935–36, after Blyth's return to Korea.

I am sitting here still translating and explaining Japanese poetry, listening to the Brahms Second Symphony. They are playing the third movement, a little too fast so they lose the sweetness and tenderness.

The verse I am now doing I will throw at you without comment—

水鳥や枯木の中に駕二梃 蕪村
(*mizudori ya karekinonaka ni kago ni-chō*)
    Water birds;
Among the withered trees,
    Two palanquins.   Buson

(Perhaps after all that is a little cruel.) On a lonely winter path stand two empty palanquins. Beside the narrow road there is a marshy pool, on which a few water birds are seen. The sky is low and grey, but it is too cold to rain.

These two palanquins,—where are the carriers, where are the passengers? What is it like to be a water bird? These questions do not arise as we stare at the colourless picture; but we know the answers, answers that are wordless.

Laotze says, 知者不言言者不知 "He who knows does not speak and he who speaks does not know." He also says, 道可道非常道 "The way that can be expressed in words is not an unvarying way." You understand what he means, I think, and your letters seem to approach that idea. I too have nothing to write about myself except that I have been reading Chinese poetry until 2 o'clock every night for the last month or two (I begin to realize why so many Japanese students wear glasses.)

You don't say very much about Dante. I hope you have not been slacking. You didn't say what you had done with your piano and what and when you were playing. My head is bunged up with half forgotten half remembered Chinese characters, so that when I am playing in the quartette my mind is not free from them.

I read an English book the other day, quite an event for me, O'Neill's *Ah Wilderness*, very good, and *Days Without End*, very bad, just religious melodrama.[27]

I have at last learned to be alone, at least in the evening; it's hard in the day time, I think; there is something in the daylight that demands society perhaps, though anthropologically one would think the opposite.

In your last letter you seemed very upset that I had not written, but after all, you receive but what you give and if you scrawl a few lines a la Laotze you must expect the same treatment.

I am sorry I never paid for the room in your lodgings. Perhaps I had better send you the money 'in kind' as they say.

Love, Reg

38

Post-1934, after Anna had returned to England and Blyth had
returned to Korea following his London trip. Dora's previous letter

noting that she was playing Mozart suggests this follows Letter #37,
in which he wanted to know what she was playing on her new piano.

Dear Dora,

I have no pain in my foot. I never go to school by taxi. I have not bought a rice field. I am not astute; my wife [Anna] bought a rice field which she left behind her.

You say you were playing Mozart violin sonatas (keyboard and violin). Who was playing the violin?

I sent my mother two fans. Tell me if you would like some.

Yesterday I played the viola in an arrangement for string trios of some of the fugues & preludes of the 48. I don't think it was very successful. I am going to write the viola part out for the clarinet. Fugal movements sound better on mixed instruments I think. There is a record of the third fugue in the 48 played on violin clarinet & piano (one finger) and it sounds very fine, intellectually anyway. This evening I play the viola in 2 Schubert piano trios. I am going to play the oboe on the radio, oboe piano violin & cello by Graun, an ancient bloke.[28]

As you imply, the statue you sent is a little florid, a little too Indian (formal or not, I like Heine very much, by the way.)

Love, Reg

39

Circa 1935? The suggestion that Dora learn an instrument other
than the piano, maybe the cello, suggests this letter follows the
previous two.

Dear Dora,

I spent yesterday evening playing the Brahms and Mozart clarinet quintets with the gramophone. The Mozart is rather easy—I mean just to play the notes, but the Brahms has too many notes to the square inch. This morning I tidied up my music—a never-ending job—and played a sonata of Grazioli on the viola. Tomorrow we play a few Mozart and Haydn symphonies arranged for quartet and flute. The next day Beethoven piano trios arranged for piano, violin and viola. Every morning before school I play the piano with one of the teachers who has a violin. We are playing the early sonatas of Mozart (not the 18). My spare time is spent in writing out the horn part of a Beethoven septet for violin.

I have just finished reading Faust again and still going slow with Japanese and Chinese. I have read a lot of French lately—*Le Rouge et le Noir* very good in parts but too long. *Paul et Virginie* by St. Pierre, unspeakably sentimental, etc. Also almost all D. H. Lawrence, who is perhaps the greatest English novelist; perhaps not.

Love, Reg.

P.S. Osaka is about as near here as Moscow is to you.
PPS Why don't you learn another instrument? Any instrument will do, that you can play in chamber music. It is a crime to have a good ear and play the piano only. I don't know what to recommend—I think the cello perhaps. To play moderately it is the easiest and very useful in all chamber music. You can buy a good enough one for 10 pounds. In a year you would be able to take part in the easier string quartets of Haydn. Let me beg you to do as I say.

40

The remark about Dora taking up the cello seems to place this letter circa 1935, not long after Letter #39.

Dear Dora,
Yesterday I had an unpleasant experience which is a sample of what I am always getting. I arranged to play two Mozart Piano Quintets. They are really for oboe clarinet horn bassoon, so I played the clarinet myself, & had a violin for the oboe, a bassoon, & a viola for the horn. It was all played terribly fast, just sound & fury, signifying nothing; the piano scrambling, the bassoon out of tune in the lower notes, the viola having to be bawled into time, the viola staying fff [fortissimo] the whole time. When I played fp [fortepiano], the pianist thought I wasn't sure of my place & kept banging out my part on the piano. Just like pigs at a trough it was. But I can't avoid this because there is no one else who can play the piano well enough. Every time this happens, I swear never to play with them again.

I hope by this time you have a cello & are halfway through Piatti,[29] and I mean that very seriously indeed. Let me tell you once more—the cello parts in most chamber music are very easy so though you may despair of cello concertos or Boccherini's sonatas you can have perfect confidence in being able to play easy quartets adequately well in an incredibly short time.

My life is given over almost entirely to music; if for no other reason I cannot afford thinking of you every day. So let me make a personal appeal to you. I myself practise the piano every day so by the time I come to England, if the worst comes to the worst I can accompany you in anything after a little finger twiddling. Don't say your fingers are small: say your will is.

Love, Reg

41

A notation reads: Miss Dora Lord, 3 Great Court Grove End Road, London N.W.8 England. Aldous Huxley's edition of Lawrence's letters appeared in 1934, so I suspect that the letter dates from the later 1930s, though it could belong to the postwar period.

Dear Dora,

I have no time to write anything much. I owe you a longer letter which has been postponed so long, I am ashamed to begin it. I hope you like the photo. What is written on the blackboard is something from one of D. H. Lawrence's letters. It was taken last winter at the [*a tear in the letter makes the name undecipherable*] University.

Love, Reg

42

Circa 1938? Blyth married Tomiko in 1937, and he is known to have started teaching French in Keijō in the late 1930s, continuing until his contract was terminated in March 1939.

Dear Ma & Pa,

This is an English Examination far removed in place and in meaning from the "English Examination" that is going on in England today.

I have to teach French at school so I am going to find some French Catholic priest who can teach me French and help to brush up my French conversation. But when I open my mouth to speak French, Japanese slips out; that is the chief difficulty!

Tomiko is well and I also hope you are both well, very well.

Love, Reg

———

43

February 20, 1939.

Dear Dora,

This is a very different letter from the one I was intending to write to you. I want your disinterested but unenigmatically expressed advice on the subject of my returning to England. As I see it, my mother will from now on, whatever happens, find her life very difficult in every way and it is my duty to do whatever I can in the matter. It is chiefly a question of money, that is, the amount of money in the bank. The cost of living, my prospects of getting a job and so on. If possible I would like to make you into a lodger but that is a matter for yourself.

As far as my own feelings in the matter, I think I would rather be in Rottingdean [with my mother] than here, though I would have to eat less and spend nothing at all. As far as the pleasure of your company and accompaniment is concerned, all the things I practice, all the laborious hours at the clarinet or piano, are all spent with an ultimate view of playing with you, so that is that. Tomiko is the next question. It is possible that she might not be able to get a passport. Maybe you would not weep for that, but still. She is rather skinny and doesn't eat much, and has the well known oriental low standard of living.

Anyway let me have a long, garrulous letter at once giving your own opinions and also your impression of my mother's outlook and psychology, please.

Love, Reg

44

Sat. March 8, 1940.

Dear Ma & Pa,

I was very grieved to hear of your phlebitis & so on. It makes all the trivial things I might write in the letter, more than usually meaningless. I hope the war will stop soon, somehow or other, & I will come back at once.

Some weeks ago I wrote about sending my money here. I think for your sake it had better stop where it is, but it would be a good idea to send the form of withdrawal here so that I could use it expeditiously, if necessary.

I usually write saying I hope Papa is well, because I have the idea, very foolish perhaps, that he will perhaps read the letter. I am sorry it seemed so odd to you.

Tomiko is well and rather fattish for such a skinny Lizzie. I am also quite well.

I write letters every week. I can't know what percentage you receive. The Post Office here seems very uneducated & letters may be sent off in all directions.

Think of you very often, but what is the good of it?

Love, Reg

45

July 11, 1940. Written while Blyth was still in Korea; his passport shows he arrived in Hagi, a port city in Yamaguchi prefecture, in July.

Dear Dora,

I think occasionally, and when unavoidable, express. I have just written to my mother one or two things which I would rather have said to you. However it seems shameful to repeat myself so you must have a look at her letter if this one makes you curious. One thing I will add and it is this. Unmotivated activity, especially of a higher kind, is very difficult. To gain knowledge without parading it, to read poetry without exhibiting the power to others, to play the piano for oneself alone is hard. I cannot yet decide whether this kind of spiritual masturbation is possible though I think it is desirable or at all events, necessary. Ulterior motives in my case are painfully absent. Perhaps the only one left to me is that of a hunter. To translate and translate and then discover some sentence which makes worthwhile the hours of dictionary-thumbing is really exhilarating and satisfying. There is something almost religious in this communion with the dead, ourselves so near death that the difference and distance are seen as nothing.

Love, Reg

46

July 11, 1940. Written on the same day as the preceding letter.

Dear Ma & Pa,

A few days ago I received a very hysterical telegram from Anna asking if there were a possibility of work for her in Korea; and also the probabilities of Insoo getting a job. I replied (by cable) that for her it was almost impossible; because if the English are defeated the English language will have very little value here or anywhere else. However, he must come back and he may as well come back cheerfully.

I am quite well and Tomiko also. One must be very thankful for that in a world like this.

I enclose a paper printed for students who asked me to read the Bible with them after school.

I began today (5th June) to read the Gospel of St. John. It seems very different to me after understanding something of Buddhism.

I hope you are able to go to the cinema sometimes. It is a great relief to forget oneself and everything else for a time.

I hope Papa is well and very well,

With love, Reg.

I am sorry for your sakes not to be with you. Up to the present, here it is safer, but we don't know where safety is until it's all over.

I received your cable, thank you. On the same day I received a letter from Insoo, saying the papers had been received on April 20. They had taken three months to go from here. So the divorce will be made final 100 days from then, about August 1st.

47

July 8, 1940. Written while he was staying in Hagi. In Europe, the German Luftwaffe was attacking England, and a German invasion was feared to be imminent.

Dear Ma and Pa,

The day before yesterday, I sent you a cable asking you to telegraph to me the date when Anna received the divorce judgement.

I did not want to trouble you with this. I sent a cable, answer prepaid, to Anna about a month ago. Ten days ago I sent a cable to Cecyll.[30] To both I received no answer.

As I explained before, I cannot remarry until one hundred days after Anna has received the divorce judgement, so this matter is of importance to us or I would not have troubled you with it.

The war must be very disturbing to you but it can't be helped. I often think of St. Augustine, the great father of the Christian Church. Few people know or remember that the last years of his life were very gloomy because the Vandals were attacking Rome. So with many people in England who are thinking how to make a good peace. They may not be asked.

I feel very sad for Dora too. She must feel very upset.

The great thing to do, so difficult as to seem impossible, is *not* to think "How is the war and its ending going to affect *me*?"

Many of us think we are worrying about England or democracy or world peace, when nine tenths is only our own private comfort of mind and body.

Love, Reg

48

September 13, 1940; from Hagi.

Dear Ma and Pa,

This summer I have moved to Hagi, Tomiko's native place. This is partly on account of Tomiko's health. The air of Keijō is bad and the climate extreme, cold in winter, hot in summer, warm in the day and cold at night. The house we have come to is at the foot of a mountain by the river; it is surrounded with trees and bamboos, to the right a famous temple of the Zen sect and half way up the mountain behind, another. This morning Tomiko has gone to a place called Ube to continue X-ray treatment for her neck. The lymphatic glands connected with the lungs had become enlarged. We brought the cat and dog safely here, but with some trials and tribulations. At Shimonoseki, the port opposite Fusan, he got out of the box in which he was sent and ran away.[31] After waiting five or six hours he came back to the station himself.

The rent of the house in Keijō was 50 yen. For this house, which is larger and has an extensive garden with orange trees etc., is 7 yen. I shall go back to Keijō on about the 21st of this month. In Keijō I shall live at the temple Myōshinji (rise at 4:30, sweep up, do zazen, gruel and soup for breakfast and the leavings for dinner), for which board and lodgings I pay 12 yen a month. I cut my foot while bathing in the river yesterday so am laid up for a bit. The water is salt, the sea is visible in the distance—about a mile. The chief drawback is the mosquitoes. They are innumerable and of an immense size. They rest neither day nor night; at one's prayers, in the lavatory, on all sacred and profane occasions they are ready and willing. I must catch the post so will stop here. I hope you are both not too badly off.

Love, Reg

PS Please send letters to Tokyo.

CHRONOLOGY

The following chronology should give a better sense of Blyth's movements within the rapidly evolving historical events of the time.

March 1939. Loses job at Keijō University.
September 3, 1939. England declares war on Germany, WWII begins.
March 1940. Fujii Akio dies suddenly.
April 1940. Moves to Hagi.
August 1940. Moves to Kanazawa to assume post there.
April 1941. Applies for Japanese citizenship.
December 8, 1941. Pearl Harbor and war with America.

49

April 18, 1941; from Kanazawa.

Dear Ma,

I received your letter today. I have not received any letter about Pa's death. You say that I do not enter into any details at the school and living conditions and so on. The reasons are rather childish and perhaps characteristic of me. In the first place, up to the present I am in almost every way better off than you, and to chortle over my comfort, and pleasant life is rather painful when I think of yours. Second, as you know very well, life is very uncertain all over the world today and to describe conditions which may in a moment be changed into something different before the ink is dry, and send the letter on a precarious two months' voyage needs a great deal of faith and optimism. Even as it is I receive Dad's letters after he is dead like a voice from the tomb—but no that is a very false way of expressing it. As you know he had something good, something charming, something pathetic about him that touches the heart when greater virtues or power would not affect it.

Anyway Tomiko is very well now-a-days; she never worries, fortunately, and that is very good indeed for me. After all as I, at times, almost seem to understand, all we have is the present moment, the past and future are a million miles away.

Thank you for writing a long letter; I hope you will do it again if it is not too tiring.

The new term [at Daiyon Kōtō Gakkō] has just begun and the new boys are very eager to learn. After a month or so, all they want to do is to get out of the school they were so made to get in. Musical boys are scarce, almost nonexistent, but many are interested in religion or poetry, so we have something in common. The teachers, as everywhere, I suppose, seem devoid of interest in anything, but very nice people indeed. The people of Kanazawa, as I think I told you, are extremely good, in the sense that they have no malice in their hearts, have a real love of peace and quietness, with no hypocrisy or false politeness. The shopkeepers show no special wish to sell anything in the shop; the love of money has few of its roots here.

I have just finished the chapters of the book Children, Old Men & Idiots, Death, and Poverty. The last [chapter] is on Animals all in relation to

Zen and English Poetry, with a very great many quotations from both, and from Japanese literature and Chinese. The only trouble is that no one will be able to understand it: I myself must read it twice when I look over some of the earlier parts. However, there are some easy bits here and there and the quotations are all worth the money.

Love, Reg

50

May 25, 1941.

14 KAMITAKAJO-MACHI, KANAZAWA

Dear Ma,

I was very glad to get two letters the other day telling of Papa's death and your receiving my letter "and liked it a little." In a day or two I will send Dora, via you, a book on learning Japanese.

I have finished my book. It contains a vast amount of quotations mostly from English literature, but also from Chinese, Japanese, Italian and Spanish (translated) and French and German (untranslated). Dora always said I would do something. Well, I have done it; it is a book of national and international importance. All that's wrong with it is that it's too good, too rich, like a Christmas pudding or a trifle—no easy or flat bits, all purple patches.

Speaking of trifles, I am always in trouble at home eating the cakes before the visitors come, or inventing tales of visitors in order to get them. Today I advanced (unsuccessfully) the plan that I eat the cakes so greedily in front of the visitors that it is better for our reputation to let me take the keen edge off my appetite before the visitors come.

Tonight a man is coming to play the violin and another the piano and I the flute for a trio to be played on the radio.

Sweets are non-existent here. Sometimes there is chocolate, and the girls at the shops kindly save some for me behind the counter, because I am rather gentle and have a pretty little dog. Tomiko is fatter and heavier than ever in her life before, you will be glad to hear.

Love, Reg

51

As his daughter Harumi was born in February 1942, this letter,
alluding to Tomiko's pregnancy, must date from the summer of 1941,
when they were staying in Hagi, or fall, when they had moved to
Kanazawa.

Dear Dora,

I received your letter a few days ago and have composed several letters in my head and one on paper, but it is somehow or other like preaching to the converted. You speak of wrens on telegraph posts and late evening thrushes as if those were the only things that really mattered. And if you realize this, what else is there left to say?

I have told you a hundred times to read Suzuki's books on Zen but you take no notice. Read Waley's *The Way and Its Power*, a translation of the greatest Chinese book ever written. The first sentence is enough; it has had more effect on me than any other in literature.

The Way that can be spoken is not the Eternal Way,
The Name that can be named is not an Eternal Name.

This is why you say "It is revolting to have *to put it into words*." Only in poetry, the revoltingness of words disappears because as in Shelley's Skylark we can say of the real meaning.

"Until we hardly see, we feel that it is there."[32]

Now nobody comes to see us partly because they might be suspected by the police, partly because I don't want anybody to come. I only practice to keep up my playing in hopes of having you accompany me. I shall never be much good on strings. The flute and clarinet and oboe come out of my belly but the viola and violin and cello are always outside. Tomiko is busy with morning sickness.

My holiday is spent thus:

At 7 I get up and let the cat in, and listen to records or the radio for 40 minutes. This morning it was Schweitzer on the organ. Then I translate the *Mumonkan* until lunch. Then I go out on a bicycle with the dog and read the *Mumonkan* in some shady place while the dog goes ratting about the rice fields (of course there are no rats, but he is an imaginative dog). Then home and listen to records on the radio till 7 when the news of the international football match is given (I am the football); then more *Mumonkan* till bed-time.[33]

Love as ever, Reg

By the way I forgot the bungalow business.[34] Of course it is all right, but please make a will yourself. I have not a penny here.

CHRONOLOGY

Blyth was incarcerated in Kobe as an enemy alien from 1941 to 1945; there are no verifiable letters from that period.

52

January 21, 1946.

Dear Dora,

I want you to read the letter I have written to Ma, and take this as adding to it. As I said to her, Anna's fabrications are rather pathetic, or perhaps financial, but it is rather a serious thing to make public statements of that kind. It might be that she could even be prosecuted for it.— But when I come to think of it again, she must have been put in a terrible position by it, with all the girls of the school asking her about it, and afraid to tell the truth, and afraid some other paper would let the cat out of the bag.

I hope I meet Miss MacGregor again. She was one of the most womanly women I have ever met, enough Scotch to keep her from being sentimental. Sometimes she nearly smacked my face when I made facetious remarks about religion, but began to chuckle instead. She was very kind to Tomiko and Harumi. Tomiko does not like many people (and I don't blame her), but she liked Miss MacGregor very much.[35]

I am very anxious that you should get my book [*Zen in English Literature and Oriental Classics*]. Of course I have outgrown it by now, but it has a freshness, a youthful unqualifiedness which cannot be recaptured. I must confess I am more concerned with religion and poetry now than I am with music. The reason partly is that I have no music at all, and never hear any except over the radio. The flute, the oboe, a third-class violin and the B-flat clarinet remain; the others are what everything will be one day. The other reason is this, that the world is in a bad way, and a proper understanding of "what men live by," and how to spend their lives living, can be given them through poetry or though religion, but hardly, I think, through music, which requires, as you know, a very special gift and talent that can hardly be cultivated, let alone supplied. I have written a book, several books, in fact, and if people are inclined or forced by some accident to read those books, they will get something out of them, the more, perhaps, the more they dislike them. If I were to write, or even to play music, I am only preaching to the converted, and though this is easy and pleasant work, it is not what the world needs.

What the western world needs is just what the east has got, not a solution to its problems, but a restatement of them in such a form that we are satisfied that the questions should remain as such, their own answers. As I said to my mother, my duty is here in Japan, to make the Japanese proud of being Japanese, to make them proud of their faithful guardianship of the open secret of Zen, so that they may not be Americanized or Anglicized, but may Japonize the Americans and the British.

I feel more at home with Americans than with English people lately. Americans are young and uncultured, good natured and easy going, very friendly, and slightly shallow. English people are a little hard, not so willing to be pleased, have an inner reserve of feeling and principle that cannot be shaken. For Japanese, everything is "mouse-color," grey; there is nothing final, no absolutely right or wrong; cause and effect are mingled; with them, as with God, all things are possible.

Going back to the music again, what I want is Bach and Handel's flute and violin sonatas, Bach's Preludes and Fugues; the miniature score of the Brandenburg Concertos. That is the absolute minimum that occurs to me at the moment. What do you mean by that very rude remark, "I hope you took your mind"—oh, I see, "Your mind with you into exile." Yes, I need an A Clarinet but that will do the year after next. I am so glad you are keeping up with the cello. Those sonatas of Bach (not the solo ones) are very nice, especially the first movement of the first. As for the Brahms clarinet quintet,

I played it once, but it was an obliging quartet that slowed up in the difficult parts. Mozart's is rather easy. Anyway, I have not played anything on any instrument for five years.

As for MacArthur approving of my appointment, I didn't ask him. In any case I have been so useful to MacArthur in quite un-educational affairs, that the thought never entered my head. Tomorrow General Dyke, head of the Educational Section of SCAP,[36] goes back to America for good, and in him I lose my best friend here. He and I had nothing in common together but he was a man who saw educational and political problems poetically, and what that means can only be understood either by having the genius for it oneself, or, as in my case, coming into contact with a man who has it. MacArthur is all right. Just leave everything to him and it will go fine. There is of course a section of the American command that want to American-ize Japan, but they are just nit-wits, assisted by Japanese nit-wits, who want Japan to turn into another Philippines.

As for explaining away your difficulties, that is easy enough to do for some-one else. In the past six months I have given a great deal of advice, had it acted upon, and always with success, but this was because, although the matters concerned the destiny of Japan, or things I was imperfectly acquainted with, I myself was not concerned with or in it, and so my judgement was good.

The Passion Music, yes, that has the whole secret of life in it, expressed clearly and finally in 12 tones of sound in certain patterns. What a beautiful example that is of the *essentially* contradictory nature of the universe, the illimitable meaning can only be expressed by limitation, in 12 tones. The final chorus I do not remember, of course I should have included the score of the Passion in my minimum requirements.

As I said to my mother, I would come home for good if I could, finan-cially, and if I could salve my conscience, or work for Japan in England with equal success and ease. But how I should explain myself out of the country for good, I don't quite know. As for a visit, I will make this as soon as practi-cable, but even for that I have no money at the moment. Why don't you get a job, a nominal one anyway, in the Embassy here? Then you could come here for nothing and be paid for it.

If and when you get my book, you will have to read it at least three times before you know what I am driving at. This is not because it is written in a difficult style; it is very readable and lucid, but the whole point of it lies in an attitude of mind. Once that is attained, the book is valueless and useless, and that is the aim of the book, as it should be of every poem and sonata and picture, to make itself as useless as a window pane, that only lets the light in from outside.

How lucky we are to have lived through this war; I'm afraid we shan't be so lucky in the next one, but to have managed to get through two of them unscathed is a matter for congratulations.

If I may suggest some books for your reading, I would suggest any books of Suzuki Daisetz on Zen, Confucius' Analects by Waley, and his translations of Chinese poetry, and of the Nō plays, particularly Sotoba Komachi. Sansom's *Short Cultural History of Japan* is very good but omits the most important thing, haiku. The books which have had the greatest influence on me are Waley's translation of *The Way and its Power*, Spengler's *The Decline of the West*, and Eckhart's works, above all this last. If you can get a translation (I think you can from the London Buddhist Society) of the Sutra spoken by Wei Wang on the "Platform of the Law" (or some such title) you have got the essence of all Eastern Culture, and the latent source of Western culture too. With the above books on your shelf you are well on your way to becoming a human being instead of, at best, a mere European.

How pleased I was to see your handwriting, and my mother's too. Even that, the strokes and the loops, the weakness and the strength, is something in common between us three.

By the way, it would be interesting to know the minimum cost of living in England now.

I think I'll stop here, and take the letters to be sent by Lieut. Bush.

Yours, with love,
Reg

53

February 7, 1946. Sent from 14 Sanbansho-dōri, Kanazawa. It is not known why Blyth was in Kanazawa at this time. Also, he writes that his daughter Harumi is four and a half years old, which she would not turn until August, suggesting that he may have misdated the letter.

Dear Dora,

I was so glad you enjoyed the book [*Zen in English Literature and Oriental Classics*]. After all, it was written for people like you, much fewer than you imagine.

I am going to "mention" a few things I want. I think I spoke about music last time. Of books, I particularly would like to see again "The Spirit of Man" by Robert Bridges, an anthology. I haven't seen it for about 15 years. I'd like some chocolate: pretend it is for Harumi. Very fortunately she is not fond of sweet things. She eats slowly and thinks fast and is very healthy indeed. Her whooping cough is over already. Tomiko is well too and learning English seriously for the first time. What I really want of course is a piano but a second hand Japanese piano, if I could find one, would cost 20,000 yen. And last but not least I want you to come out here as soon as you can. I can't like the idea of your leaving my mother, so you had better do what you have to do anyway, stop where you are for a while. I can't put it any plainer than that. How happy I would be to see you again. I have not a single friend in the world, and have long ceased to look for one, and it is now the proper time for you to present yourself, a free gift, unwanted and therefore all the more valued and acceptable. I think, I mean, I know that you and Tomiko would get on together for she is rather un-Japanese in that way, that she doesn't change her mind, war or no war, money or no money. She also has no friends and respects very few people. Dr. Suzuki is one; Mr. Shinki (if you remember the name) is another, or the other. Harumi is witty and charming; like her mother, cold-hearted. She will not soften until she falls in love, or has her first baby. She can read and write easy Japanese though she is only four and a half. Going on with the wants,—if you can, send her some shoes, and dresses. I enclose the sizes.

I have buttered you up and ought to get something for it in return. That reminds me, you will agree with Tomiko in her attitude of never praising me if possible.

I told you in the last letter that I had refused to be Principal of a University. I may be pushed into it, apparently. They are busy removing the causes of my refusal, and I shall have no excuses left to make. (By the way, I get 350 yen a month for 4 hours a week at Tokyo University, so I would have to work there 5 years to buy a piano.)

Apparently one can send post cards and "comfort-kits" to Japan from England now, but it is better to send things via Bush if possible. His wife should be here soon.

One reason I would like you here is this, that I am aware of a defect in myself that I would rather read a poem about a thing than look at the thing itself. Thomson's "Seasons" is better than the slush, winds, heat and rain of the real world. I talk too much, think too much; I need to be taken out to look at the moon and listen to the insects.

Now, doesn't that earn another bar of chocolate? I'll write another begging letter to my mother, but with the butter not spread so thick. I'm sure she doesn't have too much to spend.

Love, Reg

54

Dated with the notation "received June 21, 1946."

TOKYO, TOSHIMA KU, MEJIRO, GAKUSHŪIN KANSHA

Dear Mama,

Today Lieut Bush came with your letter and Dora's. He only arrived yesterday, so that was very kind of him. I am sorry you were given the opportunity of not being annoyed with Anna's nonsense. I suppose she did not talk about the divorce for several reasons: first, because it is nothing to be particularly proud of; second, because it might affect her position if, as the paper says, she is an L.C.C. school teacher.[37] Of course, she said too much, but that is what we all do once we depart from the truth, and I suppose she feels rather miserable about it.

After I was released from internment, we went to live, as you know, at Mrs. Bush's house in Kobe and stayed there until December last year. I went up to Tokyo several times and found a position in the Peers School. This has a primary, secondary and high school department. The Crown Prince was in a primary school at this time. I was also made a professor of the Nihon University. We came up to Tokyo in December and live in an official residence in the school grounds, which are very "extensive," and full of trees, so it is the best, perhaps the only good place in Tokyo to live in. I was appointed to teach the Crown Prince early this year, and every week also I teach seven princes separately in this house. Then I was asked by the Foreign Minister, Yoshida [Shigeru], who is now Prime Minister, to teach anything I liked in the School for Diplomats, in which young diplomats in the Foreign Office are preparing themselves for the time when Japan is allowed to have relations with foreign countries. Last of all, I have to lecture in Tokyo Imperial University on a Comparative Study of English and Japanese poetry. In addition to this Dr. Suzuki (the Zen fellow) and I are publishing a magazine called *The Cultural East*, the first number of which should appear at the end of this month. I am also a Counsellor of the Imperial Household, and in the last six months I have gone to and fro between the American Army and the Imperial Household, and engaged in all kinds of secret business which I cannot tell you about. I had an interview with the Emperor the other day, and spoke to him in Japanese for an hour and a half, a thing no foreigner has ever done. The Crown Prince himself is a plump and rather charming boy, and it is of course my idea to humanize him as much as possible, rather than teach him English. As I said, I am a Counsellor to the Imperial Household, and they have taken all the ideas I have given them so far. About two months ago I suggested that it would be a good idea if the Crown Prince could have the run of an American household with children of his own age in it. Of course that is impossible, but I proposed that they should have a young and charming American lady to teach him, because it is of the utmost national and international importance that he should *like* English. This suggestion got a little twisted in transition and they arranged to ask for an American lady of between 50 and 60 to come. However this is being modified but I don't know what will come of it.

As far as going to England is concerned, I will do so at the earliest opportunity. "Earliest" means with regard to two things, passage to England, and the earning of my living here. I am very glad you are well, and grateful to Dora for keeping an eye on you.

As you know I wrote a book that was published soon after the war broke out and I am very anxious that you and Dora should see it. There were only 500 printed and then the whole of the press was burnt down. I have only one copy, but someone has promised to get me a few and I will send it to you through Lieut Bush. The first number of the magazine also I will send immediately it is printed.

I am working very hard indeed now, every day except Sunday and on Sunday harder than any other day. I earn about 3000 yen a month, and that sounds like a lot, compared with before the war (400) but yesterday I had an ice cream for the first time in five years and it cost 9.50 yen. A second-hand Japanese piano would be cheap at 20,000 yen. A radio would cost 1500 yen so really I am earning less than before.

I am looking forward to having that house and garden; I can see it still, better than any place I know. If I had a good job in England I would be tempted to throw everything up and leave at once, but really my duty, for the time being is here. I am the only man in Japan, that is the only foreigner, who can humanize, de-Japanise, re-inspire the Japanese. On the Crown Prince I can have very little influence, partly because the time is too short, partly because I can never see him by myself alone. But you can guess the state of things, his mind-limiting, when I tell you that Prince Rei, son of Prince Li, heir to the Korean throne, and of a Japanese princess, told me yesterday that he had never been to another boy's house, nor any boy to his. (He is 13, very clever, musical, polite and amiable. I would be glad to have him as my own son).

As for the young diplomats, my influence is very strong, though they are between 25 and 27 and were educated during the totalitarian years. Also at Tokyo University, I have a "class" of 75 students (3 women) who come because they want to hear me say what poetry is, what religion is, what the unique value of Japan is and what it can contribute to world culture.

The day before yesterday was Empire Day and I attended for the first time in twenty years because Tomiko wanted to see what it all looked like.

You will find Mrs Bush a very amusing person. She has a great deal of courage, more than the average man, and ditto of humour. Lieut. Bush I met for the first time today. He has a sailor's simplicity and indifference to money, and we shall no doubt see a lot of one another.

The quotations you send are the first I have ever approved of, so either I have come down or you have gone up in the world. Especially "our stability is but balance", very different from "Rock of ages, cleft for me".

At the moment I have a very strong desire to be in Rottingdean Heights, but I suppose it will wear off in a few days. Yesterday I was Henry V and it was so poor, artistically and dramatically, that I should have cried, only the words of Shakespeare were so good. Japan is the only place where religion and poetry flourish, or rather where they have done so up to the present.

The house we are in is pretty comfortable, even absolutely, and relative to those of most people, it is a palace.

Tomiko has become a good wife. I say "become" because she has changed very much since Harumi was born. She has a very truthful nature, just as I have a very deceitful one, but she understands poetry and pictures as few Japanese do. Music she dislikes,—but how much better this is than pretending to like it, or liking the wrong things. We are always joking and kicking each other even in front of other people; we have made one international marriage a success.

I found Mrs Fujii a position in the primary department of Peers School.[38] Her five children are all grown up now. Mr. Shinki stopped at the house for a fortnight, and left yesterday. I found him also a position as teacher in a private school in Tokyo.

I buy books whenever I can find any that I used to have, but the prices are so high that I can't afford many.

Love, Reg

55

August 14, 1946

Dear Dora,

Yesterday I heard, over the radio, an Introduction and Passacaglia by (what sounded like) T. Tertius Noble. It was very good, of course like Bach's, but not so sinewy and simple. There was an Intermezzo by Delius from an opera, I think called The Walk in the Paradise Garden, but I found it tedious from the beginning to the end. Then there were Elgar's Enigma Variations which I like very much, though I could hardly remember the theme in most of them. Recently my musical interest and appreciation seems rather flabby. My blood pressure is a little low. As for the music, what I want is the score of the Brandenburg Concertos, the ordinary Novello's Matthew Passion, Bach 48 and Violin and Flute Sonatas. I have no piano and no music, so anything beyond this would be a waste of money and petrol. I once had a book called the "Spirit of Man" by Robert Bridges, an anthology. I have no Shakespeare.

It is astonishing, the number of people in the world, and the few, if any, that one cares for. Of course, some people don't like themselves, but I feel happy sometimes, just waiting around with myself. The pleasures of thought are very great, and cost little.

When the right time comes I want you to come out here. Whether you would feel at home here is a question. I feel myself to be merely "camping out" in this world, and the place is rather indifferent. In one sense, I live here because I have not yet absorbed all I can from this side of the world, and because I want to teach the people here to evaluate themselves.

What I want Buddhism as such to do, is to take from Christianity everything good in it without exception, even if it is contradictory to Buddhism itself. This will prevent any competition between the two, for Buddhism will then contain all the good of Christianity and its own as well, and a + b can't very well fight with b.

Mr Humphreys who is in charge of the Buddhist Society in London, and who has been on the International Prosecution here, is going back to England at the end of this month probably. He has been spending most of his time in unifying all the Buddhist sects here, with great success, and I am very anxious for you to meet him when he arrives in London. I will tell you a little more about it later, but don't forget in any case.

Love, Reg.

56

October 26, 1946.

Dear Dora,

Several letters have come from you in the past few days and I now hasten (Sunday morning, ten to ten) to answer. We are all well, and better off than before, because we now have access to the PX (if you know what that is) and can buy any food, cakes and chocolates and so on, ad lib.

This change was due entirely to the kindness of Col. Bunker, MacArthur's aide-de-camp, who asked the proper parties to arrange that I should be paid for teaching the Crown Prince in pounds, instead of yen. This means, in result, that my salary (total) is doubled. But we are in just the same position in regard to clothes, so we shall be very glad when the parcels from you and my mother come.

In addition, as a means of supplanting my dollar (pound) income I thought of teaching Japanese literature (in English) to the American School here. I went to the Principal and suggested this; he said he didn't know there was such a thing as Japanese Culture and anyway the boys and girls didn't know if there were any, and they wouldn't be interested, and anyway it wouldn't go into the syllabus, and anyway . . . I got very red in the face and talked to him like a Dutch uncle. He sort of apologized and said he had only been in Japan a year and a half, and what would the Board say, and what would he say if the Board said this and that. Such people are afraid of culture, and rightly, because it's alive, and will bite them. However, I can do what I want to, if I care to push the matter. What I am worried about is the boys and girls themselves; let's hope they are better than their parents.

The only music I am getting nowadays is the radio, which seldom gives anything but the most hackneyed classics or wildly improbable modern music, and piano accompaniments for Harumi. She is doing the Air on a G String in the original key; she liked it when I played it though and said she wanted to do it. She has a very good sense of rhythm, and I am going to have her taught Japanese dancing.

I hope you don't get yourself Buddhicized too much, that is, I want you to preserve your own independence, and this is impossible if you join any sort of body of people who hold certain fixed opinions, however right they may be. I would particularly ask you to read two books: *D.H. Lawrence's Letters*, edited by Aldous Huxley, and *Phoenix*, a collection of his posthumous works. Lawrence is wrong in a few places, or rather he is right, but contradicts himself too unknowingly; for example, when he says that ordinary people are only bug-like sheep (which is true enough, but as Lawrence himself would say, "a truth that kills"), and on the other hand, that each man must be what he is, a unique irreplaceable living being, that exists for itself and with no ulterior meaning. Apart from this kind of inconsistency unresolved, Lawrence is correct, I think, in taking all organizations, parliaments, nations and leagues, as mechanical devices; all ideas and ideals as unreal and therefore poisonous. Japanese students find Lawrence easy to understand. In fact, they sometimes accuse me of putting into Lawrence's mouth thoughts which come from my own understanding of Buddhism,—but this is not so, except in the sense that to understand a man we must go beyond him.

This letter is not a very personal one, and yet I am thinking of you as I write it. Please read the two (big) books I mention above. You can get some new life from them. They have changed my way of living and thinking in the past year or so.

Love, Reg

P.S. I have just received a letter from you dated 7.10.46 (today is 26.10.46). The letter I sent you "laying it on" and not mentioning my mother was sent to her by Bush's mistake. I wrote her a letter the next day. A piano (second-hand Japanese) costs now 20,000 yen, 200 before the war, but you shall have one when you come,—yet of course it would be better to bring one with you; I fancy you could make money on it. I am afraid you are mistaking the book for the person; there is no point in getting a disappointment when you meet me. It's like the problem of Shakespeare's sonnets and his plays, or the later and earlier Wordsworth. I spent many years going to the cinema *every night*, i.e., 365 times a year. "Self-discipline" is such an unapplicable word. I have lain on several beds of my own making, and composed myself to rest on them, but this was self-discipline of quite an accidental kind. I worry just as much (in fact more) over failures and disappointments, as before. That may be partly excused on the ground of the poetic temperament and general sensibility, but I am softer-hearted than ever before anyway.

I thank you very sincerely for what you are sending. I feel bad about asking for the things, and the reason is that I have what my mother would call so many blessings, internal and external, that it is inviting disaster (in the Greek manner) to ask someone to send a pot of jam

Please write as often as you can; it doesn't matter how short or trifling the contents.   Reg

---

57

Late October or November 1946, from the reference to the president of the school retiring.

Dear Dora,

Letters don't seem to be coming very frequently or regularly. I received one from you posted about three months ago, and one from my mother two months old. Did you get the magazines I sent? If not, I will send some more copies. It might interest you to know my time-table for the week.

Monday 9–4 Lecturing at Nihon University
Tuesday morning lecturing at the [Tokyo] Imperial University; after-
    noon teaching the Crown Prince
Wednesday morning teaching at the Peers School, afternoon lecturing
    at the Diplomat's College

Thursday teaching at the Peers School and a private lesson for Prince
Rikyu

Friday lecturing at Imperial University 8–10; lecturing at Nihon Univer-
sity 10:30–4

Saturday morning, lecturing at Diplomat's School 9–12; afternoon,
lecturing at University of Literature and Science [Tokyō Bunrika
Daigaku] 12:30–4:30

In addition to this I have to give special lectures, and write articles for mag-
azines in English and Japanese. This brings me about 4000 yen a month, of
which I save about 1500. I teach Tomiko English every evening; that means
another 7 hours a week. Harumi is learning to play the violin, and can play
on the open strings more or less. Somebody is going to lend us a piano for
a year; it is supposed to arrive tomorrow so that will be a great pleasure
indeed, and I must teach Harumi the piano too. Her ear is good, so there is
nothing to worry about there.

As I suppose you have seen from the papers, Mrs. Vining has arrived here,
and we are going to do our best to use her for the demoralization of the Crown
Prince, and indeed Court circles generally. She is like all American women, a
little on the hard side, but very capable and tactful and will be a great success,
I think. In her own words, she is "keeping her eye on the ball."

As I have said before, a great number of times, I am always thinking of
the time when you will be here, both for your sake and mine, and I am won-
dering if there is not some way of wangling it earlier than normal. I don't
see why you shouldn't start learning some Japanese, if you can find a suit-
able book. Tomiko is learning English pretty well. Harumi is very fond of
reading, just for its own sake. I taught her to read and write Japanese "kana"
and she reads and rereads the books I have bought her. This morning, the
first things she did before she got up, was to read through one of her picture
books. I keep trying to teach her English, but somehow it is rather difficult
to find times when both she and I are in the mood for it.

I wear glasses now for reading always; otherwise, my eyes are good. My
latest thoughts on things in general are the following: When Wordsworth
says in the *Immortality Ode*,

The moon doth with delight
Look round her when the heavens are bare,

he either means what he says or he means nothing at all. In other words, if these two lines mean that "the moon shines around when the sky is cloudless, and I, the poet, am delighted with it all," there is no poetry in them and they are of no value. Does the moon feel real delight or not? If we say yes, we feel foolish, and if we say no, things are meaningless. In the *Journal to the Western Islands* Johnson says (I have quoted it before) "That man is to be little envied etc."[39] The fact is then that we cannot always answer Yes or No to intellectual problems—"Have you stopped beating your wife yet?"—all the more it is absurd to apply this dichotomous method to matters of poetry and religion, in which, per se, the unity of oneself with the rest of things is the essential.

It is Sunday morning and I am listening to the overture to Rienzi (which the announcer says he put on because it is a nice quiet Sabbath piece). Tomiko is still in bed. Harumi is drawing golliwogs; the two cats are sitting with their ears twitching at the roaring of the radio.

You said in one of your letters that you had sent me the St. Matthew Passion.

The President of the Peers School, who has just retired [on October 15, 1946], has persuaded his son-in-law to lend me his piano for one year. It is an ancient American make but not bad, and not badly out of tune. Tuning now costs as much as three pianos before the war. The only thing is, I have nothing whatever to play. In a few days I may go to Nara and Kyoto with Tomiko and Mrs. Vining. I dislike traveling at the best of times, and nowadays it is a physical and mental pain.

As I said before, I am always looking forward to your coming here, and I hope you will make the necessary steps beforehand, because ships and things will be booked up for months ahead I suppose. I don't know if I mentioned it, but if you come across any old children's books for kids of 4–6 years old, I would be glad to get them for Harumi. You must be tired of my begging letters, but you are the only victim I have.

If you know anybody who knows anything about book publishing and copyright etc., I would be glad to get my book [*Zen in English Literature and Oriental Classics*] published in England as soon as possible. The money side has no interest for me. Mr Humphreys of the Buddhist Lodge, London, should be back soon. I cannot recommend any of their publications, except a translation of the *Platform Sutra*, which you should buy several of and give to your friends.[40]

Love, Reg.

58

A penciled notation on the letter reads "via Siberia. Miss Dora Lord, 50 Fitzjohn's Avenue, London, England." His excitement over the prospect of Dora traveling to Japan places this letter close in time to Letter #57, perhaps early 1947.

Dear Dora,

This is a very quick letter indeed. I have just breakfasted off pancakes, and am waiting for the car to come and fetch me to the Diplomats' Institute. I am looking for a suitable book on Japanese to send you, because even if you learn only a little, it is useful in a practical way, but still more so as giving you, consciously and unconsciously, an insight into the way Japanese people think. During the change of pen and ink, your dress for Harumi came. It is very nicely made and beautiful material. I would like to see you in it. It is a little on the large size so that is all right. Harumi liked it very much. She is now playing the Blue Bells of Scotland and is stuck in the variations. I am very irritable in musical matters, so I have a hard job teaching her. I am sending you a book called "Thinking in Japanese", as soon as I have time to go and buy it. Please don't send any more of your sweets. Just think of me as you eat them & that will be enough. Our servant, a girl of 18, is writing you a letter. I think you may enjoy it.

I hope you will bring a piano when you come and also your cello, also some music to play on both. I hear no music except occasionally on the radio, and this means the Japanese, because the Armed Forces Radio Network is sugary beyond imagination.

The pictures you sent Tomiko were very good. I felt when I saw them that English landscape painters, especially Wilson, Cotman, Crome, Constable, and Turner, are far better than their contemporaries in poetry Thomson, Wordsworth, and the Romantics. If it were not for haiku I should consider Art and Music as far above poetry. If you can get hold of some good and not too small reproductions of the above, especially the first three, you might bring them with the musical instruments.

I keep saying, "When you come," but it still seems rather remote. However, the world is getting a little impatient at the slowness of things, and it may be sooner than we expect. I hope you didn't suffer from the cold too much. It was painful to wonder how my poor mother was getting on, but I suppose you are warmer now.   Love, Reg

---

59

January 10, 1947.

Dear Dora,

This strange looking paper is for writing Japanese manuscripts, one character a space. I received four or five letters from you today. Mr. Bush brought them. So many letters at once made me realize that you and I have missed a lot being away from each other so long. I have thought several times that a way of getting here might be to take some sort of job in the Embassy here; the next time I go there I will ask someone about the matter. What could you do from your end?

I'm afraid you have surpassed me now in your musical appreciation, let alone your playing ability! I have heard very little and played nothing for about six years. Playing the violin with Harumi is a great pleasure, a kind of taste of the future. For her sake too, the sooner you come here the better.

Today also came *The Art of Fugue*, and part of Shakespeare and the sonnets. *The Art of Fugue* made me wish for the records I once had. They were excellently played and recorded. My mother sent the shoes and vitamins, a cat and two dresses, a strange mixture, but everyone was very happy, especially Harumi. And the addition to the family is expected about June or July this year. This was by order, not by accident. I am at the moment trying to finish the first volume of my work on haiku. It is really the introduction, and the first part shows haiku as the flower of all Eastern culture, Buddhism, Zen, Confucianism, Taoism, Chinese and Japanese painting, Japanese poetry all being mingled to produce it. I haven't received your dress creation yet, but it is very pleasant, perhaps the pleasantest of all things, to receive something for nothing. Your letters are very good indeed, quite masculine but with a strong undercurrent of tender feeling well hidden. It is a real art you have of not saying unnecessary things. The photo was very good.

You and I are so much alike in all essential matters that we rather fail to notice it. The chief difference is that I live more in thought than you do, and you more in sensation than I.

Mr. Humphreys is in England now. He very kindly sent some copies of the *Poetry Review*. Try and see him if you can.

The "Sutra of Wei Lang," a new edition by Humphreys is published for the Buddhist Society London, 106 Great Russell Street, E.C.1 by Luzac & Co. 46 St. Russell Street. My copy has the date 1944.[41] He is somewhat cold in character, but very good, very just, and very generous.

It is a great relief to me to think you are there able to help my mother when she needs it. I would like to know how much your pension is. I suppose you can get it any time now. By the way, is my writing hard to read? Yours is. Miss MacGregor, by the way, knows nothing about Japan; she was interned there for a few months, that's all. Why do you work at the Bank now? It can't be that your anti-communist feeling is so strong that you wish at all costs to support the monetary fabric of England.

This letter is all higgledy-piggledy, partly because I don't like this paper or the ink, and partly because my mind is on the book I am finishing; my mind has a kind of writer's cramp. I wish to say something sweet and charming to you, but I somehow can't. I am very grateful for the books and music, and what my mother would call "hands across the sea," but it rather unsettles me, and that is another reason why this letter is so incoherent.

I am just going to take this letter to Bush, and I'll ask him about the post bag. I should be glad to get Bach's Preludes and Fugues, or Mozart's Sonatas, or a book of sonatas or sonatinas.

Yours with love, Reg

60

Postmarked April 10 1947; c/o Bank of England, for Lieutenant Bush RNVR.

Dear Dora,

I am writing this in the early morning before Mr. Bush gets here. We both go to the Foreign Office Diplomatic Institute (but our salaries are very different). It seems very difficult to get a book published or republished here. I am thinking about America. Every author's eyes turn there in times of adversity.

They put on a part of one of the Brandenburg Concertos the other day. How glad I was to hear it. They still seem to me the best & the most cheerful things ever written, and I still dislike *all* of Chopin, and Charles Lamb and French poetry and Strauss. I shrink from them as at a bad smell of something otherwise good.

This year I am lecturing on M. Arnold and D.H. Lawrence. I have no book of reference on Lawrence. If you know of any good study of him or his works and can get hold of it I would be overjoyed to receive it. One other thing I would like (you must be thinking, and one day will say, that I ask too often, and for too much) is a collection of violin pieces for a child of 5 learning the violin. Harumi is playing the Blue Bells of Scotland with variations, but this gets a little monotonous at times. She is also playing everything in 3 sharps, a curious method of beginning, but which enables or enabled her to play on the A string as doh, making the E string soh, thus easier than beginning with the D string in two sharps or playing in C with a more difficult fingering. 3 sharps is disliked by violinists generally, but Harumi has begun with it, what Americans call "doing it the hard way."

There is nobody I know who can play the piano even badly, and I am becoming what they call "musically illiterate."

I am very impressed with some of the booklets which the Embassy hands on to me sometimes, for example, those issued by the "Council for Industrial Design and Britain Today." They speak of a life in which intelligence and beauty are playing their well-balanced parts in a slow but orderly movement towards a more diffused, rationally, controlled ideal. In Japan there are, or have been, movements of sporadic political and artistic [*missing word*] but the minds of people are still unsettled to give any sign of collective activity. When I say "still", I mean for the last eighty years, since the impact of Western thinking,—thinking that a thing cannot both be and not be at the same time. This life within, a paradox, is the essence of Japanese thought and culture. Arnold and Lawrence seem to me to represent these two poles of thought-feeling. Can the two ever meet?

With love, Reg

61

A penciled notation on the letter reads, "Received 20th Aug, 1947."
The letter was dated July 26 in Blyth's hand.

TOKYO, MEJIRO, THE PEERS SCHOOL

Dear Dora,

We have another member of the Blyth family, Nana Elizabeth Blyth, now three weeks of age. She is very well and so is Tomiko. Milk is a little insufficient, but seems to be increasing.

When Harumi was born, I was interned, so the whole business is quite new to me.

I am waiting to receive the music you have sent. I think I explained before that Harumi began learning the violin in three sharps, that is using the A string as Doh, so she can play easily in A but not in other keys. She is gradually learning two sharps.

It is so hot this evening that it is quite difficult to guide the pen. I have about a month and a half's holiday, but I work just as much or more compared to term-time.

The radio is blaring away some last movement of a symphony but I can't make any guess as to what it is. (This was Schubert's No. 2.) Yesterday I heard Beethoven's 6th. I can't say I like it,—also Brahms 4th, which I don't care much for. Most people write and talk too much. All Schubert's chamber music is excruciatingly too long.

You should read anything of Eckhart that you can lay hands on. He is the only European writer that has the depth of Asia, yet expressed in a way that is comprehensible to the Western mind. Read Nietzsche's *Beyond Good and Evil* at least once a year.

Love, Reg

62

End of September 1947.

Dear Dora,

It is indeed a long time since I heard from you. The two pieces of music you sent for Harumi came safely, and the other part of the list. I was very glad to get them. The pieces are just right for Harumi, though she hasn't got round to the flats yet. The piece she likes best is

of Bach. She plays it with energy. Her fingers are rather small, especially the little one, and she uses a 1/8 violin but she has got the feel of it, the bite of the bow, and the way the tune dances. The new baby is only 2½ months but I have a feeling she won't be musical. She looks just the image of my father, and smiles joyfully on the slightest provocation. I hope anyway she is either musical or tone-deaf. Anything half-way is painful. Two books of mine I hope to see in print by the beginning of next year. It is altogether 5 volumes of about 250 pages each. What do you think of the following; they are sen-ryū, humorous poems, like haiku but psychological and satirical rather than poetical, but not devoid of depth or human value.

朝顔は 朝寝の人にしかみつら
　　To the late riser,
The morning glory
　　Makes a wry face.

The morning glory (literally, "morning face") has withered and looks disgusted & contemptuous in its shriveled appearance.

川中をわらじであるく筏乗り
　　Walking on the middle of the river
With straw sandals,
　　The raftsman.

This verse calmly omits the raft itself.

男なら直に汲まうに水のかがみ
　　If it were a man
He would soon finish drinking,—
　　The water mirror.

These are old verses and need a little thought or explanation. Please tell me what you think of them.

Love as ever,
Reg.

63

End of October 1947.

Dear Dora,

We got your parcels today (end of October) and all the things are being put to use almost on the spot. The letter about the money arrived, and the next one also. By the way the little one's name is Nana*ko*—*Ko* is added to any two-syllabled girl's name (not, therefore, to Harumi).

I am sending you a book which I found somewhere. It contains an article I wrote about twenty-five years ago. It is like a voice from the dead.

Some people want to begin quartets again. I have no cello or viola, and am wondering about buying the latter. They say that the best thing is to buy a cheap one of thick wood, and get someone to take it to pieces and pare it down in the proper places. If you ever fall over some old Haydn or Mozart quartets I would be glad to have them. I'm sorry I can't send you the money, but perhaps I could send something in kind.

I have a holiday today, so I am going to the dentist's, to two publishers to spur them on, and various other odd jobs that will take me all over Tokyo all day.

Let me thank you once more for all you have sent. It is not only the things but the affection, the feeling that in this busy and indifferent world there is somebody that does not forget.

Yours, Reg

64

August 5, 1948.

Dear Dora,

Thank you so much for the coat you sent. It fits Tomiko perfectly and will be very useful to her. I am going to presume on you once more, and ask you if you could send us some baby's shoes. Nanako stands up by herself now (August 5) and will walk very soon. My mother sent me a lot of things. I don't know how she got so many; I am afraid she may be going out herself to send them.

Harumi is now doing scales on the violin, up to three sharps and two flats. I am teaching her English in fits and starts, and she is gradually picking it up.

Nanako is a biter, butter, and striker, when she is thwarted in any way.

I have just finished writing an article in Japanese on what the Japanese ought to read. What they *are* reading at present is just romantic and erotic magazines, and stuffy magazines about democracy.

The weather now is very hot and damp, a sort of African weather. In the evening it is pleasant to look out in the garden and see the blue-green leaves shining in the lamp light: there is something Japanese about it.

How about looking for a job with some of the firms here? I must make some enquiries. I know a Mr Turner here; he is a timber merchant but likes me just the same.

Love, Reg

65

September 13, 1948. Above the address Blyth has written, "I enclose a letter to me from the Crown Prince."

GAKUSHŪIN
MEJIRO 1 CHOME
TOSHIMA KU
TOKYO

Dear Dora
I have just received your letter about your coming here and I postpone the answer until the next letter because I am in a hurry to get the following information. How much money, if any, have I in England *in my name*? Please let me know by return of post, air mail. The reason I want to know is that I have applied not to pay back to the British government my living expenses

which they lent me during the war, and I must say exactly how much money and property etc. I possess.

Yours in haste
Reg

P.S. I have just made myself ill writing a *History of English Literature* in three weeks, two hundred pages, so please excuse the shortness of this. I will write again in a couple of days.

66

This letter appears to come after #64 and #65 based on Blyth's comment that Dora's trip to Japan must be put off, giving this letter a probable date of late 1948.

Dear Dora,

I have just received the two letters in which there is the proposal concerning the house in England, and I must write at some length to explain myself clearly.

Though I consort to some extent with the big-wigs here, I am in a position, financially and otherwise, of very small beer. We live on my salary, and are able to save nothing at all. I have no house, no chairs or tables, no clothes, nothing in the bank, plenty of jobs but only twenty-four hours in a day to do them. I have no pension. However, if things go on as they are, I have only one thing to worry about, and that is what will happen to my wife and two children in the event of *my* death, not my mother's. I have insured my life, but the money would keep them for only one year. Tomiko would have no home and no house at all to live in. She also has no clothes, one pair of shoes. Her total wealth would be a small radio, a flute and an oboe.

At the moment there is no possibility of my coming to England, for several reasons. First, I couldn't pay the fare there or back. Second, while I was away, all the jobs I have here would be snapped up by the rush of people here when the peace treaty is signed, & I myself could not come back until then. There is, as far as I know, a decreasing possibility of my getting a job in England, and anyway, my work here is of sufficient interest and importance for me to wish to stay here.

As I say, I am most concerned about what will happen upon my own decease, and to speak quite frankly, I felt a little upset by the letter my mother sent, for the money in England (I have no idea what it is) and still more the house in England are the only assets I can present my family with if I am forced to leave them for another world. That is to say, the house is of no sentimental interest to me; it represents some means of support, even bread & butter, if it were sold, to my sorrowfully bereaved family.

Now, even as far as I am concerned, I would rather live in a house that belonged to me and not to you or my mother, but for Tomiko this would be still more so.

You will wonder what the point of all this is, and I hardly know myself. It is perhaps a vague feeling that I would rather have the house in my name than in yours, for the sake of Tomiko's feelings in the matter. I have not spoken to her about it, but she is not of a very pushing or grasping disposition and would always say nothing rather than ask for anything, however simply or justified.

Not being a business man, I don't understand why it is better for the house to be in your name. If I give you full power to do what you think proper with the house, it seems all right to me,—but I am very hazy in such matters as you know. Please enlighten me here.

I fancy you must be feeling a little blue at this moment. That is only because we are communicating by letters, so take no notice of this feeling and it will go away. In regard to your coming here, it will have to be after the peace treaty is signed, I am afraid, but then I could get you a job here, at least teaching jobs, very easily indeed. My *idea* is that when you come here, you will stop, so the house business is all nonsense anyway. Life here is very interesting; it is spiritually stimulating, too much so, in fact, and that is after having been here for over twenty years.

I imagine that you will feel the same thing, that you have so much to learn, that is, unconsciously imbibe, that you won't be in a hurry to leave. In addition, there is the pleasure and profit of my daily company; Tomiko is very restful, never interferes or criticizes, Harumi is most amusing, and the baby smiling like mad all day long. For this and other reasons, I personally envisage your visit here rather as an exodus, and being pseudo-financial once more, I suppose that living in Japan on English money would be, or would become, a rather profitable way of living.

Going back to my mother, please tell her as much of this as you think necessary. Repeating myself, I would, for various odd reasons, prefer to have the house in my name. I would very much like to come home on a visit, but there must be some financial change before I can do so.

I would like to know how much money I have in England, and how much a month my mother manages to live on. We are used to a pretty low standard ourselves, so it would be a simple question of arithmetic to find out how much we could live on there.

To give you some idea of conditions here, that is, my conditions: I was paid 700 yen for my *Zen in English Literature*. That is the price of six candles. I earn 1500 yen a month for 4 hours a week at the Imperial University. Our butter ration costs 1700 yen a month. You may see from this that I ought to be, if I am not, concerned to have what I can.

I haven't read through this letter again because for one thing I never do, and for another it was painful to write it. As I said, I would like to go to England, and Tomiko is very anxious to do so. It is all a question of money, but next year things may be changed a great deal. I think you had better show this letter to Ma, because I have no time this evening to write another letter, and I shall see Bush tonight and he will post it at once. I feel my mother's position very painfully, but there is nothing I can do about it except to wait until Japanese educational & financial conditions improve. For Harumi's sake I should spend some years in England, at least four, because she has Japanese nationality and needs that time to become naturalized, politically and spiritually.

My chief job is stimulating the students. Unfortunately I can't do that without doing the same to myself, which, as my mother would say, is very wearing.

Love, Reg.

Recently we have the light cut off every evening and have to go to bed at 7 o'clock. This is very exhausting. I mention this in case you find my letter a little nervous.

67

December 27. Sent from Mejiro, Tokyo, the address of Blyth's house on the Gakushūin campus. The year must be 1947 or 1948; in Letter #69 he anticipates receipt of the Mozart and Brahms clarinet quartets he requests here.

Dear Dora,

I am sending you some books, with the ulterior motive, of course, of getting you to send me some music. What I most need is the Mozart and Brahms Clarinet Quartets (there is also one by Weber, but I have never seen or heard it). I would like the Bach flute and violin trios (there are two). I have the clarinet part only of Brahms' two Clarinet Sonatas, and Weber's Concerto and Schumann's 3 Romances. I also need Bach violin sonatas. Any of these or the like; even if the solo part is missing it doesn't matter.

We passed Christmas very pleasantly, entertaining a lot of children. I am not very good at that sort of thing. I like to look at them as from a philosophic distance and though I know it is wrong I doubt whether I could "ascend to their heights."

I am sending you a very fine calendar, in fact quite a variety of things but they will arrive some time after this letter. If there are two of anything, give one to my mother.

Things are much dearer, and it is difficult to do more than eat and drink. Our austerity is more like squalour, I am afraid, but I am useful here and feel myself to be if not indispensable, at least irreplaceable.

We are very grateful for all the things you have sent. They are all used and reused in one way or another. In the next letter I hope to send you some more photographs.

Love, Reg

68

Autumn–winter 1949. The first haiku book appeared in August 1949, the senryū book in November. An Anthology of Nature in English Literature also appeared that year. Laurence Olivier's film version of Hamlet was released in Japan on September 27, 1949.

Dear Dora,

I haven't had a letter from you for a long time so I will try to earn one by writing myself. I want to have your frank opinion of the haiku book; I suppose many people will think that literature should be treated more *in vacuo*, so to speak, without dragging in Christianity or Zen or anything else. That is *just* where they are wrong. You, as a Wordsworthian, will be inclined to agree with me, I hope. The senryū book, which you will soon receive, will interest you in a more human way, but haiku and senryū between them represent the Way, that is the way in which we must view the world and conduct our lives in it, destructively and constructively at the same moment, in a sense transcending the life and death process, and yet sharing in it.

I have spent some time and thought on the nature and value of women, and though I have not reached any very new or original conclusions, I feel I "understand" women now,—in the same sense that I understand the spring breeze, or gravitation, or bed-bugs. It makes life easier. I have begun to teach Harumi the second violin part of the Bach double concerto. Of course she plays in the first position most of the time but she'll soon be able to manage the second movement. Then I'm going to teach her the second violin part of one or two easy minuets of Mozart's quartets and she will enjoy those.

I am sending you a copy of a book on English Literature which I wrote in a fortnight; you may like to glance through it. The "Anthology of Nature in English Literature" was written too quickly but there are few such books in English. The other day Mahler's Symphony was performed; I did not hear it, and a German teacher, a very clever and musical man, enjoyed it very much. I asked him if he would like to hear it every day and he said, "No," and as we grow older, this is a good test of anything. Hamlet is very popular here (I mean the film) and I myself enjoyed it very much. Ophelia I don't care for, on or off the stage, but the grave-digging scene (in the spirit of senryū) was very good indeed.

The winter holidays are just going to begin, giving me an opportunity to work harder than ever. I grow less lazy every day.

Love,
Reg

69

Probably spring of 1949.

Dear Dora,
I have just received your letter saying that Bush had come and gone. I shall be overjoyed to get the Brahms and Mozart. I have sent you various books and things which you will get in due course. I enclose a letter to Humphreys,

so I need not talk about that matter here. Mr. Yoshida, the Prime Minister, kindly found me a rich and patriotic chap who is willing to put up a million yen (!) to publish my four volumes of haiku translations (500 pages each) so they will be out this year. Harumi is going on well with the violin. She has a teacher now, a very good man, who teaches her *musically*, not mechanically, so I am very satisfied. I think you will find it difficult to get any music for here. I bought a piano, or rather, I borrowed a hundred and fifty thousand yen from the Peers School and am paying it back with the whole of my salary. The cherry blossoms are falling; they did their best. By the way, I think I told you I was bringing out several small books, *Thoreau's Journals, Emerson's Poems, An Outline of English Literature, An Anthology of Nature Poetry, Selections from Hazlitt,* and now I am beginning one that you would like best of all, a selection from Dorothy Wordsworth's *Journals*. Get them, especially the Tour in Scotland, 1803. Fancy going to the Italian lakes! I am always criss-crossing all over Tokyo, where no prospect pleases and man is sometimes rather vile, but I feel somehow at home.

Love, Reg.

Letters to Robert Aitken

70

January 16, 1947.

TOSHIMA KU,

MEJIRO, TOKYO

GAKUSHŪIN KANSHA

Dear Aitken,

Yesterday, the 15th of January 1947, Mr Blake came with your six months old letter.[1] Many times I have imagined you appearing at the front door in a military uniform and your unmilitary face, but you have chosen a much wiser path in delaying your coming here until you are more qualified.

I liked Mr Blake very much, and I think we may be useful to each other. I am very busy indeed at the present. I teach at three universities, the Peers School and the Training School for Diplomats under the Foreign Office, the Crown Prince, my wife (English) and Harumi (the violin).

The book I am writing on haiku has assumed such enormous dimensions that the publishers suggest that the introduction be published as a separate volume. It may be being printed by the time you arrive here.

With regard to your coming here, it is possible that Mr Blake and I, or rather, some of the people I know, may be able to do something at this end. I think we should correspond on this matter, for one cannot begin too early to make arrangements of this sort.

I found your letter a little difficult to read, but then I remembered what your writing was like before, and I could not help thinking it must have improved a great deal.

Don't be disappointed at a cold reception of anything poetical. If you can find, as I did, one or two people who appreciate what one has written, that is enough reward for years of labour. Things of real value are handed on as from torch to torch; there is no bonfire. I am afraid, from the looks of them, that Nisei and their ilk are not much good, culturally I mean, of course. You cannot make peace with the world until you have made peace with yourself, and they especially, to whom the opportunity is given of being human beings, only want to be 100% Americans, and this is not possible.

We moved from Kobe very soon after the end of the war, and I am very glad I did so, because Tokyo is the only place to be for alive people. I still use the razor blades you gave me, and all the other things have been extremely useful. I have bought borrowed and stolen a few books but it is rather a pitiful library that I have. Sometimes I feel a little resentment against . . . humanity in general, when I glance at it.

Remember me to Mortimer when you see him.[2] There are quite a lot of people I would like to see again, just for a short time. I look back on that internment camp with pleasure. I remember the green mountains and the bright morning sunshine.

I hope your asthma is in abeyance. I am well and so is my wife and Harumi. We are all looking forward to seeing you. I feel a little apprehensive, that is all; you will know a lot more Japanese than I, by the time you get here.

Please write immediately. Work hard, but don't overdo it. Think kindly of the stupid and malignant.

Yours, R. H. B.

71

Dated simply March 13; the year is 1947, because Blyth refers to the birth of his second daughter, Nanako.

GAKUSHŪIN KANSHA
GAKUSHŪIN MEJIRO TOKYO

Dear Aitken,

I was very pleased to get your letter. Just now the spring sunshine is getting bright on the white paper screens and somehow I often think of Futatabisan [ed. the internment camp in Kobe]. The air and the irresponsible life made it something to look back to.

I like both Col. and Mrs Blake.[3] They are about the best Americans, I mean in gentleness and quietness, that I have met so far.

As for your marriage, you must make a success of it. At present it is not possible for you both to come here, otherwise I would suggest that you do so. I cannot give you any good advice and would not if I could. I will only repeat what I have said before, that a man (or woman) has no rights, and should demand nothing of other people and less from his wife.

I think we, that is, Col. Blake may be able to find you a job in the Educational Section here. Col. Blake seems pretty confident of it, but of course you would be stuck there from 8 to five every day, not running around doing as you like. We expect you to make good, as they say. This sounds a little patronizing but it is meant paternally. No doubt he or Mrs Blake will write to you more in detail concerning what you should do at your end in the way of sending particulars and applications, etc.

I do not find myself in sufficiently financially straitened circumstances to make it necessary for me to squeeze out my personal experiences in a book on Za-zen. (This sounds a very cold sentence.)

I have not heard about Gordanier. From what I know of the person he married, I should say he is better without her. I am sorry to hear about Henning; but somehow he seems one of those people made for unhappiness.[4]

Due to various causes I have improved in two ways, as far as knowledge is concerned. One is in world affairs, I mean in opinions about suicide, Communism, marriage, etc. This is due to discussions with Foreign Office Officials at the Diplomats Institute. The other is very different. It is the ability to grasp and retain at one time in the mind the contradictory elements of things, faithfulness and justice, life and death, self-salvation and that of mankind, the ephemeral nature of things and their eternity of meaning, cruelty and compassion. I begin to see how life progresses by the necessary aid of these. It is all contained in Ryōkan's haiku:

The leaves
    Fall,

And lie as they fall.

With regard to the reprinting of *Zen in English Literature*, which shows no signs of being reprinted here, I will send you the power of attorney and a corrected copy of the book; you will then please do what you like with it.

Things here are not so unobtainable as fabulously expensive. A day or two ago I found, to my great delight, and bought for 300 yen, a dictionary. Its published price was 10 yen, and 300 yen is my salary for teaching at the Imperial University four hours a week. My wife is having a baby, May or June or July, I forget exactly when but she seems to need wool and flannel, both of which are unobtainable here. Any kind of sweets, especially chocolate, I would be very pleased to get. The only things you can buy here are made of some kind of saccharine, some of it dangerous. Any book on Japanese literature I want I will ask you later to bring with you. I don't know much about Hawaii, what you have there and what you haven't. My wife says they haven't any wool there because it's a hot place.

I have just started reading *Marius the Epicurean* and like it very much so far. I have to lecture on Matthew Arnold and D. H. Lawrence next. Any books you could send me on the latter especially would be very helpful.

When you come you may bring some reproductions of Wilson, Crome, Cotman, and the 18 cent. English landscape painters. Do you have *such* things in Hawaii, I wonder.

Yours,
R. H. B.

P.S. My wife just says the great thing that she needs, and what is unobtainable here, is laundry soap.

72

April 25, 1947.

Dear Aitken,

I am sending you a copy of *Zen in English Literature* and a power of attorney to do whatever you like with it. The publishers, the Hokuseido, asked me to tell you that they hope to receive the proper royalties, whatever they may be in such a case, for the reprinting. There seems to be little hope of getting it reprinted here at the moment, though all the metal plates are ready. The paper shortage is so acute that very often the newspaper is no bigger than this sheet, and only one at that.

The day before yesterday I met Colonel Orr at a tea party and he mentioned having received a letter from you. He said that at the moment there was nothing suitable in the C I and E,[5] but he was most impressed by your letter (he repeated this several times) and had sent it on to the 8th Army (Yokohama). I telephoned this to Colonel Blake and he'll do his best for you, I know. Apparently there is to be a considerable change in June & July. There are also several other places, the Education Centre for example, which will be needing people. In the C. I. and E., they require rather specialized people rather than those with general qualifications.

It seems that another publisher is going to print my book, "Haiku, Their Nature and Origin." I think you will find it very instructive.

Colonel Blake tells me that civilians here are not supposed to receive books, and it's better to send them to him. I shall be sorry if I don't get the Lawrence.

It was very sweet of you and your wife to go out and buy the things for me. I would like very much to see Mary, but, as Colonel Blake will have told you, it does not seem possible for the time being.

The letters I write to you must seem rather empty, at best a little suave, the reason being that what with writing books and giving out virtue in lectures, I take letter-writing rather lightly, as a kind of pleasant holiday from painful thought.

The two Blakes (I haven't seen the son yet, but they will be coming here in a day or two) are the best Americans, together with Colonel Bunker, MacArthur's aide, that I have met. They both combine sensitive kindness with calmness and a wise firmness. I am, as you know, intellectually firm but weak in practice, sensitive, but misanthropic, so I appreciate them very much and try feebly to imitate them in various ways.

I hope to see you soon, by hook or by crook. It is just a question of getting a round post in a round hole.

Yours,
R. H. Blyth

73

October 21, 1947.

GAKUSHŪIN, MEJIRO,
TOSHIMA-KU TOKYO.

Dear Aitken,

I received your letter and the parcel of baby things from your mother. To receive such things from someone I have never seen is very affecting. They are unbuyable here, and if they were, I could not possibly afford them. It is indeed impossible to thank you and your mother enough for them. The baby is very well indeed, a month heavier than she should be, from Mrs B's milk and clothed in fine raiment from you and yours.

The MS on the *Origin and Nature of Haiku*, as well as that of the translations and commentary, is in the hands of the Japanese publishers. When I have finished it, however, I am going to send you the MS of another, translations and commentaries of Senryū.

The day after I received your letter, I went down to Kamakura to see Dr Suzuki, and asked him for a copy of each of his books, and for some of his Japanese works also. It so happened that he had received the day before several boxes of his books, though they were damaged by the flood (you remember hearing of it perhaps) in Kobe just before the war. If you don't mind the covers being unstuck, I will send them, in fact I will send them anyway, and try and make up in some way or other a more or less complete edition of his works.

I think the delay in coming here may be all to the good, as you say; the time will pass quickly and usefully.

You ask if I ever got the things you and your wife sent. I certainly did, and you apparently did not get the letter I wrote about it. So let me thank you again. My wife and I could just imagine you both wandering around looking for them.

May I recommend you to read D. H. Lawrence's letters in toto. In general, letters are miserable things to read, and in Huxley's edition too more than half might well have been omitted, but they are worth wading through to pick out some remarkable thoughts.

I have made no friends (and also, no enemies) since I left the internment camp. If only one of the students listening knows what I am talking about, I feel that continued existence is justified, and life has a meaning. Though I agree with Lawrence that Christ led us into a fine cul de sac, I can faintly glimpse that Christ came to die for Messrs Tojo and Stalin and Truman and the packs of neurotic army brats. People like Nietzsche and Lawrence, for all their genius, are unable to see the value of these "half-men", the masses of vulgar and brutal people that make up the greater part of humanity.

Well, I had better stop sermonizing and giving you pokes in the ribs. This next Sunday I shall go down to Kamakura and get the books for you, and send them off per the Blakes. Mr and Mrs Blake are the best pair of people I have ever met. They have no "cracks" in them, always the same in all weathers. I am afraid that on their account I think much too highly of American people, but it can't be avoided.

By the way, can I send you any Japanese books on any subject? Let me know at once.

My wife sends her heart-felt thanks, and kind regards to Mrs A., both junior and senior, and to yourself.

Yours,

R. H. Blyth

Signing my name and beginning the letter is a very self-conscious business. But there it is.

———

74

Written February 15; the year is probably 1948.

Dear Aitken,

I was very glad to get your letters. As for the Zazen, nothing could be better, and what a wonderful thing for your wife too. The whole point is to go on with it when it has lost its novelty, and begins to look like a waste of valuable time. You keep on moving, geographically, and I really haven't the faintest idea where you are, but as long as the postman knows, that is enough for the present.

I had a very interesting, if depressing experience today. I went with Mr Blake to the American School, and saw the Principal, Maj. Ingraham, and offered my services as occasional teacher on Japanese literature and culture. He said he didn't know there was anything of value in Japanese literature, and that anyway, it couldn't be fitted into the syllabus, and anyway, the children weren't interested in such things, and anyway . . . I got rather angry and said what I thought. He took it very meekly, apologized for his ignorance, and began to wonder what the board of directors would say about it. He wants me to draw up a plan of studies, explanatory, so he knows that Haiku is not the name of a man, etc., etc., but I feel unwilling, at the moment, to push matters any further. Like so many men in such positions, he is a coward, afraid most of all of culture, because he feels it is alive and might bite him.

I am going to send you off various books on Zen in Japanese, and the first will be the most difficult. It is two copies of Suzuki's address before the Emperor. (You will be able to imagine how little the poor chap understood of it.)

We have Mr Blunden with us now, a most clever, sensitive, modest, and warm-hearted man.[6] I am going to write a letter to your wife. My friends are few and far between, and I need to cling to those I already have. Let me recommend you as strongly as paper and ink can, to read Lawrence's *Letters*, edited by Huxley, and *Phoenix*, a big volume of his posthumous works. Lawrence is perhaps the last of the list: Darwin, Freud, Spengler, Bashō, Enō [*Hui-neng*], Lawrence. It proceeds, as you see, from Law, biological and psychological, to Liberty, cosmic, personal, human and once more universal, but not abstract or cumulative. Lawrence has the "thusness" of Eno but with a certain Western energy that is seldom felt in the East.

The MS of "Haiku *Its Nature & Origins*" will be sent in a few days (today is 15th Feb.) The Senryū book ought to be a best seller, if I can find someone to illustrate it.

By the way, I am able to buy now from the American Occupation shop here, so we are well off for food, though clothes are, up to the present, unpurchasable.

Yours,

R. H. Blyth

P.S. As for *Z. in E. L.* or any other stuff of mine, please do as you think fit, without consulting me at all. As you know, I trust you implicitly and if you make mistakes, I don't care.

March 30, 1948.

THE GAKUSHŪIN MEJIRO TOKYO

Dear Aitken,

I sent you late a rosy wreath, or rather, Mr Blake did. (I can hardly express how kind and helpful Mr and Mrs Blake are in a variety of ways, material and spiritual.) What I am trying to say is that the MS of the *Introduction to Haiku*, which has been re-named "Eastern Culture and its Culmination in Haiku" was sent off a few days ago.[7]

Please do what you can. The illustrations are rather good, I think, though whether they still have any popular appeal is another matter. Taken chronologically, they represent the development of Eastern Culture from the drawing-room to the kitchen.

I am trying to make up my mind whether to send the senryū MS to you or have it printed here. The chief difficulty is the illustrations. Unlike haiku, senryū seem to have no accompanying pictures until we get to the Meiji Era.

I'm sending some Japanese books on Zen at the same time as this letter. They are rather hard to come by now, as the second hand shops have sold most of their good books by now and there are no reprints so far, or in prospect.

I would like to know how your Zazens are going on. Aren't they a cause of marital strife? Changing the subject very quickly, and referring to the magazines you so kindly sent, I think that people should be discouraged from writing, whether it is short stories or essays or newspaper articles. Radios should be shut off for all but a couple of hours of the day, say between 2 and 3 a.m. There's only one more ghastly thing than reading tripe, and that is writing it. Almost nobody has anything really to say. It is this incessant reading and writing and talking that makes the past the golden age.

I think I have given sufficient reasons for now bringing this letter to a close.

Yours,

R. H. B.

I hope your wife will write again.

76

Dear Aitken,

It is very kind of you to spend so much of your time and notepaper on me. The people you have to deal with seem to me (and seem to seem to you) rather crotchety. They talk a lot, but I never seem quite to know what they mean. For example, Mrs Sasaki says that *Z. in E. L.* is impossible to print in this country and earnestly hopes the Japanese will do it. Does she think the Japanese are stupid enough to do what the Americans are too clever to do? Or does she mean that American printers would not be willing to print the originals? In any case, it is only a question of making money. The fact is, anyway, that the Hokuseido wishes to reprint it, and have the old matrices, so it can be done rather cheaply. (I think.) I told you they are about to print a book of mine on senryū. I must say I feel as you do about Mrs Sasaki, but if she would send me some dollars in exchange for some bits out of *Z. in E. L.* I would be very pleased. However, you do just as you like about it,—I mean just enjoy yourself as much as you can with all those funny people.

Referring to the Haiku books, I'm afraid we got a bit mixed up. There are two manuscripts as you know, one in your hands, *Eastern Culture* or something or other, and *Haiku, the Flower of Eastern Culture*, a 1000 page anthology of Haiku, now in the hands of a printer here who is hesitatingly beginning to print it.[8]

You say you will send back the other manuscript if you don't hear from me. If you have already sent it, that's all right; I'll try and get it published here. It may not be difficult because it is a reasonable size. Or if you haven't done so, please see what you can do with it there.

I just telephoned to Mrs Blake. She seems unwilling to let Mrs Sasaki get away with it, so to speak. I rather agree with her, but take a less abstract and more mercenary view of the matter.[9]

I would now like to write something about your affairs, but that seems impossible. On the radio, two days ago they were asking for teachers part-time as well, for Camp Drake, where a lot of Americans live. So keep on trying to come here in some capacity or other (together, I mean). The holidays are about to begin, so I will have time to get you some more Japanese books; that is the best way in which I can thank you for all your trouble.

Mrs Blake is still going full steam ahead doing good things for everybody. The other day her son brought a young man to look at our radio, I mean to improve it and so on. Somebody stole his shoes while I was denouncing Stokowski's conducting. After great efforts Mrs Blake managed to buy some shoes for him. This is a very significant story, showing my character and that of the Blakes. I must add that the Blakes seem to like me in spite of an unbroken succession of similar incidents. The only thing I am afraid of is that they may leave here.

This is my longest letter so far. I hope it doesn't sound "anxious" or anything. In any case, I never had, in fact, come to think of it, *we* never had the experience (so far as I know) of misunderstanding each other.

Yours,
R Blyth

77

Circa 1948, when Blyth was trying to get the first volume of the haiku series published.

Dear Aitken,

The last letter I sent contained no reference to the prospects of your getting a position here, because I was still thinking about ways and means, but, as Mr Blake has no doubt told you, there is little or no hope of filling any job here for the time being, except in the American school. I have heard that a second one is now opening, and teachers are being applied for. I strongly urge you to make repeated applications for this job, for there seems no likelihood of any other. You must think that we are doing nothing for you here, but this is not so, and, as I have told you before, it is impossible to come out here in any other than an official position under the army or government service. Every penny of my money, by the way, is spent on food and nothing else, and we live on food about one seventh as good as the occupation forces have.

I have an idea that might be of service to you in the interim by sending you over Japanese books that you need or would like. I hope you weren't disappointed with the condition of the books I sent you. No others are affordable, and these cost nothing. The books you sent, especially the one on Japanese in Hawaii and "One Nation" were very stimulating, and useful in my work. As I say, I can get any Japanese books for you, especially Dr Suzuki's. I intend to write a life of Suzuki, and he has agreed to do something that you suggested I should do, give an account of his experiences in Japan, and of his satori. I have never done anything like this before, and feel an unwonted lack of self-confidence in the matter.

The firm that was going to publish the MS on "Haiku, its Nature and Origins" kept the MS for about two months, and when I enquired what they were up to, they said there was a sit-down strike which would take another two months to settle. They said they were sorry for me, and I replied, yes, I was sorry for myself, and took back the MS. I am having a copy of it made, and when it is finished I will let you have it. Please see what you can do with it.

I feel well, and cleverer than I did while we were interned together. Don't be too ambitious. Get some work that is not uncongenial, with not too many hours, and spend your spare time in doing what you really want to do. Remember that I wasted the first forty years of my life, though of course I have made use of that waste since then. Wisdom is a kind of stupidity, a kind of insensitiveness to all the things that used to loom so large and be so annoying.

Let me thank your mother once more for her kindness. Get your wife to write me a letter. Are you thinking of having any children? I can highly recommend it. Please write again immediately, especially if you have nothing to say.

Yours,
R Blyth

78

Late 1948 or 1949. Suzuki's lectures to the emperor, Bukkyō no daii, *were published in 1947; an English version,* The Essence of Buddhism, *appeared in August 1948.*

Dear Aitken,

I received your letter a few days ago. You seem to be a little discouraged in your job, and rightly no doubt, because the sort of work you want and need, is what you would do if you didn't need the money, that is to say, work which has profit to oneself, like lecturing or preaching or exploration. For your wife also to work, I mean earn money, has its advantage, no doubt, but there is something biologically unsound about it. This sounds old-fashioned, but so is nature.

I am sending you, by the same post, a copy of Suzuki's Address to the Emperor, in Japanese and English; they don't exactly correspond. Also Jimbo's exposition of the *Mumonkan*.[10]

This is the best from the scholastic, but not from the inspirational point of view. Also included is a volume on Zen, with some account of the experience of foreigners doing Zazen; I have not read this.

The day before I took the manuscript to Mr Blake to have it sent to you, a man saw it, and borrowed it, and the next day, the present owner of the Hokuseido (who published *Z. in E. L.* and are trying to make a reprint of it) came and said he very much wished to publish it, so I let him do it. You will be both pleased and sorry.

I wish you would write more often. You change rapidly, so it is impossible for me to write blindly, as to a set and stable character.

Yours,
R. H. B.

79

The letter is dated December 8; Blyth's references to his publications suggest that the year is 1948.

GAKUSHŪIN
MEJIRO, TOKYO

Dear Aitken,

I have just received your very original Christmas card. I am much more original, in that it has never yet entered my head to send a card to anybody. This paper, by the way, is being used (the back of it, I mean) for the boys to write their examination answers on.

I keep writing and you keep saying I don't, but this is another try. To repeat myself, the Zen book is being published this month. The senryū book is being proof-read. The haiku books will follow. I have written a short history of English Literature (200 pages), which will be published by March next year. I published an edition of *Will O' the Mill* (I hope you have read it) and have almost completed one, abridged to about 200 pages, of Thoreau's book on the Concord and Merrimac Rivers.[11] This is exceedingly difficult to annotate. If you could possibly find an annotated version and send it to me *at once*, it would save me publishing a great many mistakes and slips.

Dr Suzuki is well. Why don't you write to him? I have often told him about you. Address the letters to Enkakuji Temple, Kita Kamakura. He is going to give a lecture to the Emperor on the current situation on the 22nd of this month. The Blakes are in Okinawa now. I miss them.

Love to your wife,
R Blyth

80

February 1, 1949.

MEJIRO, TOKYO

Dear Aitken,

I haven't been down to see Dr Suzuki lately, but I am glad you have written to him. You say you want some advice. I suppose growing wise means gradually feeling less and less competent to give it, and if so, I must be getting wiser. However, before the horse has learned to live on no hay at all, I suggest, as a practical measure, that you should be a sort of Dr. Jekyll and Mr. Hyde, and throw yourself into your work wholeheartedly, and then have leisure hours in which you meditate, or read Thoreau, or relax in a still more human and domestic way. Mr Blake seems to have landed himself in a funny place; it all comes of being too ambitious. (Oh, I forgot to add to the advice, put your wife's happiness above everything else.)

I am sending you some books etc., but with an ulterior motive. I need some music for myself and Harumi, and I wrote to my cousin in England for it but it is quite unobtainable there. They are not even printing any now, and none is coming from Germany. I have written a long list in the expectation, or fear, that you may be able to get very few, or none of them.

The *Zen in Lit.* is reprinted, but still lacks the title on the cover. Tell me if you need any and how many. The Senryū book is still going along. I suppose it will take another two months.

Please let me know, specifically if possible, what books I can send you. Is there anything I can do for you in the Moiliili line?[12]

Yours,

R. H. Blyth

[APPENDED LIST]

Bach:	Sonatas for violin and piano
"	" " two violins (violin and flute) and piano
"	" " Cello and piano
Mozart:	" " violin and piano
Handel:	" " two violins and piano
Mozart:	Clarinet Quintet
Mozart:	String Quartets
"	String Quintets
Brahms:	Clarinet Quintet
"	Clarinet Trio
"	Clarinet Sonatas with piano
Weber:	Clarinet Concertos
Hayden:	String Quartets
Beethoven:	" "
Bach:	Concerto for violin in E and A minor ✓
"	" " two violins

I have a feeling you can't get any of them, so I may as well add the miniature scores of Bach's Brandenburg Concertos (6 of them) or any of the above. If you can beg, borrow, buy, or steal any of these I shall be grateful, and you must let me know the cost.

81

Before Letter #82, when Colonel Blake had already left Japan.

I have just received your letter saying that you are "coming" to Honolulu. I feel that that is the right place for you, at the moment, I mean geographically of course.

Mr. Blake expects to leave in December some time. I think they also would have done better to go to Hawaii. Dr Suzuki is now in Kyoto, and I have not seen him for a long time. He is bringing out another book on Zen, but it seems to me rather chewing the same old cud. As Emerson says of his own Transcendentalism, (in *Xenophanes*), of apparently diverse things: "bring them to the mind, they dull its edge with their monotony",[13] William James and Lawrence were quite correct in their attack on Monism.

Yours,
R Blyth

82

Aitken inscribed "1948?" on this letter, but it probably dates from autumn 1949, the year Blyth's book on senryū and Outline *(not* Short Introduction*) of English Literature appeared.*

Dear Aitken,

I was quite surprised to get your letter, because I had deluded myself into thinking that I had written a letter to you recently. The book on Senryū is being printed, *Z. in E. L.* is to be reprinted very soon, the publisher has promised to print the two books on Haiku, and the publisher is printing *A Short Introduction to English Literature*, about 200 pages, which I wrote in three weeks during the summer holiday. So you see I have nothing to complain of in this matter, and as far as you are concerned, I am very grateful for what you tried to do for me, and when I compare your financial position with mine I have reason to count my blessings once more.

I think you may as well keep the *Z in E. L.* Of course I will send you some more when it is reprinted. I am about to begin to write a *Short History of*

Japanese Literature. This is a piece of presumption on my part, but the excuse is that there is no good book on this subject. I intend to make it about 200 pages. This seems about the best size for printing and selling now-a-days.

You don't ask me to do anything for you; please do so. Mr Blake has already gone, and Mrs Blake will leave about the middle of next month. I shall miss them in very many ways. What you said about the policeman aspect of the matter was very apposite.

I enjoy your letters more than anyone else's, partly because I always feel your unexpressed affection for undeserving me, partly because I understand what you saw and I think you do the same for me. As I said once to you (if I may also garble the *Analects*) if even one person understands in the morning, we may die without regret in the evening.

Yours,
R. H. B.

I often think also of your wife; please tell her so.

83

Autumn–winter 1949, the year the Kamakura Bunko publishing house declared bankruptcy.

Dear Aitken,

I owe you three letters, and the book that accompanies this of mine. I am anxious to sell as many copies as possible, because the publication of the 3rd and 4th volumes may depend on the sale of the first and second. The Kamakura Bunko, the publisher of the 1st volume, has gone bankrupt and the Hokuseido will publish the others, but the advertising of the 1st has fallen between two stools. If you could devise some way of selling a few in Hawaii, I would be much obliged.

As I have asked you for a favor, this is a good time to say something complimentary to you, and that is, you are, I know, of a rather sardonic turn of mind, but never, in all our relations, have you exercised it towards your humble servant. You pay me the greatest compliment it is possible for one person to another, that of always being your best self to me. For this reason, I always find your simplest epistles affecting.

Changing the subject again, I will send you the senryū book as soon as they let me have some copies. It is a very fine production from the book-binding point of view.

I think the Bashō idea is very good, especially if you include all his spiritual environment. Bashō is the greatest of the Japanese and (so) the most human. You should bring in Issa and Buson by way of comparison and contrast. I would suggest you study the best of Bashō's haiku first, then a chronological selection, then one of his diaries, or rather, two, including *Oku no Hosomichi*. Then you might relate him to Wordsworth, giving a brief account of the attitudes to nature of Chaucer, Shakespeare, etc., for comparison with Bashō's. You must not omit Emerson and Whitman and a subtle differentiation of Thoreau and Bashō would be especially illuminative.

I am afraid I have written rather pontifically about this, but you know I mean well. As you know, I am a great believer in quotations, and I hope you will make a great many (short ones).

The music I will be very glad to receive. I particularly want the Bach double concerto, because Harumi will be able to play the largo with me.

Please remember me to your wife.

R. H. B.

84

1949–50. Senryū: Japanese Satirical Verses, which he says he will send to Aitken, was published November 1949.

Dear Aitken,

I have just received your letter, and, having an examination, am writing you on the extra paper. You are very kind to me as always, and your criticisms are just, at least as regards slovenliness or immaturity in fine distinctions of vocabulary, and "behindness" in reading. But I don't want to go to America, because of a simple fact, namely, that what we say & think and feel depends so largely on the audience we address; one must not have to *explain* what cannot be explained & should be taken in freely and intuitively. I am sure that I would begin to think of my *career* and of what Beelzebub and Nightmare (or whatever their names are) are saying and thinking, if I had to speak to a hundred people instead of twenty. I should just fall to pieces. Poverty and austerity, not only the material, but of a social, literary, musical, and even cultural kind, are necessary for the integrity of a man who has not Shakespearean power and universal comprehensiveness. To be a best-seller, even to make a small profit on one's writings is rather an evidence of failure, not because the average man is a fool or vulgar or sentimental, but from the nature of the spiritual life itself, which is always individual, unlikable, uncatchable, breaking through all modes of thought, shaking all that can be shaken, volatile and fantastic yet strong enough to support the slings and arrows of outrageous fortune. Ask me to remove what offends, what causes "public reaction", and the whole book collapses.

I don't like people who like Zen; I don't like scholars, as you rightly say. What do I want? I want every man to make every judgment a poetical one, and what is meant by "poetical" has nothing to do with "denotative and connotative meaning" whatever that is. You read some haiku while you were interned, and you wrote some, and good ones too. To write, or to breath heavily when you read them,—this is poetry. Is this deep breath and shining face denotative or connotative?

By the way, the publishers do not do a fine job. They did everything wrong that they could. They put the frontispiece the wrong way round, and when they changed it and printed a thousand copies, they left out the title page altogether. So please give me the credit, even if I don't understand what you mean by "textual analysis tradition."

You will notice that I am a little irritated; I suppose it is because you see too clearly the faults of the book. But you know, when we love people or books, we love them, at last, for those very faults rather than for their virtues, for the mistakes and hyperboles, the conceit and the vulgarity, have something *living* in them, something human and touching. You say I need competition (this refers to a certain smugness in me) but I think not. The world of grace that we build in the world of nature (i.e. competition) has nothing competitive about it. It is so difficult to hold on to one's faith, whatever it may be, that one can hardly afford to go knocking about taking and giving intellectual kicks and blows. To get to know that the book which is on the table is *not* on the table is exhausting work, and it is easily forgotten. Lawrence says, "Avoid people; it is like a poison gas they live in. And one is so fragile in one's subtle air of life." This, you will tell me is but half the truth. That is so, but in some ways it is the most difficult half, at least in the modern world.

One of my students wrote a letter to me about a climb up a mountain and back she took *alone*. It was in Japanese; she quoted, at the end of her walk, as she turned to look back at the evening hills, Byron's

> To bend once more
> Upon the mountains high
> The quiet of a loving eye.[14]

She wrote it in this haiku form, and I began to blubber like mad, I am happy to say. (I am indeed an anti-scholar.) She is one of my closest friends, but I see her seldom, and indeed do not like to be with her.

You are lucky to get this long letter, just because I wrote the answer immediately after reading yours. I am sending the senryū book off also today or tomorrow. This at least will be rather new to you. John the Baptist has changed into Pilate.

I hope you read the Bible often. Hamlet is very popular here. People are not so bad really. I don't expect them to read the haiku book, and it seems rather cute of them not to. But, at the same time as I realize this, that to be modest, like Shakespeare, "Truly sir, I am a poor fellow that would live." This applies equally to the Emperor and a bed-bug and to

Yours,
R. H. Blyth

P.S. Thank you for the music. Did Mr Yonquist send you 10 dollars?

85

June 11, 1950. Blyth was making efforts to support Aitken's study in Japan—nominally of haiku, but probably mainly of Zen.

GAKUSHŪIN, MEJIRO
THE PEERS SCHOOL

Dear Aitken,
I was very pleased to hear about the baby; I hope both are doing well. How does it feel to be a father?[15]

I asked Dr Hisamatsu, head of the Japanese Literature Department of Tokyo University, to write a letter for you. He did so, but forgot twice to bring it. The third time he sent me a post card saying that as Mr Nambara, head of the university had written to you, at his instigation, it was quite unnecessary for him to write specially.[16] I hope everything is then all right. If not, write to me again at once. By now you should have had an invitation from Mr Nambara.

Yours in haste
R. H. B.

86

Postmarked August 8, 1951, this postcard from Numazu was probably written when Blyth was staying at Osezaki in Shizuoka prefecture. He published a translation of the Zen master Ikkyū's poetry in Japanese[17]; it was later included in his Zen Essays. Aitken was probably living at Ryūtaku-ji in Mishima at this time, studying with Yamamoto Gempo Rōshi or his successor, Naka-gawa Sōen Rōshi.

NUMAZU

Dear Aitken,

We hope to come and see you on the 10th. I hope you are quite well now. Do you know whether the roshi can tell me anything about the works of Ikkyū Zenji—I mean which are the real ones?

See you soon, RHB

87

Postmarked June 14, 1953. The "special circumstances" probably refers to the collapse of Aitken's marriage. This same year, he would leave for Los Angeles to resume his Zen practice with the Rinzai teacher Nyogen Senzaki (1876–1958).

Dear Aitken,

Instead of trying to give you some good advice, almost certainly inapplicable to the special circumstances in which you find yourself, I think it would be better to write about my own affairs, and leave you to pick out what relevant and useful points may accidentally appear.

My chief virtue is a passionate respect for what is good in the world. I have had the aim, and am on the way to achieving it, of becoming a human being. I have the necessary spirit and wish others to share in the feast of good things. My chief defect is that I am apt to arouse in others, particularly of course in the opposite sex, a love of myself which becomes a nuisance to me. Yet to talk to a charming and affectionate and intelligent woman is not only one of the greatest pleasures of life, it is the most fundamental and necessary. It stimulates us even in our higher faculties, to the greatest possible extent. I have always kept myself unspotted from the world; though I am a perfect leopard as far as my own spots are concerned. I don't think I could be of any use as a social unit. I am a Robinson Crusoe by nature and I can teach others how to be another one. There is something poisonous, something odious about Zen, and about all those who have anything to do with it, don't you think so? The great thing to avoid is any kind of satori. All we have to do is to get into the habit of thinking about other people and not ourselves. Avoid, if possible those (many) you dislike. Always keep your eye fixed on other people. Swallow them up like an octopus and digest them, if you must be in their company. Defend nothing. Attack with a kind of kindly carelessness. Never feel ugh! about anything. Just swallow it down. Be careful not to live for people or things. Live in and around them and make them live on and through, not for, you. I intended not to write any advice but there it comes oozing out.

Please write again.
R. H. B.

88

A notation on the letter dates it to September 21, 1953.

Dear Mr Aitken,

I have, and have had for a long time, some books to send you, rather a lot, but I want to know if I have the right address or not. I sent you a letter some time ago in reply to an urgent one of yours, but I got no answer. I suppose no news is good news. Mr Nabeshima said he saw you on his way back to Japan, and that you seemed well and happy. Please write to me at once, and I will send the books off.

I'm busily happy and happily busy with a book on Eastern and Western culture. I suppose I have bitten off more than I can chew, but I am not sufficiently aware of the fact to make me stop writing. I have the MS of another book of haiku and of senryū, but not enough time to put them in order. I have to write about Buddhism, which I dislike, and especially about Zen, which I have completely forgotten. Such are the trials of a "Mr Know-All." If you have any advice on this or any other matter please let me have it.

Yours rememberingly and affectionately,
RH Blyth

89

Circa 1954, after Aitken had gone to work at Perkins Oriental Bookstore, a bookseller in South Pasadena owned by P. D. Perkins that specialized in Asian books; hence the requests Blyth makes for books both here and in subsequent letters.

Dear Aitken,
As I told you, or as I didn't, I am writing a book on World Satire, in Literature and everything else, so I would like you to suggest some books on the following

1. Satire in German, French, and Spanish, and Italian literature, in those languages would be best of all.
2. Any book or booklet on satire in music
3. A book on satirical art (I have, by the way, *A Treasury of Satire*, by Edgar Johnson, quite good.)
4. Satire in Chinese Literature would be useful, if such a book exists.

Of course humour would do, but I must pick out the critical parts in that case. It occurred to me today that there is a considerable amount in the *Mumonkan* etc.

You once recommended me to read (and gave me a copy of) *The Theory of the Leisure Class*: I was reading it the other day & was surprised at its brilliance. By the way, do you know any cheap edition of Italian books? I have 40 or 50 of the Spanish "Austral" edition; I need a lot in Italian.

What do you think of Lincoln, by the way? and Hemingway? and Emily Dickinson? Of all the people in Am. Literature I dislike it is Mark Twain I dislike most. I spent a lot of time on Thoreau a few months ago. He is one of my favourite authors. How about you? Is there a collection of Thoreau's poetry? His verse has a peculiar charm, an earthy taste like mushrooms. Write soon.

Yours, RHB

90

Postmarked March 5, 1954. The letter alludes to Aitken's illness, said to have been pneumonia, for which he was hospitalized at this time.

Dear Aitken,

I was most pleased to get your letter. Have you ever tried a chiropractor as a remedy? I have nothing wrong with me, but recently a Japanese has pummeled me and my family about and I feel there is something good in it. Nanako, for example, who did nothing but catch one cold after another, has not caught cold for a year. This may be, certainly is partly due to taking cod-liver oil during the same period. I would like to recommend both to you. Seventh Day Adventist people are very good and clever and kind, except in their religion.

I am glad you are going to postpone the Zazen and the degree (which are about footlingly equal) and let your charity begin (and end) at home. When your letter arrived I was reading about the Aztec civilization, and felt rather sick. They were so horribly right in their worship of cruelty and death. By the way, you mentioned in a previous letter, that you knew of a book which treats of the influence of Hinduism and Buddhism on Thoreau and Emerson. I would be glad to order it if you tell me the details. Thank you so much for the book on Shakespeare. You are always an angel to me,—what I mean is that your attitude to me is always and infallibly right and good. I remember that big hat you wore when I first saw you digging & planting at Futatabi.[18] I think the stories idea is excellent. Work some of the haiku into them.

Yours, RHB.

Postmarked June 14, 1954.

Dear Aitken,

I got your letter today saying you had sent me your copy of Eckhart. I thereupon went out and ordered 國訳禅学大成 [*Kokuyaku Zengaku Taisei*], twenty-four or twenty-five volumes.[19] Each is about 500 pages and has *kana* throughout. They will be sent off some time next week I suppose. Of course they are second hand but nobody reads them, so they will be the same as new. I asked the man to look for a *nempyō* [chronology]. I have just bought an interesting book, 漢字の科学 [*Kanji no kagaku*], which gives the origin of each Chinese character. I must get you one. The first character, one, 一, is interesting as being horizontal instead of vertical as the Western 1. The author suggests it comes from the Chinese horizon. By the way, I want a book on the Gnostics. Also by the way, send me your wife's address; I owe her a letter.[20]

Yours,
RHB

P.S. A very good book is: Melville's *Quarrel with God*, by Thomson, Princeton, 1952.

I am not used to writing on this kind of paper,[21] so I didn't realize I have a bit more room. I have never met Mr. Perkins. What sort of chap is he? A book worth reading is *Witchcraft*, by Pennethorne Hughes, Longmans. Also any books by Rudolf Otto, in particular *Mysticism East & West*, Macmillan. Also *The Irish*, Sean O'Faolain, Pelican. Also *Stoic, Christian, & Humanist*, G. Murray, George Allen. I bought Spengler's *Decline of the West* the other day; I don't know what I shall think of it this time.

Postmarked June 21, 1954; addressed to R. B. Aitken Esq., c/o P. D. and Ione Perkins, P. O. Box 167, South Pasadena, California.

R H BLYTH

GAKUSHŪIN MEJIRO

TOKYO

Dear Aitken,

We are quite pen pals now, aren't we? I think you are right about the thing of Hu Shih and Suzuki, so let it fall into oblivion.[22] I want a book or even some books on Satanism and demonology. What I mean is this. I want a book, and not a small one, on the history of the worship of the Devil. I have come to the conclusion recently that the Devil is as important as, or perhaps more important than God, and intend to do Him the justice He deserves. I have a catalogue by Orientalia 11 East 12th Street New York, 3., but there is only one book in it, on "Occultism", which is not quite what I am talking about.

Another book I would like is *Readings from the Mystics of Islam*, Margaret Smith, 1950, $2.25. [*interlineal notation by Aitken: Luzac 12s6d*] (When women have anything to do with mysticism it always turns sloppy, but I suppose I can evade it.) It is convenient to have Mr Perkins in Kyoto, so that I can pay him directly if there is no other way.[23] By the way, one of the best, perhaps the best writer on mystical subjects is Rudolf Otto, especially *The Idea of the Holy*. I am looking forward very much to the Eckhart. I can read him like a duck taking to water. The Blakes are in Spain at this moment, it seems. As Dr Johnson says, "How little foreign travel adds to the facilities of conversation in those who have been abroad." What have you been reading recently? Don't you think *mayoi* [illusion] is better (more interesting) than *satori*?

Yours RHB

93

July 28, 1954. The works Blyth mentions wanting here were for a study of Western mysticism in which he was engaged during this period of his life. Carus is Paul Carus, the work presumably his History of the Devil and the Idea of Evil *(1900). The mystical treatise* Theologia Germanica *was also known as* Theologia Deutsch. *Pandemonium was a name invented by John Milton for the capital*

of Hell in Book 1 of Paradise Lost; *the only record I found of a book
by that name is* Pandemonium, or a Glimpse into the Modern
Inferno, *by Asmodeus from 1850.*

Dear Aitken,

I hope you have received the books by now. I will look for Vol. 7 of the Bashō.
By the way, there is a Vol. 9; I will send that too. I would like the Carus; but
the Gnostics are too dear. It's odd about the *Theologia Germanica*, because it
is or was in the Golden Treasury Series with a preface by Charles Kingsley,
edited by Winkworth, London, 1907, 4th Edn. This is a translation from
Pfeiffer's edition of *Theologia Deutsch*, 1851, which I would like too, that is
to say, any German edition. Dionysius the Areopagite ought to be found in
some Catholic edition, though the Catholic Church has always feared and
hated the Mystics. The *Pandemonium* I must look up; I don't know anything
about it yet. I shall be glad to get the Plotinus & Traherne.

I have nothing much to say in this letter because you didn't reply to my
"pertinent questions" (though I have not a very clear recollection of what
they were).

What I feel very much now, and keenly is that the world is ununder-
standable in its nature, but that we have to see more & more clearly what
that confusion and contradiction is.

I am hoping for a more personal letter from you next time. To me you
are always self-less, and I never get a chance of seeing your bad points.

Yours,

RHB

94

September 9, 1954

Dear Aitken,

I have received several more books from you recently. Carus on the Devil was
particularly useful. The only book I really want to see now is some selections
from Dionysius the Areopagite, because he was the father of all the Medie-
val Christian Mysticism. Will you please send me—something awful—the
whole bill, and I will try to pay it right off, like drinking medicine.

You seemed disturbed about your "personal" letter. I have almost forgotten what was in it. Anyway you must do your best with your own life, leaving nothing to reproach yourself for. I rather envy you in your job, but I suppose everybody envies everybody else. Dr. Suzuki has come back and I was to see him last Sunday but couldn't. Tonight I have to see DeMartino and a Miss or Mrs. Bruce or Hart or something or other. I will give them a dash of Satanism and see how they like it. With regard to the slapping story, I can say nothing, because I don't know the psychological or psychical state of the parties concerned. It seemed to me, however, a good example of the Roshi's judgement. After all, the other chap might have had toothache or a dislocated neck; it seems a little dangerous. In any case it should be kept a deadly secret. Please keep writing. You are the only person I care to hear from.

Yours,
RHB

95

November 16, 1954

Dear Aitken,

The Eckhart has just come. That sentence by Eckhart quoted in the Preface is so good: "He who knows the truth, knows that I am speaking the Truth." Today I bought Buckle's *History of Civilization*; *Auden & After*, by Scarfe; *Anthology of Spanish Poetry* (Harrap); *Religious Development Between the Old and New Testaments*, Charles; *Tragedy is Not Enough*, Jaspers; and some organ music, pre-Bach.

Two weeks ago I sent you two books of mine which perhaps you didn't have. The *Short History* is to be reprinted, & has a lot of misprints in it. A week ago 25 or 6 Zen books were sent off. Tomorrow I am sending you the Kanji explanation (etymology) book. Tomorrow evening a man called Graeffe is coming to see me after giving a lecture at the International Christian University on "Zen in Occidental Music."[24]

Today I said to the students something I thought yesterday: "No man can live truly & happily with a *particular* woman, unless he is able to live so with *any* woman." Of course I don't know all, in fact hardly any of, the circumstances, but I can't understand why you don't take your marriage as a koan. If love (i.e. Zen) means to give everything and ask for nothing, what is to prevent you from being blessed and your wife being happy? Falstaff said, honour can't cure a broken leg; can't Zen cure a broken marriage? Or can it only cure a broken heart? Kindly enlighten me, for I am troubled by all this.

Yours,
RHB

96

Postmarked May 23, 1955.

Dear Aitken,
Your letter was full of (undeserved) kindness and tact. The whole business was just a mistake. I told my wife to pay the bill to Perkins' representative in Tokyo, and I thought she had done so, but she forgot. It will be paid tomorrow, the 22nd of May. I am writing to Mr Perkins to apologize for the delay. I was very busy in the last few months because I was intending to go to England to see my mother for two or three months, but it has at last all fallen through (I intended to take a Japanese girl, who has lived with us for the past 5 years, to England as a companion for my mother) because I am unable to buy enough pounds. By the way, there are two books I want, one I think easy to get: *Autumn* (the VIIth volume) of Thoreau (Houghton, Mifflin). I have the other volumes I bought here, 890 yen each. Also I want to have the original Chinese of Fung-Yu-Lan's *History of Chinese Philosophy*; I have the translation, two volumes by Bodde. The Chinese was published in China in 1934. The title is 中国哲学史. I think he also published *A Short History*; it is not this. I'd like to know if it is available, and the price. The translation was 3,000 yen a volume, I think. Please write soon, and as personally as possible.

Yours,
R. H. B.

97

Postmarked June 6, 1955.

Dear Aitken,

I have sent off the letter to Mrs Rajagopal.[25] She will expect to see something with wings.* I think it's a good idea to change from Perkin's, though it may be a loss for me. Please apologize to Mrs P[erkins]. and tell her it was all a mistake; I thought my wife had paid the bill long ago. I'm afraid you may be disappointed with the children at first. Your job will be, like mine, resistance, resistance to the scientific, national, explanatory, soul-destroying attitude of the rest of the staff; the world the flesh and the devil. As for a fellowship and all that stuff, I have too much dignity, or malevolence, to ask for it. As for what I am studying, I am writing five books: a second book of senryū, including world satire; a history of American literature (puzzle: find it), the 5th book of Haiku, and last but not least, World Culture!! I would like you to get me the following:

1. *Anthology of Contemporary Latin American Poetry*
   Ed. By D. Fitts, a New Directions Book. Norfolk, Conn.
2. *Treatment of Nature in German Literature*
   Batt (Bett?) Chicago 1902

---

* Dear Mrs. Rajagopal,
I find it is a little difficult to write a letter of recommendation for Mr. Aitken, for he is my best friend, and I feel almost as if I am praising myself. I was interned with him during the war in Kobe, under conditions which show pretty clearly what a man is made of. He has a cool judgement and a warm heart. He delights in study and despises "vain delights." Like Chaucer's Clerk, "gladly wolde he learne and gladly teche," and he is eminently fitted for the life of a teacher, knowing human nature so well and yet not thinking unkindly of it.

That he is diligent and conscientious in all that he does, and worthy of respect in his moral character, goes without saying. An excellent brain, unthwarted by any fanaticisms, is combined with fairness, broad-mindedness, and goodness of heart. His knowledge of Oriental culture and literature gives him a great advantage over teachers who know only their own.

I can only conclude by saying that if ever I became a head master—which God forbid!—I would choose Mr. Aitken as my second in command. Anyway, Mrs. Rajagopal, have no hesitation in appointing him to the position he aspires to.

Yours sincerely,
R. H. Blyth
(Tutor to the Crown Prince of Japan)

3. *Roman Satire: Its Outlook on Social Life*
   J. W. Duff Univ. of Cal. Press 1936
4. *Martial and the Modern Epigram*
   Nixon New York Longmans Green 1927
5. *Lucian: Satirist and Artist*
   Allinson, F. G. New York Longmans Green 1927
6. There is a book about Thoreau and the East; I have forgotten the name, but it deals with the Eastern influences on him.

I have very high-class dreams sometimes. The other day I finished a (dream) lecture and woke up remembering only the last sentence, which was:
God himself is patient with a patient man.
By the way, I wrote to Mrs Galoopy, or whatever her name is, saying that you were my only friend. I suppose it is true.

Yours, RHB

———

98

Postmarked November 1, 1955.

Dear Aitken,
It is a long time since we wrote to each other. Thank you so much for the nut-grinder. It touches me that you should be so thoughtful. As for the bill for the books, I am paying Mr Perkins in yen, because it's so difficult to send dollars to the USA, especially as I have to send some pounds to my mother.

As for the books I am reading at the present time, they are: *Forerunners & Rivals of Christianity*, 2 Vols, Legge (very good), *Philosophie de la Valeur*, Ruyer, v.g., *Wuthering Heights* (connected with Satanism), *Scepticism and Animal Faith*, Santayana (just begun), *Lessons in the Egyptian Language*, Budge (just looking at the pictures), *Origin of the Family*, Engels (so obstinate they all are), *The Wandering Scholars*, Helen Waddell, the *Eclogues* of Virgil, etc., etc. What are you reading? I have found that it is better to read some good, old-fashioned book like Mill on Liberty or *Beyond Good and Evil* of Nietzsche, than these new cheap Pelicans or Penguins or what not written by little university professors. Dr Suzuki is leaving here on the 15th. I ought to see him before he goes, but he has got a beautiful young secretary and half his attention seems to be for her.[26] Of course I am partly jealous, but the hand in hand business is too much for me. Mr. DeMartino invited me to go and see him this Friday.[27] He wrote a review of Senzaki & McCandless' *Buddhism and Zen* in *The Review of Religion*. I think their book is odious, so self-complacent and know-all-ish. Please write soon. You are my one and only correspondent.

R. H. B.

———

99

Letter #100 (late 1955) is a clear follow-up to this letter's request for the Bode edition of Thoreau's poems, and the request for Shelley and Platonism *is followed up in Letter #101 (December 1955), indicating a late 1955 date for this letter as well.*

Dear Aitken,

Thank you for your long letter. Your modesty will cause you to be surprised when I say that yours are the only letters I read (the others I skip) and that they give me some kind of new life. By the way, before I forget it, I want a book, a rather large one, called *Shelley and Platonism* (or is it *Platonism and Shelley*), author forgotten, publisher may be Oxford Univ. Press. Emerson said he found it difficult to read the *Timaeus* (or rather he found it difficult to find the right day on which to read it) and I think just as with Zen, it is better to go to Platonism through or with the poets. Also a book called *Thoreau & Asia* or *the Orient, Thoreau and the East*, or some such title.[28] I have *Emerson and Asia* by Carpenter (Harvard U.P. 1950) and it is very good. You speak, by the way, of Fung's deflection; do you mean defection? I know nothing of either; or supplement: what is it?[29] I would like *The Collected Poems of Henry Thoreau*: C. Bode, 1943.

Thoreau seems to me the worst poet who ever lived, but one of the most rewarding if we concentrate on his pre-poetic meaning. As far as Zazen is concerned, I would like to suggest to you that you are wasting your time, because you are already enlightened. All you need (or almost all) is to know that you needn't do it: Our trouble is that we are always trying to get somebody else's enlightenment. I have an enlightenment which even Buddha did not have; I want his too, of course, but why doesn't he want mine? Is his also not a little defective, or deflective? By the way, I feel happy writing to you. I feel at my best. And I don't care what I am writing. Speaking of dollars, I will write to Dr Derk Bodde, but I think I had better ask him to send the book to you (otherwise I find payment difficult) to your home address. By the way, I have daily less and less belief in the Buddha nature, and this has some connection with what you asked about Zen and organisation. Organisation is bad enough when it is meetings and committees and what not, but *intellectual* organisation is far more dangerous,—the idea of satori for all, for example. Life is will. A Haiku is an act of will. A student (lady) asked me the other day to define "will." I said, "I *will* not." Will is resistance. Resistance to what? To all other will. That is why the teacher cannot have a disciple. "The falling out of faithful friends is the meaning of love", but this love is simply a means of the renewing of the falling out.[30]

Yours,
R. H. Blyth

100

Late 1955. The discussion of Yanagi Sōetsu continues in the following letter.

Dear Aitken,

I received your letter about the books. Tomorrow, I am sending you eight or nine books that I have two of. They are not what you asked for or what you particularly want, perhaps, but I am sending them quite off the list of exchange books, so you won't mind, I'm sure.

The first books I will send you are part of a Series of the works of Yanagi Sōetsu. His book of Tea must be one of the best on the subject. Look at the titles of the others, and I will send them if you want them. Once you asked me for a concluding volume of *Bashō Kōza*: there are 9 in all. Which haven't you got?[31]

By the way, as far as the exchange business is concerned, I'm afraid I may be a little richer than you, so you must tell me when to stop. Also you must keep the accounts and see that they are level. I will write the prices in the second-hand books, and the new books have the prices in them. I read an extraordinarily good piece of fiction yesterday, *Mr Fortune's Maggot* by Sylvia Townsend Warner, Penguin. If you can find any more books by her (I think there is a collection of short stories) I would be glad for you to send them. I haven't got enough pluck somehow to write to Brode or Bode or whatever his name is; I wish you would do it. I was glad to hear about your Bashō book. Bashō will never be popular, like Shakespeare, but there will always be people who like him better. Thank you for the Embassy writing. It makes things much easier for me.

RHB.

101

This letter is postmarked December 14, 1955, and is a follow-up to the preceding letter.

Dear Aitken,

Two days ago I sent you a couple of books you asked for, or the nearest I could get to it. Yanagi Sōetsu's book on Tea is about the best there is, I should think, in Japanese or any other language. He knows all about Zen, but it is not *Zen-kusai* [that is, it doesn't "stink of Zen"]. If you want any of the other books of his, in that series, please bill me and I will send them. The haibun was more difficult. There are two extremes, complete haibun with no explanations (or more difficult than the originals) and snippets for schoolboys with full & easy notes.³² The one I sent you is something between the two. Kamo Chōmei's other works are hard to come by but will turn up soon.³³ You didn't tell me what books of *Bashō Kōza* you didn't have; it goes up to Vol. 9. I am writing a history of English Literature at the moment. I have got up to Burton; and 15 days more to go. I note what you say about financial matters. I would like the book on Shelley and Platonism but after that let me send you anything you need. I think I am richer than you. I am sorry I have no words of wisdom for you this time, except to say that I think that even God himself gets confused and miserable when he wonders about the meaning of the universe, so it is quite reasonable that we should also. Your last letter was so humble that it made me feel quite splenetic about the world. Please write a little oftener. Your letters always breathe a sort of goodness and gratitude which I need when I am feeling a bit down. Of course, I can do without them, but that is precisely why I ask you to write.

Yours,
R. H. B.

102

Robert Aitken and Anne Hopkins were married in 1957 and soon after went to Japan to study Zen. This letter probably dates from that period.

Dear Mrs Aitken,

It was an unexpected pleasure to get a letter from you. You evidently see through (part of) your husband already. If I were to give you some advice, I would say, never listen to him (or anyone else for that matter) when he talks about Zen. What Zen he has in him, or gets in him, will infallibly produce its effect on you, and vice-versa. I am sorry you don't like snakes, etc. It's a great pleasure, indeed a kind of double pleasure to be fond of them, the feeling and the consciousness of it. Don't allow yourself to dislike cities unnecessarily. People are the only good things in the world. As for Koans, the biggest and most urgent is your husband. If you can solve him, you will hear the sound of his one hand. There are some lines from Arnold's *Resignation*, which I will make you a present of, more perhaps for their tone and cadence than their Buddhist philosophy (they speak of "God"):

. . .

To whom each moment in its race,
Crowd as we will its neutral space,
Is but a quiet watershed
Whence, equally, the Seas of Life and Death are fed.

Yours,
RH Blyth

Aitken inscribed a date of June 21, 1957, on this letter. The book on English versification, How to Read English Poetry, *would appear in 1958.*

Dear Aitken,

I am sorry I delayed writing to you, the more so because I am now going to ask you if you can bring me the L.P. records of Bach's 48 Preludes and Fugues. I went today to buy them but they have never been brought to Japan, the shop said, except for customers' special order. It is very late & you may have too much luggage already, but if you could manage to bring the two or three records it would be a lucky thing. I would like the piano, not the harpsichord ones. (I have just looked at the catalogue and it seems to be 6 records, not two or three). If there is no piano one available the harpsichord will do, but it goes *pin-pin gata-gata* in my ears.

I will meet you at the airport if I can. If not, at the Imperial Hotel. I am now busy finishing a third book on Humour, East and West, and translating Hakuin Zenji's *Hannya Shingyo* Commentary[34] and a book on English versification, and the fifth book of Haiku, so I feel a little confused.

Give our kind regards to your wife and tell her we are waiting to see her and to let her have as good a time as possible here.

Yours,
R. H. B.

104

Circa 1957, when Aitken and his wife Anne were in Japan studying Zen. By Anne Aitken's account, this trip was by way of a honeymoon. Having no interest in Zen herself at this point, she contented herself otherwise while her husband sat sesshin at Ryūtaku-ji, in Shizuoka prefecture, under his teacher, Nakagawa Sōen. Sōen afterward took both the Aitkens to Tokyo in August 1957. The two men went off to sesshin at Taihei-an, Yasutani Rōshi's training hall in Nerima Ward in northern Tokyo, leaving Anne behind at their lodgings. Impressed by the fact that the old lady hosting her would also be attending, Anne decided to join in and thus took part in her first sesshin.

Osezaki (Ose-saki), a popular summer resort, in Shizuoka prefecture, is located on a promontory reaching out from the Izu peninsula into Suruga Bay, separated by an inlet from the port of Numazu. From around 1950, Blyth and his family spent part of the summer at Osezaki so he could continue tutoring the Crown Prince, who stayed at the Numazu Imperial Villa located not far up the coast.

Dear Mr. Aitken,

To get to Ose-saki you must first go to Numazu Station, then take a taxi to the Port; Numazu Minato it is called, but it's a very miserable little place which looks like a local station. From there you buy a ticket to Ose-saki and get on one of the several small boats that go to and fro between there and Numazu. If the sea is rough and they don't go, you must return to the station (it only takes about 5 mins.) and go by bus, which takes much longer than the boat. The enclosed post-card shows the times of the boat and the bus.

I hope Mrs Aiken is not finding the temple too templish. Or maybe it is you who is getting secretly tired of it. Do you both need some books to read at Osésaki? If so, tell me and I will take some.

Yours,

R. H. Blyth

105

1957, the date Kenneth Yasuda's The Japanese Haiku *was published.*

Dear Aitken,

Thank you for your letter. I sent off the books the day after you left here, and another one separately a few days after. With the letter goes the huge one-volume *Buddhist Dictionary*, which has been cut down in size and weight (I once sprained my wrist on mine) but which is identical in contents.[35] I am planning to send a few more, but on these principles: (1) I would like the book myself, so you can send it back if you don't want it; (2) It shall have

Kana [Japanese syllabary] so that you can read it without a Kanji dictionary. By the way, Tuttle has just published *The Japanese Haiku* by K. Yasuda, 1500 yen, a book which of course you *must* have, but I won't send it until I know that you have not yet bought it. It has a full bibliography with no mention of my books—a palpable hit. Japanese recorders are post postponing [*sic*] themselves more and more, the latest is the middle of next month. A concert programme announced that German recorders had arrived. I rushed there the next morning to be told that they were *tsu-kan* which I thought must be "now being played", but which means going through the customs. I ordered a bass one from them and came away punctured in soul. The *Mumon Oshō Goroku* seems to exist in Mr Jimbo's imagination, but I am still trying.[36] Don't on any account become misanthropic. We have to go one further than Christ himself, and love not only our enemies, which is easy, because they are only wasting their time hating our lovely selves, but love the hypocrites and whited sepulchres. *That's* an interesting and amusing cross-eyed puzzle. Of course one has also to be what *Will O' the Mill* was, "an inscrutable talkative young man" and retire into one's invisible crab-shell. I peep, peep, peep, waiting for recorders. [Small drawing of weeping face with recorder inserted here.]

Love to Anne.

Yours,
R. H. B.

106

Aitken dates this February 2, 1958.

Dear Mr Aitken,

I was, as always, glad to get your letter. You punctuated an empty tire with your remarks about the *D. Litt.* But apparently empty tires need to be punctuated occasionally to make sure they have no wind in them.

May I ask you to send me a 10 dollar soprano Küng baroque [recorder] *two double holes*. I have just heard that a book has been published by Hisamatsu, *Zen in Pictures* (Japanese) or something like that, 3,000 yen, well criticized in newspaper.[37] Would you like one if I think it is good enough to buy one for myself? I made up my mind to send you the haiku book by the phony Yasuda,[38] but I thought I had better get your unwilling permission first. Or shall I send it to you to pass on to Mrs White, the za-zen woman I told you to write to? The trouble with books, as I have said before, the books I find that you want, I want, so I have either to find another, or sacrifice myself and get a biblio-neurosis. I am just as keen on recorders as ever. I am getting ready to play the fourth Brandenburg Concerto, which Bach wrote, as few people know, for violin and two recorders.

Yours,

R. H. B.

P.S. Get Issa's haiku *The Autumn Wind*, Mackenzie, Wisdom of the East Series.

———

107

Blyth's reference to his book Oriental Culture *seems to be a mistake for* Oriental Humour, *which appeared in May 1959.*

Dear Mr Aitken,

Just received, five minutes ago, your long-awaited letter. Now I can send my coals to Newcastle, the new splendiferous book *Oriental Culture*. I didn't send it before because I was afraid you had joined the unemployed and had also become placeless as well as timeless. (Parenthetically, I like your faithfulness better than your Zen,—or is that the same thing?) I feel very much out of it when you write so familiarly of all the experts and Zen-men. I'm afraid I have succeeded too well in becoming a kind of Robinson Crusoe. I feel recently like writing an article entitled, "Is there something beyond Zen?" but perhaps it is only a sort of cunning way of jumping around islands as the Americans did the South Pacific. Tomorrow I am going to see a Roshi to ask him to look after a girl student who periodically goes a little bit off her [*illegible*]. The cause is, what is wrong with every one of us, an excessively high opinion of other people and a desire to be loved by them. I am just in the middle of beginning to write a series of books on Zen for the Hokuseido, but somehow or other I feel rather half-hearted about it. If they asked me to write a series of books *against* Zen I think I could do that pretty well. Perhaps anyway that's what it will turn into. What is popular is always wrong, and what is wrong is always popular. Give my love to your wife. I am exceedingly pleased you get on well.

RHB

108

Aitken's notation dates this November 7, 1960.

Dear Mr Aitken,

I intended writing you for a long time past, particularly to praise the pamphlet you sent me. It was so extraordinarily well written as literature, and as chief part of that, it omitted all that should have been left unsaid.[39]

As far as the 1st Volume of *Zen and Zen Classics* is concerned, I don't quite know what the objection may be to it, except that it is too weak and watery (most of it was written during internment, I think). However, I am doing the second volume, very unwillingly, and I think it will be better for your criticism of the first, so be a good boy and read it.

Many people seem to think that zazen is a kind of cure-all, for example of mistakes of Watts and sentimentality of Ross (whoever she is).[40] I heard that Kapleau[41] tells an interesting story of a monk who beat the village dogs like mad before he got satori, but after satori beat them even harder and without discrimination, but I did not hear his explanation of this interesting fact. I must say reciting sutras and all that sort of stuff turns my stomach over. You say you have lost a few rough edges. "I would that I could utter the thoughts that rise in me", and put them back again.[42]

As far as the Japanese mind is concerned, it is just full, or nearly full, of all the human sentimentality, self-love, prejudice, nonsense, and pride that we find in ourselves. I teach my students by insulting them; they don't mind it, because I look as if I don't care if they do. They feel I am giving more than I take away. As for respect for elders, it hardly exists any more in Japan proper, lingering in the colonies apparently. I never suffered from the disease myself and laugh it out of others. Oddly enough, however, and perhaps as a result of this, one of the post-graduate students answered quite seriously, when I asked her what God was, "Mr Blyth, you are."

I have only half a page in which to expound to you my recent philosophy of life, or rather mode of conduct. It is to be one in correct thought and good taste and profound emotion and poetical judgment with another person, preferably a woman. It is very hard work, a 24 hour labour. Of all writers I like Thoreau best, who never even thought of such a thing, and never felt alone.

Yours, as ever,
R. H. B.

109

Aitken has penciled in "1961, about June" on this letter.

Dear Mr Aitken,

As I have said many times before, yours are the only letters worth reading, and answering. If I can do anything for Mr. Kenichi Fukuda I will, but it is a little difficult to get in touch with him, because I live at Ōiso now. The address is

Kanagawa ken,
Ōiso
Higashi Koiso, 567.

It is one hour and twenty minutes from Tokyo in the Osaka direction. I bought a house and land there about two years ago. It is an ideal place for me.

I am very glad to hear how unsettled you are; it shows you're not dead yet. I must give you my own secret confidences, which are known I think to the public at large. I'm afraid the letter will be a long one because it must include what I have actually done, and what I think I ought to have done (which in this case are the same thing; perhaps they are so in everyone's case).

About a year and a half ago I met one of my old students, of about 12 years ago. I fell in love with her, as I have done so many times before, but with some difference, in that the relation seemed to have, or rather, had, a sort of philosophical or religious or universal or practical or profound or creative meaning. Like you, I have always been alone, in the most intimate relations, and Zen did not help me in this respect, for as you know I went to Zen as an escape from unrequited love (of my present, still present, wife). Thoreau says that the only remedy for love is to love more, but after all, one must love one's (more or less) equal, not the human baboon that most people turn out to be. The theory of the matter is this: two persons, heterosexual by preference (this is rather Nature's preference, and mine too, but . . .) must have, or better still perhaps, be going to have, be just about to be going to have, the same (right) feelings and the same (right) thoughts about everything in the world including themselves and one another. To be more specific, two people must love Bach and Bashō and Hakurakuten [Po-chu-i], and Eckhart and Cervantes, *in the same way*; this is the catch. Further, and equally important, they must hate the same things, and the same persons especially, for the same reasons, for example all the same monsters and plutocrats and Rep-tiles[43] and money and fame and whiskey and lawn and Zen and ambitious people and modern times generally. I forgot the most important part, the sexual parts. The two people must be in love with each other's bodies, the appetite growing with what it feeds on. The two objections to this are: 1. that two such persons can hardly be found, in other words, that the whole thing is impossible; and if partial, it is only what we (are supposed to) find in the case of every fairly happily married couple. No. 2 is that even if possible, it would be horribly monotonous, just like heaven. In other words, one small difference, and it is the little rift in the lute, that slowly widening silences all. And if there is no difference there is no variety, no spice. Answering these objections, the smaller the difference the more odious and unbearable. There is pleasure in agreeing to differ. Further, the differences in sex, in body, in nationality, or bringing up, these all have to be overcome, and to overcome difficulties is the real spice of life, not variety. Nature kindly prevents ennui by making our span of life sufficiently short. The first objection includes the idea that we shall deceive ourselves as to our agreement in taste and opinion. Without such self-deceiving, marriage and society itself could not exist. This makes training in psychology, particularly practical and dramatic psychology necessary, if we are not to live in a fool's paradise. As for the possibility of finding a person who loves animals, has a good musical ear and taste, can distinguish poetry from romance and sentimentality, knows what distinguishes a good photograph from a good picture (knows that the Family of Nations is all bilge)—this is only doubling the difficulty of being like this oneself in the first place.

But I wish to add something a little more original to all this. As you know, in the West, not in the East, women's position and function has been a sort of means (*hōben*) by which they may attain to Godhood or the Absolute, or at least great works. (I have been thinking lately about Zen, what it is for, what it aims at. Of course it is supposed to be an end in itself, but it is the nature of man to ask for an end beyond an end. I have thought of two people doing Zazen together, certainly not separately, for man is a social animal and finds his meaning and value in relation, not in mere existence as other things do.) I have begun to suspect that the aim of music and poetry and art is, to put it rather bluntly, a sexual one, that is to say, these things are a way of uniting the masculine and the feminine, Thoreau to Nature, Christ to his church,—a man to a woman, in other words.

To go back to practical matters, I now live in 3 rooms of a house with A[kiko]. The other rooms are inhabited by my wife and two daughters, who have a character perhaps similar to your former wife. . . . Shizue, the servant, who is still with us, was formerly of the other party, but now seems to be veering over to our side. She has vulgar tastes herself, but she can tell nobility when she sees it.

As far as Zen is concerned, I have never thought that peace of mind, or efficiency in one's work, or the solution of one's intellectual problems, were of moment. I have always thought a poetical mind of infinitely more importance than a so-called enlightened one, even of God himself. To suffer and to reign, with Christ, alias Christina, alias Akiko, seems to me really to live. Of course I have you, and especially your wife in mind as I write this. But I myself am struggling and agonizing in ways that I have not explained to you for they are not intrinsic to the subject, but life is suffering and, as Buddha did not realize, suffering is life.

Yours,
R. H. B.

110

Aitken has written August 24, 1961, on the letter. Japanese Life and Character in Senryū *appeared on February 15 of the previous year.*

Dear Mr Aitken,
I have just received your entertaining letter. I am so glad you are coming. I wrote you a long letter about three weeks ago. I have nothing special to add

since then except I have written a lot of essays on Zen and Reason, Zen and Grammar, Zen and Music, etc. which will be published in Vol. VII of the Zen series which I was too serious about at first.

I am very anxious to show you and Akiko to each other,[44] and of course to your wife, but I don't know whether the natural cattiness of women is so revealing. Have you got the last 600 page book on Japanese Life and Character in Senryū? It is waiting for you here. Last night we played, that is I and Akiko on two cellos, and Shizue (the servant) and Nanako on two violins, some of the *Art of Fugue*. You shall hear it when you come, also a Bach fugue of 4 organs. By the way, I want you to bring me a good, a really good F Recorder (English fingering) with two double holes for D# and C#, when you come. Two would be better, but you have to pass them off as your own. The best thing is to cut your name on it, or "*Baka yaro!*" ["You idiot!"] would be nice for the customs people. Anyway you can put it in your pocket, but it's all right to kick it round the room a bit. I don't care what it looks like but get the best you can. I play the recorder every day, that is, every day I play it.

Yours,

R. H. B.

111

Aitken has inscribed two dates above the letter: December 26, 1961, and October 8, 1961. He and his wife Anne were in Japan at the time.

Dear Mr Aitken,

Your letter arrived this (Saturday) afternoon. Please telephone your telephone number. I should be glad to meet Miss P. [Aitken has written in: Pauline Offner] some time and hear about women's Zen.[45] You can drop Mr S by the wayside. The manuscript herewith. You need not use it if you don't think it suitable. Nipping people in the bud is not the intention of the author. You ask how Akiko makes me happy: there's only one way to make a man happy and that is by agreeing with him. That is Paradise. Even to pretend to agree gives him a fool's Paradise. "Agree" means to be willing to live under a railway bridge with him. It means seeing through him as he sees through himself.

Your letter was interesting as always. Remember me to Mr. Goodman. [Aitken has written in: "Gooding."⁴⁶] He seemed to like me; I can't think why.

R. H. B.

Akiko insists that I write that you should telephone in the evening, but please telephone when you like.

112

Postcard from December 19, 1961. Nakatsuchi Jumpei, the president of Hokuseido Press who photocopied Aitken's letters for me in the 1960s, deciphered two postmark dates on the postcard: December 19, 1961, and December 20, 1961.

Dear Mr. Aitken,

Forgive the colour of the ink, which has no symbolic meaning. We would like to come and see both of you, and the two rōshis if possible, on Friday morning this week.⁴⁷ I have to go to the Crown Prince's party in the afternoon. Please write or telephone.

Yours RHB

113

Postmarked December 27, 1961. Aitken has jotted on the letter: "while we were in Japan."

Dear Mr Aitken,

Your postcard arrived on Sunday afternoon. Some officious person had written Ishikawa *ken* [prefecture] on it, in English, in pencil, and this was partly the reason it came so late. If you would kindly write once more, getting somebody to address the letter in Japanese also, and tell us when to come, we'll be there without fail, or with-fail, next time. I hope your asthma is all right and (no meaning in the close conjunction) Anne also.

Yours,

R. H. B.

114

Postmarked December 18, 1962.

Dear Aitken,

I received your book some time ago, and thought it excellent.[48] It could not be better, for the purpose, and in itself. I would like to urge its use as a textbook in Buddhist universities here. If you can, send me a few sample copies. As to the haiku, I think it would be better to publish them by themselves, but if you can't find a publisher, I will make use of them.

Two or three weeks ago, I met Mr Watts here.[49] Now I have seen everything. Now I know all the Zennists in the world. He seems to have been a protégé of Mr Humphreys. He dare not contradict anything I said, laughed uproariously at my feeblest jokes, and sank himself in a hundred fathoms of water as far as I am concerned. Only you and Dr Suzuki remain floating.

I won't forget Joyce Cary, of whom (I think) I know nothing.[50]

You say you are "on edge, too defensive, and too — neurotic." I myself am always on edge, on the edge of life and death. It's a pretty good place, perhaps the best. "Defensive." Well, we have to defend ourselves against the not-ourselves. As Lawrence said, it is a poison gas they live in and we are so few and so fragile. "Neurotic" somehow reminds me of the monk who brought a basket when the roof leaked. I suppose the universe is neurotic, and we are the nerves.

I thank you deeply for your unasked-for, unneeded, unrequited affection. I am just beginning to think I might begin to love somebody, perhaps two or three people, a little. I have an idea that love is just around the corner. I sometimes catch a glimpse of it.

Make much of your wife. She already has a lot.

Yours,
R. H. B.

115

September 6, 1963.

567 HIGASHI-KOISO
ŌISO, KANAZAWA KEN

Dear Mr Aitken,

We often talk of you, but I am writing especially because I want to know how to get two books very necessary for me. One is by an Englishman whose name I have forgotten, a translation of the *Hekigan-roku*, yes, Dr Shaw. If you could get it for me that would be fine. The other book is by Father Dumoulin. I have forgotten the name but it was published this year in America, concerning the History of Zen.[51]

I am always worried about you, surrounded as you are by cowardly numskulls. I am always afraid you are going to have *kensho* and turn into a complacent humbug like the rest. I have got up to Case 31 of the *Mumonkan*, and am going at full speed. The first Volume of a *History of Haiku* will be published soon, and the 2nd Volume of the Zen Series this year I hope, the history of the Seigen branch of Zen. Mumon I respect nearly as much as Ummon.[52] He has nothing cheap-valleyish about him: I have not caught him out so far (up to 31).[53] How is Dorothy Wordsworth Aitken? Looking after you too well?

Is there anything I can send you? I have just finished correcting Suzuki's Sengai Calendar for 1964.

Yours,
R. H. B.

116

October 8, 1963.

567 HIGASHI-KOISO
ŌISO, KANAZAWA KEN

Dear Mr Aitken,

I am more "suitably impressed" with you than with the letterhead, but I am delighted that you are so well fulfilling your duties as man as a social animal. As for fooling people, the more you do that the better, like the leaf and twig insects. I have sent you the last volume of the *History of Haiku*; the 2nd will be published next spring. I have just received, this afternoon, October 8, the Dumoulin book. It is very interesting. I wish a Zen priest would write a history of Christianity, just for fun, I mean, as Dumoulin writes just for seriousness. By the way, Dorothy Wordsworth was more poetical, in my meaning of the word, than her brother, so you should not be more insulted than necessary. I am struggling with the modern haiku, which I dislike, and know nothing about. I have never met one; I don't like even their photographs. Suzuziki is a little like my spelling of his name, but still has the best appearance of any man I know. I progress, in bits and by fits and starts, every day, largely owing to Akiko, who is always happy because I am fond of her, and needs nothing more.

Yours,

R. H. B.

117

March 12, 1964

567 HIGASHI-KOISO

ŌISO, KANAZAWA

Dear Aitken,

I have been intending to write for a long time, but waiting to say I had received the *Hekigan-roku*, but I have not yet. If you tell me the publisher and price I will do what I can myself. I know well that you have done your best. Some time ago I bought the *Bi-Yän-Lu* by [Wilhelm] Gundert, 1963, but it looks more difficult than the original Chinese. It is only thirty three Cases, however, in 550 pages. I must begin on it soon, I mean my own translation. The third volume of *Zen and Zen Classics* will be published in a few weeks. Mr Nakatsuchi has the MS. of the *Mumonkan*, and I have finished yet another volume. I am in the middle of a (3rd) *History of Japanese Humour*, but at the moment I am translating haiku and senryū concerning mushrooms for a Mr Gordon Wesson who is to give a lecture to the Asiatic Society on the subject Mushrooms in Japanese Culture.[54] You will be interested to hear that there are at least four hundred haiku on mushrooms (Issa has 56 and about the same in senryū). It is deeply significant that no other literature, even including Chinese, has even one poem on the subject.

Yours,
R. H. B.

118

A notation dates this 1964.

567 HIGASHI-KOISO
ŌISO, KANAZAWA KEN

Dear Mr Aitken,
Akiko has reproached me I don't know how many times with not writing to you, "especially after you received that book," she says. I must confess I like the *Platform Sutra* of the old form better than this new one. I used to love the Sixth Patriarch, but this new version makes me dislike him as much as the author himself.[55] This is a sort of looking a gift horse in the mouth, but it can't be helped. Dr Suzuki lent me his copy of the Shaw *Hekiganroku*, and I was not displeased to find how feeble it is. Another volume of the Zen series will be published in a few hours or days or weeks, and you shall have it immediately. The 2nd volume of *Haiku* should follow almost at once, and the *Mumonkan* is being proof-read.

Dr Suzuki is very well, though he grumbles at not being able to concentrate. He relies very much on my judgment now-a-days and I cannot help feeling pleased at this. He recently wrote an essay on Zen speech in which he made the following mistake.[56] He said that Zen was the place-time in which the intellection, and the aspirations, imaginations and so on, are one. This is correct. And he gave as an example Baso's answer to a monk who asked him about the meaning of Daruma's coming from the West: "I am tired today; go and ask someone else."[57] This is also correct, and a splendid example. But then he said, "This answer of Baso is not poetry or music or religion, but pure Zen." This is not so. "I am tired today," when Baso says it, is as much poetry as when Bashō says, "the sound of the water." It is music,

Wordsworth's "music of that old stone wall." It is religion, since it is the Voice of Man, which is the Voice of God. It is also humour, never to be forgotten.

I am sorry to sound or perhaps to be, bumptious, but that's how it goes sometimes.

Yours gratefully,
R. H. B.

119

Postmarked August 12, 1964. The "script" that provoked this letter was apparently a manuscript written by the photographer Francis Haar, a member of the Diamond Sangha, Aitken's Zen group, concerning preparations that were being made to have the Zen teacher Yasutani Hakuun Rōshi come and teach in Honolulu. The cottage referred to is probably one the group had been preparing for Yasutani. When Yasutani withdrew from the arrangement, Aitken seems to have considered repurposing it for Blyth to live in if he came to Hawaii.

The script is sentimental and vulgar. There is no Zen in it. Give up Zen. Don't do Zazen; you may become like Okada or Kapleau. Read, write, and write books on haiku; it is your forte. Don't get buggered up with Yasutani. Smash something! Burn down the cottage and collect the fire insurance. Live a happy and simple life with your wife. (Think of her sometimes; she is always thinking of you.) Faithful are the wounds of a friend. Write to me *often.* I will never, never, never go to Hawaii.[58]

Yours lovingly,
R. H. B.

If you need the script I will return it.

Letters to Daisetz Suzuki

120

October 28, 1962

567 HIGASHI KOISO ŌISO
KANAGAWA-KEN

Dear Dr. Suzuki,

I was ever so pleased to get your letter. I will print what you say about the frontispiece in the second edition, if I may. Ikkyū's *dōka*, p. 192, I now understand, thanks to you.[1] This will change in the next edition.

You praise my translations as against yours, but I assure you, as an expert of English, that you are wrong. A deeper understanding of the original always shows itself clearly in the translation.

The very slickness of the translation shows a lack of understanding of the original which itself is not slick,—cannot be slick, or it would not be worth translating. There is nothing "immature and awkward" about your translations.

Please send me your translations of the *Hekiganroku*, though it will take me some time to go over them. I myself have to do the whole of the *Hekigan*, and I would like to save some labour by using your translations when I come to it.

You say that $0 = \infty$. I would like to believe this, but my mind is not very philosophical. I would rather say something with more 行 [activity, action] in it: Zen = good taste.

This admits no taste, for example being tone-deaf, but not bad taste, like Chopin or Schubert.

You will be pleased to hear that the Crown Prince is getting better every week. So am I, and I think there is some connection between the two. I would very much like you to give him a talk on Zen, if it would not be tiring to you. Please tell me if you would consent, and then I will get them to ask you.

I cannot conceive of myself as being anyone's disciple, or as having disciples myself, but I must say that one of my self-congratulations is that you and I have never disagreed about anything, at least about Zen. I felt that the 7th Book of the Zen Series was rather heretical, and that it would find more supporters among the layman than the "professionals." I am weak enough to feel some need of reassurance from you only. Zen means my Zen, or his Zen, but the Bible says, (rightly enough, for man is a social animal) "Where *two* or three are gathered together in My name, I will be there with them," so that truth seems to be triple in nature, impression, expression, reception, mutual understanding of "something" by two persons, not one only. What Buddha said on his birth day is therefore wrong, and satori by one person alone must be incomplete at best, and unhealthy at worst. If you don't agree with me, you are wrong, and if I don't agree with you, I am wrong, and if we don't care what the other thinks, that is Hell for both, "for God so loved the world . . ."

Tell me what you think.

Yours,
RHB.

121

Blyth asked Aitken for a copy of Shaw's Hekiganroku *in Letter #115, dated September 1963, and later informed Aitken, in Letter #118, which I date to 1964, that Suzuki had loaned him his copy, placing this letter sometime in between. The Introduction to Sengai is presumably an early version of the essay that later appeared in* Sengai, The Zen Master *(Faber and Faber), a book not published until 1971.*

567 HIGASHI KOISO ŌISO
KANAGAWA-KEN

Dear Dr. Suzuki,

I thought the Introduction to Sengai very good,[2] and I hope you will send me the other essay. I think the extracts from the *Hekiganroku* are necessary, but a little too long. Some people may stop reading the Introduction as a result of this. As you know, the important thing is to get people to realize that there is something they don't know that they should, that there is something beyond them which is better than anything they have hitherto attained.

Anyway, Sengai seems the best person to introduce Zen to the West, and you are the best person to introduce Sengai.

By the way, when I got home I found a letter from Mr. Aitken, the friend or disciple of mine who has been instrumental in getting Yasutani to Hawaii. I asked him about four months ago to get Shaw's *Hekiganroku* for me but after a lot of delays and mistakes the book seems to have gone out of print. I would be very glad if you could lend me your copy, but perhaps you are using it. I would like to read it through if it is in any way possible.

The Introduction to Sengai I just corrected here and there as to the English. I did not go through the translation of the *Hekiganroku* quotations as such because it will take much time, as I must compare it with the original. In any case the *agyo* especially, or only, should be explanatory rather than literal, precisely because of the "humorous" attitude of the writer.[3] Humour is a dancing of the mind, so we must make Engo skip and jump if we can.[4]

Yours, RHB.

———

122

May 1964.

Dear Dr. Suzuki,

As I always say to your secretary, you are too greedy and ambitious. The article is full of concentrated power, and nobody but you could have written it. It is a great success. Thank you for the promise of the *Hekiganroku* translation.

The 1st case, yours, will be sent in a day or two.

There is just one paragraph of The Zen Language which I think should be rewritten.[5] You say, rightly enough, that there are two worlds, 1, that of reasoning and logic, cause and effect, why and because; 2, (on page 15) the world of instincts, aspirations, imaginations, intuitions. You say that Zen is the meeting of these two worlds, their union, or rather, their original oneness which is never really broken. And you say that Baso's "I'm tired today" is neither 1 nor 2 but the very voice of their unbreakable oneness. This is so, and there is nothing more to be said.

However on page 24, you equate the "instincts, aspirations, imaginations, intuitions" with "poetry, music, and religion." This is wrong. Poetry and music and religion (not a religion) and humour are the result of the marriage, or rather, the re-marriage of the intellect and the non-intellect, of determinism and free-will, of the relative and the absolute. Baso's "I'm tired" is poetry in the same way that 水の音 ["sound of water," from Bashō's famous haiku] is poetry; it is humorous; it is musical (the Voice of Man); and it is religion; it is Zen.

It is both words and non-words. It has no symbolism and no (separable) meaning. All this is what you have taught me.

Yours, RHB

123

July 26, 1964

Dear Dr. Suzuki,

I hope you are not too tired after your journey. I have been in bed ill now for two months, unable to read anything or write anything. I am a little better in the past few days, but I have been suffering from two "diseases." I have a perpetual headache, probably from over-work of brain and nerves, and resistance to everybody and everything. Also I have had a food-phobia which has prevented me from eating, a distaste for the thought or sight of food. This is part of a general fear of everything, illness, pain, noise, past present & future, pain and death. The cat (the universal) has bitten me severely. And how can I write anyone about Zen, without satori, without understanding Mu—*please answer this question*. Also I am worried about earning a living. I have no money, only this house, and I am not sure whether I can teach any more, or write any more books. It will take me at least two more months to recover. You are the only person to whom I can write of all my un-Zen, my fears and "angst."

Will you please transcribe and translate the enclosed from Sengai? I wish to use it as the frontispiece for my *Inchiki* [phony] *Mumonkan*.[6]

Yours abjectly,
R. H. Blyth

I think the [*here Blyth makes a drawing of Sengai's calligraphy of a circle, a triangle, and square*] are the three fundamental forms of the universe.

———

124

August 21, 1964

Dr. Suzuki,
I am in great need of spiritual and material help. As for the first, Dr. Kondo is coming on Saturday. As for the second, I wrote to Mr. Yamanashi, my best friend, as I supposed, explaining my domestic situation. He wrote back today saying that if I separate from my wife or divorce her, I cannot expect to continue to teach at the Gakushūin. His letter ends with these words, which I believe to be inappropriate.

AS TO YOUR LADY SECRETARY; SHE IS STILL HEALTHY AND CAN GO ANYWHERE SHE LIKES BY THE ADVICE OF HER LAW-FUL PARENTS: PERHAPS SOME AMOUNT OF GIFT FAVOURED TO HER SHALL SMOOTH THE PROCEDURE SAFELY.

Please write soon, immediately if possible.

Yours, RHB.

———

125

567 HIGASHI KŌISO ŌISO
KANAGAWA KEN

Dear Dr. Suzuki,
Thank you for your exceedingly practical letter, though what I need also

is some affection. I am suffering from chronic masochism, with a dash of hypochondria.

Mr. Yamanashi changed his mind completely after I had written to him. He's a good and faithful friend.

Dr. Kondo came. He is a pork butcher, shouting at me and telling me I hate everybody and so I am ill and have a perpetual headache. He hates me for myself, and because I am (like all other) "British Gentlemen." (The grammar is bad but can't be helped).

As I told Mr. Yamanashi, to Hell with the Gakushūin. The Imperial Household has done nothing, and will do nothing for me except give me a 4th class *kunshō*.[7] Mr. Yamanashi loves and respects me, and I am the best teacher in the Gakushūin, and in Japan, and I have done more for Japan than any other foreigner. Forgive my violence of expression but I cannot control my pen.

As to how much I need to cover my monthly expense, I have not the slightest idea. I don't know how much my salary from the Gakushūin is, and never will.

As for my "private" life, I must support four people, myself, my "lady secretary," my daughter Nanako who is not clever or cunning but a good and honest girl who wishes to live with us, and my "wife" who has left the house forever.

I am hasty in everything, but I have no ambition, except to write books and the practical, financial situation must take care of itself. I am, as Mr. Kondo kept vociferating, a British gentleman. Before the war I tried to become a Japanese subject, but was rejected, on no grounds whatever.

It must be cool in Karuizawa; I hope my letter is as warm as it is here. I would like to add my dedication to the next Zen book, *The Mumonkan*:

To Suzuki Daisetz
The greatest man living

This will give you no pleasure and that is what makes it true.

Yours, Hamlet
(not Iago).

By the way, the reason I did not divorce my . . . wife before is, believe it or not, because I am as Kondo rightly-wrongly says, "A British Gentleman." . . . and I sacrificed Akiko to this—what a fool!

P.S. One good thing has happened. I now have another secretary, "a gentleman secretary," a graduate of the Gakushūin. If you want to hear the truth about everything you may call Nanako, (Mr. Yamanashi questioned her when she took my letter to Hakone), or you may call Mr. Inoue, who will speak of everything and arrange everything. He will live here 4 days a week.[8]

126

Dear Miss Okamura,[9]

Thank you so much for your most kind and understanding telephone messages. I have not vomited for ten days now, and can eat most things, but the headache remains the same. I don't think Mr. Kondo would be much good (I have met him).

For books, it is as follows:

1. *Mumonkan*, 340 pages, to be published in October.
2. 2nd Part of the history of Chinese Zen, 250 pages, 9/10 finished.
3. *Hekiganroku* (*soku* only) 200 pages, not begun.
4. *Zen Sermons on Christian Texts*, 200 pages, 1/3 finished.
5. *A Zen Catechism* 200 pages, not begun (translations from *Zenmon Kōan Taisei*).
6. *The Humour of the Japanese* 400 pages, 1/2 finished.
7. *Postulations and Expostulations* (quotations with commentary, on religion, poetry etc), 400 pages materials already collected.

The Hokuseido has promised to publish any book I write.

Dr. Suzuki's idea of my going to England is an excellent one, but if I had the money to do this I should have no worry about living in Japan. I can eat beans and baked potatoes. Anyway I have decided to go to Hokkaido or Kyushu as soon as I am better, and in any case I cannot! leave Akiko, who is my secretary, real wife, nurse, and comforter. My legal wife & my daughters live in the same house, for economy's sake, more or less in harmony but they are quite indifferent to my health and happiness.

I feel that I have done much for Japan politically, educationally, and propagandistically in Zen and literature. Some individual or society should do something for one now. The Imperial Household will no doubt give me a *kunshō* after nearly twenty years of service. The Crown Prince got Princess Michiko to make some ice-cream and sent it to me but I could not eat it.

I am so sorry I cannot do anything for Dr. Suzuki at present.

Yours gratefully,
R H Blyth
P.T.O.

P.S. If I have repeated myself please forgive me. I cannot remember what I wrote in the last letter. I think ○ = finite infinity, △ = fixed law, □ = humanity, the house, the castle, the city, the state 国, vulnerable.

Even the thought of it makes me weep. What I need from him is an encouraging letter. I suppose that in my heart I wished to be his successor but I am afraid I am too heterodox for him to acknowledge me.

As you say, I do not wish to teach unpoetical nit-wits any more. My plan [*sic*] If Mr Doi or anybody else could tell me the cause and cure of the headaches, that would be fine, but it is unlikely. Dr. Tominaga, head of the Shinkei-ka of the Daiichi Byōin, came to see me about 10 days ago, but all he could say was, have hot baths (I have not done so, but intend to begin today) and walk a little every day. I take a "green" pill to sleep every night, and have begun to take headache pills during the day (by which I am able to write this letter.

Please beg Dr. Suzuki not to come and see me; I could not bear it

Letter to Alan Watts

127

Circa 1960. I thank Joan Watts for providing this letter to her father.

THE PEERS SCHOOL

MEJIRO

TOKYO

Dear Mr. Watts,

Please make any use of any of my books that you wish. I at least shall read it with pleasure and profit, and as you know, one reader is enough. I am writing a 2 volume book on Humour, East and West, and I take the view that Zen is the funniest thing I have found in the world. Whether we die with laughing or laugh with dying, laughter is wisdom and tears are folly, though I must confess that never a day passes but what I shed some tears, half a dozen or so. But just as satori is mayoi and mayoi is satori,¹ so saliva and the salt water of weeping are the same thing. This is becoming unhumorously transcendental so I will stop;— As for "my personal reminiscences of my study of Zen," you must be joking. I read a few pages of *Zen in the Art of Archery*, but I couldn't stand it. I can't say why, but my instinct, my intuition, is against it, so inhuman so humorless. As we grow older, we ought to grow lighter in mind as we should also in body, until the wind of death blows both away, almost unnoticed. Sometimes I think Zen is the only thing that makes life worth living, for it is precisely the worth of life. At other times I think it to be a tremendous swindle, a carrot before the donkey's nose. No doubt both views are equally correct. Thoreau is my ideal man, no optimism, no pessimism, gratitude without servility, no grumbling at the universe.

Please look after your health; live long, and give us as many books as you can.

Yours,
R. H. Blyth

PREFACES AND
INTRODUCTIONS

R. L. Stevenson's *Will O' the Mill*

*The book was one of a dozen or so works Blyth published as student
textbooks (Tokyo: Hokuseido Press, 1948).*

THERE IS A GREAT DEAL OF ZEN IN STEVENSON'S WRITINGS. THIS
comes from his feeling of the "loneliness" of man; his poor opinion of the
intellect; his love of paradox; his acceptance of all that life brings us good
and bad; his rejection of morality as a guide to life; his humour; his desire
for absolute freedom; his energy; and above all, his courage. These qualities
may be seen everywhere in Stevenson's life and works, most explicitly per-
haps in the *Fables*, but also in such books as *Treasure Island*, in which the
story seems everything.

Yet though he knew that words are not life, that "Weisheit ist nicht mit-
telbar,"[1] he made himself a writer by unremitting efforts, scarcely to be paral-
leled in the annals of English literature. Words are nothing, and yet they are
everything; truth is inexpressible, and yet it is expressed. Here again is the
paradox that draws Stevenson unwittingly rather to eastern than to western
thought-feeling. We can only imagine the surprise and joy that Stevenson
would have had in the *mondō* of the Zen masters, the simplicity of Bashō,
the poignant pleasures of Issa, the realism of senryū, the romance of the
Manyōshū. When we read Stevenson, as also D.H. Lawrence, and Emerson,
we feel that their differences from the Japanese poets only intensify, only
vivify the elements of their common experience.

Stevenson is well-known for his doctrine of cheerfulness. He thought, and
perhaps rightly, that if a man has nothing invigorating and manly to say, he
should be silent. When he was still an unknown writer, people supposed him

to be a healthy young animal, but they found out that he wrote of cheerful-ness while gasping for breath and spitting blood. "Cheerful" is itself an inter-esting word, unique perhaps in its meaning, for it implies happiness in spite of all the good reasons we have for being sad and dejected. It is indeed a word of Zen, a word of abounding courage.

I want now to try to explain why I think this story is one of the most meaningful short stories in the English language. It is not a very exciting story; it lacks that very "quality of incident" which Stevenson himself said was all-important in fiction. It is not especially well-constructed. The style is most suitable but not brilliant. It has no pathos, little humour, few if any apophthegms or quotable passages. Yet there is something strange about it. It is a story of peace, and success in a way of living, but it leaves us with a feeling of anguish. Again, it raises many problems of life, and the most important of all, the relation between a man and a woman, yet it does not answer these problems, but moves serenely to its end, old age and death. There are books which raise problems, and books which solve them. This does neither. The problems are with us; life, our living solves them in one way or another, but the problems and their solution are not external to us. They are not separable. They can never be abstracted from life and looked at "objectively." As Thoreau says, anticipating Stevenson,

All fables, indeed, have their morals; but the innocent enjoy the story.

Will O' the Mill is a kind of fable, both in its intention and spirit, and the style also takes us into a world which is not realism, and not romance, but that of a fairy tale which is truer than anything written in the daily newspaper.

The two problems raised in the story are, first, should we live in the world, and be of it, or should we as far as possible withdraw from it? The latter was after all the attitude of poets such as Saigyō and Bashō. Second, should a man live in married bliss or single blessedness? This latter again was chosen by the Japanese poets. Will's refusal to go down into the world is represented as a poetico-religious matter, as a renunciation of something to which, as Arnold says,

We have no natural right.

In the valley, from its natural conformation, Will was able to see what is usually hidden from us by the complexity and confusion of nature, that all changes, "all flows," all flows downward. In this fact perceived there occurred a kind of natural *satori*, a bodily perception of a living truth. Then, at the hands of the fat young man, Will had another kind of *satori*, not so different as it seems from that of Enō [Hui-neng], the Sixth Zen Patriarch, when he overheard the words of the *Diamond Sutra*:

Arouse the mind without fixing it anywhere.

This line may be divided into two parts, which are nevertheless equivalent to each other. "Awaken the mind," means "live fully," "live God's life." "Without fixing it anywhere" means "without attachment to anything, without ambition, without an (intellectually explicit) object." The fat young man uses the stairs (or do they use him?) to show Will that "we are in a rat-trap." This is the Buddhist Karma, the (scientific) world of cause and effect, "the squirrel cage of duality."[2] We cannot escape from this by going down the valley. There is no difference between one place and another. All is eat or be eaten. Will says, "The shepherd who makes so pretty a picture carrying home the lamb, is only carrying it home for dinner."

The alternatives given are "the squirrel turning in his cage," or "the squirrel sitting philosophically over his nuts." These mean the attitude of the man of action, the soldier, the explorer, the pure mystic. To put it another way, it is the difference between the man who attains happiness by increasing his possessions and him who does so by decreasing his wants. The stars, "the vast army of unalterable law," convince Will of his own insignificance, in Buddhist language, of his "emptiness," and he becomes "a kind, talkative, inscrutable young man." To be talkative and yet inscrutable is a sign of some kind of genius.

After nature and man comes woman. Will's third *satori* comes from his contact with Marjory, the parson's daughter, who is a counterpart to Will, not a contrast, except in so far as she is above all a woman, as he is a man (not merely a male animal).

She is described by Stevenson in words which are as lovely as the girl. She is "a soul beautifully poised upon itself, nothing doubting, nothing desiring, clothed in peace." The language reminds us of the noble yet womanly women of the Old Testament, devoid of introspection and subtlety, whose thought and body are undivided and indivisible. We realize in her the truth of Blake's words:

Body is a portion of Soul discerned by the five Senses.

At first Will felt in her company an "agreeable dismay," then, by a change of emphasis, a "grave beatitude." He felt that Marjory gave him what the outer world had tempted him with. Everything became illumined with

The light that never was on sea or land.

His love for Marjory was deep and real, but already "sublimated," as the psychologists say. She had entered into him, and pervaded all his thoughts and feelings, yet at the same time she was in every fish and tree and stone and winding stream, his marriage was already consummated. He was born old, in the sense that he had attained to godlike union with the world, and inhaled and exhaled the serene air of eternity while yet in his thirtieth year. She it was that lifted the inanimate into the animate, that gave the trees and plants voices, that made the fish of human significance, and men and women to walk the world like gods. But we have no reason to seek out nature. It is always with us and in us and around us like the air; for this reason "it seemed as if he avoided her rather than sought her out."

In the flower-plucking scene Stevenson brings out, with great simplicity, the difference between men and women, that is, between Will and Marjory. The girl says that the flowers say to her, "Come and do something with us," but when she has cut them they lose their power over her and her mind is easy. This has a fairy-tale profundity. The reason she wishes to cut or pluck the flowers may be the biological fact that to women all forms of life are ultimately or potentially inimical to the one they cherish, that of their children. Men alone are able to be free of this ulterior view, and this is indeed what happens to Will. He sees suddenly that *he wishes to pluck her*. Most men remain in that dilemma that Meredith had expressed once for all in *Love in the Valley*:

Fain would fling the net, and fain have her free.

Will wishes not to possess himself of her, just as he does not want to go down into the plain below. Is it possible to have one's cake and eat it too?

When Will decides that marriage is "not worth while," his previous haiku-like life changes to an atmosphere of senryū. In spite of all Will's mysticism, woman detaches herself from nature, and becomes a distinct and independent entity. Will's strength is met by hers. He looks upon her as he does upon the stars. When he shouts up to the sky in the evening, the stars seem to radiate light to one another, and a corner of the blind is lifted and lowered. But when he tells her the next morning that he does not really wish to marry her, he finds he is not talking to the stars or to a female saint, but to a real solid woman, who can take command of a difficult situation and extricate herself from it with dexterity and self-assurance. Will for his part begins to admire her for just those qualities which he desired to suppress and finally exterminate in himself. Yet he sees also that she could not walk in the way he had chosen, this path of "artificial calm."

For three years she shares with him this unnatural, platonic, love-at-a-distance, then suddenly marries someone else. This leaves Will in an unsettled state which is resolved by Marjory's death a year later. Will sees her on her death-bed, but we are not told what they said to each other, nor do we wish to know. But this is Will's fourth *satori*, and it is the deepest and strongest of all, for when he comes to die, he says to Death, "Since Marjory was taken, I declare before God you were the only friend I had to look for." What is called in Zen "The Great Death," has these four stages, the death of each thing as it passes down the valley, the death of ambition, the perception of the fact that we are not to "pluck" things or people, and the final realization that we have no right to "life, liberty, and the pursuit of happiness." After this there is nothing but the procession of the seasons, the wind in the pine trees, the shining of the sun by day, and the stars by night.

Will says himself, at the age of fifty, "I am a dead man now; I have lived and died already." His death, in his seventy-second year, is described by Stevenson with the same skill in personification as is shown in *Markheim*. And death alone has the power to make Will leave his valley, and go at last upon his travels.

The two problems are: should he have left the valley? should he have married Marjory? The deep sincerity of Stevenson is shown in the fact that it is very difficult for us to answer yes or no to either of these questions. Is the story a tragedy or a comedy? This also is difficult to say; it is perhaps something beyond either. A man cannot live two lives. He must choose one and reject the other. He cannot live in a state of both single and wedded bliss. A man must make his bed; the question is not which bed, but how he lies upon any.

Thoreau's Journals

Another textbook published for students (Tokyo: Daigakusyorin, 1949).

HENRY DAVID THOREAU WAS BORN IN CONCORD IN 1817. THE SCENery in which he grew up was one of slow rivers, great trees, small lakes, low ranges of hills, and fields and undulating country with a rich flora and fauna. As a boy he was grave in manner but active and fond of the open air. After trying and giving up teaching, he earned his living chiefly by manual labour, especially surveying. In 1839, together with his brother John, whom he loved dearly, he went for a week's voyage on the Concord and Merrimack rivers, an account of which he published, at his own expense, in 1849. In 1834 Emerson settled in Concord, and the two men profoundly influenced each other; Emerson was then thirty-one and Thoreau only seventeen, but Thoreau matured at a very early age.

In 1842 his brother John died, and Thoreau was deeply and permanently affected. But in a letter to a friend a month later, he writes:

Only Nature has a right to grieve perpetually, for she alone is innocent. Soon the ice will melt, and blackbirds sing along the river which he frequented, as pleasantly as ever. The same everlasting serenity will appear in the face of God, and we will not be sorrowful if he is not.

To Nature he gave already that submission and faith which never ceased to the last moment of his life. With children and rough farmers he was on the best of terms, but any kind of snobbery, affectation, cant, hypocrisy or subservience roused him to an uncompromising opposition.

In the spring of 1845 he borrowed his friend Alcott's axe and began to build a house or hut by Walden Pond; it cost him twenty-four dollars. Every day he walked far and wide, in all seasons and weathers. He read much in Greek and Latin, and in English literature, especially Chaucer and the seventeenth century religious poets.

In the summer of 1847 he returned to the village, well satisfied with his experiment, "reality rather transcendentally treated," he says in a letter of 1852. In 1854, a great event occurred in the history of American literature,—the publication of *Walden*.

Between 1846 and 1860, Thoreau went on several journeys, to Cape Cod, to Canada, to the Maine Woods, to the White Mountains of New Hampshire, but his health began to fail; his mind was always stronger than his constitution. Three years before his death he spoke ardently and incisively on the trial and execution of John Brown, the slave-abolitionist.

Thoreau's death is memorable for his absolute obedience to the will of Nature, and for three great sayings concerning it. The first is contained in a letter written three months before he died:

I may add that I am enjoying existence as much as ever, and regret nothing.

When asked on his death-bed if he had "made his peace with God," he replied,

"I have never quarreled with him."

When someone wished him to speak about religion and the next world,

"One world at a time!"

he answered.

Thoreau is the most remarkable, perhaps the greatest man America has produced. His life-work was the *Journals*, begun in 1837, when he was twenty years old, and coming to an end in 1861, the year before his death. During these twenty-four years, Thoreau put the whole of himself into almost daily records, which when printed, for the first time, in 1906, edited by Torrey and Allen, comprise fourteen volumes of about 500 pages each. The present selection is based upon Blake's *Early Spring in Massachusetts, Summer, Winter, Autumn*, published between 1881 and 1892, but arranged chronologically, as in Shepard's excellent *The Heart of Thoreau's Journals*, 1927. This last work was of the greatest use in preparing the present book.

Even in the present short selection, it will be clear that as Thoreau grew older, there was a gradual decrease in poetic and intuitive power, corresponding somewhat to that of Wordsworth. In Wordsworth it was theology that represented the stiffening of the mind, the ebb of poetic life. In Thoreau it was science,—not so much the scientific spirit, as the mechanical collection of mere objective facts, that smothered the poet in him. Thoreau is not great as a naturalist. Many other men have had as much or more patience, impartiality, industry, respect for law. Few, if any, are as deeply *religious* as he. And this "religion" has the unique quality of being as much concerned with all the aspects of nature, the sweet and the savage, as with the aspiring soul of man.

Thoreau is great also, together with Emerson, in combining Western independence and self-respect, the deep sense of differences in things, with the spirit of the East, its weak sense of the ego, its mystical feeling for nature and the sameness of things. Thoreau has his limitations; at times he may be priggish, obstinate, uncouth, misanthropic, pedantic. But in his depth no man goes deeper; the truth takes place as he walks and feels and thinks; his silences are more significant than the most eloquent periods of other men. There is nothing weak, snobbish, sentimental or cruel in him, and in his tenderness towards his parents, his defiance of the mob, his complete devotion to nature, and painful desire of deep and pure friendships, he is a pattern and example to young men and women of any time and place. Nevertheless, like the other transcendentalists, Thoreau had no disciples, founded no school, taught no doctrines. No less than the muskrat and the snapping turtle, every man is to follow his own light, however dim and faint it may be, so that at last he will come to say, with the vastness and the particularity of Thoreau himself,

I will not doubt the love untold,
Which not my worth or want has brought,
Which wooed me young, and woos me old,
And to this evening hath me brought.

The Poems of Emerson:
A Selection

This introduction accompanies a selection of Ralph Waldo Emer-
son's poetry published in 1949 in Kenkyūsha's Pocket English Series.
The English poet Edmund Blunden was a friend of Blyth's and, like
him, taught and lectured in Japan both before and after the war.

A FEW DAYS AGO, MR. BLUNDEN, ON MY ASKING HIM WHAT HE
thought of Emerson's poetry, immediately quoted some lines of his and
said that he considered Emerson greater as a poet than as a prose writer.
Mr. Blunden did not expound, but I suppose he meant, not that Emerson's
transcendentalism is better expressed in his verses than in his essays, but
that his poetry as poetry is better than his prose as prose. Indeed, Emerson's
verse is worth careful study even from the technical point of view, for its
very irregularity and frequent uncouthness is expressive. To a large extent
Emerson's aim was that of Thoreau,

a style in which the matter is all in all, and the manner nothing at all,

but in so doing Emerson attains an all the more characteristic and signifi-
cant style. Nature is "all in all,"

And in their vaunted works of Art,
The master-stroke is still her part.   (*Nature, II*)

This idea Emerson repeats in his *Journals*, December, 1841:

All writing is by the grace of God.

Four months before, he says that when he went out into the fields he perceived

That the finest rhythms and cadences of poetry are yet unfound, and
in that purer state which glimmers before us, rhythms of a faery and
dream-like music shall enchant us, compared with which the finest
measures of English poetry are psalm-tunes. I think now that the very
finest and sweetest closes and falls are not in our metres, but in the measures of eloquence, which have greater variety and richness than verse.

In Emerson's verse we find certain elements of his character, which we surmise in his prose works, plainly and explicitly expressed. He has a certain
ruthlessness, akin to that of Nietzsche and D.H. Lawrence, which he finds
also in the universe. In *The World-Soul* he says, of Destiny (a word he uses
somewhat in the same sense as Spengler):

He serveth the servant,
The brave he loves amain;
He kills the cripple and the sick,
And straight begins again,
For gods delight in gods,
And thrust the weak aside;
To him who scorns their charities
Their arms fly open wide.

There is the same thought, a transcendental "Might is right," in *Fate:*

One thing is forever good;
That one thing is Success.

In this connection a passage from his *Journals* (September 29, 1839) is very
interesting:

When I was thirteen years old, my uncle Samuel Ripley one day asked me, "How is it, Ralph, that all the boys dislike you and quarrel with you, whilst the grown people are fond of you?" Now I am thirty-six and the fact is reversed,—old people suspect and dislike me, and the young love me.

Like Robert Louis Stevenson, Emerson appeals to the young, and to the poor. His ideas are vital, a fountain springing up into eternal life, and eternal life is the youth of the soul. He is one of those

> Olympian bards who sung
> Divine Ideas below,
> Which always find us young,
> And always keep us so.   (*Ode to Beauty*)

In *The Tables Turned*, Wordsworth says:

> Come forth into the light of things,
> Let Nature be your Teacher.

This was in 1798, but he gradually turned from this "Nature" to the light of orthodox Christianity and reactionary politics. Emerson has no other teacher but Nature, the nature within and without. Thoreau is even more consistent, "watching his own moods as a cat does a mouse" and obeying nature without question. In Emerson, even the most difficult and complicated intuitions are derived, implicitly and explicitly from nature. For example, *To Rhea*, one of his most profound and "symbolic" poems, is derived from the solitudes of the spring woods:

> Listen what the poplar-tree
> And murmuring waters counselled me.

These two lines are not a poetic fancy or figure of speech; they are not another way of saying, "Listen what I thought sitting under the poplar by the stream." What appears as beauty in the poplar and mobility in the stream, manifests itself in the rhythm and fluidity of his thinking,

His own symmetry with law.   *(Guy)*

It should be especially noted in this connection that Emerson says in verse what Thoreau says in prose. There is a strong and fundamental similarity between *Woodnotes*, for example, and *A Week on the Concord and Merrimack Rivers*.

Like Thoreau, Emerson was always seeking ideal friendships, and the apparent coolness of their relations with many people was undoubtedly due to the height of their standards. In a poem called *Dirge* Emerson expresses obliquely the pain he felt at the death of early friends of his:

> I touch this flower of silken leaf,
>> Which once our childhood knew;
> Its soft leaves wound me with a grief
>> Whose balsam never grew.

In two memorable lines he eternalizes them:

> The strong, star-bright companions
>> Are silent, low, and pale.

But the great grief of his life, one from which perhaps he learned most of the nature of things, was that of his young son Waldo, aged five, in 1842:

> A boy of early wisdom, of a grave and even majestic deportment, of a perfect gentleness . . . Every tramper that ever tramped is abroad, but the little feet are still.

> Sorrow makes us all children again,—destroys all differences of intellect.

> The wisest knows nothing.

In *Threnody*, he says, what is intolerably true,

> The eager fate which carried thee
> Took the largest part of me:

For this losing is true dying;
This is lordly man's down-lying,
This his slow but sure reclining,
Star by star his world resigning.

The death, one by one, of those we love, is our own gradual decease.

Emerson holds, implicitly at least, the Buddhist idea that the Buddha-nature belongs to all things, both animate and inanimate, and this Buddha-nature, the power and tendency to become Buddha, is "the meaning of each feature."

And the poor grass shall plot and plan
What it will do when it is man. (*Bacchus*)

Emerson is an optimist, persuaded by the beauty and meaning of things in spite of the frequent indications of individual and general chaos:

Silent rushes the swift Lord
Through ruined systems still restored,
Broad-sowing, bleak and void to bless,
Plants with worlds the wilderness,
Waters with tears of ancient sorrow
Apples of Eden ripe to-morrow. (*Threnody*)

Emerson's models in verse are Milton, Herbert, Marvel, and to a lesser extent the Elizabethan poets, whose singing quality he did not even try to emulate. To the seventeenth century religious poets, however, with their dry wit, moral tone, brevity and simplicity, Emerson felt a deep affinity, for he also is "religious" in every word he wrote. He is far from emotional, but it is a mistake therefore to call him an intellectual poet. It is an imaginative spirituality which infuses his life and work, and from his high place he does not "descend to meet." There is no concession to human weakness, to sentimentality, to the desire to impress, to hyperbole; but he is not cold in himself or towards his reader.

For Emerson, as for Shelley, the poet is the only real man. History is the history of poets; "poets are the unacknowledged legislators of mankind"; they do not create, they discover, uncover for us truths and values which speak through them to us. A poet is not necessarily a writer of verse, for "words and deeds are quite indifferent modes of the divine energy." Indeed, Emerson says that even such poets as "Homer, Milton, and Shakespeare do not fully content us," for poetry is a part, and not the whole of life, that is, of life as it is lived at the present time.

Emerson has not only a theory of the poet, but a theory of poetry, expressed characteristically in both verse and prose. In *Merlin*, he says the words of the poet are

> No jingling serenader's art,
> Nor tinkle of piano-strings.

They are blows which are

> Strokes of fate
> Chiming with the forest-tone.

This is one of the reasons for the irregularity of his metre, in which beauty, however much produced, is not the first concern. Life creates beauty, and just as inevitably destroys it, and so in Emerson, as with Bach, beauty comes almost as an accident, and for this very reason is the "more endeared." Nevertheless it is quite clear that Emerson spent much time and care in the revision of his verses.

> All were winnowed through and through,

and yet the spontaneity remains unimpaired, and to the end of his life the same scrupulousness of inspiration is found; in a characteristically elliptic line, he tells us how he does not fail to

> Obey the voice at eve obeyed at prime.

Emerson's literary judgements are interesting in themselves, and for the light they shed upon his own practice. Landor, Goethe, Carlyle and Wordsworth were the modern writers in whom Emerson was most interested. What attracted him particularly to Landor was something that is characteristic of Emerson also:

We do not recollect an example of more complete independence in literary history. He has no clanship, no friendships that warp him.

Landor's compact, condensed style no doubt had a considerable effect upon that of Emerson, who constantly read the *Imaginary Conversations*.

Goethe Emerson admired for his genius, his "range of thought and catholic mind," but felt him to be "the poet of the actual, not of the ideal," and thought the fault lay in the shallowness of his moral perceptions.

With Carlyle he was intimate, and respected him as one of the few men who always kept his eye fixed upon "the gracious Infinite which embosoms us." But Carlyle ends by wearying us, which Emerson does not. Again, the power which Carlyle worshipped has something tyrannical and monstrous in it, but for Emerson the universe is implacable yet benign.

While English critics were arguing about Wordsworth's poetic diction, his theory of poetry and choice of subjects, Emerson was appraising him from a far loftier point of view.

> Early in life, at a crisis in his private affairs, he made his election between wealth and a position in the world, and the inward promptings of his heavenly genius; he took his part; he accepted the call to be a poet, and sat down, far from cities, with coarse clothing and plain fare, to obey the heavenly vision. The choice he had made in his will, manifested itself in every line to be real.

Montaigne and Shakespeare were always in his hands. Their all-inclusive, humanistic, uncensorious, humourous attitude Emerson made his own.

Coming to the question of the scansion of Emerson's verse, we may first quote from *Merlin* two lines which show Emerson's conscious avoidance of merely melodic beauty. Speaking of the bard, he writes:

> He shall not his brain encumber
> With the coil of rhythm and number.

Unfortunately, the reader of Emerson, that is to say anyone who wishes to read his poetry aloud, must know which syllables to accent and which not, and how to squeeze out the requisite number of stresses in each line. Sometimes, indeed, we are reminded of Skelton:

It was never for the mean;
It requireth courage stout.
Souls above doubt,
Valour unbending.   (*Give All to Love*)

The first two lines also have two accents each, on "was," "mean"; "requireth,"
and "stout." On the whole, in any given poem, the number of syllables is gen-
erally kept, but the varieties of rhythm are innumerable. For example, in *Each
and All*, the eleventh and twelfth lines are:

All are needed by each one;
Nothing is fair or good alone.

This has a strong trochaic rhythm; but the first line is:

Little thinks, in the field, yon red-cloaked clown,

And this seems to have five accents, until we see that the line is anapaes-
tic, with only four.

A foot of one accent is common in Emerson, for example, from *To Rhea*:

Í have cóme from the spríng-wóods.
His swéet-héart's idólatry.
Ánd the gód, háving given áll.

From *Woodnotes II*:

Hé shall néver be óld.

But how shall we scan line 60 [from *To Rhea*]:

Not for a private good:

One of the most difficult things in Emerson is the way in which the same
word, in consecutive lines, sometimes bears an accent and sometimes not;
for example, from *To Rhea*, lines 24–6:

Yét thou érrest far and broad.
But thóu shalt do as do the gods
Ín their cloudless periods.

This alternation of accent is heart-breaking sometimes; Emerson should himself have marked the accents, since the thought may always break the rhythm, which is the servant, not the master. It should be noted that from this conflict of rhythm and thought arises a feeling of freedom and a feeling of humour. This comes out most clearly in *Fable*, and in *To Rhea*, which has a kind of cosmic humour. In any case, we are never lulled to sleep by music or monotony.

Chronologically, most of the poems included in the present selection belong to the earliest of the three collections of 1846, 1867, and 1883, the last a year after his death at the age of seventy-nine. To the second collection, *May-Day and Other Pieces*, published when he was sixty-four, belong: *Brahma, Nature, Days* (which Emerson thought his best poem), *Compensation, Unity* and *Worship*; the rest are from the first collection, entitled *Poems*, published when Emerson was forty-three. The order in the present book is approximately that of difficulty.

In this selection, I have chosen only those poems which seem to me to have poetical worth, or, by felicity of expression, to contain that super-literary value which Emerson, like Thoreau, was always aiming at. The notes are full and conscientious; there are very few cases where I have pretended something was easy because I could not understand it.

A Shortened Version of
A Week on the Concord and Merrimack Rivers

A student textbook published by Hokuseido Press, 1951.

ON THE 31ST OF AUGUST, 1839, HENRY AND JOHN THOREAU SET out for a trip on the Concord and Merrimack Rivers. They started from the village of Concord in their boat the Musketaquid, which they had themselves built in the spring of the same year, and carried with them a tent, guns, fishing gear, etc.

Travelling down the sluggish River Concord, they reached the town of Lowell where it flows into the River Merrimack, a broad, clear, and swift-flowing stream. They rowed up the Merrimack as far as the New Hampshire capital, another Concord, and went on foot to the source of the river in the White Mountains. Hawthorne speaks of the boat they used in *Mosses from an Old Manse*.

There are two rivers in Concord, the slow-flowing Musketaquid (the River Concord) and the swifter Assebet; they meet at the north of town. The sea is twenty miles away, and there are several ponds, Walden, Sandy, and White Pond to the south, and Bateman's to the north.

Thoreau had an older and a younger sister, Helen and Sophia, and an elder brother John, three years older than himself. This brother, who accompanied him on the trip, Thoreau loved more than any other human being. In February 1842, John Thoreau died suddenly and painfully from lock-jaw, and years afterwards, Henry could not bear anyone to speak of it. In the spring of 1845 Thoreau built himself a hut on the shore of Walden Pond and there edited the *Week* from his *Journals* of the time. It is worthy of note that though this was three years after the death of his brother, he nowhere mentions him by name, and speaks of him almost as though he were a spirit being. So God is never named in the *Inferno*.

The *Week*, which appeared in 1849, was Thoreau's first volume. Published at the author's expense, it was well reviewed, but did not sell well. In 1853 the seven hundred remaining copies of the thousand printed were sent to Thoreau, who tells the story in his own whimsical yet manly way. Literary history has few more interesting anecdotes. He writes:

> I have now a library of nearly nine hundred volumes, over seven hundred of which I wrote myself. . . . I can see now what I write for, and the result of my labours. Nevertheless, in spite of this result, sitting beside the inert mass of my works, I take up my pen to-night to record what thought or experience I may have had, with as much satisfaction as ever. Indeed, I believe that this result is more inspiring and better for me than if a thousand had bought my wares. It affects my privacy less and leaves me freer.

That this book of five hundred pages was appreciated by only a very few readers is not surprising in view of the fact that it is highly transcendental, and in addition, is disjointed, without any kind of order, a mixture of pantheism, literary criticism, descriptions of nature and anecdotes of the journey. Thoreau left behind him thirty-nine volumes of *Journals* and from these the *Week*, and *Walden*, published in 1854, five years after the *Week*, the only books published during his life-time, were composed.

The present book is not an abridgement, except in the sense that it is only two-fifths of Thoreau's *Week*. It is a revised, pruned edition, in which is omitted all that Thoreau should himself have omitted; the tedious verses; historical and topographical details; certain conceited or affected passages and forced symbolisms; translations of Greek poets; extracts from ancient Hindu writings; and the like. To make it consecutive, to organize it, to make it an ordinary book, is of course an impossibility; the material is too varied. And yet as Thoreau himself says, when we compel our spontaneous, momentary thoughts into a system, we are destroying their life, their variety. All their natural hue and flavour disappears. Even the abrupt transitions, then, the changes of subject, and heterogenous material, preserve something that is lost in works intellectually organized. And may not that be the best of all, "that something that infects the world"?

The best thing said about the *Week* was by Thoreau himself in his *Journals*:

> I thought that one peculiarity of my *Week* was its hypaethral character, to use an epithet applied to those Egyptian temples which are open to the heavens above, under the ether.

Thoreau has this same hypaethral quality when we are with him; the combination of the transcendental with the practical gives us a sensation of open air, of the sky that is so near and yet so far. The *Week* is a book of an imponderable lightness. It has a kind of artless art; like Pepys' *Diary*, it was written to please the author, not the reader. It reminds us of the sermon of a Zen abbot, a conversation between himself and the silent Buddha, with the assembled monks overhearing it.

Thoreau had a deep appreciation of literature, but he put life and living before all things. Of himself he says,

> My life has been the poem I would have writ,
> But I could not both live and utter it.

More generally:

> The breath by which the poet utters his verse must be that by which he lives.

Indeed we feel deeply in him all that is lost when pen is put to paper; all the bloom and perfume of the world which vanishes when it goes "under the roof." Thoreau says in the *Week*:

> Unfortunately, many things have been omitted which should have been recorded in our journal; for though we made it a rule to set down all our experiences therein, yet such a resolution is very hard to keep, for the important experience rarely allows us to remember such obligations, and so indifferent things get recorded, while that is frequently

neglected. It is not easy to write in the journal what interests us at any time, because to write it is not what interests us.

If we compare the *Week* with *Walden* we note certain differences. The *Week* is fresher, less dogmatic and didactic. This is due partly to the fact that there is five years between the two, but still more to the difference of the circumstances under which they were written. The *Week* was composed amid changing scenes, on the water; *Walden* in a hut, on the land, to which only the weather and the seasons brought variety.

His view of poetry, implicitly and explicitly despised by his critics, is one that will come ultimately to be accepted. He always read through the poetry down to the ground of it, the poetic experience without which poetry is only ornament, parasitic, non-organic, a graceful pretence. Emerson says of him,

> He was so enamoured of the spiritual beauty that he held all actual written poems in very light esteem in the comparison.

Thoreau's own verse is some of the worst that has ever been penned; much of it is irregular, impossible to scan, wooden in form and prosaic in idea, but there are lines that reveal the poetic life that lay buried so deep under the clumsiness of expression, for example, the last lines of *Inspiration*:

> Now chiefly is my natal hour,
> And only now my prime of life;
>   . . .
> I will not doubt the love untold
> Which not my worth nor want has bought,
> Which wooed me young, and woos me old,
> And to this evening hath me brought.

No more religious lines than these have been written. They have the "natural piety" which he shares with the early Wordsworth.

What Thoreau says about music shows that he understood it profoundly:

> Let us hear a strain of music and we are at once advertised of a life which no man has told us of, which no preacher preaches.

But even deeper is his relation to nature.

> Alone in distant woods or fields, in unpretending sprout-lands or pas-
> tures tracked by rabbits, even in a bleak and, to most, cheerless day, like
> this, when a villager would be thinking of his inn, I come to myself, I
> once more feel myself grandly related, and that cold and solitude are
> friends of mine. . . . I come to my solitary woodland walk as the home-
> sick go home.

Wordsworth said "Let nature be your teacher," but it was not long before he
allowed orthodox Christianity, conventional morality, political reaction, in
a word, sterile rationality, to usurp the place of nature. Thoreau, even more
than Emerson, practised what he preached.

Many have criticised Thoreau for an alleged lack of humanity, of human
feeling; they accuse him of downright coldness, and quote from his letters
and diary to convict him out of his own mouth. For example, in a letter to
Mrs. Emerson, May 22, 1843, reversing what Confucius says at the begin-
ning of the *Analects*:

> Is it not delightful to have friends coming from afar?

Thoreau writes:

> Nothing makes the earth seem so spacious as to have friends at a distance.

The year before, after the death of his brother John, he writes to Mrs. Lucy
Brown:

> Soon after John's death I listened to a music-box, and if, at any time, that
> event had seemed inconsistent with the beauty and harmony of the uni-
> verse, it was then gently constrained into the placid course of nature by
> those steady notes, in mild and unoffended tone echoing far and wide
> under the heavens. But I find these things more strange than sad to me.
> What right have I to grieve, who have not ceased to wonder?

It is only a shallow mind that will take such words as evidence of a hard
heart. Thoreau is writing, as always, to and for himself.[1] He is telling us, if we

care to overhear him, what he wishes to be. And he continues in a strain that is far beyond tears and lamentation:

Only Nature has a right to grieve perpetually, for she only is innocent. Soon the ice will melt, and the blackbirds sing along the river which he frequented, as pleasantly as ever. The same everlasting serenity will appear in this face of God, and we will not be sorrowful if he is not.

Elsewhere he writes that "the smallest seed of faith is of more worth than the largest fruit of happiness"; he estimates the worth of life not by its happiness at all, but according to some quite different standard: "our sadness is not sad, but our cheap joys."

> Packed in my mind lie all the clothes
> Which outward nature wears,   (*The Inward Morning*)

says Thoreau. In the *Kegon-kyō* [*Flower Garland Sutra*] we read:

The triple world (material, sensuous, and spiritual) is but one Mind.

Take also the following:

See how I can play with my fingers! They are the funniest companions I have ever found. Where did they come from? What strange control I have over them! *Who* am I? What are they?—those little peaks—call them Madison, Jefferson, Lafayette. What is *the matter*? *My* fingers do I say? Why, erelong, they may form the topmost crystal of Mount Washington. I go up there to see my body's cousins.

Compare this to the second of the three questions asked by Ōryō (Huang-lung, 1002–1069), a Chinese Zen master:

1. Everybody has his place of birth, and where is yours?
2. How is it that my hands are so much like those of the Buddha?
3. How is it that my legs are so much like those of a donkey?

In the following passage we see a Zen that is akin to the transcendentalism of Chuang Tzu:

> You *fail* in your thoughts, or you *prevail* in your thoughts only. Provided you *think* well, the heavens falling, or the earth gaping, will be the music for you to march by. No foe can ever see you, or you him; you cannot so much as *think* of him. Swords have no edges, bullets no penetration, for such a contest. (Letter to Mr. Blake, Sept. 26, 1859)

This reminds us of the same hyperbole (which is yet sober fact) of the 50th chapter of Lao Tzu's *Tao Teh King*):

> The rhinoceros finds no place in him to thrust his horn, nor the tiger to fix its claws, nor a weapon to insert its point. Why? Because there is in him no place of death.

Here is one more passage of the same mystical yet matter-of-fact kind:

> It is after we get home that we really go over the mountain, if ever. What did the mountain say? What did the mountain do? (Letter to Mr. Blake, Nov. 16, 1857)

A little further on we see Thoreau's natural humour, that is, the humour of nature: his own mountain is a very strange one:

> I keep a mountain anchored off eastward a little way, which I ascend in my dreams both awake and asleep. Its broad base spreads over a village or two, which do not know it; neither does it know them, nor do I when I ascend it.

What many people forget is that the transcendentalist is looking for the same thing as the "practical" man; he is looking for something to stand on, something permanent and unfailing, and Thoreau makes a just and final judgment here:

> This, our respectable daily life, in which the man of common sense, the Englishman of the world, stands so squarely, and on which our

institutions are founded, is in fact the veriest illusion, and will vanish like the baseless fabric of a vision; but that faint glimmer of reality which sometimes illuminates the darkness of daylight for all men, reveals something more solid and enduring than adamant, which is in fact the corner-stone of the world. (Letter to Mr. Blake, May 2, 1848)

Thoreau was one of the few men who achieved what little independence it is possible for us to attain in a world where every act is determined, and this freedom comes, as it always must, from a willing and cheerful acquiescence in what is about to happen, and an absolute reliance upon our deepest experience.

I know of no redeeming qualities in myself but a sincere love of some things, and when I am reproved I fall back on to this ground.

Thoreau's anarchism is one of his fundamental characteristics; it is a somewhat un-american and unenglish quality. We are reminded of Shelley, Lawrence, and Nietzsche.

If our merchants did not most of them fail, and the banks too, my faith in the old laws of the world would be staggered.

Thoreau's anti-social feeling is very strong, even violent. He says that this failure of the banks is as "exhilarating as the fragrance of sallows in spring." His economic theory is very simple, but few people have enough serenity of mind to attend to it:

If thousands are thrown out of employment, it suggests that they were not well employed. Why don't they take the hint? It is not enough to be industrious; so are the ants. What are you industrious about?

But the greatness of Thoreau lies after all not in his literary judgements, however just, nor in his criticisms of society, truly sane though they may be, but in his ever-present knowledge of that which is important and that which is not.

What, after all, does the practicalness of life amount to? . . . I could postpone them all to hear this locust sing.

Thoreau is always "mindful that the earth is beneath and heavens are above him." Everything in him begins in nature. When the final account is made and God closes the books, it may be found that Thoreau was the one real man that America produced.

We may conclude this introduction by a quotation from the diary of another traveller in a far-distant time and country. At the beginning of his *Oku no Hosomichi*, a poetical account of a journey of about fifteen hundred miles, and of not one, but of twenty-three weeks, Bashō writes:

Days and months have been travellers through ages past; the years that come and go are travellers too. Those that float away their lives on boats, those who grow old leading the mouths of horses, journeying every day; their dwelling place is travelling itself. Of the ancients there are many who passed away while on a journey, and for some time past I also, a tattered cloud wafted along on the wind, could not keep myself from thoughts of wandering.

In the autumn of last year, loitering by the seashore, I swept away the ancient cobwebs of a hut by the river. The year drew to its close, and with the floating mist of spring in the sky, I felt I would like to pass through the Barrier of Shirakawa. Somehow or other, as though possessed, I felt restless; I could settle down to nothing, beckoned by the God of the Road. (Written in 1689, when Bashō was forty-six years old, five years before his death.)

R. L. Stevenson: *Fables*

Blyth provided the introduction and notes for this volume (Tokyo: Nan'un-do, 1953). A postscript he appended to the introduction is dated April 14, 1952.

THE FABLE IS INSEPARABLY ASSOCIATED WITH THE NAME OF Aesop, fl. c. 600 B.C., who was so misshapen and tongue-tied that he was the closer to the animals that he used as his mouth-piece. Socrates spent his time in prison putting Aesop into verse until his death in 399 B.C., and it is said that Aesop also was executed for the political wisdom contained in his fables. Their social and moral wisdom too, if a man attain to them, mark him as a graduate in the school of humanity.

In a papyrus dating from 1200 B.C. we find an Egyptian version of the fable of the Lion and the Mouse. In fact, as Ernest Rhys tells us in his Introduction to the Everyman *Aesop's Fables*, it is to India that we must go, as for so many things, to find the earliest collection of fables, the *Hitopadesa*, translated by Sir William Jones in 1851.[1] This was known in its earliest form as the *Panchatantra*, a Sanskrit collection of fables, from which are derived the *Fables of Bidpai*, or *Pilpay*, the Arabic version. These were translated into English in 1852. Babrius, a Greek of the first century B.C., made metrical versions of Aesopian fables. They were first discovered in 1842 in a monastery on Mt. Athos. Another name connected with fables is that of Phaedrus, who lived in the first half of the first century A.D., and suffered also for the political implications of his metrical fables.

More fabulous than his own fables in Arabic is Lokman, said variously to be a nephew of Job, a councillor of Solomon, a king of Yemen, a tailor.

His stories were collected by Barsuma at the end of the 13th century, and translated into English in 1869. Russian fables by Kriloff, written between 1809 and 1816, were translated into English by Ralston in 1868, and those of Tolstoi in 1872. Welsh fables were rendered into English by Edward Williams, the "Welsh Shakespeare," in 1848.

In English literature, fables begin with the first printed books, Caxton's *Aesop*, 1485, although Chaucer's *Canterbury Tales*, a hundred years before, contain the well-known fable of the Cock and the Fox, the Nun's Priest's Tale. A little before this, soon after the middle of the 14th century, we find fabulous stories in the *Voiage of Sir John Maundevile*, for example the Fable of the Bees. Dryden's *Fables, Ancient and Modern*, published in 1699, are verse paraphrases of fables by Chaucer, Boccaccio, and Ovid. About the same time, between 1692 and 1699, we have Sir Roger L'Estrange's translation of Aesop's fables. In 1727, John Gay brought out the first series of his *Fables*; the second appeared in 1738, six years after his death. They were very successful. The greatest literary expression of the fable however is in France, that of La Fontaine, who between 1668 and 1694 used the fables of Aesop, Phaedrus, Pilpay, etc., to create the human world of courtesans, merchants, priests, and peasants of his own and all time.* In a note to the *Fables* in the Skerryvore Edition of Stevenson's works, Sir Sidney Colvin tells us,

> By the winter of 1887–88 Stevenson had enough of these by him, together with a few others running to greater length, and conceived in a more mystic and legendary vein, to enable him, as he thought, to see his way towards making a book of them.

In 1888 he went to Samoa in the South Seas, and wrote a few there, Nos. XIII and XV, but only enough altogether for a slender volume of forty odd pages, which never appeared. Nevertheless, in profundity and practical significance,

---

* Mention should be made of *Fables for Our Time*, 1939, by James Thurber, "Surprising wise and witty" criticisms of modern men and women, often using animals. The morals are very original: "Early to rise and early to bed makes a male healthy and wealthy and dead." "It is better to ask some of the questions than to know all the answers." "You might as well fall flat on your face as lean over too far backward." Another modern work of permanent value is *Archy and Mehitabel*, by Don Marquis, 1927. (Archy is a cockroach, Mehitabel a cat.)

not to mention style, several of them, particular The Poor Thing, The Touchstone, and The Song of the Morrow, are perhaps the best things Stevenson ever wrote, even excelling such masterpieces as *Will O' the Mill* and *Markheim*.

Stevenson has not the age-old simplicity and universality of Aesop, nor his worldly wisdom; he has not the psychological truth and naturalism, the gaiety and charm of La Fontaine; nor the artistic detachment and humourous faithfulness to human nature of Chaucer. But he has more earnestness, more power and passion, more Zen than they; and yet there is in some of his fables a perfect balance between art and nature, between the depth of the thought and the justness of its expression:

> But he was like the hunter that has seen a stag upon a mountain, so that the night may fall, and the fire be kindled, and the lights shine in his house; but desire of that stag is single in his bosom.

Stevenson uses human beings or supernatural creatures instead of animals for his fables, which would perhaps be more exactly denominated parables, since they are "fictitious narratives by which moral or spiritual relations are typically set forth." But considered more profoundly, every story is a fable, every life a dramatic allegory. At first we may suppose, the fable was simply a story, a story for its own sake. Then gradually it began to take upon itself various meanings, political and moral, as in Aesop, literary and poetical, as in La Fontaine, other-worldly and eschatological as in the parables of Christ. But when the moral and the fable are separated, when life and its significance are not one, we feel both to be lacking; the story is a mere succession of events, the meaning is a purely abstract principle without power or practicality. Looking through Stevenson's fables, we see a tendency towards the reunion of fable and moral, so that in the last one, The Song of the Morrow, we cannot say what the moral is, so closely are the events and the meaning knit together.

The best stories, the best fables, the best lives, are those in which the meaning and the events are indivisible. "Do not, I beg you," says Goethe, "look for anything behind phenomena." This is why Irish fairies are "beings so quickly offended that you must not speak much about them at all." Things cannot bear to be explained.

Jūroku Nenkan no Oshiego ("My Student for Sixteen Years")

Asahi Gurafu, tokusatu, 1963. I have translated this brief article, which appeared in a special issue of Asahi Graph, *one of the leading weekly magazines of the time, for the bit of light it throws on Blyth's relationship with Crown Prince, later Emperor, Akihito, whom he had by that time tutored for almost eighteen years.*

IT HAS NOW BEEN SIXTEEN YEARS SINCE I FIRST BEGAN TUTORING the Crown Prince. Every Thursday I went to the Imperial Palace to teach him, so I came to think, "Thursday is the Crown Prince's day." Perhaps the Crown Prince thought, "Thursday is Blyth Sensei's day." To be completely truthful, for the first eight or nine years I did not have a favorable impression of the Crown Prince. The Crown Prince later told me that he had felt the same way about me. This may be owing to the very different circumstances of our everyday lives, work, and interests.

The Crown Prince is interested in science, which I believe to be the enemy of mankind. I love poetry and religion, which his Highness was at one time more doubtful about, thinking that they could easily be used to hoodwink mankind. However, over the past seven or eight years I have grown to like His Highness. I think it was because I gradually came to feel the human warmth buried deep in his heart. My own character also changed greatly over that time, and one of the reasons for that was owing to the "many things I had learned from His Highness. For example: not to overstate or exaggerate things, not to go to excess, to consider all questions from both sides, not to condemn or feel hatred for others, to give careful consideration before making a decision, and not to tell lies.

Crown Princess Michiko also sometimes attended our classes. In such cases, the characters and relationship of husband and wife were clearly revealed, so during the classes this is what I learned about them.

One thing I saw was that Crown Princess Michiko did not marry the Crown Prince because he was the Crown Prince. She married him for the same reason that I was teaching him. That is, because the Crown Prince was a gentleman of worth and merit. Another thing that I was surprised to find was that the Crown Princess was a wonderful wife and wonderful mother, and even more so, the Crown Prince was a wonderful husband. Intellectually- and theoretically-minded, he does not easily become disturbed about things. There was only one time when this was not the case. It happened after a Thursday class when I said something that offended the Crown Princess, and the next week the Crown Prince took me strongly to task for it. For me, that Thursday was a very happy day.

BOOK REVIEWS

A Wanderer in Japan

Blyth's comments were printed on the dust jacket of this book by the poet Edmund Blunden (Tokyo: Asahi-shimbun-sha, 1951).

THESE SKETCHES ARE NOT IN THE FORM OF A CONTINUOUS NARrative broken into chapters, but a record of those hours which the memory of the poet chose to retain and give significance to out of all the multitudinous events of several years.

They range from Hokkaido to Nagasaki, from the Imperial Palace to octopuses and oysters.

They have a background of about 25 years, for it was this number of years ago that Mr. Blunden first came to Japan and fell in love with a country and people he has served so faithfully and so well.

As the first article shows, he came back to this country with an almost painful eagerness, he left it with equal reluctance in order to fulfill his obligations to the London Times.

He seems to have regretted the ruined condition of Japan and the distress of the people almost as if it had been his own country. To the poet, misery anywhere, whatever the cause, is misery. Ypres, London, Tokyo destroyed is just a dead loss to the world and a weight upon the minds of all its poetical inhabitants.

We feel in these sketches what Mr. Blunden had himself and what he wanted to bestow on Japan, "a lyrical joy or awareness in life, and at the same time, a steady, clear, and courageous kind of thinking."

The word "bestow" is unsuitable for so modest a man.

A Very Important Person said to me the other day, "Mr. Blunden was modest to the point of extinction."

I replied, "He was modest to the point of genius," and it is one of the strangest things in a very strange world, that the less a man thinks of himself, the more we think of him. But in Mr. Blunden this remarkable humility was combined with, or perhaps even based upon, an equally remarkable courage, seen not only and not chiefly on the field of battle, where he won a remarkable fame, but in the most delicate of his poetical perceptions, by which he eagerly penetrates into the minds of men and the forms of nature.

So at the end of a poem included in this book, Ainu Child, he says, of one of the children with speaking eyes,

> She implores that strange woman to challenge her fate,
> And take her and break for her all the locked gates.

These "locked gates" of the Ainu world are to be broken for her by the poet's wife; the girl is to be given all the opportunities of a free and poetic life, instead of the monotonous and gloomy pleasure of killing bears dragged from their forest haunts.

This energetic tenderness of character reminds one of the ideal man envisaged by the English more than a thousand years ago in the character of Beowulf:

> Of man he was mildest, and most beloved,
> To his kin the kindest, keenest for praise.

This tenderness of mind is seen everywhere in the present collection of his writings, for example in *Tokyo Seclusion*, concerning the preservation of the stump of a burnt tree (p. 84):

> A few tiny snails, a few fungi, an occasional bird or moth find that it helps their difficult lives.

In this single word "difficult," we see clearly his more than Shakespearean sympathy with all things animate and inanimate.

He flits like Ariel, like a hummingbird, from one thing to another, and as he does so we call to mind a saying from the *Zenrinkushū*:

The water that a cow drinks turns to milk;
The water that a snake drinks to poison.

He is able to see books in stones and good in everything. He has a catholicity of taste, a willingness to be pleased, a mind rich with the stores of a vast reading, yet a mind so subtle and leaping that his style often becomes overparenthetic.

This characteristic style of his has been influenced, I think, by his understanding of the Japanese language and literature, for example on page 79, lines 17–21, where past and present, here and there, are blended in the oriental manner.[1]

Indeed, every line breathes an unspoken love of Japan; he remembers or knows instinctively what Blake says:

Never seek to tell thy love
Love that never told can be.

The best of the pieces in this collection is, I think, *The Sea Speaking*. It is full of the most delicate poetry and tender feeling; the voice of the Pacific Ocean, its sea-speech, the low talking of the waters, profound even on windless days; the puppy-dogs with their "finds" on the sea shore; old thoughts reviewed by the ever-young ocean; his faint grief for the little crabs and fishes snatched from their narrow dwelling places by small boys.

This piece is too personal, yet universal; speaking of self without self-consciousness; pity without patronage; love without sentimentality; an absence of strain, a latent power, an untapped reservoir of thought and feeling which gives balance and depth to the most trivial remarks.

"The sea is salt everywhere" goes the Zen saying, and in these sketches there is not a paragraph without that keen yet mellow flavour, that clear but soft tone, that delicate and strong sense that at once soothes and stimulates.

Mr Blunden knew even before he came to Japan three things that the Japanese knew long ago: that if you want to reveal something, you must hide it; that there is nothing greater than the smallest things; and that, to use his own words, "we should allow life to meet us without the barrier of previously formed convictions."

Zen Buddhism: Selected Writings

Blyth's review of this book of Suzuki Daisetz's writings (Garden City, NY: Doubleday, 1956) appeared in Japan Quarterly, *1958.*

IT IS HARDLY POSSIBLE TO CRITICISE, TO ADD OR SUBTRACT FROM the works of Suzuki Daisetz. During the thirty years from his first *Essay in Zen Buddhism* in 1927 to the latest of his writing, there is no development such as we find in Shakespeare or Mozart, but from the beginning all is sublimely true, indeed infallible. Just here and there are slips, but of the pen, not of the soul. For example in the present selection, on page 121, George Wither's line, "In some other wiser men," should be "man." On page 284, Bashō's date of birth is given as 1643. I think it should be 1644. The Introduction, Zen for the West, by William Barrett, is very competently done, though with a little too much emphasis on the differences of East and West. I wish to return to this point later. Our great fault, that is, of Mr. Barrett and myself, is that we wish, as Mencius says, to be teachers. Suzuki Daisetz, like Edmund Blunden, does not want to be brilliant, to lay down the law, to startle or convert. He is just his own natural self, speaking of what he has experienced in the right (not the best) words. This is the highest art, and the most difficult thing in the world. I also am not able to attain to it, but can only add the following "legs to the snake," and relate the work of Dr. Suzuki to world religion, and show how he is a link of the great chain that might bind together a broken world. This is not the so-called East-West division, but that of intellect and intuition, science and religion, reason and poetry, art and life. This conflict is found in every country, in every man, and we must say that world wars, hot or cold, have little direct connection with it.

The Indian statement some three thousand years ago of the animistic unity of all things has been the most stimulating and potent of all the spiritual forces that have been brought to bear upon the stupidity and egoism of mankind. It may have been behind the miracle of the sudden rise of Greek culture; it was essential for Christian mysticism; it resulted in the poetry of Wordsworth and the transcendentalism of Emerson and Thoreau; it was the foundation of the later Buddhist doctrine of the Buddha-nature of every creature animate and inanimate.

But an even more wonderful thing occurred in China in the 7th and 8th centuries A.D. In contradistinction to the dichotomy of Christian theology, Buddhism had asserted the divinity of man. In the words of Blake, himself one of the distant beneficiaries of the teaching of the Upanishads:

Thou are a Man; God is no more;
Thy own Humanity learn to adore.

But this was still an intellectual, verbal, *understandable* statement of the fact, a fact, which is living, which is beyond words yet includes them. This activity is not one thing, as Buddhism asserts. It is not two things, not the relation of man and God, as Christianity states. This activity is what is called in grammar an uncountable noun; it is Zen, the great discovery-invention of the Chinese people. Zen, like poetry, like humour, is here, is there, is unmistakable, but is unobjectifiable, or rather it is subject and object as both one and as two. Zen is poetry. It is a thing meaning, and when a thing means, it is all things. It means because it is all things.

The great Chinese Zen monks, such as Hui-neng, Yun-men, and Lin-chi, without leaving the framework of the life of ordinary Buddhist monks, were able to act in it, to be free in it. Most remarkable of all, they were able to *be* this activity even while they spoke, briefly, *of* it. Note this word "of." We talk about the meaning "of" something, the colour "of" the sky, as if these things were separate or separable from each other. This is the kind of illusion created by speech, by the intellect. A thing means; it does not have a meaning. More strictly, a thing does not mean; a thing *things*. But speaking most strictly (which is really, I suppose, not speaking at all) it simply does not matter what we say; any nonsense will do, as Carroll and Lear showed us, provided that we are acting freely and unseparated from the words themselves. As I write at this moment, the ideas and the ink flow in a single stream that continues unbroken in the reader's mind. "All flows." We see a new and deeper meaning in these ancient words. What flows is the All. Nothing does not flow. What does not flow is nothing. When we flow we are All. Only when we are All do we flow.

How can we flow? For most of us this is only possible by imitation, by contagion, or better, just as ice is melted by warm water. The writings of Suzuki Daisetz are like this. To borrow Arnold's lines concerning Wordsworth, written a hundred years ago, he also

> Had fallen on this iron time
> Of doubts, disputes, distractions, fears.
> He found us when the age had bound
> Our souls in its benumbing round;
> He spoke, and loosed our heart in tears.

The odd thing about East and West is that it is the active West that finds the Universe too dreadful to accept as it is and has tried to sentimentalize and romanticize the "iron face of God." But the East knows that the Universe is not dreadful, that the sky is not blue; we make it so. The passive East declares that it is the mind of man which creates truth. But here we must beware of this comparing and contrasting of East and West; Dr. Suzuki himself is not entirely innocent of it. Byzantine religious art, Anglo-Saxon poetry, German music are not to be confused with the Hebrew moral dichotomy or the Greek intellectual antitheses; but neither are they to be separated from them. As Emerson says:

> All are needed by each one;
> Nothing is fair or good alone.

Again, where Zen is so right is in its absolute refusal to take questions seriously, that is, as separable from the answers to them. After all, when we ask the question properly, there is the answer; the question answers itself. Each fact, each action is perfect. It is only when we try to detach the purpose, the meaning, the cause, the effect, from the activity that we get question and answer. But questions are not wrong, nor are answers; it is taking them as matters of urgency, of life and death that is bad, that is blasphemy of the wholeness of each infinite and unique event. Things are timeless, but it is not wicked to carry a watch. However, to think of the Universe as a watch and of God as a watchmaker is to insult both.

Japanese Court Poetry

Blyth's review of this book by Robert H. Brower and Earl Miner
(Stanford, CA: Stanford University Press, 1961) appeared in Japan
Quarterly, *April 1962.*

"THIS IS THE FIRST TIME THAT METHODS OF MODERN WESTERN
analytical criticism have been employed to any length in dealing with an
Asian literature." This is perhaps true; the question is, should they have
been so employed? Two American scholars write with an almost painful
sympathy and admiration for waka in its palmy days. The poetical creed
of the authors, as far as lyric is concerned, seems very similar to that of the
waka poets. The analyses of the individual poems are excellent, minute,
but keeping in view the background and the atmosphere. It is a first-class
account of a first-class form of culture. What then is wrong with the book?

Just after the end of the War, there was a saying, "Culture is not shiny."
This book is shiny. It has something slick and sleek about it which is dis-
agreeable to a certain taste. But, it may be said, waka themselves are shiny.
This is true, and it is why the authors and their subjects are so well suited.
What Bashō did was to take out the shininess of waka, and replace the
glossy with a matt finish. In dealing with waka we should underplay the art
and artificiality, just as we dress a thin woman in a horizontal pattern, or to
some extent de-sentimentalise Schubert. This is of course especially need-
ful in translation. Homer is plain. Milton should not be read with pomp,
and Shelley should not be read quickly. Haiku has not much rhythm. We
may give it a little more. To add beauty to waka, to gild the lily, and, as the
authors themselves confess, sometimes "make poor verses seem better than

they are," may not be altogether reprehensible, but this practice spoils the best verses which become sicklied o'er with a kind of artiness and excess of beauty. An example is the following:

> Haru no no ni
> Kasumi tanabiki
> Uraganashi
> Kono yūkage ni
> Uguisu naku mo.

This is translated:

> Now it is spring
> And across the moors the haze
> Stretches heavily
> And within these rays at sunset
> A warbler fills the radiant mist with song.

The last two lines of the original simply say: "In these rays of the setting sun, an *uguisu* sings:" Another example:

> Yo no naka ni
> Taete sakura no
> Nakariseba
> Haru no kokoro wa
> Nodokekaramashi.

This is translated in the following way:

> If cherry flowers
> Had never come into this world,
> The hearts of men
> Would have kept their tranquil freedom
> Even at the brilliant height of spring.

The last two (three) lines say only; "Hearts in spring would have been at ease." And what is "the brilliant height of spring," if there were no cherry blossoms?

In many of the best waka we feel something beneath the beauty of things and words; it comes out in the translation only when it is literal. There are several references to the "something" (which I call Zen) in this book, which show that the authors belong to that pitiful group of people who not only think they know what Zen is when they don't, but understand it upside down and inside out. We are told that the following, by the ex-Emperor Fushimi, "exhibits one kind of Zen enlightenment":

Itazura ni
Yasuki waga mi zo
Hazukashiki
Kurushimu tami no
Kokoro omoeba.

When I consider
The sufferings of the mass of people,
I am filled with shame—
At myself who am all too prone to live
In the languor of my easy days.

To take Zen as humility for one's self and sympathy for others flatters Zen, but the following is more relevant to waka:

So the Zen priests approached the mysteries of Buddhism with symbols, when it was necessary to approach them at all; for in the fourteenth century at least, priests did not go out of their way to symbolize unless pressed by ardent disciples. If someone had the temerity to ask, "What is the ultimate principle of Buddhism?" the only reply was something like, "The cypress tree in the courtyard." And perhaps a sharp rap on the questioner's tonsured head.

The essence of Zen (and of poetry) is the experience that each thing has an intrinsic value in relation or use. Nothing is symbolic of anything else. Even Goethe said, to Eckermann: "Do not, I beg you, look behind phenomena; they are themselves the meaning."

Most interesting is the section "Japanese Poetry and the Western Reader: The Problem of Limitations," in the last chapter. Waka, not Japanese poetry, are compared to all European verse, drama, epic, lyric, narrative, etc., and the conclusion is:

> And so, ultimately, and as a whole, we prefer our own poetry to the Japanese. But this is an ultimate choice, and one which really need not be made.

Then why make it? The conclusion, however, will please everybody, Japanese and Americans alike, but that is just what is wrong with it. What an American thinks of Japanese literature, or what a Japanese, as a Japanese, thinks of it is interesting, but repulsively so. Wherever and whenever there is poetry, of any kind, I want it. It is the only reason for learning foreign languages, or dead languages, or even one's own. And ultimately (I also have an ultimate) what is wrong with Japanese who like their own literature best, and like Americans to like their own American literature best, and Americans who do ditto, is that they are all insincere, because it is not the human attitude. This comes out inadvertently when the authors say, "All art is a feigning of reality, and the question to be asked is not of its autobiographical 'sincerity,' but of its success in moving our minds and feelings."

To sum up, this book is the best possible introduction to waka as one form of Japanese verse. If, however, we think of the waka writers as prophets who foresaw the Heavenly Kingdom, the Promised Land of Haiku, though they themselves never entered into it, this book will seem unsatisfactory. To put the same thing in another way, waka are Japanese, haiku are human, just as Tennyson is English and Shakespeare is not. Anyway, perhaps the best and only things to do with any foreign poetry is to translate it as literally, yet as "kindly" as possible, and let the reader make the best of it he can. All we can really do is to take the horse to water.

ARTICLES AND ESSAYS

Two Autobiographical Essays

Blyth wrote these two essays for the Eigakusei Shimbun, *a news-paper with information and brief articles for Japanese students of English. They were published, with a Japanese translation, in vol. 1, no. 2 (December 1947) and vol. 2, no. 2 (February 1948), under the common heading "When I Was a Schoolboy in England."*

1. "BLOODKNOT" WAS VERY FOND OF TEASING BOYS

In the primary school I was always at the bottom of the class. This was partly because I was completely unable to do any kind of sums; even now I cannot add up a row of figures without making a mistake. Partly it was because I found nothing interesting in what the teacher was saying. The only good thing about school was the ending of the day's lessons.

However, I was always a very "good" boy. I sat up straight, looked at the teacher's face all the time—but never listened to anything he said. When he found this out, he became very angry with me; I suppose he felt insulted.

I should mention here that my mother and father never said anything to me about being at the bottom of the class. This was very wise and kind of them, for it is useless to force children to study before the desire to do so arises in them spontaneously.

When I went to the secondary school, I began to find certain subjects interesting, English literature, and French, and a few things in geometry. I can remember even now the first day on which I found an English poem of deep and inexplicable meaning. I now worked very hard, and strangely enough the chief reason for this was to please my parents, who would never have reproached me for poor marks. I was already very interested in insects and religion. These two subjects are more connected than many people may suppose.

If I am asked that difficult question, what the difference is between English and Japanese schools, the only answer possible is that in England the boys and teachers are English, not Japanese. In other words, it derives chiefly from the home life which makes both what they are. What I learned at home had a stronger and more permanent effect than what I was taught at school.

In class, arguments between the boys and the teachers were not uncommon. In particular, one of the teachers of English was a Socialist. He was also an atheist, and I often talked about religion until his red face seemed to be getting larger and larger and fill the room.

This particular teacher was very fond of teasing the boys, often making them cry with his sarcasm. His real name was Goodspeed, but his nickname was the rather horrible but not altogether unsuitable one of "Bloodknot." I don't quite know what it meant.

I must tell you something more about him. He used to teach music as well as English, and used to beat time with a cane on the softer parts of the boys, so that it must have looked more like a dancing than a singing lesson.

Quite different from Japanese boys, English schoolboys are always eating sweets, in school and out. When "Bloodknot" caught any boy eating sweets in lesson-time, he would take away the bag of sweets from the boy, and eat all the sweets in front of the class, teaching meanwhile, smacking his lips and making all the boys' mouths water.

This happened so often and annoyed the boys so much that they decided to have their revenge on him. They bought some chocolates, took out the insides, and filled them with pepper. That afternoon, a certain small boy in the front row began to eat something ostentatiously. "Bloodknot" immediately made him hand over the bag of chocolates, and began to eat one with great relish. Gradually, his naturally red face began to get redder. Gazing fiercely round, however, he continued to eat the chocolate and swallowed it. He said nothing about it at all, but no boy ever dared to eat sweets in his class again.

This story shows, I think, the justice of the teacher, for he realized that he had teased the boys too much. There is a certain quality of manliness also, in both boys and teacher, and I think this is perhaps the most necessary thing in the Japanese middle school. Manliness for the boys and womanliness for the girls,—is there anything better?

2. ENGLAND IN WINTER

England is a small country, but has a great variety of climate, scenery and architecture. There are cities, towns, villages and hamlets, and the winter is different in all of these. In the cities, the seasons are hardly noticed. In the south of England it may not snow, and hardly freeze, and yet one may have to light a fire in the middle of summer. For the schoolboy, winter is the season of football, as summer is the season of cricket. Only occasionally the ground freezes, and makes the game impossible.

I was born in Ilford, Essex, a flat country north-east of London. Ilford itself is seven miles from the center of London, and now included in Greater London. The winter landscape of the Essex countryside is not beautiful in the picturesque sense, but the checker-board of fields, the great bare elms, the cabbages in silent rows, the misty distance and the sodden hedges,—all these things have a poetry, a solitary harmony that makes the Alps and the Grand Canyon look like picture post-cards.

Sometimes (but rarely on Christmas Day) it snows in earnest. Snow is the same all over the world, but no city is so transformed in an hour or two, as is London, by a snowfall. Sometimes, too, it freezes hard, and people get out their skates and wait anxiously for the ice to thicken. Every school playground (made of asphalt) has long slides, and the boys with blakeys (iron nails) on their boots slide along faster than anyone.

It may be well to mention here the fogs of London. More or less foggy days are many in November and December, but real "pea-soup" fogs are infrequent. When they occur, however, they produce a very strong impression. To be completely lost in a great city, electric lights blazing but invisible, all sounds blanketed, one's eyes and throat stinging with smoke, eyebrows and clothes damp with mist,—this is an almost terrifying experience.

The most important part of winter, for schoolboys, is the winter holidays, and everything leads up to Christmas Day. When we compare this to New Year's Day in Japan, we find many differences. For adults, as for the children, Christmas means eating and eating and eating, and going for long walks to get up an appetite for more eating. What a world of difference, too, there is between Christmas pudding, into which go raisins, currants, spice, apples, bread-crumbs, butter, lemon-peel, orange-peel, sugar nuts, milk, and so on,—and "mochi," made of rice. There is another difference also.

Christmas Day is for the children. My mother and father fairly slaved for days on end, making Christmas decorations, preparing the puddings and pies and jellies and custards and cakes, buying the presents secretly and hiding them up somewhere, setting up the Christmas tree, inviting relatives,— all for me, an only child. I remember even now the chimney up which I called in a hoarse and trembling voice, for Santa Claus to send me a Punch and Judy Show (a kind of small marionette theatre). After Christmas, there is only a melancholy waiting for going back to school. New Year's Day is hardly kept in most parts of England.

In winter we feel above all things the value of home, of the fire-side. When I was young, I once said that my idea of heaven on earth was to lie on the hearthrug in front of the fire, with a dog, eating sweets and reading a book. I am afraid that I have not risen very far above this. The sun in summer, the fire in winter, these are two fundamental things in the life of temperate zones. Castles in the fire, the wavering shadows on the wall, the sound of the cold wind outside,—we can never forget such things, any more than the billowing clouds of summer, the glittering sea, the hot roads.

Winter enters into the English character far more than the other seasons. It is not cruel, but stern: it teaches a man to "grin and bear it." Nature is not bountiful, but willing. It seems that those peoples whose own languages are difficult, are good at foreign languages. It may be that the "difficulties" of the English climate have enabled Englishmen to bear the heat and cold, rain and snow, of all parts of the globe.

Winter means to English people grey skies, bare branches, umbrellas and heavy boots; it means the warmth and cheerfulness of the fire-lit room, the cat with his paws on the fender, the kettle hissing on the hob. It is by such things that an Englishman is made, and in such things his character may be seen. Perhaps his silence and reserve, "an absence of outline, impreciseness, a subtle variousness, unobtrusive kindliness and tolerance" are not unconnected with the English winter. Winter is not the death of the world, it is a sleep, and in the very depth of winter we feel there is life within the trees and earth. From this again comes perhaps that common proverb, on the lips of ordinary English people, which expresses the spirit of England: *Live and let live.*

Freedom

This short piece, like the two preceding ones, was written for the Eigakusei Shimbun (*vol. 2, no. 9, May 15, 1948*).

WHEN WE THINK ABOUT THE SUBJECT OF FREEDOM FROM A JAPA-nese or Eastern point of view, we find ourselves using the method of con-tradiction. On the one hand we are to live for others: on the other hand we must live for ourselves, according to our own nature. If my daughter (aged six) says, "Let's leave some of this for papa, because it is so delicious," this is one kind of freedom, the expanding, social variety. If she says (as she did) on being asked to say something about her dear papa's character, "He's very greedy," she is not only telling the truth, but expressing her freedom from all human relationships, as an absolute, independent existence.

It is a strange but interesting thing that both these two extremes of free-dom have something repulsive about them. A man who is always "thinking of others," a woman who "lives for her children," is not an entirely pleasant sight. And it goes without saying that people who are entirely selfish and self-centred have something inhuman about them.

But if we say that a man should think partly of himself and partly of oth-ers, this suggests a divided and vacillating mind that is not a unity. What then is the real freedom? It is like a hand that has a back and a palm. The palm is altruism and unselfishness, keeping to the left side of the road, hav-ing no black market, acting as a social being. The back is doing, saying and thinking what we like, submitting to no tradition or convention, seeing faults and imperfections in God himself, if there are any. But real freedom is the hand, not the back plus the palm. It will not allow itself to be defined or explained, but it may be lived at any time and in any place. As Marcus Aurelius said, it is possible to live the good life even in a palace, and Bashō put this into practice when he was invited to the mansion of a daimyo. Sometimes we have the feeling, the experience of freedom. It comes quite unexpectedly and unbidden. We do not attain to freedom; it takes up its abode in us when it will to do so, after we have prepared for it.

How can we prepare for this freedom? It is to some extent an act of faith that, as the English say, "Honesty is the best policy"; that finally our own best interests are identical with those of other people. It means following, in our minds, the greatest extremes of both kinds of freedom, without reservation or reluctance; individualists like Blake, Byron or Nietzsche, social workers and thinkers like Matthew Arnold, Karl Marx or Gandhi are all followed and absorbed to the very limit. Perhaps the opposite of freedom is meanness, a coldness of mind that dulls and stifles the energy that flows outward and inward.

The aim of life, its only aim, is to be free. Free of what? Free to do what? Only to be free, that is all. Free through ourselves, free through others; free to be sad, to be in pain; free to grow old and die. This is what our soul desires, and this freedom it must have; and shall have.

Thoughts on Haiku

From an undated, rather beat-up typescript found among Blyth's posthumous papers. I can find no record of it ever having been used, though the paper and handwritten Japanese characters would seem to date it to the early postwar period.

THE WORLD-VIEW OF HAIKU

The world-view of senryū and that of haiku are explicitly opposed. Haiku gazes out on this world,

And builds a Heaven in Hell's despair.

Senryū shakes all that can be shaken, but implicitly there are things which cannot be laughed away, and the scorn of pretence, lies, snobbery, selfishness is after all based on the love of truth and goodness. If we put together a haiku and a senryū which express their respective world-views, we see something profoundly in common between them.

Fotoritaru   nomi wo tsubuseba   harami-ori

A fat flea;
Cracking it,
It was pregnant.

(*Kenkabō*)

Takotsubo ya   hakanaki yume wo   natsu no tsuki

The octopuses in the jars:
Transient dreams
Under the summer moon.   (*Bashō*)

In both we feel the transience of life, its meaninglessness, its "indifference." Both show us this world of eat and be eaten, but the senryū leaves us there, whereas the haiku spreads over all the pain and failure the beauty of the summer moon. This is not throwing a veil over the imperfection and ugliness of reality. Indeed, the real beauty of the summer moon comes out only when we see, *at the same time*, the ephemeral and tragic nature of sublunary things.

The world-view of haiku is not something that can be put into words either than those of the haiku themselves, and even here, the words point to something which is wordless. One must admit that it lacks the completeness and universality of Shakespeare's or Goethe's view of life. But what it loses in breadth it makes up for in depth. The passion of love, its triumphs and despairs; the heroism and horror of war; all the grotesqueness and humour of human life—these things are omitted from its scope. But just as nature is contained in man, man is contained in nature, and we feel that the Way of Haiku, though in a sense a narrow one, is not a mere by-path, but leads us to an acceptance of the world and all that goes on in it. In other words, we read the newspaper (or do not read it) with the spirit of haiku. We meet disaster and death, our own and that of others, with the calm that Wordsworth expresses in the most remarkable of all his poems, ourselves also

Rolled round in earth's diurnal course
With rocks and stones and trees.

HAIKU IN WORLD LITERATURE

Japanese literature stands or falls by haiku, in my opinion, but its unique characteristics make it a difficult matter to assess its position in world literature. It is not merely the brevity, by which it isolates a particular group of phenomena from all the rest; nor its suggestiveness, through which it reveals a whole world of experience. It is not in its remarkable use of the "season word," by which it gives us a feeling of a quarter of the year; nor its faint, all-pervading humour. Its peculiar quality is its self-effacing, self-annihilative nature. Just as we are to be in a state of *muga*, selflessness, when we compose haiku, so the haiku itself is not a thing of beauty and a joy forever, but a single-post, a raft unwanted when the river is crossed. If, like waka, the haiku itself has literary charm and value, we are distracted from the real region of haiku, the experience, the mutual life of poet and things.

Many readers must have had the experience of reading haiku which have not seemed very good or striking, and yet, for some strange and unknown reason, were unforgettable. To take some examples:

Roku-gatsu ya   mine ni kumo oku   Arashiyama

　　In the Sixth Month
　　Mount Arashi
　　　　Lays clouds on its summit.　　　　　　　　　　(*Bashō*)

To explain the poetic spirit of this would be very difficult. It lies partly, no doubt, in the personifying of the mountain, or rather, realizing the "life" of it, but the simple sublimity of the verse is Homeric; it is that of the cloud-capped mountain.

Inazuma ya   kinō wa higashi   kyō wa nishi

　　Summer lightning!
　　Yesterday in the East,
　　　　Today in the West.　　　　　　　　　　　　(*Kikaku*)

There could be nothing less "poetical" than this bald statement of meteorological fact, and yet we feel the vastness of nature together with the underlying willing acceptance of man. The position which haiku has, or should have, in world literature may be brought out by comparing and contrasting Bashō with Shakespeare, Homer, Dante, Goethe, and Cervantes. If he can hold his own with these, the 17-syllabled haiku may well claim to be on an equality with the world masterpieces of epic, of drama, and lyric.

Bashō has not the grim strength of Dante, but he also sees how

The little flowers, bent and shut by the chill of the night,
Soon as the sunlight whitens them,
Erect themselves all open on their stems.   (*Inferno* 11, 127–129)

He has not the power to create "forms more real than living man," but has the universality of

Truly sir, I am a poor fellow that would live,

As applied to all the things in the world,—for example:

Yoku mireba   nazuna hana saku   kakine kana

   Looking carefully
There is a shepherd's purse
   Blooming under the hedge.

He has not Homer's grasp of the primitive nobility of men and women, but he has his pleasure in the plain and elemental things of life:

Sake nomeba   itodo nerarenu   yoru no yuki

   I drank wine,
But all the more could not sleep,—
   A night of snow.

Goethe's understanding of science was to Bashō unknown, but he shares with him the knowledge that there is nothing behind phenomena: "they are themselves the meaning." On the other hand, Bashō is an idealist like Cervantes, but he does not tilt at wind-mills either real or symbolical; he does something just as destructive however, in taking away from things their (apparent) heavy, stupid meaninglessness and shows us them as the world of grace and nature in one.

In what point is Bashō equal or superior to these great men? In his touching the very nerve of life, his unerring knowledge of those moments in time which, put together, make up our real, our eternal life. He is awake in the world that for almost all men exists as a world of dreams.

Bashō gives us the same feeling of depth of Bach, and by the same means, not by noise and emotion as in Beethoven and Wagner, but by a certain serenity and "expressiveness" which never aims at beauty but often achieves it as it were by accident. This comparison between Bashō and Bach may seem to be far-fetched, and in a sense is so, for there is nothing whatever in common between them,—except their profound understanding of death, and as Confucius implies, he who understands either death or life understands both. The hymn says:

Days and moments quickly flying
Blend the living with the dead,

but Bach and Bashō felt this so deeply, each in his own way, that the average mind finds the one too intellectual, the other too simple. The so-called intellectuality of Bach consists in his saying different things at the same time, thus expressing the fugality, the diversity in unity of the universe. The so-called simplicity of Bashō is his saying the same thing at different times, seeing heaven in every flower however wild. There is indeed in this identity perceived in two such different characters, and modes of artistic expression, something that reassures us about the universe that produced them.

HAIKU AS POETRY TRANSCENDED

When we compare haiku and waka we feel a difference that is hard to express but it is deep and strong nevertheless. Waka are beautiful, haiku not. A haiku effaces, even annihilates itself, in pointing unequivocally towards what can of its nature never be said, and yet is the commonest experience of mankind: So it is that a badly translated waka has no value; a haiku, however poorly translated, still has something, and in a sense, enough of the original meaning.

A haiku presupposes great faith, great courage on the part of the reader, who is to recreate in his hours of tranquility what the poet experienced in his moments of excitement. What is difficult is to trust what we call the "poetical emotion" we undoubtedly feel, for our ordinary emotions lead us astray so often that Hamlet was forced to rate such a man as Horatio above the poet. And how close and yet how far away are the worlds of poetry and of sentimentality. We look at the moon when we feel happy, and ascribe our gladness to her, colour her with our minds. This is sentimentality. We look at the moon when we feel happy, and see the gladness inherent and intrinsic in the moon. This is poetry.

> The moon doth with delight
> Look round her when the heavens are bare.

If this means, "the moon shines in the cloudless sky, and I am delighted," there is no poetry here. If it means what it says, it is, scientifically and intellectually speaking, nonsense, or rather, false, untrue, a lie. This dilemma is one that constantly faces us in all our judgements, in our daily life. It is a world of law, of cause and effect, rigid and immovable, for all our cries to Heaven. It is also a world of freedom, unknowable and unpredictable. The moon is a cold, silent, dead mass of stone. But it is

> a globe of dynamic substance coagulated in a vivid pole of energy.
> (*D.H. Lawrence*)

It is no good, we have to make up our minds about it. We must either take what the poets say as truth, or reject it as falsehood and non-vital ornamentation. There are two ways of explaining everything, the intellectual or rational, and the poetic or religious. These run parallel but never meet. Why does New York have sky-scrapers? "Because land space is limited," say the architects. "Because of the desire for infinity," says Spengler. Why do fishes swim in shoals? "Because of the habit engendered by food being in one place," say the ichthyologists.

> A magnetism in the water between them only,

says Lawrence. Why does the river flow? "Because of the slope of the land," say the geologists,

> The river glideth at its own sweet will,

says Wordsworth. What makes the sun and moon shine? The impact of atoms, and reflected light, the physicists say.

If the Sun and Moon should doubt,
They'd immediately go out,

says Blake.

Which of these are we to choose? But this "which of these?" again is an intellectual question, and

The Questioner who sits so sly
Shall never know how to Reply.   (*Blake*)

The poets are right, but the scientists are not wrong.

According to Lawrence, there are two kinds of poetry; indeed, we may say that there are two kinds of art, two ways of living. One is the classical, conventional, conservative, that looks towards the past (still more imaginary) perfection, and towards the future and its (still more imaginary) perfection. Its form is symmetrical, regular and recurrent. The other is that of "free verse," in which

The whole tide of all life and all time suddenly heaves, and appears before us as an apparition, a revelation. . . . There must be mutation, swifter than iridescence, haste, not rest, come-and-go, not fixity, inconclusiveness, immediacy, the quality of life itself, without denouement or close. (*D.H. Lawrence, "Poetry of the Present"*)

To which of these two does haiku belong? Let us take a modern example by Takahama Kyoshi:

Ame ni nure   *hi ni kawakitaru*   *nobori kana*

Wet by the rain,
Dried by the sun—
The banner!

This might be taken, in both the Japanese and the English, as referring to the past. The banner has hung there in rain and sunshine—that is how the poet looks at it, as having within itself all the nights of dew and days of wind. This also is poetry, of the first kind, but it is not the meaning of the haiku, which is much more simple, and yet, not more profound, but more *alive*. A passing shower has just wetted the banner, and the hot, midday, summer sun has dried it again. This is all, but it is also all that God offers, and God never offers less than all. We may say then that haiku also looks before and after, but does not pine for what is not. Lawrence says of Whitman:

The clue to all his utterances lies in the sheer appreciation of the instant moment, life surging itself into utterance at its very well-head. (*"Poetry of the Present"*)

Onitsura says:

A baby at the breast,
Smiling up at the cherry blossoms,
Pointing to the moon.

He means that haiku is to be on the one hand earthy, belonging to our daily life; on the other hand it is celestial, leading the mind out of itself into another world than this. The only poetry which is really satisfying is that which at one and the same time does both. But this "at one and the same time" does not mean doing two things at once; it means—how can one explain it?—it means the state in which a single thing, a stick, a stone, a flower, a toad, is seen as containing the whole universe within it. When we say this, it can be labeled "mysticism"; it can be thought of as something eccentric, aberrant. It refers, however, as pointed out above, to experience which ordinary people are having every day, but do not attend to. It is in this sense also that Yun-men's "Your ordinary mind—that is the Way!" is true. There is a similar contradiction underlying Nietzsche's words:

The more abstract the truth you wish to teach, the more you must allure the senses to it.

In haiku the senses are fully engaged, and there is nothing present but pure sensation, but at the same time, the most "abstract" truth is conveyed, and in an entirely non-intellectual form.

The *means* of English poetry is to a large extent *words*. Robert Bridges speaks, in his essay on the poetry of Keats, of

The power of concentrating all the far-reaching resources of language on one point, so that a single and apparently effortless expression rejoices the aesthetic imagination at the moment when it is most expectant and exacting, and at the same time astonishes the intellect with a new aspect of truth.

In a great a deal of English poetry, words are used rather as ends than as means. In Japanese poetry, waka very often has this quality, but haiku is different. Right at its inception as a popular and independent form of art, Onitsura said,

> The Great Way of Haikai does not consist in perfecting words, nor in learning to make the outward form of verse. It is just our ordinary, every-day mind and spirit, rejoicing on the high plain of Heaven, finding plea-sure in the truth, the reality of clouds, moon and flowers. If you know these spiritual marvels, walking in ecstasy, without a touch of the foot, over the invisible floating Bridge of Dreams will be an everyday thing.

The scope of English verse is (in intention) universal; that of haiku is limited. Vast subjects are rare. Violent passions, dramatic situations, vague fancies and philosophic meditation,—these are almost completely absent. On the other hand, we find many things in haiku which would not be con-sidered as of poetic worth in English verse. This is due to lack of attention to such things on the part of English poets, and to the absence of a tradition which teaches us, beyond our will, to know that poetry is depth.

What haiku has endeavored to do since its beginnings, is not to extend the range of subjects, which was indeed unnecessarily limited by a fixed poetical calendar, but to see the poetry of what is apparently flat and taste-less, to register the most fleeting impressions, to get blood out of a stone. It leaves the pounds to take care of themselves, and concerns itself with the pennies of life. Like practical Christianity, like Zen, haiku finds its significance in the daily round, the common task. It goes directly against the opinion of the critic brought up upon Greek and Roman models. The Western world thinks that there is an objective greatness and grandeur in the external universe and the poet "cannot make an intrinsically inferior action equally delightful with a more excellent one by his treatment of it" (Arnold).

The Eastern world thinks that "Packed in my mind lie all the clothes / Which outward nature wears" (Thoreau, *The Inward Morning*). What this mind sees deeply is profound; slight but unforgettable things have thereby infinite value. Like Chaucer's Parson, it can

In litel thing han suffisance.

One other difference that may be mentioned again is the all-pervasive, imperceptible but invariably present quality of humour in haiku. On the negative side humour is closely allied to brevity; humour has the tendency to shorten our verses; it deletes the bombast; the isolated beautiful phrase finds itself unwanted. On the positive side, it shows us the double, paradoxical nature of things, the meaninglessness of their meaning; it lets us see the pathos of the universe, the dignity and value of scraps of paper and empty tin cans. The seventeen syllables are perhaps themselves a kind of joke; how can a whole world be seen in a drop of ink, or heaven in three lines of verse? To give an example of how subtly revolting and anti-haiku the absence of humour can be, we may quote as the spirit of "impure haiku of the lowest order," the climax of Edward Shanks' *Night-Piece*:

So far ... so low ...
A drowsy thrush? A waking nightingale?
Silence. We do not know.

Japanese people have an instinctive preference for the small and simple as against the large and ornate. This is often attributed to geographical reasons, or lack of material resources, but the preference coincides suspiciously well with the universal aesthetic rule that we should have a minimum of means with a maximum of effect. Internally, it is a kind of streamlining of the mind; externally it appears as brevity and plainness. The brevity of haiku springs from the same (human) nature that Mr. Weller understood so well in regard to writing to a lady:

She'll wish there was more, an' that's the great art o' letter-writing.

Three haiku of Bashō will bring out this tendency:

Haru nare ya   namonaki yama no   asa-gasumi

Yes, spring has come;
This morning a nameless hill
Is shrouded in haze.

Sanjaku no   yama mo arashi no   kono ha kana

Round three-foot mountains also,
Leaves of the trees
Are blown about.

Kiri-shigure   Fuji wo minu hi zo   omoshiroki

A day of misty rain,
Mount Fuji unseen,—
A day of pleasure.

These three all have to do with hills. In the first, it is a mere hill, unnamed and with nothing striking or picturesque about it. The second is a small hump three feet high. The third is Mount Fuji, conspicuous by its very invisibility. Imperfection, asymmetry, even the complete absence of things bring us somehow closer to life than certainty and finality.

This fact was expressed long ago by Yoshida Kenkō, 1288–1350, in his *Tsurezuregusa*, chapter 82:

In general, perfection in anything is bad. To leave something unfinished gives interest, and the "life" of the thing expands.

[The typescript ends here; the remaining text has apparently been lost.]

The Position of Haiku and Senryū in World Literature

This appeared in Contemporary Japan, *vol. 19, 1950.*

PERHAPS THE BEST WAY TO TREAT THIS SUBJECT IS TO SHOW THAT haiku and senryū have elements in common with all the greatest works of world-literature, and that they also have special and unique qualities equivalent in value to those special and unique qualities that make Homer, Dante, and so on, the greatest writers of all time. And last we may refer to those circumstances which have prevented or delayed the recognition of Bashō, Buson, and Issa, and the writers of Old Senryū, as world-figures—in other words, explain why this article requires to be written.

Beginning with Homer, what is memorable in him is not so much the fighting and killing, but a kind of poetical piety, the way in which for example Odysseus bids farewell, in the Thirteenth Book, to Queen Arete:

> "Fare thee well, O queen, throughout all the years, till old age and death come, which are the lot of mortals. As for me, I go my way, but do thou in this house have joy of thy children and thy people and Alcinous, the king." So the goodly Odysseus spake and passed over the threshold.
> (A.T. Murray translation)

There is here a religious solemnity, a freedom from what is trivial and transitory in the very midst of ordinary life, which we feel in the following verse of Bashō, the first in *Oku no Hosomichi:*

(When selling his cottage to a man with several daughters)

> Times change,
> And my grass-thatched hut also,
>   Into a house with dolls.

Or take the following, the grief of a son for his dead mother when he meets her in the other world:

> My mother, why dost thou not stay for me, who am eager to clasp thee, that even in the house of Hades we two may cast our arms each about the other, and take our fill of chill lamenting?
>   [*The Odyssey*, Book 11, Murray translation]

Bashō has far fewer words, but is his grief less poignant, less universal?

> My old home;
> Weeping over the umbilical cord,
>   At the year's end.

This was written in his native place, at the age of forty-five, as he grieved over the physical bond of love which once united him to his mother. Bashō has also another poem of Homeric qualities, pleasure in the plain and elemental things of life:

> Drinking sake
> All the more I could not sleep:
>   Snow falling at night.

It is Bashō's samurai origins which make us feel something Spartan and noble—in a word, Homeric—in this amiable, monk-like, poetic missionary of three hundred years ago.

Coming to the Bible, a religious anthology of a thousand years, history and poetry, law and morals, we cannot help being struck by the difference of the genius of the Japanese and the Jewish peoples. Take the following passage from Psalm 102:

Of old hast thou laid the foundation of the earth: and the heavens are the work of thy hands. They shall perish, but thou shalt endure: yea, all of them shall wax old like a garment; as a vesture shalt thou change them, and they shall be changed: But thou are the same, and thy years shall have no end.

When we compare haiku to this, to Wordsworth's pantheism in *Tintern Abbey,* or to the poetic glories of the Chinese genius Li Po, we find a reticence that has in itself a deep meaning. Such a haiku as the following by Bashō is exceptional:

> A wild winter sea;
> And stretching across to the Isle of Sado,
> The Galaxy.

Japanese people feel, perhaps rightly, that there is something vulgar about the grand in nature. It may be noted here in passing that Japanese poetry is not an abbreviated imitation of Chinese poetry. Their aims and achievements are incommensurate, because entirely different. Both may be called poetry, it is true, but compare the following, by Li Po:

> Tonight I am staying at Feng Ting Temple:
> If I raise my hand I can touch the stars;
> I do not dare speak loudly,
> Lest I disturb the Dwellers of Heaven.

and contrast it with a verse by Issa:

> A day of mist and haze:
> The Dwellers of Heaven
> May well feel bored and listless.

Bashō's religious feelings also find a different expression from the Chinese and the Jewish poets, more earthly, more subdued:

> The leaves of the willow tree falling,
> The master and I
> Listen to the sound of the temple bell.

Even to cherry-blossoms
At their height in this world,
We murmur, "*Namu-amida-butsu!*"

What the Bible says *fortissimo*, with angel-trumpets, haiku says *pianissimo*, on a bamboo flute. St. Paul says in Romans 8, 22:

The whole creation groaneth and travaileth in pain together until now.

Issa says the same thing, but how differently:

For you fleas too,
The night must be long,
It must be lonely.

Senryū is yet more grim, more truly religious in its feeling of the meaninglessness of our lives:

A fat flea:
Crushing it,
It was pregnant.   (*Kenkabō*)

This senryū is one half of the meaning of the Book of Job. God crushes us all, fat or thin, barren or pregnant. "To see the world in a grain of sand" has always been the aim of Japanese culture, and with a rare self-control, the Japanese have kept their eye on the grain of sand, and the "world" which is seen in it is never allowed to be separated from the grain of sand—as indeed it is not and cannot be.

In the following, we have a whole Elizabethan tragedy in seventeen syllables:

He hanged himself
At Ueno
Facing the Yoshiwara.

The violence of tragicomedy here is Hogarthian. To commit suicide is a terrible and ghastly thing, but to do it because of some wretched prostitute is a kind of parody. But the parody also disinfects the scene of all falsity, eternal love and other sentimentality. We see a human being stripped bare of all but his painful life and solitary death. There is also another element (seen in the place of his suicide), of exhibitionism, of which not even the greatest men are free.

Some more senryū which have this concreteness, depth of meaning, and universal validity are the following:

> Worn out with domestic work,
> She looks at her sleeping husband,
>   His bald patch.

It should be noted that in this caricature, it has some sense of tears in it, "the still sad music of humanity"—somewhat out of tune.

> He keeps on flattering
> His wife:
>   She does not smile.

This is one of those frequent and disagreeable episodes between husband and wife, which, accumulating, lessen the sting of death.

Senryū also, in their humourous way, give us the essential nature of things; for example,

> As if after thinking it over,
> A raindrop
>   Falls.

This expresses the apparent hesitation of the raindrop before it falls to the ground.

> The fallen leaves
> Call the sweeper
>   Back again.

In both the above senryū may be seen the strong tendency of senryū toward (conscious) personification. In haiku this is never found, for the simple reason that the life, the existence of every thing in nature is felt in a personal way. The next example is nearer to haiku:

> The stealing cat
> Looks at her steadily,
> And runs away.

The original is more humourous; it says, "looking enough to bore a hole." We see here the real nature of the cat, a wild animal that only pretends to be tame, and to love us, but which lives a purely selfish life, calculating coolly the distance, presence of weapons or missiles, necessity of speed of retreat, and so on.

Senryū is poetry in many ways, and first, it is poetry in reverse, in showing us so clearly what is *not* poetical; yet Shakespeare would have appreciated the following:

> Quite well,
> But his nose
> Has fallen off.

Venereal disease is not commonly accepted as a subject for literature, especially poetry, but it is a disease of the body that has its own secret correspondence with love, which is the health of the soul. When we look at the man's face, we see Venus inside-out, and remember, if we may, that

> Every error is an image of truth.[1]

Second, senryū is poetry in the sense that haiku is, though with different and grosser material. It shows us the essence, the characteristic feature, the symbolic point, the "life" of things and human nature. For example:

> The one who beats the ash-tray
> So harshly,
> Is the master.

Old senryū have a poetry in them which is "far beyond singing." By despising the poetical, by disdaining all its artifices and subterfuges, its half-truths and silent omissions of the poetically intractable, senryū attains a region hardly capable of description in terms of the geography of the mind. It goes down to the dark, secret life of things, the compulsion, the destiny which moves us, from whence come

> Airs, and floating echoes, that convey
> A melancholy into all our day.   (*Arnold*)

To many people, all this may seem too great a claim for these expressions of the *trivia*, these *membra disjecta* of our daily life, but as Blake says, such things are "portions of eternity too great for the eye of man."
One more example of the poetry of senryū:

> A black dog
> As a lantern,
>   Along the snowy road.

On the white landscape, the black dog acts as a lantern does on a dark night. Compare this with lines from a modern English poet, William Davies, speaking of the skylark:

> Day has her star, as well as Night,
> One star is black, the other white.

Coming now to Shakespeare, in the grave-digging scene in *Hamlet*, the knocking at the door in *Macbeth*, we see the destructive elements of nature portrayed, the all-transcending, all-mocking spirit. When King Lear is dying, gazing at the body of his dead daughter, he says in the purest spirit of senryū:

> Pray you, undo this button; Thank you, sir.

Cleopatra, looking at the asp which she has put to her breast, feels the poison working in her veins, and says:

> Dost thou not see my baby at my breast,
> That sucks the nurse asleep?

Shakespeare's contemporary Cervantes created a character, Don Quixote, the secret of whose character is that he lives by Zen, at least in the first part of the book. The lives of Saigyō, Bashō, Ryōkan, Ikkyū, Issa were also as lacking in so-called common sense as that of Don Quixote, but the latter speaks for all of them when he says (Part II, Chap. 17):

Let me tell you that I am not so crazy and half-witted as you take me for.

One of the profoundest sayings of Don Quixote is the following (Part I, Chap. 11):

It may be said of knight-errantry what is said of love, that it makes all things equal.

This is the very work of haiku and senryū, to show that there is nothing high or low, that all is "interesting":

The *uguisu!*
Even before His Lordship,
That same voice!   (*Issa*)

For Bashō and Issa, like Don Quixote, there was but one work to be done, and that was to make common men more imaginative, more poetical, to bring eyes to the blind and ears to the deaf. This missionary spirit infused the haiku poets, and they might say as Don Quixote said, when Sancho told him they were outnumbered two to twenty:

"I am worth a hundred."

The English metaphysical poets of the XVII century have much in common with the earlier *haijin* (haiku poets). Their expression of occult resemblances in things far removed in form and nature from each other finds a parallel in the mysterious relations of things adumbrated in haiku; for example, the following:

At the flower-vase,
The butterfly too seems to be listening
To the One Great Thing.   (*Issa*)

A camellia flower fell;
A cock crew;
Another fell.   (*Baishitsu*)

The temple-bell dies away,
The scent of flowers in the evening
Is still tolling the bell.   (*Bashō*)

Many verses of the period approach senryū in their mocking spirit, for example in Marvell:

The grave's a fine and private place,
But none, I think, do there embrace.

But in the same poem there is a return to the deeper tone of haiku:

But at my back I always hear
Time's winged chariot hurrying near.

Compare this to the verse of Buson:

Slow days passing, accumulating—
How distant they are,
The things of the past!

When we come to the nineteenth-century English poets, to Wordsworth, Shelley and Keats for example, the parallels between haiku and their best lines are striking enough. If we compare the following, we shall be surprised and pleased at the resemblances, and still more surprised and pleased at the shades of differences, the nuances of tone and tempo distinguishable in superficially similar poetical experiences.

I cannot see what flowers are at my feet,
Nor what soft incense hangs upon the boughs.   (*Keats*)

What flowering tree
I know not—
But ah! The scent! (*Bashō*)

The blue deep thou wingest,
And singing still dost soar, and soaring ever singest. (*Shelley*)

The river-boat:
Skylarks rising, singing,
On the right side, on the left side. (*Rankō*)

The temple-bell dies away,
The scent of flowers in the evening
Is still tolling the bell. (*Bashō*)

Over his own sweet voice the Stock-dove broods;
The Jay makes answer as the Magpie chatters;
And all the air is filled with pleasant noise of waters. (*Wordsworth*)

Through the skylark's singing
Comes the beat
Of pheasants' cries. (*Bashō*)

With a full but soft emotion,
Like the swell of Summer's ocean. (*Byron*)

The sea of spring.
Rising and falling,
All the day long. (*Buson*)

Where great whales come sailing by,
Sail and sail, with unshut eye,
Round the world for ever and aye? (*Arnold*)

Flowers of rape;
No whale approaches,
It darkens over the sea. (*Buson*)

With my inward Eye 'tis an old Man grey;
With my outward, a Thistle across my way.   (*Blake*)

   In the flower of *u*
May be seen
   The white hairs of Kanefusa.   (*Sora*)

In this last verse by Bashō's disciple, the white head of Yoshitsune's faithful retainer is seen in the snowy flowers of the *Deutzia scabra*.

It may be interesting to take some haiku and senryū on the New Year, and compare them with English verses on the same subject. When the lunar calendar was in vogue in Japan (that is, from A.D. 604 to 1872), January 1st was what is now about the first week of February. Plum was blooming in sheltered places, and the life of man no less than the life of nature was felt to begin again; it was an annual renaissance. The renewal of life in ourselves is often a seeing of old things in a new light, when the "film of familiarity and selfish solicitude" is somehow taken away. Whitman tells us, in *Crossing Brooklyn Ferry*, how he saw one day that wonder of wonders, common humanity:

   Crowds of men and women attired in the usual costumes, how curious
   you are to me!

Raizen, a poet of the 17th century, has the same experience, but of nature:

   The stream through the fields—
Ah, the sound of the water!
   It is New Year's Day.

So often, however, poets go back to the past on this day which looks to the future. Bashō says:

   The First Day of the Year:
I remember
   A lonely autumn evening.

This resembles lines from a poem by Wordsworth, also written in early spring:

> In that sweet mood when pleasant thoughts
> Bring sad thoughts to the mind.

Fitzgerald says, with the Persian poet:

> Now the New Year, reviving old Desires,
> The thoughtful Soul to Solitude retires.

Chora, in a similar mood, living the life that the English poet speaks of:

> The First Day of the Year:
> I long for the voice of the *uguisu*
> Of past times.

A yet profounder comparison may be made between Matthew Arnold's lines in *Resignation*, when he speaks of the poet as he gazes over the fields in the early morning:

> In his ears
> The murmur of a thousand years;

and the following verse of Onitsura, a contemporary of Bashō:

> The Great Morning;
> Winds of long ago
> Blow through the pine trees.

But the poets go back still farther, on this day, to the most distant times. Moritake, an early haiku poet, says:

> It is New Year's Morning;
> I think also of the Age
> Of the Gods.

This reminds us of Arnold's lines in *The Strayed Reveller*:

The Gods are happy.
They turn on all sides
Their shining eyes;
And see, below them,
The Earth, and men.

Some poets, however, like Issa, live deeply and entirely in this particular day of days; the following verses are by him:

New Year's Day:
What luck! What luck!
A pale blue sky!

My spring too,
What luck! What luck!
The plum blossoms!

These have the spirit of elation expressed in Nash's well-known poem, beginning:

Spring, the sweet spring, is the year's pleasant king.

Though the New Year may seem to be a joyful time for the young only, it has something special for the old, too, that is seen in a verse by Ryōto:

That is good, this is good—
New Year's Day
In my old age.

This is what Wordsworth calls

Years that bring the philosophic mind.

Most senryū on the New Year have a different quality from haiku on this subject. There are verses, nevertheless, in which we feel something similar, for example:

> On New Year's Day
> The dust is picked up,
>   And thrown away.

On New Year's Day, no sweeping or work of any kind was done, so dust and dirt had to be picked up, not swept up. Again, no violent noise or quarreling or weeping was countenanced, and we get the following verse:

> Those who cry
> On New Year's Day
>   Are not yet six years old.

The feeling of such senryū is seen in English poetry in poems concerning Christmas. So Milton in the *Ode on the Morning of Christ's Nativity* speaks of the universal peace that reigned on that day:

> No war or battle sounds
> Was heard the world around;
>   . . .
> The winds with wonder whist,
> Smoothly the waters kist,
> Whispering new joys to the mild Ocean.

But after all, Christmas or New Year's Day, Buddhism or Christianity, the Occident or the Orient—these are all one to the Wisdom and Spirit of the Universe;

> They know not well the subtle ways
> I keep, and pass, and turn again.

Coming now to the reasons for the lack of recognition in other countries of the supreme value of haiku and senryū, this is due to several causes, partly intrinsic and partly psychological and accidental. First there is the apparently excessive brevity by which they isolate to an unparalleled degree a particular group of poetical phenomena. Then there is the suggestiveness which arises from this, through which it reveals the depths of a whole world hidden under a mass of dead material. The use of the season-word in haiku should be noted here as a kind of poetic algebra, and the fact that in one sense the season *is* the subject of the verse. This makes each haiku a much bigger thing than the foreigner would suspect. The faint but all-pervading humour of haiku, and the insistence of senryū upon the humourous nature of reality should be noted also as a very special feature of the two kinds of verse. But what makes haiku distinct from all other forms of literature, Oriental and Occidental, ancient or modern, is its self-annihilative character. When we compose haiku (and the same may be said of senryū) we are to be in a state of *muga* [non-self]; we are ourselves to be nothing, mere instruments of Amida, God, Nature, the Over-Soul—if such things indeed exist. In the same way, the haiku composed is not "a thing of beauty and a joy for ever," but a finger pointing, a hand beckoning, a raft that is not needed once the river of insensitiveness and stupidity is crossed. If, like waka, the haiku has intrinsic charm and value, we may be distracted from the real region of haiku, which is the poetic experience, the mutual life of things.

The great power and merit of haiku and senryū thus being in their leading us away from themselves to the life which gave them birth, above all other forms of art they "catch the winged joy *as it flies*." They aim at the very creative work of God himself, at the Buddha-nature of all things, and in this sense, though there is no word of God or Buddha, Heaven or Hell, they are religious poetry as Dante's *Commedia* and Milton's *Paradise Lost* are not. From this comes the idea of the Way of Haiku, the realization that the real poetry is in our life as we momentarily live it, not in the mere composition of verses.

Lastly we may say that the delay in the recognition of the world-value of haiku and senryū has been also caused by the peculiar attitude of the Japanese people themselves. On the one hand they are (or were) proud of their poetry, and thought it unequaled in world literature. On the other hand, they feel it to be so wonderful that a mere foreigner could never hope to penetrate into its mysterious essence. This is a contradictory but not altogether inexcusable attitude, for they felt, quite rightly, that Japanese culture has something very special about it, but they forgot that this "something special" is not something specially *Japanese*, but specially *human*. They may henceforth be proud of their culture and of themselves, and at the same time with modest confidence expect an increasing number of poetical and enlightened foreigners to agree with them, when they claim that Japan has a poetry inferior to none, and that Japan has done what Bernard Shaw said was the mark of an honest man, put as much into the world as she has taken out of it.

Buddhism and Haiku

Monumenta Nipponica, 7: 1–2 (1951).

IT IS A COMMON IDEA, BOTH AMONG SCHOLARS AND ORDINARY people, that the Japanese were originally a light-hearted, pleasure-loving people, who were changed by the advent of Buddhism into a melancholy, fatalistic, pessimistic and indeed morbid nation. If this was so, it was a heavy price to pay for Japanese culture, which is all Buddhistic, in spirit, if not in form. Compare for example the following, the first a waka from the *Manyōshū*, the second one of the best known of Bashō's haiku, written nine hundred years later:

春すぎて夏来るらし白妙の衣乾したり天の香具山

Spring has passed away
And summer is come:
Look where clothes
Are spread in the sun
On the heavenly hill of Kagu!   (*Manyōshū*)

枯枝に烏のとまりけり秋の暮

On a withered branch
A crow is perched
In the autumn evening.   (*Bashō*)

This crow is sometimes taken as representing Bashō himself; it might be taken as the crow of Buddhism gloomily surveying a world of pain and grief.

I do not understand the matter in this way at all. Buddhism was developed in India as a spiritual philosophy. It passed into China, where it was blended with Chinese practicality, and then, passing through Korea, entered Japan where it was for the first time put into practice in the daily life of the people. This latter of course took a long time, and is the popularization of what began as purely aristocratic pursuits, *chanoyu, ikebana, renku,* etc.

This putting of the principles of Mahayana Buddhism into practice in eating and drinking, in walking, and talking, is in evidence, indirect, but all the more conclusive, of the fact that the Japanese people were Buddhists before Buddhism ever came to Japan.

They took to Buddhism "as a duck takes to water." The duck is not converted to the water; it is a *water-bird.* To illustrate what I mean clearly, I will take an example from my own experience, not unrelated to Buddhism. When I was eighteen years old, one day a man said to me, "Do you eat meat?" "Yes, of course," I replied. "Don't you know that you can live quite healthily without having animals killed for you to eat?" he asked. "Why, yes, I suppose so . . ." I mumbled,—and from that day to this I have never eaten any meat or fish. It is quite clear from this anecdote that I was a vegetarian before the man asked me these two simple questions, that I was a born vegetarian, or to express it in the language of Zen, in a transcendental way, I was a vegetarian *before* I was born, beyond time. In the same way I mean that the Japanese were Buddhists. For that reason Buddhism still exists in Japan, and not in the country of its origin. The Japanese are Buddhists in the same sense that they are Japanese.

If what I have said is true, the description of "a Buddhist" and that of "a Japanese" should more or less coincide, and I propose to try to show that this is so. Many people may object to this from the outset, as being too complimentary to the Japanese, but a true Buddhist could not do so because according to Buddhism *every* man is at bottom a Buddhist. Again, it may be urged that to describe the nature of Buddhism may be fairly easy, but to give an account of the characteristics of a typical and representative Japanese is extremely difficult. This is so, and I think it will therefore be advisable to limit the description of the Japanese culture, and indeed to one aspect of it, namely haiku. I hold haiku to be the flower and culmination of all Eastern culture, and that it occupies the same position in one half of the world as Homer, Dante, Shakespeare or Goethe do in the other half of the world. Let us look then at Buddhism and haiku, taking haiku as representing the national character of the Japanese as expressed in 17 syllables.

1. Just as Buddhism in India took over a great mass of pre-Buddhistic experience and philosophy, so Buddhism in Japan absorbed much that existed in Japan prior to the sixth century. Such haiku as the following show the primitive Japanese animism which was a kind of spiritual democracy in which animals on the one hand and the gods on the other were conceived in a human way, and as lying close above and close below human beings.

留守の間にあれたる神の落葉かな

    The god is absent;
Dead leaves are piling,
    And all is deserted.   (*Bashō*)

The god has gone to Izumo for the yearly meeting, and the shrine has a deserted air, dead leaves remaining unswept.

さまづけに育てられたる蚕かな

    Bringing up the silkworms
They call them
    "Mister."   (Issa)

The word ""sama"" ["Mister"] implies some gentle, pious, familiar attitude to the silkworm.

2. The feeling of the transitoriness of life is found everywhere in the world. Buddhism gave a variety of means for its expression. In the following verse, Bashō tell us, indirectly, that human life is unreal with nothing permanent in it.

たこ壷やはかなき夢を夏の月

The octopuses in the jars:
Transient dreams
    Under the summer moon.   (*Bashō*)

3. Selflessness is the essence of Buddhism, as it was of the Japanese artist. It was the good element in Emperor worship. One of the most interesting examples of this selflessness in haiku derives not from Buddhism but rather from Taoism. Wafū (和風) says:

蝶消えて魂我に返りけり

The butterfly having disappeared,
My spirit
    Came back to me.   (*Wafū*)

A few days before his death, Bashō composed the following, lying in bed:

秋深き隣は何をする人ぞ

It is deep autumn:
My neighbor—
    How does he live, I wonder?

How is he passing through this world, Bashō wonders. There is the same interest in the world of trees:

五六木よりてしだるる柳かな

Five or six,
Drooping down together,—
    Willow trees.   (*Bashō*)

4. Loneliness may be thought a specially Japanese quality rather than a Buddhist, but compare the following passages from the *Zenrinkushū*:

兀然無事坐　　春来草自生
樹密猿声響　　波澄雁影深

Sitting quietly doing nothing,
Spring comes, grass grows of itself.

The cries of the monkeys echo through the dense forest;
In the clear water, the wild geese are mirrored deep.

Bashō is the master of the loneliness of nature and man suffused with each other:

うき我や淋しがらせよかんこ鳥

Ah, *kankodori*,[1]
Deepen thou
　　My loneliness.　　　　　　　　　　　　　　　　　　　(*Bashō*)

The loneliness of Buson is that of Nature alone:

葉の花を鯨もよらず海くれぬ

Flowers of rape:
No whale approaches:
　　It darkens over the sea.　　　　　　　　　　　　　　(*Buson*)

The loneliness of Issa is that of Bashō, but with less of nature and more of man:

苦の姿婆や桜が咲けばさいたとて

A world of grief and pain:
Flowers bloom:
　　Even then. . . .　　　　　　　　　　　　　　　　　　(*Issa*)

The loneliness of Shiki is that of Buson, more inclusive but with less serenity:

梨さくやいくさの後の崩れ家

> By a house collapsed,
> A pear tree is blooming;
> Here a battle was fought. (*Shiki*)

5. Buddhism is often considered fatalistic and lacking in a positive spirit, but the grateful acceptance of whatever happens means cooperating actively with life as it moves towards its far-off and unknown goal. Buson has a verse expressive of his complete and life-long acceptance of destiny:

西咲けばひがしにたまる落葉かな

> Blowing from the west,
> Fallen leaves gather
> In the east. (*Buson*)

Ryōkan has a more tragic verse:

たふるればたふるるままの庭の草

> The grasses of the garden—
> They fall,
> And lie as they fall (*Ryōkan*)

There are two verses by Issa which show the interrelation of man and nature in daily life:

山水に米をつかせて昼寝かな

> I take a nap,
> Making the mountain water
> Pound the rice. (*Issa*)

Issa makes the mountain water pound the rice while he is asleep.

扇にて尺をとらせる牡丹かな

> The peony
> Made me measure it
> With my fan.   (*Issa*)

The peony makes Issa measure it with the fan he carries.

6. In India Buddhism seems to have been a highly philosophical thing, and this tendency increased in China, but at the same time there was an opposite tendency, culminating in Zen and Jōdo, towards simplicity and non-intellectuality. There is a verse by Ryōta which illustrates this:

ものいわず客と亭主と白菊と

> They spoke no word,
> The visitor, the host,
> And the white chrysanthemum.   (*Ryōta*)

7. Mahayana Buddhism is essentially paradoxical, and the great merit of the Japanese people was their realization (making real) once more in daily life of these contradictions which once, far away and long ago, were derived from practical life in Buddhist and pre-Buddhist India. The best, or at least the clearest and most concrete example of this in Japanese culture is that of the movements of *waki* and *shite* in Nō, and those of the Tea Master, for all their walking is a no-walking. They

入林不動草、
入水不立波

> Entering the forest, do not disturb a blade of grass;
> Entering the water, do not cause a ripple.   (*Zenrinkushū*)

Issa feels strongly the contradiction between mind and body, absolute and relative, ideal and real:

柴の戸や錠の代わりにかたつむり

    A brushwood gate;
For a lock,
    This snail.   *(Issa)*

Compare also the following by Dansui (團水):

御幸にも編笠ねがぬ案山子かな

    Even before His Majesty
The scarecrow does not remove
    His plaited hat.

8. One of the criticisms made of the Japanese is that they have never fought for and obtained freedom, especially political and social freedom. Some people connect this fact with their being Buddhists. It this is so, it does not conflict with my present thesis, namely, that Japanese are Buddhists by nature, that their Buddhism springs from within and is not something which changed them from without. Freedom is, however, a very elusive thing; it is almost synonymous with life itself, and may and does exist apart from its (proper) social expression. Indeed, it is something in the nature of the Japanese character, to be subservient, even servile to authority, to rush from one extreme to another of fashion and philosophy, and yet at the same time to preserve some kind of inner, secret life that shows itself only in the arrangement of some branches in the *tokonoma*, or in the veiled criticism and humour of senryū. The freedom of haiku comes out in many odd ways. For example, there is the freedom from what is usually considered dirty or unseemly.

秋の夜や夢と鼾ときりぎりす

    An autumn night;
Dreams, snores,
    The chirping of crickets.   *(Suiō)*

I think it would be difficult to find any serious poem in English in which snores were introduced.

夕顔の花で洟かむ娘かな

> The young girl
> Blew her nose
> In the evening-glory.

(Issa)

鶯が梅の小枝に糞をして

> The uguisu
> Poops
> On the slender plum branch.

(Onitsura)

9. Japanese people are often said to be deficient in a "sense of sin." Most Japanese will admit this to be so, and they do not seem very ashamed of this either. Primitive Buddhism and the Hinayana insist strongly upon the importance of morality, but the Mahayana is transcendental in its attitude to everything and indeed the difference between morality and religion lies simply in this fact, that morality is relative, things are good and bad; but religion is "beyond good and evil." So in haiku we have such verses as the following:

犬を打つ石のさてなし冬の月

> Not a single stone
> To throw at the dog,—
> The wintry moon.

(Taigi)

凩や二十四文の遊女子屋

> The autumn storm:
> A prostitute shack,
> At 24 cents a time.

(Issa)

10. This mark of a man of false, pretended culture is that he is subtle concerning matters to which he should have an attitude of simplicity. Eckhart, the great German mystic, says:

What God loves, that is: what God loves not, that is not.

When we read this we are not to try to define God, or love, or existence but take the simple statement in its deepest but simple meaning. Bashō's verse is to be taken in the same way:

道のべの木槿は馬にくわれけり

    The Rose of Sharon
By the roadside,
    Was eaten by my horse.

Issa has a similar but more subjective verse:

うまさうな雪がふうわりふうわりと

    I could eat it!—
This snow that falls
    So softly, so softly.

This simplicity is something special and native to the Japanese. It is seen clearly in Shinto, but also in Buddhism:

出門逢釈迦
入門逢弥勒

青山自青山
白雲自白雲

Go out, and you meet Shakamuni;
Go home, and you meet Miroku Buddha.

The blue hills are of themselves blue hills;
The white clouds are of themselves white clouds. (*Zenrinkushū*)

11. The love of Buddhism and the love of Christianity are somewhat different. The love of Buddhism is selfless, not so passionate. It is closely associated with the *sabishisa* [loneliness] that takes away some of the energy and activity and gives it a somewhat detached, contemplative, pitying character. Christianity is love of God; Buddhism is love of the Universe, of the Devil as well as God, of *nankinmushi* [bedbugs] and crocodiles as well as flowers and nightingales. Love begins, as always, at home.

渋いこと母が喰ひけり山の柿

Mountain persimmons;
The mother is eating
The astringent parts. (*Issa*)

But in Issa this love goes out to all things, yet includes himself as well, for Issa rightly counts himself among the pathetic creatures struggling in this world.

The following is perhaps the most Buddhist verse ever written. It is by Issa, the most Japanese of all the Japanese who ever lived. And here Buddhism shows us the real nature of man, just as the most Japanese of men is the most human. When the last human being has disappeared from the world, the following verse should remain engraved on a shaft of bronze, a testimony to the greatness and weakness of mankind:

蚤どもも夜永だらうぞ淋しかろ

For you fleas too,
The night must be long,
It must be lonely. (*Issa*)

Buddhist Sermons
on Christian Texts

*This book, published in 1952 by Kokudosha in Tokyo, has largely
escaped the notice of Western readers. Blyth decided to revise it in
his final years and add it as a volume in the* Zen and Zen Classics
*series. The abbreviated version given here includes about one-third
of the original text. Blyth, from a Nonconformist background,
attended Bible study classes from an early age and knew a good deal
of the Bible by heart. The passages he quotes here cannot always be
traced to any known version of the Bible. He may, in such cases, be
quoting from memory or improving on existing translations.*

INTRODUCTION

One of the chief reasons why it is necessary to interpret Christian intuitions
by Mahayana concepts, and not *vice-versa*, is that Buddhism, in China and
Japan, has realized how inexpressible, how crude, how treacherous words
are. We may lay side by side utterances from the Bible and from the Sutras,
and see the identity of experience that originated them. But formally, ver-
bally, they may involve contradictions of an apparently clear-cut, logical
nature. Only a mind free from this intellectual bondage, yet exactly con-
scious of what it is doing in overstepping the laws of thought, is capable of
holding fast to conflicting facts, of grasping the inner essence of a paradox
without making the fatal attempt to "vocabularize" the so-called "truth"
that reconciles the contradiction. The mistake which so many sages have
made, the illusion which Zen alone is ever on guard against, is that of sup-
posing that there is such a thing as error as opposed to truth. Even in the
above sentence, this same mistake is apparently made, yet only apparently,

for it is impossible in words, as opposed to experience, to avoid making the mistake as we warn ourselves against it. The moon must be pointed at; the finger is inevitable, and consequently the mistaking of it for the moon itself.

In regard to words, we go through three stages. First, words and facts are presumed to correspond. But once expressed, the truth seems somehow dead, unmoving, and we enter the second, in which our minds leap out beyond the words into another realm, wordless but not silent. Last of all, the words themselves once more regain their value and power. We recognize the life that is in the words, the significance that the finger itself has apart from its pointing at the moon.

The same thing applies when we compare the anthropomorphism and symbolism of Christianity with the airy transparency, not to say elusiveness of Zen. Once we have "seen though" such things as the transcendence of the Deity, the contradictions of the Trinity, the fall of Adam and his redemption by Christ, we can perceive their own intrinsic value. In Buddhism too, of course, we have a pantheon of gods, the mystic Kannon and the symbolical Fudō, but these do not come home to our business and bosoms as do the Ancient Worthies of the Old Testament and the miraculous elements of the New.

The progress of religious thought in Christianity and Buddhism has been from one point of view entirely opposite. Indian spirituality and hyperbole was modified by Chinese and Japanese practicality. Jewish warmth and earthiness was influenced by Greek clarity and abstraction. In fact Greek culture has proved a mixed blessing to Europe. Abstract concepts have been the most useful and at the same time the most dangerous of all human inventions.

The only power which can perceive the essential that lies beneath these diverse elements of coarseness and subtlety, personalization and etheriality is that of poetry, but abstractions are also necessary, otherwise we are apt to miss in not expressing it, what unifies all the diverse phenomena. We must avoid the two extremes of the merely "poetical" life of registering movements of vision as they come and go, and the merely "religious" life of other-worldly contemplation. We must live in the true poetical-religious life in which we not only mark the flashes of insight but endeavor to perpetuate and increase them; we strive to make every action, to see everything suffered or done as significant, not only to ourselves but to the flow of life in the world. In Christian language, our daily, hourly life is to mean something to ourselves and to God. We are to share with Him in the task of sweeping rooms and breaking bread, doing for Him what could not be done without us, for in us He moves and lives and has His being.

The title of the present book is interesting, but rather misleading, because the texts are not interpreted according to orthodox Buddhist doctrines (whatever they may be), but according to the principle laid down by Emerson in *Self-Reliance*:

> Speak what you think now in hard words and tomorrow speak what tomorrow thinks in hard words again, though it contradicts everything you said today.

SERMONS

Blessed are they that mourn, for they shall be comforted.
Matthew 5:4

If life is a good thing, if it is better that the universe exist rather than not, (and this is the whole problem and the only problem), mourning is good, rejoicing, its inevitable counterpart, is good. If there is rejoicing, there is mourning; if there is mourning, there is rejoicing. When we take the individual case, a certain person, in that place, at that point of time, the mother with her dead child, nothing is clear, all is dark, and silence and tears are our only offering. But when we look over vast tracts of time and place there is a painful sense of meaning, that is, of Comfort in the absolute sense. However slight it may be, it is this realization that enables us to continue living.

Blessed are the merciful, for they shall obtain mercy.
Matthew V, 7

If you are merciful to a tiger, the tiger will be merciful to you. How will the tiger be merciful?—But first of all, how will you be merciful to the tiger? By willing it to be what it is, acting as it does, according to its Buddha-nature, in running after you so gracefully. You with your Buddha-nature run away from it as fast as you can, not quite so gracefully. How do you obtain mercy? When the tiger pounces on you and eats you up, you are eaten alive, obeying Virgil's command, *Inferno, V, 22–4*:

> *Non impedir lo suo fatale andare;*
> *Vuolsi cosi cola, dove si puote*
> *Cio che si vuole, e piu non dimandare*

> Impede not his fatal coming:
> Thus it is wished where he can perform
> That which is wished; and ask no further.

("His" is the tiger's, in a limited sense, but really refers to the Buddha.) Part of our Buddha-nature is our eatableness-by-a-tiger. Towards the potential or actual eater in time and space we are to have mercy, and we shall infallibly and instantaneously receive mercy. Then we can say with Christ:

> No tiger taketh my life from me; I lay it down of myself.
> *John X, 18*

Thou shalt worship no other God: for the Lord, whose name is
    jealous, is a jealous God.
Exodus 34:14

In Zen this is expressed quite otherwise:

纔有是非粉然失心

> If there is the slightest trace of this and that
> The Mind is lost in a maze of complexity.   (*Hsinhsin-ming*)

But the more the expression changes, the more the meaning remains the same, or rather, the more vivid and alive it is. If the word "jealous" seems more of a hindrance than a help, consider fire and ice; these are jealous and merciless things. The "maze of complexity" is polytheism.

Looking for that blessed hope and the glorious appearing
of the great God and our Saviour Jesus Christ.
Titus II:13

Ultimate ends are always preposterous, whether it is the Western Para-
dise, or the golden streets of Heaven, or the Buddhas on their Lotuses,
Perfection and Bliss, universal attainment of Buddhahood,—what a ter-
rible prospect! And yet it is this very prospect that keeps the whole thing
going. In fact the "going" is this movement from one blank, void inanity
to another. Under the category of time, therefore, without which we are
incapable of thinking, nothing is comprehensible, all is paradoxical. Reli-
gion, morality, progress, all destroy themselves in their consummation.
Not only eternity, but thought itself can "tease us out of thought," and
this glorious hope of salvation is seen as an illusion even by the temporal
eye. So we say,

My thoughts are not your thoughts, neither are your ways my ways.
Isaiah LV:8

The truth is that it is not the "far-off divine event" (which will never come,
for the far can never be near), but the looking which matters, which alone
matters, a looking which is now and here, that is, timeless and placeless,
though its object may be past, present, or future, in one place or another,
according to the character or mood of him who looks. This "looking" is
the glorious appearing. He who looks sees God; God sees in him. This is
Buddhahood, for with a look we are saved, lost again in a moment when
we cease from looking at that which is non-existent, never-to-be-attained.

Without faith it is impossible to please God.
Hebrews XI, 16

Faith means the courage to gamble and the strength to fail in staking your
comfort and happiness, such as it is, upon the possibility of attaining heaven
here and now. Life is one fear after another. To gain peace of mind, the pearl
of great price, we must get rid of every wish and will for even life itself. Thus
only can we please the divinity within and without us. When we say, "to

please God," we are saying something most profound in (scientifically) inadequate and (to the unpoetic mind) misleading words. Milton says,

> Silence was pleased,

and if you understand this, you understand Paul's words. If you do not, no one can explain either to you.

Whatsoever thy hand findeth to do, do it with all thy might.
Ecclesiastes IX,10

"To do" includes also what is more difficult, "to be done to." To accept, with all one's might, all that happens, to be silent and inactive, to be the servant and stand and wait,—when this is done properly we have the highest form of activity.

行亦禅坐亦禅　語默動静體安然

> Walking is Zen, sitting is Zen; whether speaking or silent, moving or
>   quiescent, the Real Self is at peace.   (*Cheng-tao ke*)

Doing nothing at all with all our might, busied about many things, yet knowing that they are of no importance whatever,—this is the immovable wisdom, 不動智.

For God so loved the world that He gave His only-begotten Son, that whosoever believeth in Him should not perish, but have everlasting life.
John III, 16

God so loved the world.

Everything in the world loves itself and every other thing. The love of some things is so violent, like that of Othello, or so subtle, like that of Iago, that it needs great courage to perceive it. But it is the same everywhere, the stream that laps the sand-banks, the axe that makes the oak shudder, the shadow that loves us and will not let us go,—all these feel the love of

God for each other, an attraction that works through repulsion, that kills everything it makes alive, whose only law is perfect freedom, and whose one steadfast and immutable principle is change. Mother and child, murderer and murderee, the ice of winter and warm spring winds, the yeast and the flour, the bullet and the lungs, Christ and the Pharisees,—if we do not see these things as the love of God, how shall we love God or be loved of Him?

That he gave his only-begotten Son.

God gives himself completely to us, to all things, though He is not received by all equally. In every flower, in every dust-filled corner of neglected closets, He is the only begotten Son, born again and again,

that the Universe may for ever renew its youth. (Marcus Aurelius 7:25)

Nothing is hidden, nothing is revealed. When we see the autumn moon, when we hear the words

Let him deny himself, take up his cross and follow me,

Matthew XVI, 24

we know ourselves, we shine with the moon and stagger with the Saviour. In this, the Son is given. It is love that makes the world go round, but it is the knowing of it, love in its self-consciousness that is the giving of the Son by the Father, the *Will* in the love that makes it really human at last.

That whosoever believeth in him.

God gives you this table, this unique, never-to-be-repeated, only-begotten table; do you *believe* in it? Do you believe it has four legs and an oblong top, that it supports your elbows, that it will float on water and burn you alive, that it will stand imperturbable while love and hate, wisdom and folly flow round it? Do you *believe* all this, or do you only think it, suppose it, agree indifferently to it?

Should not perish, but have everlasting life.

The days and hours, above all, the moments we waste in time, when we might be living in eternal, timeless time!

He that believeth in the Son of God hath the testimony
of God in himself.

1 John V, 10

Whether it be the Brandenburg Concertos or the Essays of Emerson, the
death of Socrates or the landscapes of Sesshū, we know it without any
proof, without any evidence, for the expression is not different from it, and
is identical with ourselves. It is thus clearer than our own existence, closer
than any physical sensation.

I am the Vine, ye are the Branches.

John XV, 5

No analogy surpasses this. I am the whole, you are the parts. The "I" is as
personal as the "Ye"; the "Ye" is as soul-less and devoid of ego as the "I". If
we go farther and speak of the stem, the roots, the flowers and fruit, every-
thing is spoiled, and from the realm of the organic we have descended to
that of the mechanical.

I beseech Thee, show me Thy glory. And He said, Thou canst not
see My Face: for there shall no Man see me, and live.

Exodus XXXIII, 18

A sword cannot cut itself, an eye cannot see itself. No one can know what
life is; it is a mystery of mysteries.

> No man hath seen God at any time.
>
> *John 1, 18*

But this is only because we think about it. Cut off all intellection as intellec-
tion; only live fully, and,

> The only begotten Son, which is in the bosom of the Father, he hath
> declared Him.
>
> *John 1, 18*

We shall be like Him; for we shall see Him as He is.

1 John III, 2

Every eye shall see Him.

Revelation 1, 7

Life is known by living it.

Fear not, for I have redeemed thee.
Isaiah XLIII, 1

What is it that we fear, or rather, what is it that we do not fear? Suffering that teaches us, the death of loved ones that matures us, our own death that perfects and completes what was once begun. Who or what can redeem us, give us back our native innocence, the time when we looked neither before nor after, when we did not pine for the impossible?

We can lose our fear only if we feel deeply that the universe within and without us loves us deeply, not shallowly and sentimentally, not us as us, but us as branches of the vine, as leaves and blossoms that the wind loves to sweep away, that the waters love to engulf and the mountains to overwhelm. This is the love we are to have towards God, and he will love us exactly in the proportion that we love him, and with the same quality. In Christ, the young hero, we catch a glimpse of this fearlessness which is one with love as an eager, self-abandoning, self-giving joy. But the last word is not with the New Testament, but with the Old:

Though He slay me, yet will l trust Him.

Job XIII, 15

The meek will He guide in judgement.
Psalm XXV, 9

Pride cannot co-exist with a realization of the impermanence of all things, in the sense that our self is deeply felt and experienced as a non-ego, a nothing. Pride is the one and only deadly sin, in that it sets up a hard, dead, unchanging core of self-existence in a world whose nature is fluid and yielding where it seems most fixed and immovable. Meekness is the essence of the iron that strikes, the flint that is struck, the spark that rises upwards. Meek in denunciation, gentle in refusal, mild in condemnation,—and we manifest clearly Whose judgement it is with which we judge.

Teach me the way, O Lord.
Psalm XXVII, 11

This is the only kind of prayer permissible. Even the "Lord's Prayer," with its modest request for the necessities of life, still looks towards the dubitable future and seeks to influence what is within the power of accident. This is a part of legitimate human hope rather than of prayer, but "Teach me the way" is a prayer for bread which teaches us the Way, and it is a prayer for no bread which no less teaches us the Way.

The end of all things is at hand.
1 Peter IV, 7

It is not only at hand, but present with us at this moment. The world is now being created, in every bud and blossom; Christ is being born again in every heart. Life goes smoothly on, and miracles are done. Death and destruction overshadow all things, and the whole creation is crucified while we draw a single breath. This does not mean that among the myriad things of the universe some are being born and some are dying. It means that each thing dies as it is born, dies to be reborn, at every moment and in every place.

In my flesh shall I see God.
Job XIX, 26

We have five senses, and they are "given us" to perceive God with. We have also a brain; what is this for? It is to *know* that we perceive God through the five senses. In the Communion, God is eaten and drunk. Issa says:

涼しさやここ極楽の這入口

> This coolness!
> It is the entrance
> To Paradise!

Who shall separate us from the love of Christ?
Romans 8, 35

This is such a platitude and yet so profound, so obvious and yet so little believed, that one hardly knows what to say about it. What can separate us from the love of Christ? All that we think and feel and do is the life of Christ, and He is love. All our sin, our fancied isolation, both through the eye and through the mind, is his vision and our delight. The love of Christ is so much closer than any of us suppose. He is not behind nature egging it on to manifest himself but before it leading us into it. Because of his love of us, he himself makes himself nothing, that we may be everything. But this "love" includes death and disease, heartbreak and madness. This is the "love that will not let me go."

We love Him because He first loved us.
1 John IV, 19

Ikkyū has a somewhat similar thought:

本来の面目坊が立姿　　ひとめ目しより恋とこそなれ

The figure of the Real Man
　　Standing there,—
Just a glimpse of him,
　　And we are in love!

Paul finds Christ as personal as we are: Ikkyū finds the Buddha no more personal than we. In Paul the idea of reciprocity is somewhat astonishingly expressed, but Paul was, after all, a poet. In Ikkyū the words are shallower and more fanciful, because the idea is too profound for expression, since the love is in reality, as Coventry Patmore says, "A female vanity," a kind of self-love, or rather, Self-Love, that is felt in the self.

Consider the lilies of the field, how they grow.
Matthew VI, 28

"Consider," "grow," are the two poles of thought in this verse. "Consider" can mean "just look at" as Peter Bell did at the primrose. It can mean "think about" as a botanist or as a moralist. It can mean "feel about," overlay with various emotions. It can and should mean *interpenetrate*, so that their life and ours is indistinguishable. The lilies look and think and feel, —but as flowers would if they could. We bloom with sincere colour, and are still yet aspiring. We grow and the lilies consider,—so we say, but there are no such things as poles or axes, only the turning of the earth in infinite space.

The foxes have holes, and the birds of the air have nests,
    but the Son of Man hath not where to lay his head.
Matthew VIII, 20

Not a doctrine that can be asserted, not a principle to live by, no man to reverence or God to adore. Adrift on the ocean of life for a few years, then darkness and silence. Even the pillow we lay our heads on is swiftly falling to dust, the head itself wrinkling and decaying in the most peaceful slumber. This is so, and it is good so. Our souls are not ours, let alone our heads. We own nothing, there is nothing to own and nobody to own it, and when we realize this, not as a doctrine but in all our *instinctive* activities, we have our hole, our nest; our headlessness is laid to rest on that non-existent pillow. Only when this is so can we understand Paul's words in their real meaning:

> All things are yours; whether Paul, or Apollos, or Cephas, or the world, or life, or death, or things present, or things to come; all are yours; and ye are Christ's; and Christ is God's.
>
>   *1 Corinthians III, 22–23*

What need then have we of beliefs, of friends or a friendly universe?

Peter followed Him afar off.
Matthew XXVI, 58

This is what we all do, and it is not altogether reprehensible, because it is human nature to avoid suffering, to avoid the truth itself when, as usual, it is painful. This "human nature," which is made the fatal objection to socialism and every idealistic system, is also the great objection to Christianity and Buddhism. How to be both blessed and happy is what nobody can tell us.

My strength is made perfect in weakness.
2 Corinthians XII, 9

Imperfection has in it a deeper meaning than perfection, growth than matu-
rity, because it has movement, movement towards some end that is never
attained, but always will be, shall be. The very name "Unfinished Sym-
phony" endues it with a secret power more subtle than the symmetry and
finality of perfect masterpieces. The willful irregularities of Korean pottery,
the asymmetry of Japanese flower arrangements, the blank space of Chi-
nese landscapes, the brevity of haiku, and the ellipses of poetical language
generally, illustrate the principle that each thing is capable to every possible
use, may be an instrument of life or death, goodness or badness, is itself All
Things. Thus its relativity is the only guarantee of its absoluteness; its finite-
ness and evanescence are essential for its infinity and eternity.

Whatsoever things are true . . . think on these things.
Philippians IV, 8

Why? Because

> such as are thy habitual thoughts, such also will be the habitual charac-
> ter of thy mind; for the soul is dyed by the thoughts.
>
> *Marcus Aurelius*

And what are these eternal principles, indubitable truths of universal valid-
ity? There is only one, and that is that there are none. But *things* are true,
true to themselves and us. Let them go their way. Go with them on the Way.
Your own body for example, with all its functions of so-called honor and
dishonor; St. Theresa says:

> Christ has no body on earth but yours, no feet but yours; yours are the
> eyes through which to look out Christ's compassion to the world, yours
> are the feet with which He is to go about doing good, and yours are the
> hands with which He is to bless us now.

Everything is full of blessings. Think on everything, and thus will our souls
be dyed with things, with all things, with truth.

If we suffer with Him, we shall also reign with Him.

2 Timothy II, 12

Suffering and reigning seem such different things that when we say that they are one thing, and that one without the other is impossible, we are saying something fanciful and paradoxical. In the realm of the intellect, we assert and understand,

> Better to reign in Hell than serve in Heaven

but in the realm of poetry we know something that cannot be said or understood, that losing is winning, that endurance is power, that in so far as we share in the suffering of Christ, we share in his conquest of suffering; his submission to destiny, and its consequent subjugation; his doing the will of God, and his unity with the Godhead; his suffering in time, and timeless reign.

Mortify . . . your members.

Colossians III, 5

Even monkeys over-eat, eschew vitamins and mineral salts, pick out the crumb and leave the crust. This is due to a greediness so deep and ancient that it must be something good, something Good. Excess is often not so much for the pleasure proposed as to get rid of the pain of desire. But to escape from the power of things, is to give up the things themselves, to cease living, for just as

> Without human beings there are no Buddhas,
>
> *Platform Sutra*

so without things there are no human beings, for these three are one. Further, since

> We are members one of another,
>
> *Ephesians IV, 25*

if we mortify our members we are killing other creatures and ourselves in the bargain. Thus here as on every subject, reason leads us to dilemma and contradiction that only life can and does solve, the golden mean where both mortification and self-indulgence are laid aside and forgotten.

My God, my God, why hast Thou forsaken me?
Matthew XXVII, 46

The greatest poet, the greatest moral teacher and religious teacher is dying the death for crimes against God and man. He is dying alone; his words will be forgotten; his followers, dispersed and disillusioned, are in any case ununderstanding, and what is worse, misunderstanding. The world is dark with false ignorance and useless knowledge, and the Light of the World is being extinguished. Christ could not realize that though God had forsaken him, Chance had not, that his life and its teaching would live on because of the very stupidity and weakness of his disciples. And had the authorities rounded up the few cowards that were hiding in their homes, Europe would now be either Mohammedan or Buddhist.

Behold, I stand at the door and knock; if any man hear my voice, and open the door, I will come in to him, and will sup with him, and he with me.
Revelation II, 20

This is the kind of ghost story or detective problem, for he that knocks without is already within, and though the room is empty, there is a feasting going on, for the clatter of dishes and smacking of lips is clearly audible in the 48 Preludes and Fugues and the symphonies of Mozart.

Beloved, let us love one another: for love is of God; and every one that loveth is born of God, and knoweth God.
1 John IV, 7

Buddhism fears above all things attachment, but Christianity, much more profoundly, is afraid only of weakness of attachment. Hamlet and Othello are great, because of the depth and persistence of their attachment. The alleged object of attachment is indifferent, whether it is Mrs. Gamp's gin bottle, or "the disciple whom Jesus loved."

The time is short: it remaineth, that both they that have wives be as
though they had none; and they that weep, as though they wept
not; and they that rejoice, as though they rejoiced not; and they
that buy, as though they possessed not; and they that use this
world, as not abusing it: for the fashion of this world passeth away.
1 Corinthians 7, 29–31

In the *Diamond Sutra*, we read:

"Subutai, what think you? Is the Nyorai [Tathagata] to be seen as a body-
form or not?" "No, World-honored One, the Nyorai is not to be seen as a
body-form. Why is this? Because according to the teaching of the Nyorai,
body-form is a non-body-form." The Buddha said to Subutai, "All form is
illusion. If all form is seen as no-form, the Nyorai will be seen."

When we know that "the time is short," when death is imminent, a matter of
moments, we marry, we laugh and cry, we purchase things and go about our
daily life just as others do, but as though we did none of these things, not in
a dream, but realizing (that is, doing everything in such a way) that the doer
and the done are not divided into this and that, I and the action, you and I,
short and long, today and tomorrow.

First the blade, then the ear, after that the full corn in the ear.
Mark IV, 28

It is precisely those things which are most logical, most purely cause-and-
effect, most scientific, which are most miraculous, because we can never
know why this particular cause has this particular effect, why the mind sees
the things in this order and relation, and no other. All we know is that there
is an exquisite satisfaction in it. Buson says:

白露やいばらのとげに一つづつ

White dew
On the bramble,
A drop on each thorn.

Religion and science are for the moment united.

The Lord God Omnipotent reigneth.
Revelation XIX, 6

When I was young, it was not uncommon, in the religious circles I was compelled to frequent, to debate the question whether God could tell a lie. If he could, he was not all-good; if he could not, he was not all-powerful—this was the dilemma. The fact remains, however, as St. John remarks, that the Lord God Omnipotent reigneth, and we are all his obedient or (apparently) disobedient subjects. Somehow or other, God's will is done at all times and in all places.

Though we feel something of the old tribal fear expressed in the words of our text, we turn with relief to an omnipotence of a different character, such as that in the following lines from Emerson's *Worship*:

> This is he, who, felled by foes,
> Sprung harmless up, refreshed by blows.

> This is Jove, who, deaf to prayers,
> Floods with blessings unawares.

He that keepeth thee will not slumber.
Psalm CXXI, 3

See how the toast burns when you forget it; how the clock stops when you don't wind it up. All is change and decay, nothing is constant; but there is "something" that never sleeps, that is immortal and omnipotent. It is beyond all conception, all expression, all proof, yet when we are in painful or joyful union with "it," we feel and know that

> Underneath are the everlasting arms.
>
> *Deuteronomy XXXIII, 27*

Zen and Mysticism

This two-page essay appeared in The Young East *(Winter 1954).*

THE ETYMOLOGY OF THE WORDS MYSTICISM AND ZEN BRINGS OUT clearly the difference between these truly similar states of mind and forms of life. Mysticism seems to be derived from the Greek word *muein*, to keep one's mouth shut, and as with the pagan Mysteries, the Christian mystic was told not to "utter or divulge the heavenly mysteries unto the uninitiate" (Dionysius, *The Divine Names*, 1.8). In Zen this sort of thing is impossible. We can say what mysticism is, but no one has ever said or will ever say what Zen is. In fact the expression of Zen is more mysterious than silence about it, for silence might be regarded as not saying what could be said, but to pull a man's nose, or say "Kwatz!" or merely to repeat the question—how can these do anything more than increase the observer's confusion?

Zen derives historically to a great extent from the spiritual experiences of the Indian race during the first millennium before Christ, for example, the last words of the *Taittireeya Upanishad*:

I am this world, and I eat this world.
Who knows this, knows.

This expresses, or records, a state of mind in which, first, there is no division between I and not-I. The relation of myself to the universe is not a problem, intellectual or emotional, because *I am it*. There is no good and evil, true and untrue, beautiful and ugly, enlightenment and illusion. Second, this state is not a passive, but an active one, a state of eating, a perpetual Holy

Communion of eating one's own body and drinking one's own blood. In other words, the whole affair is interesting; I enjoy *myself*.

This experience was repeated again and again in (later) time and (a different) place, that is to say, it was carried from India to China, to Korea, to Japan, the carrier being Buddhism, a non-religious, atheistical, intellectual, unpoetical system which nevertheless could provide the innocuous and necessary moral and philosophical framework within which the poetico-religious life could develop.

In the same way it was intellectual Hellenism which was the rational basis of the supra-rational mystical intuitions of Plotinus, the father of Christian mysticism though himself not a Christian. His transcendentalism he derived partly from Plato, partly from the Egyptian, Greek, and Roman mysteries, but there can be no doubt that Indian and Persian thought influenced him and his contemporaries greatly. Plotinus must have met many Indian travellers in Alexandria, his native place, and wanted to get first-hand information on Indian mysticism. For this reason he endeavored to reach India by accompanying the army of the Emperor Gordian against the Persians in 244 A.D. However, the Emperor was assassinated, and Plotinus was forced to turn back from Mesopotamia and arrived in Rome late the same year. The fact that Plotinus does not mention India or Indian philosophy in his works shows nothing, for he does not say anything about the Christianity by which he was surrounded, nor does he mention his teacher Ammonius Saccus from whom he learned for eleven years, until he was thirty-nine. This probable historical connection between Zen and Mysticism, corresponding to that between Bashō and Wordsworth, explains the similarities between them. (Thoreau is even closer to Bashō than Wordsworth, this being again partly due to the Indian writings which he received from an English friend, and which gave him that philosophic background needed for all poetical and religious experiences.) The differences between Bashō and Wordsworth are those between the Chinese-Japanese mind and the German-English mind, the latter always moving from the particular to the universal, the concrete to the abstract, the former never leaving the particular and the concrete however much the universal and abstract may be implicit in them. In a sense, Zen and Bashō are better (that is, deeper) than mysticism and Wordsworth, but we do not really *know* this, in other words, it is not actually so, until we have studied occidental philosophy and poetry.

From the above point of view, Zen and Mysticism may be said to form a bridge, both historical and spiritual, between Occident and Orient. Indeed the Japanese educational system might well be aligned to it. We have India as the chief fountain of world culture; the two streams running east and west, the eastern with its Chinese and Japanese art, poetry and religion; the western and its Italian art, German mysticism and music, English poetry. (In addition to this, there are two more tributaries; the Greek, philosophy and drama; and the Christian, a combination of the Greek, the mystical, and the Jewish.)

To repeat, in all this, the most vital, the most religious, the most poetical element is Zen and mysticism and their Indian origins. And in addition to this intuitive activity we need the scientific clarity of the Greeks, the common sense of the English, the *mens sana in corpore sano*, without which we might merely wallow in general theosophy or wander in individual eccentricity.

Buddhism in Senryū

This article was published serially in two parts in The Young East, *vol. 3, nos. 3 and 4, 1956.*

WE HAVE TO CONSIDER THE RELATION BETWEEN BUDDHISM AND senryū, the one a so-called religion originating in India of the 5th–6th Century B.C., the other a form of literature, of poetry, that flourished in Japan in the 18th Century. In India itself the primitive Buddhism gradually changed as time passed, assimilating the very Hinduism against whose excessive spirituality it was a reaction. Passing to China, the practicality and poetry of the Chinese people left their mark upon it, and when it arrived in Japan, a thousand years after the death of Buddha, it was a very different thing from his pseudo-scientific and moralistic teachings. Then for another thousand years and more it suffered another island-change, being mingled once more with the superstitions, the animism, the poetry of the Japanese people. The Japanese accepted Buddhism easily and gladly because of the Hinduism with which it was mixed. The poetical animism of the 6th century Japanese people (seen in its simplest form in Shinto) welcomed the spiritual view of the world held by the Indians long before Buddhism began to moralise and systematize and *atheise* it. It is indeed my opinion that all Japanese culture is, not derived from, but stimulated by the mysticism of Hinduism, seen in the Upanishads, and that Buddhism was merely the carrier, the pedagogue that brought the Japanese to Nature, not to the beauty of nature, but to its inner life and meaning. It was this which fed the poetry of waka and haiku, and is not entirely absent in kyōka and senryū.

As I said before, the Indian Buddhism that had come through China and Korea, was changed still more after it reached Japan. At the hands of Dengyō Daishi and Kōbō Daishi in the 9th century, Shinran, Eisai, Dōgen, and Nichiren in the 13th, various Japanese sects were created, and by the 18th century Buddhism as we know it today was already fixed.

Senryū, which seems to appear rather suddenly about 1760, has actually a long hidden history behind it. From its very beginnings Japanese literature was rich in humour, of a rather primitive kind it is true, but just as in Greece we have the tragedies of Aeschylus developing from the ancient spring festivals and fertility rites, and the comedies and farces of Aristophanes from the buffoonery and phallic ceremonies of the same processions and dances, we find it in the *Kojiki*, the various *Fudoki* and also in the *Manyōshū*: A man named Ikeda no Ason wrote a satiric waka about the excessive thinness of Omiwa no Ason. In answer to this, Omiwa no Ason wrote:

Hotoke tsukuru   masō tarazuba   mizu tamaru   Ikeda no aso ga
        hana no ue wo hore

   When making a Buddhist image,
If you should be short
   Of red colouring,
Just dig on the nose
   Of Ikeda no Ason.

This humour is a very simple one, but what is remarkable is first that such a verse should be included in the *Manyōshū*; second, that the senryū of a thousand years afterwards are latent, are potential in such waka. The spirit of humour, of senryū, is further nourished in the *Makura no Sōshi* [*Pillow Book*] of Sei Shōnagon, in the *Tsurezuregusa*, in Kyōgen, and also I think by the Chinese humourous and erotic stories that were translated in increasing numbers during the 17th and 18th centuries. In the 15th century the character of Zen master Ikkyū, the anecdotes told of him, the *Kyōun-shū* and the *Dōka* also had their effect in determining the state of mind that later produced senryū.[1] An example is the following:

Umarete wa   shinuru nari keri   oshinabete   Shaka mo
     Daruma mo   neko mo shakushi mo

     Being born
We die and are gone,
     Shakamuni and Daruma also,
The cat too,
The ladle as well.

Ikkyū's view of death is no different from that of senryū. From the Genroku Era, 1688–1703, a great number of *Waraibanashi*, comical anecdotes, began to be published, but just before this time a book called *Karukuchi Otoko* appeared, in which we find the following story:

A certain Buddhist believer had been a vegetarian for many years, but one day eating some fish he found it delicious. Turning to the statue of the Buddha he said: "If it is wrong to eat fish, please grumble at me. If it is all right to do so, just say nothing." It is said that he ate fish from that time onwards.

Almost all haiku have some faint but unmistakable humour in them somewhere. Bashō made haiku serious, one might almost say religious, but kept something of the wit, punning, and word-playfulness of the older haikai masters Teitoku and Sōkan. The followers of Bashō, particularly Kikaku, Taigi, Kitō, and Issa have many comical or satirical verses. For example, a verse by Kitō, Buson's pupil:

Mugiaki no   kutabire-goe ya   nenbutsu-kō

     The autumn of the barley:
In weary voices,
     Their invocation of the Name.

In early summer the farmers are tired out, and when they meet at the temple their chanting of "Namu-amida-butsu" sounds sleepy and somewhat lifeless.

Kyōka, or mad waka, also had their effect in the emergence of senryū, though the best of these comic waka poets, Shokusanjin, 1749–1813, comes a little after the flowering time of senryū. An example from Shokusanjin, or Yomo no Akara, is the following:

Sōshū mo   neko ni owarete   unasaren   Kochō to narishi
haru no hi no yume

Chuang Tzu too
Will moan and groan
  Having become a butterfly,
And pursued by a cat,
  In a spring day dream.

This of course refers to Chuang Tzu's dreaming himself to be a butterfly, and wondering on waking whether he was a butterfly dreaming he was a man, or a man dreaming he was a butterfly.

The aim of senryū is to bring out into the open the sentimentality, affectation, swindling, and hypocrisy in the world; to expose the unobserved or purposely overlooked contradictions in what men say and what they actually do; to lay bare all the hidden motives, the secret shame, the useless wisdom and foolish misery of mankind. Without fear or favor, senryū does this with regard to Buddhism and Buddhists. However, unlike the medieval and modern critics of Christianity the senryū writers have no destructive or anti-religious attitude. They simply test truth with humour, with a polite and good-natured ridicule. For Japanese people, the great sin is rudeness. Nature is never rude. The sun shines, the rain falls, weakly or strongly, but never insultingly or contemptuously.

One more point should be noted. In the 18th century political criticism was dangerous, but religious beliefs were relatively free. There were no blasphemy laws such as still remain on the statute book in England. Even in ancient Greece religion was sacred, and we are reminded in Kenkabō's verse:

Sokuratesu shikei   Koshi shitsugyō   Shaka yukidaore

Socrates was executed;
Confucius lost his job;
  Shakamuni died on a journey.

Coming to the world-view of senryū, which is of course implicit rather than explicit, we must call it agnostic, even atheistic. But primitive Buddhism was so, and in this both senryū and Buddhism show their common critical and rational attitude. Unlike European satire senryū is neither destructive nor reformative, but in the following we see it at its most severe:

Tsujigiri wo   *miteowashimasu*   *jizō-son*

> Murder at the cross-roads,
> Jizō calmly
> Gazing on.

Jizō neither helps the innocent man slashed to death, to test a newly bought sword, nor does he punish the villain. In *Macbeth*, Malcolm, whose wife and children have been slaughtered by Macbeth, cries:

> Did Heaven look on
> And would not take their part?

The cool politeness of the senryū is more scathing than the agonized questioning of Malcolm.

Unlike Buddhism and Christianity senryū asks and expects nothing,

Shimbutsu ni   *temaegatte wo*   *mōshi age*

> They beg and pray
> To gods and buddhas,
> According to their own convenience.

Senryū has the true humility, which perceives the impossibility of changing things from what they are. It has even some pity for God:

Ningen no   *fuman ichichi*   *kamikikezu*

> How can the gods fulfill
> Everybody's wants and wishes
> About this that and the other?

(*Shūsen*)

The following senryū mildly satirize the Buddhist concepts of Heaven and Hell. The first gives us the essential democracy of all poetry:

Kawahaba mo   *onaji sanzu no*   *fusha hinja*

> The width of the Styx
> Is just the same
>   For rich and poor.   (*Takeo*)

The next is more witty:

Tobikonda   *toko ga sanzu no*   *kawa no ue*

> Jumping in,
> He found himself
>   In the Styx.   (*Shugyo*)

Committing suicide by throwing himself into the river, he found himself in the river which must be crossed by all the dead. The next shows up the humbug of descriptions of heaven:

Gokuraku wo   *mitekita yō ni*   *oshō toki*

> The priest talks about Paradise
> As if he had been there,
>   And seen it all with his own eyes.   (*Tadaichi*)

But next is more penetrating. The truth is that we don't want to go to Paradise at all; we want to lead an interesting and happy life on this earth:

Gokuraku wa   *taikutsu rashii*   *akubi nari*

> Ah, Paradise!
> But it seems rather boring,
>   They are yawning.   (*Namboku*)

The senryū writer suggests perhaps that instead of talking about Heaven and Earth Buddha should have told us to "cultivate our gardens," so that this world should be as happy a place as it is possible to make it. The best of life indeed consists of listening to music and eating; death does the rest. And coming now to the senryū view of death:

Nana-korobi   ya-oki ku-korobi   sore de shini

> Seven times we fall
> The eighth time we get up!
>   The ninth time, it's all over with us.   (*Kenkabō*)

Whatever success or fame we may attain to, the result is the same. As Ikkyū said, even Christ cannot live for ever. But what is most remarkable, senryū notes, is our power to dismiss death from our conscious minds:

Itsumademo   ikite iru ki no   kao bakari

> All their faces look
> As if they think
>   They're going to live for ever.

Shinu koto wo   wasurete itemo   minna shini

> All forget
> About dying,
>   But all die.   (*Bentenshi*)

To the eye of senryū ordinary religion is little more than a mass of superstitions fitted for old men and women who need something to pass the time that hangs heavily on their hands. Thoreau agrees with this:

> I see that the infidels and skeptics have formed themselves into churches and weekly gather together at the ringing of a bell.   (*Journals*, 1857)

In other words, it is the least really religious people that infest the temples:

Odangi wa   kikitashiyome wa   ibiritashi

> She'd like to hear the sermon,
> But she also wants to bully
> Her daughter-in-law.

Senryū is not like haiku, nature-power, but it has an unexpressed respect for nature as against the works of man:

Butsudan ni   hi ga sashikomu to   yasuku mie

> When the sun shines
> On the Buddhist altar
> It looks a bit cheap.   (*Kotarō*)

Senryū sees Buddhist images in the same way. Nature, in this case human nature, is better than art or religion:

Busshiya wa   Amida no kubi de   ko wo ayashi

> The Buddhist image maker
> Humours the child
> With Amida's head.

This is indeed a true Buddhism. Amida would be glad to have his head used in this way.

Ori-ori wa   hihataki ni naru   ishijizō

> The stone statue of Jizō
> Sometimes serves
> To knock out the dottle on.

In this verse also we see the Zen of senryū, the understanding that all things are to be used in all ways, that nothing is holy because all is so.

Coming now to senryū criticisms of the priestly tribe, the question of sex arises. According to primitive Buddhism and Christianity, the act, the talking, the thinking of it even is forbidden. Buddha deserted his wife and children; Christ never married. St. Paul said, "It is better not to marry." Christ tells us that there is no marrying or giving in marriage in Heaven, from which we may conclude that sex, if not positively bad, is not good. I would call this attitude blasphemy against, not the Holy Ghost, but something as important, human nature. If you cannot be united with your brother or sister whom you have seen, how can you be so with God whom you have not? Senryū agrees with D.H. Lawrence that there is nothing so important in the world as sex, but it does not make the mistake of taking it too seriously. Look at the following:

Kore made to   oshō karakasa   uchinagame

"Here is far enough,"
Says the priest, looking at her
Under the umbrella.

It is raining, and the priest has been seen off by his concubine. "Go back now," he says as they get near the temple, and stands in the rain looking at her, his face more human than Buddhist, more vulgar than noble, more human than divine. But humanity is the one thing that senryū will forgive. In the next verse, the priest has a little too much perhaps:

Bonsai ni   kane wo tsukashite   go ni fukeri

Immersed in playing checkers,
He gets his wife
To ring the temple bell.

For the priest, as for all of us, religion, in the ordinary sense of the word, is not the most important thing in life. We see this in the next four senryū.

Kuchi de kyō   hara de o-fuse wo   shoke wa yomi

With his lips, reading the sutra:
In his heart, the priest
Estimates the fee.

Danna-dera   kuwasete oite   sate no ii

    The family temple:
After giving them something to eat,
    "Well, I'm sorry to say that . . . ."

It is difficult to refuse to contribute money after you have been feasted.

Hi no koromo   kireba ukiyo ga   oshiku nari

    On wearing the scarlet robe,
He begins to hold dear
    This transitory world.

Toshitotte   hōi no iro wa   wakaku nari

    The older he gets,
The younger the colour
    Of the priestly robe.

The next senryū combines in a most clever way Mongaku, who killed Kesa Gozen and became a monk, and Zen master Ikkyū:

Mongaku to   Ikkyū atama   nite susume

    Mongaku and Ikkyū
Both made their appeal
    With a skull.

In the 12th century, Mongaku showed to Yoritomo his father Yoshitomo's skull, urging him to destroy the Heike. Ikkyū, three centuries later, went round the streets of the capital on the first day of the year, carrying a skull and telling people,

Kadomatsu wa   meido no tabi no   ichiri-zuka
Medetaku mo ari   medetaku mo nashi

New Year's pine decoration
Is another milestone
    On the way to Hades;
A time for congratulation,
    And a time for condolence.

The senryū shows how a skull has various meanings. "Go and kill your father's enemy!" it says, and at the same time, it tells us as in the hymn:

Brief life is here our portion,
Brief sorrow, short-lived care.

The next senryū also deals with Mongaku:

Bonnō no   kesa wa bodai no   zenchishiki

Worldly passions for Kesa Gozen
Became the good means
    To salvation.

This is the Zen doctrine that "Worldly passions are salvation, illusion is enlightenment," but expressed with some cynicism of course.

Coming last of all to a few verses about Zen, here senryū finds itself in some difficulty. Zen is so impalpable, so intangible, yet so all-pervasive, that whether we criticise Zen or praise it, we are in great danger of merely showing our ignorance or misunderstanding of it. Here are a few that rush in where angels fear to tread:

Kōban e   honrai kū ga   tsukidasare

"All is originally emptiness"
Is taken off
    To the police station.

In Zen we often hear *muchimotsu chū mujinzō*, "to have nothing is to have everything," but in actual fact, *ex nihilo nihit fit*, "nothing comes out of nothing." In the senryū, a man eats a meal in a restaurant, knowing that he has no money to pay for it. In England, to be without visible means of support is itself a crime. In other words, what Zen says has a spiritual meaning only, and here is a defect. If a priest, if Buddha himself goes to a restaurant without money in his purse he will soon find himself in the clink. This weakness of Zen, or perhaps rather of the teachings of Zen, comes out in the next two examples:

Dō satotta ka   *zenso mo*   *tameru nari*

> What was his enlightenment?
> The Zen priest also
> > Has begun to save money.

Zenshu wa   *zazen ga sumu to*   *nomi wo tori*

> In the Zen Sect,
> When they have finished zazen
> > They catch the fleas.   (*Kenkabō*)

The fleas which have been tormenting them, they now catch and kill with unbuddhistic glee. Zen says, "When you feel hungry, eat," and so on, but zazen has something artificial and unnatural about it. Of course it is an unnatural way of becoming natural—but that is precisely the criticism of the senryū.

Gejigeji ni   *zazen no oshō*   *tobi-agari*

> The Zen priest
> Leaps in the air
> > At the millipede.

Kenkabō, the greatest senryū writer of the last hundred years and more, is perhaps making a mistake here. He seems to think that a Zen adept should not be so alarmed at a small millipede; he feels that the priest's enlightenment is not deep enough. This is not so. Buddha also must jump in the air if a millipede makes its appearance. The Zen is shown in the *way* he leaps, in his state of mind and body as he avoids pain and death as far as he can.

In conclusion I would like to say that senryū, the Way of Senryū, is a test, is *the* test of religion. Senryū after all is a kind of poetry in that what it does not destroy is poetry. That which remains behind after senryū has done its damnedest I will believe. It shall be my religion. But even this I will not believe fanatically, solemnly. As I said before, truth does not need our firm belief. It will stand of itself without our recommendation. And so to conclude:

Mō owari   chikai okyō no   arigatasa

    Ah, how edifying
The holy sutra
    That is coming to an end!   (*Tōfū*)

In Praise of Suzuki Daisetz and Zen

Published in Today's Japan, *vol. 9, no. 2, May 1957.*

THE FIRST TIME I MET SUZUKI DAISETZ WAS IN KANAZAWA, HIS native place, just before the beginning of the Pacific War. I had read his books and done zazen (practicing Zen while seated). I was in the middle of *Zen in English Literature*, and my mind was full of the question, "What is Zen?"

When Dr. Suzuki asked me to go and see him at the inn where he was staying, I was of course most excited. I pictured him as a very fierce-looking person, something like Daitō Kokushi, who would rap me over the knuckles and ask me that most unanswerable of questions, "What is Zen?"

Anyway, I prepared my answer and went to the inn. I found him to be a very gentle, sympathetic person, more interested in me and my life than in philosophizing. He reminded me of the minister, Mr. Hayhoe, in T.F. Powys's story, *The Only Penitent*:

> He never spoke to any for the purpose of teaching them, for God chooses His own time for that, but was always ready to speak of the most trifling matters, for who can tell through what little corners the joy of religion may enter the soul?

Dr. Suzuki asked me how I came to be interested in Zen. I answered eagerly that it was through his *Essays in Zen Buddhism*. He bowed his head and I cannot say how much that action impressed me. It was not modesty, hardly gratitude, rather a kind of expression of the inevitable. At last I said to him, "Dr. Suzuki, I thought you would ask me what was Zen was, and I see I was mistaken, but as I have prepared the answer, I will tell you anyway. The answer is 'There is no such thing as Zen.'" "Yes," he said, smiling, "that is true; there is no such thing as Zen."

The second anecdote relates to after the war when he was living in Engakuji Temple. I often went to see him there. I had now published several volumes of translations and commentaries of haiku, and one day an old man from—I have forgotten where—wrote a long letter to me saying that I did not understand haiku at all, neither the particular haiku nor the spirit of haiku in general. I have never been so angry before or since.

I continued to be angry for three days, and then went down to Kamakura. I told Dr. Suzuki all about this, and said that whatever I knew about haiku, at least I had no understanding of Zen at all. I finished my story and sat back to hear his reproof, teaching, and advice. He said, "Mr. Blyth, people with poetic minds are more sensitive to things than others are, and they take longer to forget them." I burst into tears. To praise instead of blaming,—this is Zen.

The other day I was talking with some students about the Seven Ancient Wonders of the World—the Pyramids, the Colossus at Rhodes, and so on, and at the end of the class I asked them, "Don't you think there is something vulgar about wonders, especially huge things?" Some agreed, some did not. I then asked, "What, in your opinion, is the most wonderful thing in the world?"

The students looked dubious. I suggested haiku. They looked surprised. I suggested the music of Bach. They looked miserable. I then said, "Well, I will tell you what the most wonderful things in the world is: it is Zen," and at that moment I felt the truth of what I had said. Zen is not only the greatest thing in the world, it is the only great thing. It is that which makes things great. It is greatness itself.

Suzuki Daisetz is a great man, in the same sense that Aristotle, Paul, Spinoza, Eckhart, and Nietzsche were great men. Each of these did something that no other man had done before, or has done since. What then has Suzuki Daisetz done? He has explained the inexplicable; he has shown us the greatness of the greatest thing in the world.

Dr. Suzuki "understands" Zen better than any man who has ever lived, better than Lin-chi or Hui-neng, better than Daruma, better than the Buddha himself. Let us look at the matter with reference to literature and art and music.

An impression, in order to be a real impression, must be expressed. Without expression there is no impression. And these two are not consecutive, but simultaneous. As soon as the impression begins the expression is there at once. As long as the expression continues, the impression is still active.

But this expression itself is not *mere* expression, in a vacuum; it is expression *to* someone. Even in the case of Robinson Crusoe, it is still expression to some desired or recollected or imaginary person. The solitary hermit expresses himself to God. Thus life must see itself: the indivisible must be divided; the inexpressible must express its own inexpressible nature.

There must be a duality without losing the unity, a unity which exists only because there is at the same time a duality. When Bach is playing the organ in the empty church, he combines in himself the three functions of impression, expression, and reception,—composer, performer, and listener.

God creates the world, and finds it good. But besides giving us this view of the artistic activity that derives from Zen, Dr. Suzuki has quieted all our intellectual agonies by showing us that the world is not an intellectual thing, or at least is only subordinately so. As Swift says, perhaps "reason reflecting upon the sum of things, can, like the sun, serve only to enlighten one half of the globe, leaving the other half, by necessity, under shade and darkness."

Since the world is not rationally apprehensible, that intellect is to be used merely as a regulative faculty, not as an organ of truth. All our philosophical worries, real and pretended (and chiefly the latter) are now at an end, but our emotional troubles remain; they can be resolved only by ourselves.

There is one other way in which we may appreciate the greatness of Dr. Suzuki. In literature we often talk of a great poet. Matthew Arnold spoke of "the grand style," thinking of Homer, Dante, and Milton. But there is too much emphasis here on quantity; quality is more important. As Ben Jonson says:

In small proportions we just beauties see;
And in short measures life may perfect be.

A great writer is great in one sentence, in each sentence; a great man is great in every action; the sea is salty in every drop of its water. And so it is that in all the innumerable works Dr. Suzuki has written in English and Japanese, I cannot disagree with anything he writes—not a sentence—just as I cannot with anything Mozart composed, or Paul Klee painted, or D.H. Lawrence wrote.

When we compare Buddhism, especially Zen, with Christianity, we cannot help being struck by a certain lack of warmth, a want of human emotion in the former. Take the following hymn by Charles Wesley:

Jesus, lover of my soul,
  Let me to Thy bosom fly,
While the nearer Waters roll,
  While the Tempest still is high:
Hide me, O my Saviour, hide,
  Till the Storm of Life is past;
Safe into the haven guide;
  O receive my Soul at last!

Jesus loves me; I can go to his Bosom when in trouble. He will hide me, save me, and when I die, will welcome me into Heaven. There is nothing of this kind in primitive Buddhism, in Zen, in *jiriki* (self-power) Buddhism. There is no Jesus; love is attachment; "me" is an illusion. It is no use hiding; no one can save another. My dying is consequent upon my being born, and neither is my true state. Heaven is here and now, in moment's eternity.

All this is true enough, and orthodox Christianity is (intellectually speaking) wrong, no doubt, and yet we feel that Zen is too inhuman, too lacking in human warmth. The trouble with some of the practitioners of Zen is that they are transcendental all right, but never seem to have had any emotion to transcend.

Just as Christianity has fallen into sentimentality and hypocrisy, so the followers of Zen have not been free from indifference, rudeness, and downright cruelty. (And do not these two extremes meet?) I used to go to do zazen every night at Myōshinji Betsu-in in Keijō, and during the winter—the temperature often falls below -20—when we entered the temple we often had to step over the bodies of beggars sleeping under the Great Gate of the temple.

Sometimes, as we came out, full of Zen and satori and transcendental bliss, one of the beggars would be really asleep, frozen to death. No doubt this kind of thing could be paralleled outside the cathedrals of Northern Europe, but it remains a defect of Zen that it is too little concerned with human suffering, especially of the physical kind.

From this coldness Dr. Suzuki has been saved by his deep understanding of *tariki* (other-power) Buddhism. The essence of the Shin and Jōdo Buddhist sects is that we are stupid, sensual, obstinate, lazy, and self-deceiving. We cannot save ourselves: we cannot even ask Amida Buddha to save us. But if we realize that we are unsavable He will save us, for He has vowed to do this very thing.

This impossible task is what Amida has promised to achieve; our powerlessness is His omnipotence. Dr. Suzuki sees the *jiriki* of Zen and the *tariki* of Shin Buddhism as one thing. Power, pure power, not power over others, is true love, love which is not sentimentality but a pitiless pity, an *amor fati*.

Pain and death and even annihilation come from God's loving hands. To what extent the Jōdo sect owes, historically, its doctrine of absolute submission to Amida, to Christianity, will perhaps always be an unsolved problem, but in seeing into both Jōdo Buddhism and Zen, Dr. Suzuki has avoided the inhumanity of Bushidō with its excessive emphasis on death, and made Zen a less monkish, more universal, more human thing, without in the least degree vulgarizing or popularizing it.

There is one question which Dr. Suzuki seldom deals with—the relation between Zen and peace and war, Zen and socialism and capitalism, Zen and daily life. I wish to rush in where angels fear to tread, but I should first like to say that those who love peace most speak of it least, and that a good society is to be composed of people who have little interest in the distribution of wealth, because they are not interested in wealth itself.

War is caused by two things, a deficiency of food, or its unequal distribution; and differences of religion, i.e. of world view, of the idea of what makes life worth living.

These two are not so different, so separate as they seem, for the idea of the equality of distribution of the necessities of life, is itself a "religious" idea. It should be noted further that Zen has been connected with war rather than with peace simply because there has been far more war in the world than peace, up to the present time.

Zen does not bring about peace or war. It shows us how to live properly in either. Zen does not show us how to be all of the same belief, but how to live with any, or none. In any case, peace demands that all shall work and eat, and be more or less of the same opinion about what we work and eat for. Zen will of course deal with both these problems as one.

The United Nations charter says rightly enough that peace or war is decided in the minds of men. Zen, that is, the Zen experience, tells us that though I am I and you are you, I also am you and you are I, so that when your stomach is empty, mine is empty too, and when I kill you, I fall in death together with you.

This is always so, whether we know it or not, but this "know" is knowing with the stomach and the hand rather than knowing in the head. If we thus "know," most social and political and national and international troubles are at an end, for my troubles are yours, and yours are mine . . . well, not quite at an end, for there are not only human beings but many other creatures and even mindless things in this world of ours whose joys and sufferings, rise and fall, existence and non-existence, we must also share.

In other words, the universe was not made for happiness and can never achieve it; our lives may have peace, but they must always have sorrow.

The most remarkable thing about Zen is that it should be able to solve the problem of fear (of the suffering and death of ourselves and others) without a *deus ex machina*, indeed without any power, human or divine, *jiriki* or *tariki*. As Blake says:

> Man was made for Joy and Woe;
> And when this we rightly know
> Thro' the World we safely go.

That is to say, when we really see the dichotomy, when we "rightly know" it, when we become it, we are safe in our lack of safety.

One last thing about Zen. It is not really mystical. Mysticism is a return to Nature, to God, from which we have emerged. Christ comes down from Heaven so that we may rise up to Heaven, man becoming God.

Zen is not a reunion with God: there is no return to Nature; there is no going back to anything at all. We go to Heaven, it is true; we transcend the relative and grasp the absolute, but only to come back and live our true life on earth. God becoming man. To quote Blake once again:

> Thou are a man: God is no more:
> Thy own Humanity learn to adore.

Everything is pure egoism, pure will, pure subjectivity. As Lawrence said, "Life is what you want in your soul." But what we really want is by some odd chance the will of God and the inevitable course of Nature.

The Way of Senryū

Published in Today's Japan, *vol. 3, no. 10, October 1958.*

SENRYŪ IS THE MOST REMARKABLE PRODUCT OF THE JAPANESE mind, surpassing even haiku in its breadth and depth, since the Way of Haiku would hardly be possible in a prison or if blind and deaf, but the Way of Senryū exists precisely because of (spiritual) blindness and deafness.

Tragedy is always taken as profounder than comedy, tears than laughter,—but is this really so? The poet says with a painful depth of feeling,

> It was because you did not weep
>> I wept for you.

Not to weep is thus better than to weep. And may we not also say:

> It was because you did not laugh
>> I laughed at you.

The conclusion is that weeping is folly, and something that arouses in the end derisive laughter. We may parody another, the even lesser poet who said,

> Laugh, and the world laughs with you;
> Weep, and you weep alone.

This is simply not true: the fact is,

Weep, and the world weeps with you;
Laugh, and you laugh alone.

Real laughter is as uncommon as real love or real poetry. This is what makes senryū so remarkable. Senryū was (at length) born at a time when the warrior class (humourless and weeping in Japan as elsewhere in the world) was trying to preserve itself and its ideas without war. The tradesman of Edo and Naniwa (Osaka) saw the folly of this, but also, had the gift which Burns prayed for, to see themselves as others saw them, no less foolish, cosmically speaking, than those they laughed at. But the sword is always mightier than the pen. We laughed tyrants off their thrones, but we ourselves are wept (patriotically) into prison, or at least into silence. The Way of Senryū existed at its best for a short time only, let us say from 1765 to 1790, the time between the appearance of the first volume of *Yanagidaru* (a series of selections of senryū published between 1765 and 1837) and the date of the death of the first and best selector, Senryū Karai.

Senryū, like all literature, is a kind of poetry, in this case with the same form as haiku, 5, 7, 5 syllables. We must say outright that humour which is not poetical is not (in some way) humourous, is not real poetry, but a collection of *purpurei panni*, purple patches, and sublime nothings.

Religion is being in love with the universe, and poetry is no less. But love without humour is an odious, a hot-house, an Othello-Desdemona-like thing. And humour is just as necessary in religion and literature as it is in love. In haiku this cosmic humour is so much involved into the poetic attitude that it is almost impossible to point to the humourous element without thus overemphasizing it. But humourless haiku is mere photography or sentimentality or sermonizing. To take a haiku of Buson that has a good deal of humour in it:

我水に隣家の桃の毛蟲かな

　In our water,
A hairy caterpillar,
　From the neighbor's peach tree.

The water here may be of a small pool, or some other water-holding receptacle. The peach-tree of the neighboring house is not only tantalizing with its fruit, but its overhanging branches drop caterpillars into the water in *our* garden. The hairy caterpillar is itself a rather comical creature, but its comicality is only implicit here, whereas in the following old senryū, it becomes explicit:

花の幕毛蟲一つで座が崩れ

> Within the flower-viewing enclosure;
> A hairy caterpillar!—
> And the party breaks up.

A long parti-coloured curtain is drawn round the merry-makers, but a caterpillar falls from the cherry-tree above and the fair scream with half-simulated fear, and even the brave are disconcerted.

Senryū has to Western satirical verse somewhat the same relation as haiku has to European nature poetry. In haiku and senryū the general is far more subsumed into the particular, so that the concrete case alone is visible, the philosophical or psychological law being entirely implicit. Thus, oddly enough, Bashō resembles Burns far more than he does Wordsworth, as we see when we read the comparison Hazlitt makes between Wordsworth and Burns:

> Nothing can be more different or hostile than the spirit of their poetry. Mr. Wordsworth's poetry is the poetry of mere sentiment and pensive contemplation: Burns's is a very highly sublimated essence of animal existence. With Burns, "self-love and social are the same"—"And we'll tak a cup of kindness yet, For auld lang syne."

Haiku is "a very highly sublimated essence of animal existence," in its relation to nature, senryū being exactly the same "essence" in its relation to man and society.

The special character of senryū as a form of humour is that though it is satirical it is never wantonly cruel, it is never insulting. Chinese humour is often ruthless; it treats people with derision. Senryū always preserves a certain propriety and suavity. It is never angry like Juvenal; it has not the misanthropy of Swift, or the disappointed love of Aldous Huxley. The Japanese cannot hate nature, though it take the form of pestilence and earthquake, and neither can they hate human nature, though treachery, murder, and rape be among the least of its habitual failings. It might be said that Japanese people do not laugh because of their own superiority over others, but at the inferiority of others. This is a delicate distinction. The European laugh (of Hobbes) is a laugh of victory. The Japanese laugh (ideally speaking) has some sadness in it. It is more laughing (together) with than (down) at. To express it in other words, there is less sadism in it, or to put it more exactly and less complimentarily, Japanese cruelty does not come out in their humour. Besides the laughter of superiority there is that of surprise, the most simple being the surprised delight when someone presses the spring of a Jack-in-the-box. Far more exhilarating than a chance revelation of something hidden is the unmasking of hypocrisy, and, most intriguing of all, the disclosure of self-deception. It is hardly possible to deceive others unless we have first deceived ourselves. All pride, boasting, affectation, self-consciousness and shame are forms of self-deception, and are naturally enough humourless. The great asset of the Japanese is their ability to deceive themselves to death, without which fanaticism it would probably be impossible for the Japanese to get the material necessary for humour. We see this brought out in the literary field by Lafcadio Hearn's humourless romancifying of the sentimentalism of the Japanese. It is to be seen in the neo-Shintoism of Fujisawa Chikao, who humourlessly philosophizes the poetry, the physico-spiritual intuitions of the Japanese into a vainglorious "Sumeracracy."[1]

The fact is, as Matthew Arnold said, that the world long ago decided to live, to live for comfort, for a higher and higher standard of living, for "peace," and not for poetry or value or depth of experience. The Way of Haiku is being trodden by almost nobody now, and the Way of Senryū, which is a sort of parallel road, leading to the same unattainable goal, must become equally disused, since poetry, that is, quietness, greed-lessness, is the essence of both.

Oriental Humour

Published in Today's Japan, *1959. A brief editor's note prefacing this essay reads, "A 600-page book,* Oriental Humour, *will be published by Mr. Blyth at the end of April. This article, however, is not taken from the book, but was written specially for* Today's Japan.*"*

THERE ARE FIVE KINDS OF WORLD LAUGHTER: THE HOBBESIAN, of superiority; the Kantian, of shock; the Freudian, of release; that of Shui-lao, of enlightenment (he laughed when kicked in the chest by his master Ma-tsu, d. 788); and that of Mahakasyapa, given in the *Mumonkan*, the 6th Case, of perfect satisfaction. Of course the last is the best, but all are good. It should be remembered, however, that laughter is not essential for humour. Laughter is the result of the element of surprise. Humour is a tickling of the mind, a tickling that may be intellectual (puns) or poetic (cosmic paradoxes) or of course a mixture of these.

For the origins of so many forms of culture, East and West, it is necessary to go back to India, but perhaps this is not so in the case of humour. Chinese humour, like literature everywhere, is at first illiterate, that is, unwritten; it is oral, aural. Popular stories became proverbs, the proverbs were again expanded into tales of a different content. It should be noted that an unhumourous proverb is usually a poor one. Proverbs went to the court, they came from the court, undergoing land-changes; rank-changes. Bottom and Duke Theseus in ancient times were not so far from one another as they afterwards became. Of many proverbs the original stories are known, for example, "To cover the ears when stealing a bell is to deceive oneself."

In the state of Chin, in ancient China, 265–419 A.D., some robbers killed a man and wanted to carry away a bell, which however was so heavy they decided to break it up. When struck it made such a noise they feared that people would come and see what was going on, so they covered their ears to deaden the sound. Another proverb which seems to have no story behind it, but which expresses a piece of ancient humourous wisdom: "Feet that resound like a drum will be poor all their life," that is, big and heavy feet are a sign of a poor brain.

It was the early Taoists, Chuang Tzu and Lao Tzu, that received from and gave to the Chinese their sublimest form of humour. But let us take first the unpromising Han Fei Tzu, forced to commit suicide in 230 B.C. He was said by Ssu-ma Chien to be fond of penology, epistemology, law, and statecraft. Many literary men have had a legal or medical background, but Han Fei Tzu's mind *was* this background. However, his exceedingly acute mind causes us a kind of joy, like that from an acrobat or a conjurer, who make us laugh at his skill. For example, in Chapter XVII, "Guarding Against the Interior," he writes:

> When the cartwright has finished making a carriage, he hopes people will be rich and powerful. When the carpenter has finished making a coffin, he hopes people will die soon. This is not because the cartwright is kind-hearted and the carpenter sadistic, but because only noble people buy carriages, and only dead men need coffins.

Then here is the well-known story of the shoes.

> A man of Cheng was going to buy a pair of shoes. He took the measurements of his feet, and went to the market place, but by accident left them behind. When he found he had forgotten the measurements, he told the shoe-maker he would have to go back and get them, and off he went, but when he returned to the market, it was shut. On someone asking him why he didn't try on the shoes, "I trust the measurements more than my feet," he said.

Going back a couple of centuries, we have the sublime humour of Chuang Tzu applied to shoes and to forgetting. The following comes from the end of the Chapter, "The Full Understanding of Life."

When the foot is forgotten, the shoe fits; forgetting the waist shows the girdle is just right. When wisdom forgets right and wrong, the heart is in the proper condition. When the inward mind does not change, unaffected by externals, the fitness is fitting. Realizing from the first this fitness, never losing the sense of it,—that is the fitness that has forgotten all about such a thing as fitness.

The humour of Chuang Tzu and the mythical Lieh Tzu is of the highest class. It is exceeded only by that of the *Mumonkan* (*Wu-men kuan*) and the *Hekiganroku* (*Pi-yen lu*). For example, in the 8th Case of the *Pi-yen lu*:

Yang-shan Hui-chi said to San-sheng Hui-chan, "What's your name?" Hui-chan said, "Hui-chi." Hui-chi said, "But that's my name!" Hui-chan said, "My name's Hui-chan." Hui-chi burst out laughing.

Hui-chi says, "Who are you?" Hui-chan says, "I am you." Hui-chi says, "But I am I, not you!" Hui-chan says, "Yes, that's so, and I am!" Why does Hui-chi laugh? He laughs, not because of a contradiction, but at the contradiction that every thing is both itself only and at the same time it is everything else in the world. A is A, and A is not A. Don't you think that's a funny thing?

There are two kinds of laughing, at what we may call second-class, relative contradictions, and first-class, absolute contradictions. They are described in the *Kaian Kokugo, "Dream Words from a Land of Dreams,"* Hakuin's commentary on the sermons of Daitō Kokushi, 1282–1336:

Those who understand jokes are many; those who understand true laughter are few.

In their written form Chinese humourous stories begin with the *Hsiao Lin*, "Forest of Laughter," in the 3rd century B.C. Here is an example from the *Ch'i-yen lu*, "The Book of Smiles," by Hou Pai, a famous scholar of the Sui Dynasty; it is called "Foolish Forgetful." (Oriental people saw a deep meaning, as Freud afterwards did, in forgetting, deeper than in remembering.)

There was a very forgetful man in Hu prefecture. One day he took his axe and went out to the field with his wife to cut wood. When he got to the wood he put down his axe and eased nature. When he stood up he saw the axe and cried out, "I've found an axe!" and danced with joy and trod on his own faeces, and then exclaimed, "Somebody must have eased nature here and forgotten his axe!" His wife, irritated by his foolish forgetfulness, said to him, "It was you who brought the axe here and laid it down. How can you forget so quickly?" The man gazed at his wife, and said, "What is your name, my good woman, and when did we get acquainted?"

This rustic outspokenness and hyperbole is typically Chinese, and excellent of its kind. A different type of story from a later collection, the *Hsueh-tao hsieh shih*, "The Humorous History of Snow Wave," by Kiang Ying-ko of the Ming dynasty:

There was once a hen-pecked husband, whose wife was angry with him about something, and decided to put the thumb-screws on him. The husband said: "There are no thumb-screws in our house." "Go next door and borrow theirs," ordered his wife. As he went off he murmured something, and his wife called him back and asked him what he was mumbling about. The husband said, "I was only saying we ought to have a set of our own."

This story may not please a jaded taste but I think it rather delicate and good.

The most famous of all Chinese collections of humourous stories is *Hsiao-fu*, "The House of Laughter," by Feng Meng-long, published in the first half of the 17th century. The following is not one of the best, but brings forth a certain aspect of Chinese humour, a forthrightness that in many cases is almost too cruel and rude for humour; and also the undefeatability of the Chinese.

There was a carpenter who by mistake fitted the bolt on the outside of the gate. The owner of the house abused him and said, "You must be blind!" The carpenter retorted, "It's you who are blind!" Taken aback, the owner replied, "You must be blind to hire a carpenter like me."

Chinese folk-songs are of an undetermined and undeterminable antiquity. The following belongs to any time when child-marriage was the custom, the wife being always older than the husband. It comes from Nanking, and is called "The Little Bridegroom":

The bride is eighteen, the bridegroom three.
Looking after his pissing, his shitting,
She holds him in her arms, and rocks him to sleep.
In the night he wakes up, and cries for milk,
Seeking with his mouth, with both hands.
"Oh, I am your wife, not your mother!"

Beggars are seen also without dislike or indifference in the following from Chekiang:

Musk melons are delicious, but far beyond me,
Watermelons are nice too, but where's the money to buy one?
Just let me stroke the watermelon,
And I'll pass the summer with the tea I'm given!

The disarming sweetness of these contrasts with the (still mild) cynicism of the following from Kiangsu, called "Lazy Together," also found in the form of a proverb:

One priest draws water and drinks it;
Two priests carry water and drink it;
Three priests—and no water to drink.

Another pair of verses from Anhwei, which express the feelings of employers and employees all over the world:

Dear Sun, my dear Sun,
Sink soon behind the hill!
Day-labor—how grievous!
My back is swollen,

My arms and legs are sore.
Dear Sun, my dear Sun,
Sink slowly behind the hill!
Day-labor—how grievous!
I have to feed them,
I have to pay them!

As in Korea, lice and fleas are as much companions as enemies, and have their own woes. A louse of Heilungkiang sings:

Farmers all wear rags,
And dry them three times a day over the fire.
Far from eating their flesh,
My life is in danger!

A flea sings:

Town people all wear fine clothes,
And change them three times a day,
Far from drinking their blood,
I can't even see their skin!

Nursery-rhymes also are the remains of some of the most ancient verse, the ancient poetry of practical experience. As with English nursery rhymes, many are extravagances:

Little boy, little boy,
Rode on mule-back,
To sell dried bean-curds.
When the mule farted
Little boy was blown
Five miles away!

A song which reminds us distantly of Wordsworth's *Idiot Boy*:

Everyone calls me a fool,
But who cares?
After the south wind, there blows the north wind.
I make the moon my pillow, and sleep;
When it gets cold, I pull the sun over me.
The Lord of Heaven is my grandpa,
The Queen of Heaven is my grandma!

The Koreans have, and apparently always had, an excellent sense of humour. I remember telling a funny story to a mixed class of Japanese and Koreans, and how at the end of it one Korean student beat on the desk in his uncontrollable pleasure. There is something indeed violent in Korean humour which gives it a special flavour. The myths and traditions are often more or less explicitly sexual. An eschatological one tells us that the sun and earth will join together again and whirl round and round as a mill-stone; only good men can leave by the hole in the mill-stone and be reborn. Another agrees with the idea that all living things come from water, even human beings, as everyone knows. Again Heaven moves, Earth does not. This is because the former is the male, the latter the female.

As for Korean humourous stories, it is not easy to tell which are original and which are imitations or adaptations of Chinese stories. One which does not strike us as very funny but which is a hyperbolical case of something very common in Korea is titled "A Lazy Man."

> A certain very lazy man felt even too tired to eat, so his wife fed him,
> putting the food into his mouth. On one occasion she had to go some-
> where for a few days, so she made a rice-cake for him and hung it round
> his neck, and said, "If you feel hungry, eat this." When she came back,
> she found her husband dead of starvation, the rice-cake still dangling in
> front of him.

As with Korea, Japan derived a great deal of its humour, particularly in the form of humourous stories, from China. What is different is first the softening of the (necessary) Chinese cruelty; second, the unique form of humour seen in senryū, in which there is an ideal blending of the explicit ridiculousness of human life and the implicit poetic tenderness. In Japanese literature, humour is found almost everywhere, at least sporadically, except in a few Buddhist books, such as the *Hōjōki*. Even in the *Hōjōki*, the first part of the book describes the natural calamities with a certain relish that is close to the pleasure in the grotesque and macabre. During the earthquake of the second year of Genreki, 1185,

> the only son of a certain samurai, about six or seven years old, was playing
> at houses beneath a roofed wall when it suddenly collapsed and buried

him, flattening him so that both his eyes were squeezed out, about an inch beyond their sockets.

The 15th century Nō *kyōgen* are the first example of literature with a specifically humourous object. The writers of *kyōgen*, like their contemporaries in Europe, attacked particularly women and priests, and also made them attack each other. However, *kyōgen* criticises not only priests but their doctrines, especially those very injunctions whose disobeying cause, in the Nō plays, all the woes of this world and that to come. For example, in "The Staghunter," Sakon no Saburō pours scorn upon the five prohibitions: taking life, stealing, impurity, lying, and drunkenness. The play ends in this way:

Priest: Whatever you may say, if you kill a stag you'll be reborn a stag.
Sakon: Oh, is that so? Then if I shoot a priest I shall be reborn a priest.
Priest: Don't you dare shoot at me! I have a three-inch image of Amida
    in my bosom.
Sakon: Then I'll cut it open and see what's inside.
Priest: That would be like the foolish man who split open the cherry
    tree of Yoshino to find the blossom (*hana* means blossom and
    nose).
Sakon: Blossom? Well, you've got a red one yourself.
Priest: Where?
Sakon: On your face.
Priest: Don't be silly! Off with you!

Humour was always more or less underground in waka; it became implicit in haiku and explicit in senryū. While this was happening, *kobanashi*, short humourous stories, were developing between 1650 and 1850, reaching their highest point in *Kanoko-mochi*, and *Kikijōzu*, both published in 1772. *Kobanashi* are not jokes. They portray aspects of human life, unnoticed just because they are so common; mistakes and lies that are far more revealing than truth and honesty. They show us human nature in undress, oddly enough far more attractive than in its ceremonial robes. Some stories are quite puzzles at first. The following is called "Thinking too much."

A girl put her face out of the window and said in a soft voice to a mushroom-seller, "I say, mushroom-seller!" The man thought she spoke in such a low tone because she was bashful, and answered in the same low voice, "They are 32 *mon*." "Ah," said the girl, "so you have a cold too."

Mushrooms are, or at least were, sexual symbols in Japan, and the man thought this was the reason why she spoke so softly. One of the best of the *kobanashi* collections was *Kikijōzu*, "Good Listening," edited by Komatsuya Hyakki in 1772. The following, *Andon*, "Paper-covered Lamps," comes from it.

> A hand-cart loaded with lamps passed by some workmen mending the road. The workmen said, "Tremendous number of lamps!" Soon another hard-cart came along, the men calling, *"Yo ho!"* The workmen said, "Such a lot of lamps is ridiculous!" The foreman observed, leaning on his pick and gazing earnestly at the lamps, "Somewhere or other it must get terribly dark."

Also from *Kikijōzu* is the following, "The Master":

> A samurai went to a small-furniture store and asked the price of a wine-decanter. "Yes, that's a nice bottle," said the master of the shop. "It will cost you five hundred *mon*." "That's far, far too dear! Lower the price!" "No, I'm sorry, that's impossible." "Isn't the master in? If he were here, he'd make it cheaper,—you are no good." "No, no, I am the master; we never overcharge." "You're no master! The other day this was priced at two hundred *mon*. You can't be the master." "Oh, yes I am!" "No, no, not you!" The master got red in the face and upset, and threw the bottle down and broke it. "Now do you see I'm the master?"

This is a very Japanese, a very un-Chinese story.

Though not heavenly like the humour of Chuang Tzu or transcendental like that of Zen, the most truly human humour in the world is that of senryū. The word-play and drollery of *haikai renga*, and the witty game *maekuzuke* combined to produce the first volume of *Yanagidaru* in 1765. The following is from this volume, and exemplifies the strict though never trenchant criticism of senryū, which cannot bear the slightest untruth, whether of hyperbole, hypocrisy, self-deception, affectation, or, as here, of sentimental sexuality.

Kurosuke e   daiku-darake no   ema wo age

> They offer the votive pictures
> To Kurosuke,—
> > Most of them vicarious.

Kurosuke was the god of the harvest enshrined in the Yoshiwara, and he was worshipped also as the god of love. The courtesans offered votive pictures, usually of a horse, when their prayers were fulfilled. But the verses written on them were not by the person concerned, but by someone else. The verse says that the courtesans were all uneducated, without hardly any exception, contrary to the (modern) romantic idea.

Oriental humour, especially that of Japan, differs from occidental humour in its being rather less misanthropic, less "mistheistic" in its satire. Swift and Juvenal, if they had been born in the Far East, would not have had the prestige and influence that they possessed in the West. But otherwise, word-play, parody, irony, comedy, farce, nonsense verses, proverbs, doggerel, fables, and jokes,—in a word, the appreciation and expression of the details of the cosmic paradox, are the most human part of us all. They are our common ground, and the only hope of the world.

Buddhism and Humour

This essay appeared serially in The Young East, *Winter 1959,
Spring 1960. I have incorporated the revisions Blyth penciled into
the printed version and added a brief essay from the same journal
titled "Zen Is Nonsense" that Blyth's notes indicate he wanted to be
appended here. A similar version of this essay later appeared in* Zen
Essays (Zen and Zen Classics, *vol. 5).*

THE SUBJECT OF THIS ARTICLE IS BUDDHISM AND HUMOUR, BUT IT
should rather be Humour and Buddhism. My own experience in relation
to both, and my relation to this relation, may be represented by the well-
known story of the Arab and the camel. One cold night a man in a tent
felt sorry for his camel outside in the cold, so he told him to put his head
inside the tent. The camel gladly did so. Then the camel asked if he might
put his shoulders in, as it was so cold outside. The man said yes. Gradually,
the camel got further and further into the tent until all his body was inside,
and the man was forced to go outside. The man is Buddhism, the camel is
humour. Thus the subject should be, not even Buddhism and Humour or
Humour in Buddhism, but Buddhism in Humour.

Religion teaches us how to "overcome the world," whether it be by sub-
mission as in Jōdo Shin tradition, by energy as in the Nichiren Sect, or by
re-union with the Divine as in Hinduism. Popular Buddhism, like popular
Christianity, is for cowards and fools like ourselves, and consists of escap-
ing from this world to the Western Paradise, or to a Heaven of some kind or
other. Humour, however, belongs very much to the world. Life is suffering.
As Shakamuni pointed out long ago, we cannot have what we want, and we

must have what we don't want, but humour is not escapist. It overcomes the world, not by ascending to heaven, but by laughing at the paradoxes of life. We overcome the world by laughing at it; we overcome it in so far as we laugh as it. Humour is thus a religion. It is religion itself. It belongs to the will, to the subconscious will, and sets its will against communism and democracy and Buddhism and Christianity, and every other will, that is, every other religion.

Buddhism, like Christianity, hates this world. The world, the flesh, and the devil are lumped together in the New Testament. In Buddhism the world is, as said before, suffering, something we hate. Perversely, Christianity and Buddhism both tell us to love what we hate, to love our enemies, to be compassionate to the things or creatures or human beings that annoy and destroy us. Humour, on the other hand, makes us laugh at our enemies, and at our friends still more, laugh at God and the Devil, laugh at ourselves. To laugh is really to love. This we see in Hamlet and Ophelia, Othello and Desdemona, whose humourless love causes their tragedy.

If we take humour to be the nature of the universe, the origin of life and its object, the antagonism of Christianity and Buddhism to humour shows their irreligiousness. Of course, when we assert the importance of humour in this serious way, humour itself is absent, and we get only one more humourless –ism or –ology. What I really want to say is that it does not really matter whether a theory of life is good or bad, right or wrong, so long as it is humourously so.

The history of Christianity in England is the history of the addition of Anglo-Saxon humour to Jewish and late-Greek fanaticism and hero-worship. So, matrimonial quarrels were inserted in the story of Noah, sheep-stealing to the Nativity. People like Christ and Socrates and Buddha and Shelley have a mania, a megalomania for saving the world, teaching the unteachable. (So have I.) It is not possible to threaten, to frighten, to cajole, to shame people into Heaven. Can they be laughed or smiled into it? This is to some extent possible, humour being such a widely-spread thing, but the object must be, not Heaven, but laughter itself. Here, as everywhere, indirectness is best.

Coming now to Buddhism in particular, Buddhism was of course criticised in India. It was persecuted several times in China, for example between 438 and 452 by the Taoist To-pa Tao, and again in 845 by Wu Tsung. The famous prose writer Han Yu, d. 824, sent a petition to the Emperor Hsien in 820, begging that Buddhism should be proscribed:

It is a barbarous religion of which antiquity had no knowledge . . . of a man who disregarded his duties as a son and a subject. And you allow to be presented to your Majesty a dry bone of that man, a dirty piece of his corpse. Ah! I beg you to have this bone sent to the executioner, that he may throw it into the water or the fire. . . . And if the Buddha learns of it and can do anything, well, let him revenge himself on me, Han Yu, who will bear the full responsibility of your act!

In Japan, at the beginning of the 9th century, Shinto and Buddhism were merged, but the Neo-Shintoism of Motoori Norinaga and Hirata Atsutane was opposed to the Indian ideals of celibacy and world-renunciation, and chose rather the Chinese filial piety and loyalty of Confucianism. However, what we want to know is not so much the semi-official criticisms and professional animadversions against Buddhism, but how the Japanese generally felt towards it. In this respect, the proverbial sayings that have come from Buddhism are extremely interesting, even more so than the personal opinions of literary people in kyōka and senryū, since they show us what the common people thought was good or bad in Buddhism, in a word, what *interested* them in it. There is of course a good deal of criticism of Buddhism in the proverbs, for example:

Amida also shines with gold.

Buddha is power, and money is power, and so . . . .

Outside, a Bodhisattva; inside, a demon.

This is used of women, but may and should be applied to nature.

A Buddha to worship, and a lavatory,—both necessary!

Equally necessary.

The evil of Devadatta is the mercy of Avalokitesvara;
The folly of Panthaka is the wisdom of Manjusri.

This saying comes in the Noh play *Sotoba Komachi*. Devadatta committed all the Five Sins and fell into Hell through trying to harm the Buddha. Panthaka (Japanese, Handoku) was so foolish and forgetful that he could remember nothing that Buddha taught him. The above saying means that evil is good, illusion is enlightenment.

> The face of Yama-rajah when giving back;
> The face of Ksitigarbha when receiving.

Our very humanity, our Buddha-nature itself, requires us to do this, so that we may and should look smug when borrowing, and malignant when returning.

> Expounding the sutras before the Buddha.

This is what this article itself does.

> Trying to improve the Buddhist statue, and breaking its nose.

All improvement is really like this.

> My Buddha is holy.

Especially Christ and Buddha are not free from this illusion.

> The Nichiren prayer in the morning,
> The Shinshū prayer in the evening.

Namu-myōhō-renge-kyō, the formula chanted by Nichiren Buddhists with the beating of the drum, is suitable for the vigor of the morning, for young people. Namu-amida-butsu, the formula chanted by Shinshū, Pure Land Buddhists, suits the evening, with its quiet feeling; it is for old age.

One more may be quoted from its similarity to something in the Old Testament.

> Dye your mind, rather than your garments.

In *Joel* II 13, we have:

Rend your hearts, and not your garments.
Life is the treasure of treasures.

This is so, since without it no good is possible.

This comes from the *Daichidoron*, "Commentary on the Great Wisdom Sutra," attributed to Nagarjuna:

Life is a dirty thing.

This is so, since to eat or to be eaten is equally odious.

Life is like a candle flickering in the wind.

But these flickering candles tease and torture and extinguish each other.

The desire for enlightenment is also illusion.

If so, the desire for illusion is perhaps enlightenment.

Look at the audience first, and then preach.

If we do this too carefully, we might never preach at all.

Religion also comes from greediness.

A desire for peace of mind, a desire to be desireless,—what a difficult world it is!

To faith, a lavatory broom also is the five hundred Arhats.

This sort of thing, even at its lowest,—the worship of the heathen who "bow down to stocks and stones,"—adumbrates the best, that is, the interpenetrative identity of all things.

The flourishing will decline;
Those who meet must part.

Is there no exception to this? No exception.

Small wisdom is a hindrance to salvation.

To Hell with moderation!

Zen, cleaning; Shingon, cooking; Monto, flowers; Hokke, offering;
Jōdo, slovenly.[1]

This seems to represent the opinion of the common man about the various
sects. The first and the last, anyway, seem to me true.

When the temple is askew the sutras cannot be read properly.

We can't study in a tent. A good building is necessary.

Eating, and chanting the Buddha's name is bit by bit.

This is interesting as an example of "physical law in the spiritual world."

The one lamp of a poor man rather than the thousands of a rich one.

There is an exact parallel in the widow's mite.

Hell also is a place to live in.

However painful our life is, it's our only life.

A deaf man eaves-dropping.

This is a definition of a philosopher.

Spitting at heaven.

It falls back onto our own face,—that is true, but let's spit anyway; it relieves the feelings.

A hand lantern and a temple-bell.

These two things look alike, but are very different in weight. But looks are sometimes heavier than weight.

Counting the treasures of next door.

All education is this, but it's better than counting nothing.

A lotus flower in the mud.

This is one of the best similes, for enlightenment is illusion, since the lily *is* the mud.

A life, even if you cry; a life, even if you laugh.

But a life without crying and laughter is not a life at all. Stoics, take heed!

Those who chant the Buddha's name, and camellia trees,—is there a straight and upright one?

The answer is, as they say, in the negative.

Poverty is the seed of salvation, riches the father of karma.

This is something the world has forgotten, and may never remember again.

Buddhism and a straw thatch in the rain,—to hear them you must come outside.

This is a clever simile for the necessity of seeing the truth objectively as well as subjectively.

The moral (and even the legal) law exists because Buddhism exists.

What is chiefly wrong with society is the hiatus between the two laws. How can an ego-less judge condemn an ego-less criminal who has "stolen" what no one can really possess?

Worldly passion is, as it is, enlightenment.

This is perhaps the greatest paradox in the world, equal to the Christian incarnation, or the Hindu "You are not-you." It must have intrigued the Japanese from the moment it was imported.

Worldly passion is the dog of the house; it does not go away though you beat it. Enlightenment is the deer of the mountain; it does not come though you invite it.

These similes are good, too good.

Renouncing the world, but not renouncing oneself.

This is the fate of all hermits, whether scholarly or religious, so the only thing to do is to renounce renouncing the world, and then we shall renounce not renouncing ourselves.

This world is the accumulation of a thousand years.

This means what Blake said, more cheerfully: "A little flower in the labour of ages."

Life is short; the will is long.

Those who are satisfied with their three score years and ten are indeed pitiable creatures.

A potato-digging priest.

This gives us a picture of a priest of a small mountain temple. It is a warm day; the priest is intent upon his potatoes; Buddhism is forgotten; the priest does not know that we are looking at him. There is a deep feeling of *lacrimae rerum*, until we remember that God is watching us just as we are watching the priest. Who is watching God?

A chestnut-bur priest.

This priest has renounced not only the world, but also all kindness and humanity, yet this has something consistent in it.

What the doctor gives up belongs to the priest.

And what the priest gives up belongs to God. And what . . . .

A toad-eating priest.

The Japanese is "a sesame-grinding priest," since when working the mortar to grind the seeds the body moves to and fro as if bowing to and flattering somebody.

A stingy priest.

It is odd that the Japanese for miser is *kechimbō*, as though the Japanese did not find out what a stingy person was really like until they saw some mean priests.

There are many popular songs, sung all over Japan, a great number being derogatory to priests. The following is an example from Yamashiro; it is a cradle song:

The temple priest likes to gamble. Amida Nyorai he takes to the pawn-shop.

The pawnshop!

Here is one from Ise, a woodman's song:

When Priest Saigyō was travelling throughout Japan, he forded the River Hosoya, and injured his foot on the backbone of an eel. Isn't there any good medicine for this? Yes, there are many: bamboo shoots at the end of the year; midwinter eggplants; mushrooms growing at the bottom of the sea: shellfish on the top of a mountain; snow in summer. Take them in your hands, warm them in water, cool them in the fire, knead them with the tears of ants, and put the mixture on the wound, which will be cured immediately.

Another example, a remarkably poetical one from Mino, a children's song, shows some pity for the life of young priests, who usually left their homes at a tender age:

A temple is seen through a clearing of the wood,
A lonely temple with one priestling.

The following is somewhat subtle, from Echigo province:

Ye . . . e . . . e . . . s! Day has dawned!
O priest who rings the temple bell,
By your favor, day has dawned.

This reminds us of Lyly's skylark,

The day not breaking till she sings.

Occasionally the criticisms of Buddhism are quite profound, that is to say, humourous, that is to say, they have some Zen in them, for example, a Buddhist Dance Song from the province of Mutsu:

Something or other seems about to happen! Something or other seems about to happen! This dance and that dance—let's dance a Jizō dance! Look at this Jizō dance! Jizō! Jizō! Why should Jizō be gnawed by a rat? A rat is Jizō. If a rat is Jizō, why should it be eaten by a cat? A cat is Jizō; then why should it lose out to a dog? A dog is Jizō. If a dog is Jizō, why should it be frightened of a wolf? A wolf is Jizō; then why should it be burnt in a forest fire? The forest fire is Jizō; then why should it be put out by water? Water is Jizō; then why should it be drunk up by a man? A man is Jizō; then why should he pray to Jizō? Jizō is Jizō. Look at the Jizō dance! Look at the Jizō dance!

The most trenchant criticisms of Buddhism, that is to say, the most humourous, come in senryū, satirical verses written in the haiku form from the middle of the eighteenth century (1765), and still being composed at the present day. The following are both ancient and modern:

> Shinkō to betsu ni ume ari sakura ari

> Quite apart from our religion,
> There are plum blossoms,
>   There are cherry blossoms.   (*Nanpoku*)

This is a double mistake, the mistake of religion, and the mistake of poetry.

> Amari hare sugite sōshiki chiisaku yuki

> The weather is too fine,
> The funeral ceremony
>   Seems out of place.   (*Santarō*)

A funeral requires a rainy day, or at least an overcast sky.

> Kasōba no kemuri mo haru wa nodoka nari

> The smoke from the crematorium too
> Looks serene and calm
>   In spring.

There is no "pathetic fallacy" in senryū, and where would religion be without it?

> Shinjin de mireba sakura wa chiru bakari

> Seen by the eye of faith
> The cherry blossoms
>   Are always about to fall.

Religion is too prone to look only on the gloomy side of things.

Shinigao de   yatto ningen   rashiku nari

    At last,
With his dead face
    He looks like a man.   (*Kenkabō*)

Perhaps Kenkabō is speaking cynically, but inadvertently at least this verse justifies the Buddhist doctrine of the Buddha-nature. Underneath all the greediness and vindictiveness and vulgarity of his life-long face there always lay the humanity at last revealed by death.

Unkei wa   hotoke no kuzu de   meshi wo taki

    Unkei boiled rice
With the shavings
    Of Buddhas.

Unkei was a famous 12th and 13th century sculptor. This verse seems to have been written ironically, but also has a symbolical meaning.

Sekkyō ni   akubi mazari no   go shinkō

    Preaching;
Yawns
    Mixed with belief.   (*Kanno*)

This is perhaps the true human nature, the nature of human truth, the true humanity of Nature.

Bōsan to   michizure to nari   satorisō

    Happening to accompany
A monk,
    I feel near enlightenment.

So carrying a book under the arm gives us the illusion of learning something.

Zazendō   aita to miete   minna rusu

The Zazen Hall;
Nobody there:
    They must be tired of it.   (*Kenkabō*)

This is rather more valid than most criticisms of Zen, which are usually
based on ignorance or false understanding. Zazen is not a means to an end;
it is an end in itself; it is the end. Yet the Hall is deserted, as though the
monks with enlightenment don't need to sit, and those without it are all
right without it.

Iro otoko   de mo bōzu dake   yowami nari

A handsome man
With a weak point,
    He's a monk.

This is an inversion of the usual way of looking at things. In Sei Shōnagon's
Makura no sōshi we get a different inversion:

The expounder of the sutras should be handsome. We look fixedly at
him and thus perceive the holiness of his teaching. If we look elsewhere,
as a result of his ugliness, and don't listen, isn't this ugliness the cause
of our sin?

Nii-ama no   ware to iyagaru   kagebōshi

The new nun
Dislikes herself
    When she sees her shadow.

It is odd that the silhouette seems so much worse than the whole thing seen
in the glass, but this verse belongs to a time when mirrors were rare.

Osho mukuchi   hanaseba Zen ni   tesshi kiri

The priest
Keeps his mouth shut,
　Or speaks of Zen only.

Mr. Blyth is like this; but this is not real Zen, which will talk of anything, even of Zen.

One aspect of humour is lacking in Japanese Zen, though not in Chinese Zen, and therefore in Japanese Buddhism, that is, pure nonsense. The *Mumonkan* is full of preposterous stories, which must have been popular in China long before "Chan" was ever heard of. It was the genius of the Chinese Zen monks of the 8th century which perceived the Zen latent in those stories, and laughed with their conscious minds as did the Chinese illiterates with their subconscious minds. But how can we laugh with our conscious minds? To do so is Zen.

What human beings seek for is a unifying principle in this apparently chaotic universe; and nonsense is one of them. The most common of these principles is science, which discovers (or creates) cause and effect. The trouble with science is that cause and effect are only too efficient as an explanation; there is no mystery, no wonder, no interest remaining. Another such principle is religion. Buddhism joins all things by giving them all the Buddha-nature, which "escalates" them somewhat mechanically to Buddhahood. Christianity marries the soul to Christ, who is one with God, but the rest of creation seems to be omitted. According to Keats, Beauty is what makes everything meaningful,—but how about the ugly things, how about ourselves even? The hymn says love is "the tie that binds" things together, but the vast empty spaces of the universe do not look particularly loving. Poetry, in the practical sense understood by Bashō and Thoreau and Wordsworth, "seeing into the life of things," is the best so far, the "life" being the existence-meaning of things animate and inanimate. Humour also is a unifying principle, since it is possible, and even desirable, to laugh or at least smile, however grimly, at all things without exception.

The most remarkable, and most unexpected, of all these principles is nonsense. Nonsense does not mean no sense whatever; it implies a sense which is imperceptible by the reason, and can be assumed and justified only by an experience of that very "sense," that is, nonsense. There is a super-natural order, in which there is no intellect, no emotion, no beauty, no morality, no unifying principle, no order of any kind, natural or supernatural. This is the world of poetry, the world of Zen, of nonsense.

It is worthy of note that there is more nonsense verse, at least in English literature, than prose. The reason for this is that the rhythm, rhyme, alliteration, and so on, being themselves purely "nonsensical," help us to escape from the unreal world of common sense. An example of this is the following:

> Who killed Cock Robin?
>   I, said the Sparrow,
>   With my bow and arrow
> I killed Cock Robin.

Sherlock Holmes could never have found out who killed Cock Robin, nor could the most astute criminal psychologist, but the poet knows: it was the Sparrow. How did he discover this? Because "Sparrow" rhymes with "arrow." Why, at the end of the poem, did all the birds of the air start a-sighing and a-sobbing? It was not because they had sympathetic hearts, but because sobbin' rhymes with Robin. And this, to a child, Wordsworth's "Best Philosopher," is perfectly satisfying, is perfectly clear. Compare this with the following *mondō* [Zen question and answer]:

> A monk one day said to Yun-men, "A man may kill his father, and kill
> his mother, and repent before the Buddha; but if he kills a Buddha or
> a Patriarch, before whom or what can he repent?" Yun-men answered,
> "That is clear."

What is clear? It is clear that the question is not as important as the monk thinks, that no question is really important. It is clear that it is all right to repent before somebody, or before nobody, or not to repent at all, or to repent of repeating. It is "all right" as Browning said, a little too complacently, for the Sparrow to kill Cock Robin. It is clear that everything is clear.

Nonsense sometimes consists of saying the obvious, with pontific solemnity. We see it in the well-known verse from "The Walrus and the Carpenter."

> The sea was wet as wet could be,
>   The sands were dry as dry.

You could not see a cloud, because
  No cloud was in the sky;
No birds were flying overhead—
  There were no birds to fly.

This corresponds exactly to the Zen saying, "The flowers are red, the willow is green." It is in nursery rhymes and ancient nonsense verses that we see the Zen of nonsense and the nonsense of Zen at its best, its freshest and most natural. In Edward Lear and Lewis Carroll, as in much of the *Mumonkan* and *Hekiganroku*, we get a conscious resistance to sense, an intellectual defiance of intellect:

There was an Old Man who said, "Hush!
I perceive a young bird in this bush!"
  When they said, "Is it small?"
  He replied, "Not at all!
It is four times as big as the bush!"

The Thirty-eighth Case of the *Mumonkan* is this:

Goso said, "It's like a cow that passes by a window. The head, the horns, the four feet all pass; why doesn't the tail?"

The answer to this question is the same as that of the March Hare when Alice asked why the two little girls drew everything that begins with an M—. "Why not?"

Nonsense and Zen both make us free, free of emotion, and intellectuality, and morality, and beauty and ugliness. They enable us to escape from this unreal world of egoism and competition and hope and despair into the real world. Nonsense and Zen destroy false sense, all sense, all science and common sense, with which the newspapers and schools are filled. Above all they keep us young and healthy. "Some nonsense a day keeps the machine away." "Unless ye become as little nit-wits . . . ."

Untitled

Manuscript of an untitled essay read on an overseas broadcast for the NHK, Japan's national broadcasting network, on October 19, 1960.

UP TO ABOUT A HUNDRED YEARS AGO, THE LIFE OF THE JAPANESE was closely connected with the seasons, and almost every day had its special meaning, national, local, or personal. The seasons were closely related with religion, with Shinto and Buddhism, and these again with eating and dancing and singing, with processions and festivals of various kinds. The word for festival, *matsuri*, connected with *matsu*, usually refers to the summer festivals, when the rice has just been planted and the hopes of the farmers are for a bountiful harvest. The autumn festival is one of thanksgiving for whatever harvest nature has allowed them to gather. Of the reaping and harvesting haiku poets were spectators, seeing indeed things which the farmers overlooked. For example a verse by Buson:

稲刈れば小草に秋の日のあたる

　The grain being cut
Small grasses
　Feel the autumn sun.

This reminds us of Emerson's words:

　[The manuscript omits the text.]

An even more tender-minded verse on the same subject by Shiki:

稲刈りて野菊劣ろうこみちかな

> The grain being cut
> The wild chrysanthemums
> Are drooping along the path.

They seem to have nothing to support them now that the corn is cut.

The haiku poets were like other literary people, detached more or less, and to their loss, from the real world of the farmers. Bashō himself writes:

世の中は稲刈るころか草の庵

> I, in my hermitage;
> And in the world outside
> The time of cutting the grain.

But the real world of the farmers was connected with the world of poetry in being a part of the world of religion. The rice the farmers harvested no less than the verses they said or sang was received from the hands of the gods. One of the most visible and indeed boisterous of the manifestations of the way in which the world of men and the world of spiritual beings are blended is the procession carrying the *o-mikoshi* or portable shrine. The *o-mikoshi*, in which the local god is enshrined, was first used in the Heian Era, in 791. It is square, or six- or eight-sided, usually of wood lacquered black with a Chinese phoenix on the roof, and has two long poles.

The long men of the district carry the *o-mikoshi* on their shoulders along the street of villages or cities in a peculiar way, zigzagging here and there, and sometimes even retreating. So we get the following senryū:

後戻りしては騒はがすみこしかな

> The portable shrine
> Excites people
> When it goes backwards.

The religious or psychological explanation of this is that it is not that the young men are carrying the shrine with the god in it, but that the god is carrying *them*. And the god himself seems undecided whether to go or not and wavers along the street as though the spirit indeed "bloweth where it listeth."

The experience of each bearer is one of possession, possessing and being possessed. A modern senryū says:

御神輿を自分のものの気で担ぎ

    Carrying the portable shrine
He feels as if
    It belongs to him.

Often there is rivalry between the bearers of the *mikoshi* of one shrine and another. The *mikoshi* are bumped together, and often heads too. We are reminded of the religious contest between Elijah and the priests of Baal.

Of course the modern mind does not take the *o-mikoshi* in a serious or anthropological way; for example, another senryū, also a modern one:

御神輿を少しゆるめるみずたまり

    The puddle
Bends a little the procession
    Of the portable shrine.

Actually, however, all the ceremonies and festivals of this season, including that of the *o-mikoshi*, are the expression of the Japanese people's desire to be, if only for a short time, united with each other, united with the gods, in a word, one with humanity in its desire to be not merely animal, but human.

What Is Poetry?

*From a typed manuscript written for an NHK overseas broadcast.
Circa 1960?*

THIS QUESTION MAY BE ANSWERED IMMEDIATELY BY ASKING another: what is the meaning of life? The answer is: Poetry. The word "poetry" may be used in three ways: (a) verse (not prose), (b) the deep meaning of any action, of art, of music, of literature, (c) the above two combined, that is, deep meaning in verse. As to the significance of the word "deep," only deep people understand what is deep. How shall we explain it to the shallow? Well, even the shallowest person has his deep moments; even the deepest person has his shallow hours.

The enemies of poetry are many besides shallowness. Sentimentality, vulgarity, hypocrisy, bad taste, snobbery,—and science. The first six are not so dangerous, because they are clearly bad things, at least in the abstract, though usually not recognized as such in the concrete particular cases. But science is *the* enemy of poetry, that is, of mankind, because it is good, or at least, it is true. Poetry however is better, and the good is always the enemy of the better. Poetry is living truth, science dead truth. When for example a leaf falls to the ground, it does so by the force of gravitation. This is true, 100% true (though what it means I haven't the slightest idea). But there is another truth, that the leaves *want* to fall, and fall because they want to. This is poetry.

Once more, what is poetry? [Bashō's haiku] *Furu ike ya* is perhaps the greatest poem in the world,[1] for one reason, because it shows us what poetry is *not*. We realize, when we look back at Bashō's and our experience in *Furu ike ya*, that poetry is not emotion, not philosophy, not religion, not morality, not beauty. Here we have no comedy or tragedy, love or hate; there is no God, no Truth expressed here; the frog is not an ethical frog, nor does the sound of the water have any moral. Above all, the frog is slightly grotesque; it does not jump gracefully into the water; the sound is not an aesthetic experience. Can we say that whenever there is no emotion or intellection or morality or beauty there is poetry? Perhaps so. Emerson says, "When half-gods go, the gods arrive."

But if we take *Furu ike ya* as *the* poem, what becomes of the Anglo-Saxon poetry of war (emotion), the love poetry of Burns (emotion)? What becomes of the philosophical, scientific poetry of Lucretius? What shall we say of the (religious) *Paradise Lost?* How about waka, which is beautiful things in beautiful words? The answer to all this is of course that poetry may and perhaps should have morality and beauty and intellect added to it, and there is no limit to these. We cannot have too much love, too much duty, too much cleverness, provided that the essential poetry is there.

It may be suitable to speak here of bad poetry. "Bad poetry" is strictly speaking a contradiction in terms, because poetry can never be anything but good, and *the* good. What the phrase really means is, poetry (if any) smothered with false (unpoetical) religion, false (unexperienced) philosophy, false (shallow) emotion, false (artificial) beauty.

To know what bad poetry is, in this modern world of sham, is almost more necessary than to know what good poetry is. To take some examples from English literature:

The world is charged with the grandeur of God.

This is by Gerard Manley Hopkins, a late 19th century poet. The "grandeur" of God is a very disagreeable thing. "Grandeur" has some vulgarity in it. "Charged" seems to be a metaphor from electricity. Milton shows us the grandeur of the universe, of Satan, of himself, but he never speaks of it directly in this odious way. Another example of false emotion, from Keats, *The Eve of Agnes:* the young lady says to the young gentleman:

Oh leave me not in this eternal woe,
For if thou diest, my love, I know not where to go.

Woe is not eternal. "I know not where to go." Go home, go to the lavatory, go to the cinema. It is the rhyme, chiefly, which induces Keats to write like this. Japanese poetry is in a way lucky in its absence of rhyme. Japanese poetry falls seldom into morality or philosophy, more often into trivialism. An example of the first is the following by Ryōta:

むつとして戻れば庭に柳かな　　　（蓼太）

> I came back,
> Angry and offended:
>> The willow in the garden.

Issa's verse:

我と来て遊べや親のない雀　　　（一茶）

> Come and play with me,
> O motherless, fatherless
>> Sparrow!

This is a disgraceful example of self-pity.

Too much beauty is the bane of waka, as it was of the poetry of Keats and Tennyson, but to give examples of excess is itself excessive.

In Japanese literature, bad poetry has been checked by the profound Japanese sense of humour. Is humour essential to poetry? It is necessary for life, and for love. How about music? Music is a form of dancing, and heavily solemn dancing is not dancing at all. We may say then, boldly, that some faint kind of humour, often quite impalpable, which cannot and which must not be separated from the poem itself, it to be found in all real poetry. In Japan this fact was known almost consciously, since the history of Japanese literature is that of a swinging to and fro between the serious and less serious. English literature has been too much concerned with greatness, the great poem on the great subject. This was itself based on the unhumourousness of Virgil, and again on the (mistaken) view of Homer, who, as recent translators have shown, was far from the solemnly noble person we were formerly taught to consider him to be.

Is poetry national or international? This is perhaps a problem of comparative literature, but it might be considered from the point of view of translation. And first of all I would like to say something about the Japanese view of translation of Japanese into English, especially haiku. Japanese teachers of Japanese literature always inform their students (I suspect) with a portentous solemnity and a fanatical look in their eyes, that haiku do not and cannot exist in any other language, because foreigners lack the special Japanese delicate poetical feeling. This may be true. I think it is true to a certain extent. The mistake that is made is this. When a Japanese reads a (very familiar) haiku in Japanese, he puts into it all the poetical feeling he is capable of. He infuses it with all the associations, linguistic, cultural, ancestral, and so on. However, when he looks at the English translation, he sees it with a glazed cold, grammatical, scientific eye (that of his English teachers in the middle school) and is unwilling to see anything poetical in it. After all, if Bashō had been born in England, he would have had to write *Furu ike ya* in English, and if he had come to Japan he might have found that it sounds even better, softer, less merely factual, when translated into Japanese, but some verses might go better in English. It must be remembered that what matters is not what is behind the haiku, but what is behind the reader. The following are from Wordsworth and Coleridge, but would any Japanese know this when they are put in their Japanese dress?

> Over his own sweet voice
> The Stock-dove
> Broods.

> The moonlight steeped
> In silentness
> The steady weathercock.

Thoreau in his prose is much like Bashō:

Over the old wooden bridge, no traveller crossed.

This last is a modern haiku with no season word.

As for the philosophy of matter, we might like to suppose that there is a primordial wordless poetic experience which is then "translated" into

Japanese or German or so on according to the nationality of the person. This would make poetry international, but I am afraid the explanation won't do. We cannot imagine matter without form, poetry without words of some kind. The early Christians felt the same difficulty about the resurrection of the soul, so they borrowed from the Gnostics the idea of a spiritual body. We may then say that there is a spiritual language, as yet undiscovered by psychologists or linguisticians, which is the fundamental and universal language of poetry.

Last, what is the origin of poetry? Of course the answer is the (apparently) individual soul, of any place and any time, but here we may take the question scientifically, that is, historically. Much of human culture comes from India, and indeed Japanese poetry and English poetry are joined through the philosophical poetry, and religious intuitions, of the *Upanishads*. Bashō and Wordsworth thus derive from the same source, flowing together with the stream of Buddhism on the one (Eastern) hand, and on the other (Western) hand, expanding into the stream of Neo-Platonism. However, rather than the doctrine of the identity of the I and the not-I, which is too transcendental for poetry, it is the animism of the *Upanishads* which confirmed the poetical experiences of Wordsworth, and supported those of Bashō. Animism in some form or other is the essence of poetry, not only of Wordsworth, but of Shakespeare, even of Milton, who is the least mystical of the great English poets. One of the most remarkable passages of *Paradise Lost* is:

> Silence was pleased

(with the singing of the "wakeful" nightingale at evening). Shakespeare's most poetical lines, in

> daffodils
> That come before the swallow dares, and take
> The winds of March with beauty.

are so animistic as to be unexplainable (but not untranslatable). Wordsworth's addition to all this is his feeling that not only are all things alive, but that they *enjoy* their existence.

The moon doth with delight
Look round her when the heavens are bare.

D. H. Lawrence is perhaps Wordsworth's only disciple.

I don't know how to finish this essay, but I will say one more thing. Poetry is our common humanity. The object of life is the communion of souls. We see this in a verse of Robert Frost's poem, *The Pasture*:

I'm going out to clean the pasture spring;
I'll only stop to rake the leaves away
(And wait to watch the water clear, I may):
I sha'n't be gone long.—You come too.

I love poetry: how can I be happy if you don't.

"Zen" and Daisetz Suzuki

Published in Today's Japan: Orient/West, *vol. 6, 3–4, March–April 1961.*

THE HISTORY OF ZEN IS THE HISTORY OF THE HUMANITY OF human beings. "Humanity" means that state of Nature in which the human part has reunited itself with the whole, speaks for it, acts for it, sings for it, poses for it, and thus makes it really alive. Real "history" is not the concatenation of cause and effect, any more than culture is an accumulation of works of art. It is humanness appearing and disappearing, apparently haphazardly, to all intents and purposes without any plan or aim, but with an intellectually indiscernible poetical inevitability. The ordinary assessment of the real greatness of so-called "great men" must be revised. If Hitler has more Zen than Lincoln, he is to this extent a "greater" man, and will occupy more pages in the never-to-be written Zen History of the World. A general or an emperor will, for merely being such, have no interest for the Zen reader; the "short and simple annals of the poor" will remain short, because though wealthiness is a vice, poverty is no virtue.

The question of the influence of one man upon another is much more difficult to make out than it seems at first sight. Even of Dr. Suzuki I have to report, not that "he taught me all I know," but that "he taught me that I (already) knew." What did Christ really owe to his predecessors and contemporaries? Here the orthodox Christian answer is (as usual) correct: nothing at all. The Anglo-Saxons were already Christians before 597, when Augustine landed in England. Or may we not rather say that after 1,400 years they are still not Christians? Or best of all, the English are Christians in spite of all that Augustine and Wolsey and Cranmer and Law and New-man could do to prevent them from being so! History must be written in this transcendental way, but not à la Carlyle, full of emotion and violence and hyperbole and symbolism.

I wish here to write about Zen, the history of Zen, the Zen history of Zen, as finding its ultimate exponent in Suzuki Daisetz—not that there will be no development of Zen henceforward. The Europeanization, the Christianization of Zen is yet to come; it is oriental Zen that Dr. Suzuki has expounded. Zen is the power which human beings have, to be both themselves and the universe which they live in. The discovery of this power, its creation, was made in India some 3,000 years ago. What makes art, music, and poetry is precisely this being both oneself and all things, which the Indian forest-hermits experienced and expressed as best they could in the *Upanishads*. Buddhism appeared, with its doctrine of no-soul, the realization of which is Nirvana, a transcendental state beyond time, place, causality, dichotomy, and differentiation. All-soul and no-soul, Hinduism and Buddhism are the Yea-saying and the Nay-saying aspects of the Indian soul. The Cosmic Suicide was performed symbolically and vicariously by Gautama under the Bo-tree.

A well-bred dog goes out of the room before one kicks him out. The death of the universe, which occurs at every moment (this "every moment" is eternity) must be paralleled, must be re-enacted by the death of the individual man, who thus becomes Buddha, who thus dies into Christ. The simile of the dog is of course faulty, since the dog is the room and also the people in it. The universe kicks itself out of itself.

In the 6th century Daruma came to China, but, more important, Hui-neng was born in 638. It is with Hui-neng that Zen, as we know it today, began. He emphasized, by the way, two things that have been little understood ever since: the unimportance, not to say the folly, of doing zazen; and the fact that illusion and enlightenment are not two different things.

After Hui-neng we get the directness of Chao-chou, the laconism of Yun-men, the beatings of Lin-chi. It is the high-tide of Chinese Zen, after which it declines, and mingles with the stagnancy of the Pure Land Sect. The Chinese took Zen about as far as it could go along the line of perfecting a monkish character, rendering an individual completely efficient by removing the obstacles of egoism and self-consciousness, intellectual entanglements and passional rubbish.

When Zen came to Japan it spread out into various forms of culture, and even affected more or less permanently the national character. The Japanese Zen priests did not develop Zen in any special way. Dōgen is pedantic and obscure, Hakuin eccentric and parochial, Ikkyū at once conventional and paradoxical; but the genius of the Japanese lay in this very defect, in their application of Zen not so much to monastic life as to music and art and poetry. Or rather, a cultural Zen emanated from the Japanese people, whereas the Chinese people produced a philosophic Zen. "Philosophic" does not mean here intellectual or metaphysical, but transcendental, in spite of its practicality. The Zen is still obvious or ostensive. To put the matter in a cheaply religious way, Chinese Zen was man becoming God; Japanese Zen was God becoming man. When Zen appears as architecture or haiku or tea-drinking, it loses all its odious professionalism. The great principle is: the less Zen the better.

Coming now to the works of Suzuki Daisetz, particularly those written originally in English: in reading these we realize that Zen is being expounded in abstract words in a modern way. The word "modern" does not mean contemporary; it is having a historical sense, a feeling of progress and a common goal of human life; there is no hyperbole or fantasy, no superstition or rant. The *Essays in Zen Buddhism*, first published in book form in 1927, were written by Zen, of Zen, and for Zen. Just as science must be spoken of scientifically and appreciations of poetry must themselves be literature, so when we write of Zen—for it or against it—the words themselves must be a "seeing into the nature of one's own being, and pointing the way from bondage to freedom." Or rather, the words must *be* the being of the speaker; the words must themselves be free. This is what happens in *Essays in Zen Buddhism*. We feel as we read them that every word is his experience at the moment of writing it. He is not trying to teach us something; he is not, as so often in such cases, trying to persuade himself into something. He is writing as the *rōshi* of a Zen temple lectures, a conversation between himself and the (apparently silent) Buddha, the assembled monks overhearing it. We feel the same thing in *Walden* and *A Week on the Concord and Merrimack Rivers*. Thoreau and Suzuki Daisetz have also the power to teach because they have no wish to—a perfect example of the Zen doctrine that only a no-teaching is real teaching. Again there is in both no understatement, no figures of speech, no beautiful words or purple patches; is not this very Zen? (Zen has no rhetorical questions.)

It would not be proper only to praise Dr. Suzuki, any more than it would be right to omit all criticism of the universe itself. The sickening praise of God that still ascends to the sky every Sunday: no wonder Elijah supposed of another God that "he sleepeth or perchance has gone on a journey." Dr. Suzuki is rather overly fond of making comparisons between Buddhism and Christianity, or between Japanese and European cultures, to the disadvantage of the latter. Certainly it is all right to speak ill of something or somebody occasionally—say once in a million years; but comparisons are always odious. However, when Dr. Suzuki explains passages in the Bible by Buddhist experiences we see what comparative religion should have been. For example, with regard to the saying, "Let not thy right hand know what thy left hand doeth," he comments that it corresponds to *anabhogacarya*, "an act of no-effort or no-purpose":

> When spirit attains to the reality of enlightenment and as a result is thoroughly purified of all defilements, intellectual and affective, it grows so perfect that whatever it does is pure, unselfish, and conducive to the welfare of the world. So long as we are conscious of the efforts we make in trying to overcome our selfish impulses and passions, there is a taint of constraint and artificiality, which interferes with spiritual innocence and freedom, and love which is the native virtue of an enlightened spirit cannot work out all that is implied in it and meant to be exercised for the preservation of itself.

The most recent, the American and European criticism of Zen is that it is amoral. There is felt to be something wrong with a Zen that makes a man kill other animals or men more efficiently, more mindlessly, more divinely. This objection Dr. Suzuki has not, to my recollection, answered explicitly in his many works, English and Japanese; but it is forestalled in the first chapter of the First Series [of *Essays in Zen Buddhism*], The Doctrine of Enlightenment, in which he points out that Buddha was a practical man rather than a philosopher, and taught that the way to deliverance is through a threefold discipline; namely, moral rules, tranquillization, and wisdom. If Zen is, as he states, the essence of Buddhism and not an aberration from it, it must include, by transcending it, morality. "By their fruits shall ye know them" applies here as everywhere, and it is not possible, in my opinion, for a bull-fighter to kill bulls by Zen, because the bull-fighter is the bull, and bulls don't commit suicide. You may say, "But men do." The answer is, "Not when they are bulls."

Dr. Suzuki's great problem has been how to introduce (oriental) Zen to the occident. The obvious way would have been via Christian mysticism, which itself came, as did Zen Buddhism, from India through Egypt and the Near East with its Neoplatonism, magic, and alchemist thought. It is only recently, however, in 1957, that he published such a work, *Mysticism, Christian and Buddhist.* He may have felt, at the beginning of his career in America, that the country that produced Emerson could take its Zen "straight." Further, the boundless compassion of Buddhism that (supposedly) underlies or overlies Zen is not altogether different from the love which is (said to be) God. The second stage, now entered, is that of temples and sutras and zazen. Involved here is the difficulty that has always lurked in the background, the relation of (the freedom of) Zen to (the formality and formalism of) Buddhism. Everyone, except a few eccentrics, dislikes the superstitions and ceremonies of others, and loves his own, but this difficulty can be overcome by judicious substitution and amalgamation, such as was done in the case of Christianity which came to a pagan England in the 7th century. But the real "East is East and West is West" problem lies in the antithesis, referred to before, between (absolute) Zen and (relative) Morality. The East—that is, China and Japan—is transcendental; it is not, and never was, concerned with the moral horror of the cat eating the rat. The East believes in harmony, the harmony of the cat eating the rat, and the rat being eaten by the cat. This perhaps is why Dr. Suzuki spends so many pages, 153, in the new edition of his *Zen and Japanese Culture*, 1959, on the subjects of Zen and the Samurai, and Zen and Swordsmanship. After all, swordsmanship is two people harmoniously trying to kill each other. The West, though accepting for other reasons an Eastern religion, has clutched at any word of Christ or Paul which suggests pity for our poor relations: "Not a sparrow can fall . . .": or holds out the slightest hope of salvation for the lower creatures: "The whole creation groaneth and travaileth—." Buddhism sidestepped the question by taking over the old poetic theory of reincarnation, but, as Darwin rightly said, it is the meaningless suffering of animals which is a (moral) mystery, rather than "Why was this man born blind?" In any case, neither Christ nor Buddha could answer such questions, and they remain to trouble the thoughtful hearts of men as long as there are men upon the earth.

The insolubility of the mysteries of life does not, however, affect the greatness of great men, and we may sum up the work of Dr. Suzuki as having been that of Daruma and Hui-neng combined. Neither he nor they nor Buddha invented Zen. No one can create or destroy what does not exist, and what does not lack existence. No one can convey from one country to another something that is not a thing, and that is beyond, to say the least of it, geography. Dr. Suzuki has done something different. He did what the Four Statements of Zen said he could not do. He put into abstract terms, in a language not his own, that which seemed to be only concrete. He made the particular general, without losing its particularity. He did what Thoreau said a writer should do—chop his experiences into words with the same sinewy hands that he chopped wood behind his house in Engakuji Temple. Every log split as it was appointed to be split. Infinitives also were split sometimes, together with infinity, in his writings.

The true history of the world, as was stated at the beginning of this essay, is the history of Zen. If this Zen history of the world is ever written, Dr. Suzuki's name will have a high place in it. And if it is a (Zen) history of the exposition of Zen, we can prophesy that the name of Suzuki Daisetz, like that of Abou ben Adhem, will lead all the rest.

Why Nobody Likes Senryū

Published in Orient/West, *vol. 7, no. 3, March 1962.*

THERE HAS BEEN A HAIKU BOOM, AND ALSO A ZEN BOOM WHICH, to mix metaphors, Mr. Koestler has scotched, but there has been no senryū boom, and this article proposes to explain why—or rather, why there never will be one.

Haiku are nature poems which are short because the experience, all experience, is short, is (supposed to be) timeless. "Nature" is a very restricted nature indeed, including only the harmless animals (with the exception of wild boars) and excluding all evil-smelling plants, and omitting the struggle for existence, death, and anything violent whatever. Most of the things are small, or are dealt with in a small way. Whales for example are not Ahab's whale, but those of Matthew Arnold, which

Sail and sail, with unshut eye,
Round the world for ever and aye?

No one, therefore, can have any particular objection to haiku. Most people pretend to some love of nature, and are willing to allow the existence of haiku, provided they may keep their television and motor-car, and continue to live a life that is diametrically opposed to the haiku way of living.

Zen is another harmless toy; you can play with the fire of Zen without burning your fingers. Of course, if you go so far as doing zazen, your legs will hurt agonizingly, but to get rid of a neurosis some inconvenience is unavoidable, and the mysteriousness, the indefinability, the very inaccessibility of Zen are attractive to the ambitious fanatic. Everyone likes the esoteric. Inside, you can exhibit your knowledge to the vulgar herd; outside, you are made to get inside. To (clever) Roman Catholics, Zen is seen to be even more poisonous than pantheism; it is a mystery that competes with the mysteries of the Trinity and the Incarnation. But after all, it has no political power or social influence, so it is not necessary to excommunicate Daruma and the rest of them. Zen does not change a man's life, and make him resign from the presidency of the whiskey company, and incommode his family; or become a pacifist and betray his country. It makes him a better salesman, a better golfer, a better public speaker, a better butcher even, of animals or men. Zen can never be exactly popular, but a smattering of it might well become one of the extra graces of an international gentleman.

Senryū are verses of the same form as haiku, but originating in the middle of the eighteenth century, in 1765 to be precise, with the first volume of *Yanagidaru*. The aim of the many authors of the senryū was to show up the hypocrisy, sentimentality, self-deception, in other words, the humanity, of other people and themselves also. Their especial object of derision was of course the upper classes, the warrior, the virtuous man, the sage, that is to say, humbug.

Oku-karō   kao wo shikameru   mono wo fumi

> The Chief Retainer of the Ladies' Quarters
> Treads on something
> > That makes him make a face.

The *Okukarō* was in charge of all the affairs connected with the ladies-in-waiting, and would be especially solemn and unbending in mind and visage, but one touch of nature makes the whole world stink, and pride goes before his gall. His face is one of cosmic disapproval, and that is the funniest, foolishest face of all, for "this dungy earth" is all God gives us.

Another verse, which shows the senryū disrespect for religion:

Tetsuke nite   mō shinboku to   uyamaware

> The earnest money paid,
> It is now respected
> > As a divine tree.

Someone has just decided on a certain tree as timber for a shrine, and paid some money on it. A label is tied to it, and from now on it looks quite different from the other trees. (The senryū writers would have parodied *The Dream of the Rood*, had they known of it.) Noted also is the vital connection between money and religion. They produce and support each other.

The following (all these senryū are from the First Volume of the *Yanagidaru*) shows us that virtue is a garment which a man puts on and takes off at will, *sartor resartus*:

Funa-yado e   kawa no richigi wo   nuide yuki

>   At the boat-hiring place
> He takes off and leaves behind
>   His domestic integrity.

Funayado was on the bank of the Sumida River, where those who visited the Yoshiwara came and hired a boat for the purpose. At this place a man stopped being a husband and a father, and became an animal.

Everybody talks too much (and writes too much, and reads too much) especially about his own interests. This general truth, or platitude, as some people like to call it, is particularized in the following:

Nezu no kyaku   ie no hizumi ni   kuchi ga sugi

>   The visitor from Nezu
> Talks too much
>   About the strains of the house.

Many carpenters lived in Nezu. When one of them came, invited as a guest, he could not keep his big mouth shut, but must talk about the badness of the building and the incompetence of the carpenter who made it.

The hero is debunked along with the rest of them. No man is a hero to his valet (but neither is he to himself, otherwise he would not commit suicide).

Kozamurai   kumo to gesui de   hi wo kurashi

> The petty samurai
> Spends his days
> With spiders and drains.

Most of the warrior's life is spent cleaning the house and its attendant drains. Even one crowded hour of glorious life is not his, but only an age without a name.

The insincerity, unfaithfulness, and opportunism of men is frequently glanced at:

Nyōbō ga   shinu to otto wa   fumi wo yari

> The husband;
> When his wife dies,
> He sends a letter to her.

"Her" is another woman that he is intimate with. "He" is you and me, if the reader is a man.

Enough examples have been given to show what kind of literature, that is poetry, senryū is. Senryū is the reality of human nature, omitting all the truth and goodness and beauty as being something that because of its own intrinsic merit does not need support or advertisement. Senryū are not so much an attack upon falsity and hyperbole and sentimentality and hypocrisy and self-deception, as a defense of truth against the attacks of human beings, for "All men are liars," except the senryū writer.

It may be urged at this point that satire is a world-wide thing, and that Aristophanes, Juvenal, Martial, Rabelais, La Fontaine, Butler, and Swift have covered the ground pretty completely. It might be further pointed out that masochism, in this case the pleasure of being criticised, is also a universal phenomenon of human nature, that as masochism is a popular sport, not stated by Hamlet, senryū also may become popular. The fact is, however, that even the most masochistic person wears armor, which senryū can pierce. We are masochistic—up to a certain point; there are limits to our painful pleasure. Self-preservation is nature's first law, and its last. "Oh, to be nothing, nothing!" the hymn says, but this is not only a psychological impossibility but a logical one also, for "to be" means "to be something." Though not in the slightest degree reformative, senryū reproves us. It never praises us for any virtue we may possibly have, but points out the defects or excesses in that one and only virtue. It keeps reminding us of all the things we want to forget. This forgetting is essential to life itself, that life in which, as Nietzsche said, illusion is as necessary as truth. The instinct of humanity is against senryū, the most humane of all its creations, and rightly so. We must have a Way to walk on, be it democracy, culture, Christianity, science, the Way of haiku, Zen even; but senryū are like holes, air-pockets, like the spaces between the rungs of a ladder.

Actually, however, senryū are not merely negative. They involve a positive philosophy, a conscious or unconscious realization that to forgive is human, but to err is divine. The Fall of Man is a more meaningful, a greater event than the Atonement. The saints in heaven can have only one pleasure—that of watching the damned squirm in Hell. Or putting it another way, those in Hell have the exquisite pleasure of watching the holy humbug of Heaven, the egoism of the Deity, and the anti-Miltonic subservience of the saints. And whatever Way of Life is proposed, senryū will laugh it out of existence, not from any nihilism or pure love of destruction, but because as Lao Tzu said, "The Way that can be called a Way is not the Eternal Way." Thus senryū can never be popular, any more than the atomic bomb, which it resembles slightly, can be popular. As far as a boom is concerned, it is the aim of senryū to prevent it, for senryū is a disintegrating force. As Emerson said, "Men are not saved in bundles," to which we may add, senryū is precisely the force that cuts asunder the bundles. As to being saved, only those who do not wish to be saved will be. "Knock not, and it shall be opened unto you."

Senryū touch all our most sensitive spots; they tell us the very things that we do not wish to know, and which we would almost literally rather die than know. Thus the only people who read senryū are those who write them, and they are an odd squad, supersensitive to the frailty and folly of humanity and their own, and yet not realizing it or not feeling deeply the dreadful cosmological consequences of their knowledge. Only certain Japanese could do this and retain their equanimity. The rest have always consciously overlooked senryū into practical non-existence. I myself read the next senryū gingerly. I never know what painful memory it will prod, what last balloon it will puncture. At every senryū my God forsakes me.

The *Zenrinkushū*

These translations from the Zenrinkushū, *"Anthology of Phrases for the Zen Forest," a collection of poetic phrases used in Rinzai Zen koan study compiled by the Myōshin-ji priest Tōyō Eichō (1428–1504), appeared serially in* The Young East *12, no. 46 (Summer 1963); 12, no. 47 (Autumn 1963); 12, no. 48 (Winter 1963); 13, no. 49 (Spring 1964); and 13, no. 50 (Summer 1964).*

IN BOTH ANCIENT AND MODERN TIMES THERE HAVE BEEN MANY books of quotations, poetical, religious, witty or proverbial. In the middle ages in Japan there were also collections of proverbial sayings and of short religious passages. We have already in the 11th century the *Wakan Rōeishu*, a selection of Chinese and Japanese verses made by Fujiwara no Kintō, who died in 1041. The *Zenrinkushū* is an assemblage of words, phrases, and sentences, from two hundred and seventeen Chinese books, the Chinese Classics, verse anthologies, sutras, records of Zen priests, and various collections of sayings and doings and commentaries on them. In particular we may note the *Nirvana, Shurangama, Diamond, Vimalakirti, Amida, Forty-two Chapter, Engaku, Lotus, Wisdom,* and *Brahmajala Sutras,* the *Sutra of the Final Teaching;* the *Blue Cliff Record,* the *Mumonkan;* the various histories of Zen; the *Analects, Doctrine of the Mean, Great Learning, Mencius, Chuang-tzu, Lao-tzu, The Book of Changes, The Book of Songs;* the *Records of Yun-men, Wei-shan, Tung-shan, Po-chang, Hung-chih, Chao-chou;* the poems of Tao Yuan-ming, Li Po, Su Tung-p'o; the *Tōshisen, Sōshisen, Santai-shi;* the *Ten Ox-herding Pictures;* the *Chen-tao-ke, the Hsinhin-ming.*[1]

The author, Eichō, a monk of the Rinzai Sect, was born in 1428, in Gifu province. At the age of five he entered Tenryū-ji temple, and afterwards visited various famous Zen monks all over Japan, especially Sekkō of Ryōan-ji, by whom he was confirmed. In 1471 he became head of Daitoku-ji in Kyoto, then of Myōshin-ji. He died in 1504 at the age of seventy-seven. The book itself was first published in 1688, just before the beginning of the Genroku Era, nearly two hundred years later. At first it contained more than five thousand entries, from one word (Chinese character) up to sixteen, then another five hundred entries were added, making about six thousand in all. The origins of nearly all the phrases are given, with some mistakes, but many of the verses have no apparent connection with Zen at all, and seem to have been inserted by the selector's whim, or taste, a very catholic one. In 1889, the original was republished, and in 1920, Yamamoto Shungaku published it complete, for the first time with Japanese readings and explanations. These are often feeble and mistaken, but better than nothing. Sometimes the attempt is made to give the Zen meaning, sometimes not. In 1953 Shibayama Zenkei published about half the *Zenrinkushū*, with comments that also are limited by the size of the page. In Volume I of my *Haiku*, pages 10–23, about seventy verses of the *Zenrinkushū* are translated, without explanation, to bring out the connection between Zen and haiku, the poetry common to both. In the following, the principle of selection is not altogether different, but the lines are chosen more for their intrinsic interest, and, in addition, as revealing Eichō's own standard of judgement and taste, that is, to try to understand why a Japanese Zen priest of the 15th century, a contemporary of Ikkyū, chose the passages he did.

Going backwards through the *Zenrinkushū*, which is arranged in order of the length of the quotations, the longest are couplets of eight characters each:

寒山拾得及第不得　　碧眼黃頭遂是難得

Hanshan and Shih-te could not pass;
Blue Eyes and Yellow Head attained it with difficulty.

This verse expresses the superhuman efforts necessary for the attaining of enlightenment, which nowadays is guaranteed by some Rōshi within ten days. Han-shan and Shih-te are the famous "mad" pair that haunted Kokusei Temple in the 8th or 9th century. The denial of their attainment is somewhat facetious and hyperbolical here. Blue Eyes is Bodhidharma; Yellow Head is Buddha.

雲門云我当時若見　　一棒打殺与狗子喫

Yun-men said, "If I had been there at that time,
I'd have struck him dead, and fed him to the dogs!"

This very un-Buddhistic remark refers to Buddha's birth, when he is reported to have said, "Under Heaven and upon the Earth I am the only World-honored One." Yun-men is not reproaching Buddha, however, for his boasting, but for his disturbing humanity, just as Christ, and pre-Christian thinkers such as the author of Job, upset the Jews in their acceptance of suffering and death. Buddha, with his talk of enlightenment and illusion, prevented people from living their old, thought-less, natural, Lao-tzean life. If Hitler had not (supposed that he) loved the Germans and (supposed that he) hated the Jews, how much better it would have been for everybody! So Yun-men says that to have fattened some skinny dogs with Buddha's carcass (but Yun-men disliked dogs) and let everybody "cultiver son jardin" (and not himself) in peace would have deserved the Nobel Prize. After all, what is the good of teaching the unteachable? People are now so, not out of ignorance, but because they are blasé, that is, they know all the answers, but don't care tuppence about the questions. (In the note in the original *Zenrinkushū*, it is said that this saying comes from the Commentary on the Verse of the 16th Case of the *Blue Cliff Record*. This is so, but it is already a quotation.)

欲能其詩先能其心　　欲能其画先能其容

Wishing to make the poetry better,
We must first improve the character;
Desiring to make the painting better,
We must improve our style.

This has little to do with Zen perhaps, but provides an interesting distinction between literary men and artists. Literature, that is, poetry in verse or prose, emphasizes the matter rather than the form, and proceeds more or less directly from the character, which must be improved to improve the writing. Art, on the other hand, stresses form more than content, and an artist should include himself also in the beautification of the world. Zen requires us to do both, to do zazen for the body, and meditate and study for the mind.

削亀毛於鉄牛背上　　截兎角於石女腰邊

Shaving the tortoise's hair,
That grows on the iron cow's back;
Cutting off the rabbit's horns
That grows on the stone woman's hips.

There are two kinds of impossibility, that of enlightenment, of the absolute, "with God all things are possible"; and that of illusion, the relative, "Joshua commanded the sun to stand still." The iron cow, the unmoving mover of things, and the stone woman who dances (she is usually coupled with the wooden man who sings) are the first. The horns of the rabbit and the tortoise hair are the second. This distinction corresponds to Wordsworth's of the imagination and the fancy. The imagination creates what already exists; the fancy pretends what cannot. In the above verse, the two pairs are combined, as in real life, that is the life of Zen, so that the rabbit has horns and the tortoise has hair (potentially, latently); the iron bull cannot move, and the stone woman cannot dance. The absolute is relative, the relative is absolute. "Eternity is in love with the productions of time." Our life has no object, no meaning. It just continues from glory to glory.

追大鵬於藕絲竅中　　納須弥於蟭螟眼裏

Following the Great Peng
In the interstices of a lotus root;
Keeping Mount Sumeru
In a creature that nests in the eyebrow of a gnat.

The Peng is the ultra-colossal bird that Chuang-tzu invented; Mount Sumeru is the great mountain in the center of the (Buddhist) universe.

Transcending is done is music, in art, in poetry, in love, and last, but not least, in thought, for example by Eckhart and some other mystics. As we think, the thought seems to burn, to radiate light, to go beyond itself and fill all the worlds, yet remain thought. But just as music, for example Baroque music, gradually becomes a mannerism, and the original poetic animism turns into metaphors, and love knows its satiety through self-imitation, so in Zen there is a great deal of repetition of what was originally experience. The present verse is so. It is constructed merely in the head, is not real "thought," and has no more Zen, that is life, that is poetry, in it than a pawn-shop.

説妙談玄太平姦賊　　行棒下喝亂世英雄

Explaining the deep, expounding the mysterious,—
A robber-ravisher of peace and harmony!
Wielding the stick, and letting off his shouts,—
A hero in this war-troubled world.

On the one hand, "I come not to bring peace, but a sword"; on the other, "How beautiful upon the mountains are the feet of him that bringeth good tidings, that publisheth peace." And this "I" and "he" are the same non-person. The verse refers no doubt to the two-fold activity of the Zen master, but it also reminds us of the double nature of truth, the way in which it blasts all our hopes and yet reconciles us to the world. Like Job we say to the inscrutably unjust universe, "Naked I came from my mother's womb, and naked I shall return; the Lord gave, and the Lord has taken away; blessed be the name of the Lord."

劍輪飛處日月沈輝　　寶杖敲時乾坤失色

The sword flies up,
And sun and moon are darkened;
When the treasure-staff strikes,
Heaven and earth blench.

It has been said that Oriental people have less ego than Occidental people, but sometimes, as here, it seems as if the reverse is true. Modesty, of course, is a virtue in both East and West, but in Zen, "Not to have a single thought, is to have everything." According to Christianity, even in Heaven life is spent praising God, and the saints cast their crowns before Him, but the Zen master is he who wields this sword and brandishes this stick, and every existence in the universe admits his omnipotence. However, when we think of the Jōdo Sect in Japan, and the fundamentalists in America, it seems that human nature is more or less the same (either self-centric or other-centric) everywhere, and only the region where these characters express themselves is different in each case.

I have never forgotten two remarks made to me by a Dr. Hattori in Korea concerning Zen. He said, "Zen is a trick of words." When we are speaking of Zen we have to use the greatest care to contradict ourselves. "Without paradox it is impossible to please God."[2] So in the *Zenrinkushū* we have such a verse as:

> The mind is not Buddha;
> Wisdom is not the Way.

These two statements are the opposite of the "fact." But when we assert that A is A, this is only the relative, logical, rational, dichotomous truth. Sometimes we realize that A is not A, that A is B; this is the mystical, super-rational, absolute truth. But this is still not the whole truth. We have to be constantly balancing ourselves between the two, putting together the two half-truths.

Dr. Hattori also said, "Zen is not everything." The *Zenrinkushū* itself illustrates this feeling, peculiarly Japanese. We might say that the Japanese created Haiku, the Art of Tea, Flower Arrangement, Bushidō, and so on because they felt that a purely religious, life-and-death-transcending, specialistic, esoteric Zen was too narrow in its scope. They wanted to put the seasons, plants, and animals into it; they wanted to drink tea with Zen, arrange flowers with Zen, kill one another with Zen. Theoretically, they should have gone on, and widened Zen to include government, social reform, love, sex, science, everything. The *Zenrinkushū* hints at this absorbing of all the elements of life and a consequent enlargement of Zen in such a verse as the following (still going through the book backwards):

> Sensitivity to the feelings of others
> Is a cause of world peace.

Zen should never think or talk about peace or war, but the very object of zazen is sensitivity, a cosmic awareness, self-sensibility of the highest degree. So Shelley says that we become more moral by being more poetical, that "poets are the unacknowledged legislators of the world."

In another interesting verse, which shows how in some ways the Japanese understood the Chinese genius even better than the Chinese themselves:

Morality, virtue, humanity and justice
Without good manners, are unfruitful.

Christ on the cross must not be violent or rude or sneering or affected or pretentious, or sentimental, otherwise his sacrifice is all in vain. To divide good manners and morality is perhaps wrong, but of the two the former is more difficult, more delicate, more spontaneous, cannot be imitated. Zen is the good manners of oneself and the universe towards each other.

Christianity gives us as many examples of Zen as the Buddhism from which Zen is supposed to have derived. This may be partly because just as Zen is a combination of Indian spirituality and Chinese practicality, (the Zen of) Christianity is an amalgamation of Jewish practicality and Near Eastern spirituality. The following verse reminds us inevitably of the Incarnation:

In heaven, a Heavenly Being;
Among men, a man.

This verse should be connected with the next:

The Real Ground
Is never contaminated.

It is Christian doctrine that Christ was wholly divine, and wholly human; that neither nature affected the other; especially that his human weakness did not impair his omnipotence, nor mixing with sinful men his perfection. The meaning of all these factually-speaking nonsensical statements is that our Buddha-nature, that is our human nature is good as it is, is void of qualities, moves unrestricted throughout the universe, cannot increase or decrease, be purified or degraded.

However, Christianity rejected the Near Eastern pantheism, and refused to things in themselves any kind of intrinsic value. God is immanent, like water in a jug; the jug has no meaning of itself. It was left for certain poets, Vaughan, Herbert, Wordsworth, Thoreau, Whitman, Shelley and so on, to put back the animism, or rather animatism, that had been omitted. In the *Zenrinkushū* we have:

The purple swallow, the yellow Korean cuckoo
Expound deeply the Real Form of things.

Vaughan says, commenting himself on the text, "For the earnest expectation of the creature waiteth for the manifestation of the sons of God" [Romans 8:19], and speaking of Bible commentaries:

My volumes said
They were all dull and dead:
They judged them senseless, and their state
    Wholly inanimate.
Go, go; seal up thy looks
And burn thy books.

He then goes on to say, in the most unchristian Christian way:

I would I were a stone or tree,
    Or flower by pedigree.

Without this love of nature, which for many ancient Chinese and Japanese was religion itself, Zen, whether Buddhistic or Christian, is a half-alive, narrow, and fanatical thing. Whitman says:

All truths wait in all things,
They neither hasten their own delivery nor resist it,
They do not need the obstetric forceps of the surgeon.

Both Buddhism and Christianity go from one extreme of optimism, the power of God, the ubiquity of the Buddha nature, to the other of pessimism, the incurable sinfulness of man, the extreme difficulty of becoming enlightened. A verse which seems to illustrate the latter is:

Shaka already dead.
Miroku not yet born.

Miroku is Maitreya, who is the next Buddha to make his entrance on the stage of this world. This verse reminds us of Arnold's lines:

Wandering between two worlds, one dead,
The other powerless to be born.

An optimistic verse:

Old Shaka has nowhere
He can hide himself.

He manifests himself in every natural phenomenon. The Catholic martyr Southwell wrote, about a hundred years after Eichō:

God present is at once in every place,
Yet God in every place is ever one.

The Buddhist lines may seem very different from the Christian in this sense, that they imply, for Zen, that every man has this same lack of capacity not to show himself in every corner of the cosmos; God is the only omnipotent being in the universe, and so am I. But Southwell goes on:

So may there be by gifts of ghostly grace,
One man in many rooms, yet filling none.

This reminds us of the *Vimalakirti Sutra* in which Vimalakirti's small room accommodates thirty-two thousand Bodhisattvas; and of Lear's verse:

There was an Old Man who said, "Hush!
I perceive a young bird in this bush!"

When they said, "Is it small?"
He replied, "Not at all!
It is four times as large as the bush!"

The bush and the bird, the universe and God, the world and man, are not inside or outside of each other. There is no prepositional relation between them. So the *Zenrinkushū* says:

Outside the mind, not a thing exists;
The blue mountains fill the eye.

The scene of the hills rising one behind the other enters the eye and occupies it completely; the eye and the mountains are one, like the Father and the Son. The mountains can do nothing of themselves, but that is so with the eye too. So we may rewrite the first line, "Outside things, not a mind exists": and the second line, "The eye fills the blue mountains," with color the form.

After all this transcendentalism and mysticism and mystification, what shall we say when we are asked (as we never are) what we really believe? The following verse answers:

Lifting up his *nisidana*, he said,
"Just this is This!"

The *nisidana, zagu* in Japanese, is a piece of cloth used for genuflection at Buddhist ceremonies, carried on the left arm for the purpose, but otherwise not in use. The original says, "This is simply this," but a capital letter, fore or aft, makes the statement more intellectually understandable: "Simply, This is this," or "Simply, this is This." Whitman once more:

And the cow crunching with depress'd head surpasses any statue,
And a mouse is miracle enough to stagger sextillions of infidels.

The aim of life is not happiness, as most people (think they) think. It is not suffering, as Kierkegaard thought. It is not a good society and a welfare state. The aim of life in general is what we see around us, what we read in the newspapers of the world so far. But the aim of my life is to know the aim of my life. This will be known after the end of eternity. How can I get to know it? The *Zenrinkushū* says,

> It does not come through the body,
> It is not to be sought with the mind.

Zazen, asceticism, philosophy, passion—all are useless. In this predicament Wordsworth says,

> Think you, 'mid all this mighty sum
>   Of things for ever speaking,
> That nothing of itself will come,
>   But we must still be seeking?

Nature is always telling us that we must be, like the Vicar of Bray, on the winning side. That is why the Japanese, whose very religion is this cosmic opportunism, are always on the side of Nature. But Nature is not such a simple thing. It often opposes itself, and we have to follow Something or Something deeper still. And the odd thing is that when we follow It, It follows us. Of this paradoxical realm the *Zenrinkushū* says:

> Striking the void, it emits a sound;
> Hitting wood, it is without a voice.

Here we go beyond sound and silence, yet things are both voiceful and voiceless, just as in *To the Cuckoo* the near and the distant are transcended, and yet, and because of this,

> Thy two-fold shout I hear . . .
> At once far off and near.

The verse from the *Zenrinkushū*, however, differs from Wordsworth's, in that it is not poetry, and therefore not Zen. Real Zen is poetical Zen. This fact was understood vaguely by the Zen masters of ancient times. They felt by instinct (as well as following even pre-Daruma custom) that their enlightenment must be expressed in verse form, in that form at least. The philosophic reason is this. When we assert, unpoetically, that upon hitting wood there is no sound, but empty space makes one, this is true, though not Living Truth; it is so to speak half, or rather one third of Truth. Poetical Truth. The second part is that wood makes a sound when struck, emptiness does not. The third is that the first and second occur simultaneously, and never separately, except verbally and paperly. A is B = A is A. Thus only when A is B, is A really A. Only when you have Pai-chiao's NO STICK have you A STICK [ed. *Gateless Gate*, Case 44]. A stick is not the same as no stick, but A STICK and NO STICK are identical. So are a stick and A STICK, and so are no stick and NO STICK and A STICK. But as said before, a stick and no stick are different. So according to this paralogic, a = A and b = B and A=B; but a is not equal to b. This is because "equality" in the realm of A and B is different from the equality and inequality in the realm of a and b. So we cannot ask the question, "Which is stronger, love or death?" because the realms are different; one is LOVE, and other is death. It may be asked, "If A STICK and NO STICK are identical, why do we write them differently?" Because we cannot help thinking of a stick as deriving from A STICK, and no stick as coming from NO STICK, but strictly speaking we should write STICK-NO-STICK. The relative stick-or-no-stick is born of this absolute, but the Son is not inferior in glory to the Father, for without a song there can be no father.

Further to refine on the matter, the identity of the absolute A STICK and the absolute NO STICK is not the same as the identity of the relative a stick and the absolute A STICK, and of the relative no stick and the absolute NO STICK. The first is the identity of two indivisible absolutes—which is a contradiction in terms that shows their absoluteness. The second is the identity of the relative and the absolute, which are at the same time divisible.

Going back to the original problem, common sense asserts that a is a. Unpoetical Zen asserts that a is not a, a is b, which really means that a is NOT-A, and a is B. But poetical Zen somehow or other states its experience that a is a and a is b—in one sentence, a sentence which is imperative rather than indicative, since all this happens in the will. It does not speak of A or A; it just says that the cuckoo's voice is both near and far, and if we wish to may explain it unpoetically and commonsensically as several cuckoos, just as theologians explain Christ's paradox about losing one's life being to gain it, as referring to physical and spiritual lives. As the Japanese say, there is no medicine to cure an (unpoetical) fool.

Our next verse looks quite popular and untranscendental, but its being so interesting must make us suspect it has some Zen in it.

A man's face looks like a thief's;
A thief's face looks like a man's.

Hui-neng asked Hui-ming, "What is your real face?" — The face you had before your birth, and that you will have after your death, and which you have at this moment — Is it a faceless face? Is it perhaps God's face, the Face of the Universe, which appears sometimes like that of the Virgin Mary, sometime like that of the Gorgon?

In order to go deeper and deeper into the already not shallow Buddhist experience, the early Zen monks found it expedient and necessary to get rid of the "Idea of the Holy," because, following the paralogic of the previous verse, just as a sound is a sound because it is soundless, so the really holy is holy because it is non-holy. So we get the following:

The old chap Sakyamuni
Has not yet the Buddha-nature.

This is like asserting that Christ was not a Christian. The verse is not, as some assume, indirect praising of the Buddha by pretending to speak ill of him. It is really condemning him. God also is not yet divine. Christ still cries, "My God, my God, why hast thou forsaken me?" This is not because he despairs of the universe, but because of the doubt that inherently and indissolubly belongs to that aspect of the divine-human nature that we call intellection. The Great Doubt can be solved either by giving up thought altogether (many people have nothing to give up), or by putting no emotional energy into it, that is, making our thinking something apart from our life. What is the meaning of the (useless) suffering of animals? Christianity does not know or care, and gets thereby the peace that passeth understanding. Orthodox Zen does not know or care, and this is (a necessary part of) enlightenment, Wordsworth's "turning his face from half of human fate," as Matthew Arnold puts it. But in real Zen, not only Chao-chou's dog, but Chao-chou, and the Buddha himself have not (yet) the Buddha-nature. The electrocution by the will of the intellect is forbidden, like suicide, in Roman Catholicism, but there is little difference between Zen and Catholic priests.

Neither really love truth, and that is why they both dress like women, who also do not know that they do not love truth. Truth is always something paradoxical, and therefore painful, and pain being due to the doubt, which priests cannot afford to have, with the paradox originating in the simultaneous identity and difference of relative and absolute.

The doubt, which we must never cease to cherish, is followed close behind by the belief, which however never overtakes it. But besides this there is Belief, which every thing has. As Blake says,

> If the Sun and Moon should Doubt,
> They'd immediately Go Out.

Thus there is no Doubt in the universe, so far, because Doubt is nihil per se. But doubt—doubt makes the world go round, that is, doubt and belief and Belief, which is love. These are the three that rule our lives, rule all existence, and this trinity is always a unity.

> Daruma came from the West
> With a mouth, but no tongue.

When we teach one thing, people learn (if they learn at all) another. Silence is louder than words, but words are louder than silence. To talk with no mouth, or be mum with one,—this is the art of Homer and Christ and Shakespeare.

> People who praise me are many;
> Those who laugh at me are few.

This is because few love me, that is, love what I love, love truth: "Whom He loveth, He chastiseth."

> He who (thinks he) gives, and he who (thinks he) receives
> Are both one-eyed nit-wits.

The ancient Indians perceived this fact four thousand years ago. The history of mankind has been the more or less successful endeavor of people to forget it. Kindness and gratitude are "flowers of the air," fictions of emotion.

The real pleasure of giving and receiving is in *movement* only, not in the illusion of getting something, or in surveying those foolish feelings in the other person.

> When a man is poised, he does not speak;
> When water is level, it does not flow.

This is why Christ and Socrates and Buddha talked so much. As Christ himself said, only God is good, that is, silent.

> Above, no Buddhas;
> Below, no human beings.

What remains? The answer is not nothing, but Nothing, and in this Nothing the Buddhas and men live and move and have their being.

> Originally, water has no voice;
> When it touches the stones, it sings.

Actually, we need not only the water and the stones, but the air and the ear and the human consciousness as well, and the oneness of the sound suggests that perhaps all these things are one, at least in relation to the sound. Further, water without stone is not water, stone reveals its nature in relation to water. No God, no man; no man, no God.

> To open the eyes is all right;
> To shut them too is all right.

Hamlet did not think so, nor do I, but this is the philosophy of Zen, of Browning, Emerson, Whitman, and Thoreau.

> A hair swallows up the Great Ocean;
> A poppy-head contains Mount Sumeru.

The most difficult of all things is not to overcome the world, but to overcome prepositions. Only humor or nonsense, in a word, Zen, can do it. The money is in the purse—how true! But also the purse is in the money.

Financially, yes, because we can buy another purse with the money, but physically, materially speaking, how can a bird be in a bush if it is four times as big as a bush? How can we apply our poetical, artistic, musical, transcendental intuitions to daily, bodily life? That is *the* problem.

Neither yearning after the sages,
Nor prizing one's self.

This is the very antithesis of Christianity, for it means neither loving God and one's neighbor, nor saving one's own soul. What then must we do? The answer, as before, is, Nothing. Simply forget God, forget your neighbor, forget yourself, and there "you" are!

Yellow-head binds his tongue;
Blue-eyes swallows his voice.

Buddha refuses to tell us whether there is a God or whether the soul is immortal. Daruma does not even say that he will not say.

If Buddha comes, strike him!
If a Patriarch comes, strike him!

Not only so, but even if truth, if beauty, if goodness come, drive them all away! Be yourself! Be free! Be an exclamation mark!

The head pillowed on Mount Ko,
The feet on the North Peak.

"The foxes have holes, and the birds of heaven have nests, but the Son of man hath not where to lay his head." Then let him lie upon the whole universe, and let God sleep in the holes with the foxes and in the nests with the birds.

Turning the Great Wheel of the Law
In the midst of fire and flame.

The aim of Zen is not peace of mind, but neither is it, as Kierkegaard thought, agony of mind. The aim of Zen is to turn the Great Wheel, and we must enter the fire of doubt and the flame of resistance in order to do it. What is the Wheel of the Law? It is said to be the Buddha-truth, which, like Indra's wheel, crushes all in opposition to it, falsehood, cruelty, snobbery, sentimentality, hypocrisy, and insensitivity. To turn the Wheel is said to be to preach the Buddha-truth, which must be by action, not words. Anger does not turn away anger, nor does indifference, nor does love, which makes the angry man feel yet more inferior. Zen turns away anger—in time, of course, and that may mean a year or fifty years. Zen is helping on the system of things, which is set in the opposite direction of anger and vulgarity and self-seeking and romance and revenge and sadism and masochism—which are the fire and the flame.

> Grasping the whole world,
> Not letting the slenderest hair escape you.

This is what God does, counting the hairs of our head, and watching how a sparrow falls to the ground. We must go and do likewise, for all that we omit conspires against us. For want of a nail a battle is lost. A dislike of cockroaches vitiates all our theology.

> Each rice field
> Has its three snakes, nine mice.

Zen belongs to human beings, but "The earth is the Lord's, and the fullness thereof." And we have to struggle with the snakes and mice for the possession of it. If men win, Zen may win; if men lose, Zen must lose.

> It is like being among the flowers,
> Their scent fills our clothes.

This verse refers obliquely to the effect upon us of our human environment, but it may be taken more profoundly concerning the religion we have been living by, more or less unconsciously, for so many years. And we may ask, what is the smell of Zen? Far indeed from having no smell, it is rather like the contents of Alice's little bottle, which had "a sort of mixed flavor of cherry-tart, custard, pineapple, roast turkey, toffee, and hot buttered toast."

A dragon has no dragon-word,
A phoenix has no phoenix-phrase.

"And the Word *was* God," it says, but this is only half true, for "The Word was (also) *with* God." God is nameless, like my cat. The gnostic doctrine of emanations was correct enough, but God, if he expresses himself, becomes not-God. A thing is not a thing until it speaks; that is true, but the speaking and the thing are different. The Father, the Son, and the Holy Spirit may be one, but this is beyond experience, true (for us) only in the abstract, in dogma. When a thing speaks and exfoliates, the original oneness is broken, and can never be regained. And the ultimate end is not oneness but difference, as Lawrence says in *Women in Love*:

"I don't want love," he said. "I don't want to know you. I want to be gone out of myself, and you to be lost to yourself, so we are found different."

Not distinguishing the master and the servant,
Not differentiating between stone and jade.

This is the false Zen that makes all things equal, that pretends not to, or cannot see the difference between killing a cow and killing a cabbage, between "the mealy-mouthed lover of nature" and the silent woodsman with his axe.

For forty years
He did not preach a word.

Buddha told no one what he perceived under the Bo-tree. Couldn't, or wouldn't? Didn't. For one thing, nobody asked him. Why not? Because they didn't want to know. I lecture on Love in English Literature at a certain university. Two students come; 19,998 students don't. When a certain Zen master was about to die, he heard a flying squirrel shriek. "That's it," he said. Let nature be your preacher.

Holding nothing inside oneself,
Seeking nothing outside oneself.

To be neither Hamlet nor Macbeth is to attain the object of life, freedom.

Entering the fire, not burned;
Entering the water, not drowned.

This is the absolute, our Buddha-nature, but the Buddha-nature is also our human nature, and the absolute is the relative, so that we must also say: "Not entering the fire, but burned; Not entering the water, but drowned." Zen is the time-place at-in which relative and absolute are one—and two.

It is like a dragon without legs,
Like a snake with horns.

Reality is the relativity of the absolute, the absoluteness of the relative. God tells us to be pacifists and vegetarians, but is himself a man of war, and takes delight in burnt offerings. He lovingly annihilates us. In his omnipotence, he wishes for our help. Indeed, he cannot exist without our admiration and affection, but he knows better than we do that to be loved is nothing, to love is everything. Reality is Lao Tzu's "uncut block" which we have to "rough-hew."

The marsh is vast, and hides the mountain;
The badger defeats the leopard.

This is Lao Tzu's doctrine of the weak overcoming the strong, both materially and spiritually. But it is a mistake to be weak *in order to* defeat the strong. To be obedient, even unto the death on the cross, is good in itself, not so as to sit at the right hand of the Father in his glory. A swamp is the most poetical thing in the world; the mountain is too aggressive, too masculine. The ugly hippopotamus is more meaningful than the beautiful butterfly. We must sit at the back because it is good to be there, not so that the master of ceremonies will urge us to come to the front. Both Lao Tzu and Christ are too practical, which means, in the event, not practical enough.

If we see a ghost as not a ghost,
It ceases to be a ghost, of itself.

This is too subjective, and it does not allow for the objective existence of things, either Platonically or materialistically. We may say that ghosts do not exist, but Zen cannot assert that they do, or do not. It says that they both do and do not, so that we may see a ghost as a ghost or as not a ghost. Either will do, but they are not quite the same, because the non-existence of ghosts is stronger than their existence, just as the lifelessness of the moon is stronger than its "with delight" looking down on us "when the heavens are bare."

Under the ear, the voice of the fountain;
Before the eye, the shape and color of the hills.

After all the paradoxes and the mysticism and the stink of Zen, to listen to the sound of water and gaze at the distant mountains—to know how to do this is "all ye know on earth and all ye need to know."

Haiku, Senryū, Zen

This appeared in the Japan Quarterly *vol. 11, no. 1, 1964.*

THE JAPANESE PEOPLE CREATED THE FIRST TWO, AND HAVE PER-
petuated the third, which was "discovered" in China. Of the three, Zen is
said to be difficult or impossible to define, and this is true, but so are haiku
and senryū. What poetry is, the poetry of Nature, and the (satiric) poetry
of man, has not yet been explained, even unsatisfactorily, and the same is
true of humour. We may suspect, then, that there is some occult and never-
to-be-revealed connection between these three—poetry, humour, and reli-
gion. The value of Japan lay and lies in its haiku, senryū, and Zen, for in
Zen we may also include the art of living, of dressing, of drinking (tea) and
eating, arranging flowers, fighting, painting, building, and so on. Since this
is true of Japan, it is of great interest also to see to what extent we can find
examples of Zen, haiku, and senryū in English life and art. In this essay it is
intended first to bring out the nature of Zen, haiku, and senryū by illustra-
tions from both Japanese and English literatures, and then to consider the
relation among Zen and haiku and senryū themselves.

Haiku is the poetry of sensation, not only of sight and sound, or even of
smell and taste, but of many other unnamed modes of physical apprehen-
sion. For example:

Kakitsubata betari to tobi no tarete keru

> The droppings of the hawk,
> Soft and sticky,
>> On the leaves of the iris.

This haiku, by Buson, gives us directly the feeling of stickiness, and indirectly the contrast between the shapeless white blotches of the droppings, and the clean-cut sword-like iris leaves. Another example, by Taigi:

Kokoro hodo botan no tawamu hikazu kana

> The peony
> Is bending very slightly
>> After the lapse of days.

Here is the feeling of weight, tension, and malleability that Taigi has expressed. An example from Thoreau's *Journal*, 1850:

> Villages with a single long street lined with trees, so straight and wide that you can see a chicken run across it a mile off.

Here we have the "sensation" of two straight lines crossing each other. In these examples there is no thought, no morality, no beauty, no desire or loathing, only an intense interest in the thing, the sensation for its own sake, its intrinsic value, that is, its poetry. It is not, strictly speaking, the poetry of the sensation, but the poetry-sensation, the sensation-poetry. If the printer could print two words simultaneously, that would be it.

Senryū are the record of the failure of men, as haiku are of the successes of Nature. If there ever was an action performed without malice, sentimentality, snobbery, stupidity, self-consciousness, affectation, vainglory, obstinacy, hypocrisy, greediness, self-seeking, in a word, without humanity, senryū will take no notice of it. How little indeed of human life senryū omits!

Sōbetsukai kenji kanashii koe wo age

> The farewell party;
> The master of ceremonies
>> Raises a sad voice.

We may compare this with what the seventeenth century lawyer John Selden said:

The Tone in preaching does much in working upon the people's affections. If a man should make love in an ordinary Tone, his Mistress would not regard him; and therefore he must whine.

Zen is the un-symbolisation of things, dealing with nothing as means, but as ends. Blake says that:

He who kisses the Joy as it flies
Lives in Eternity's sunrise.

The Joy is the droppings of the hawk on the irises, the bending of the peony, the chicken running across the road, the master of ceremonies raising his voice. It flies, it comes once, and never again. When we kiss this Joy, that is, do not appropriate it to ourselves, but just look and listen and smell and touch, we live in Eternity's sunrise. Eternity's sunrise: that's an interesting expression! Eternity means timelessness; sunrise is time. Timeless time, timeful timelessness,—to live in this is the aim of human life. It can be done by kissing a Joy, listening to the music of Bach, painting pictures, building a dog-kennel, teaching children, refusing to drink with people, being a vegetarian, reading haiku, reading senryū, doing zazen. There seems to be an affinity between the last three, between poetry, humour, and Zen. If we equate Zen to poetry and humour to lunacy, we may remember what Hamlet says, "The lunatic, the lover, and the poet . . ." in which one thing is seen under three aspects, and then we may go on to Polonius' words:

To define true madness,
What is't but to be nothing else but mad?

Polonius seems to mean that it is foolish to define madness; it is madness to try; only a madman can do it. Only a madman knows what madness is. Only a poet knows what poetry is, and in explaining what it is he ceases to be a poet. Only a man with a sense of humour knows what humour is, and he is the last person in the world to attempt to explain a joke.

The fact is that the (real) poet cannot help falling into Zen. Though he tries to be lachrymose and sentimentally subjective, Zen will keep breaking through. And for (true) Zen, poetry comes together with it so that we can hardly distinguish one from the other. Yun-men said:

"The ancient Buddhas and the temple post are always having relations with each other; is this subjective?" The monks were dumb. Himself replying, "When clouds rise over the Southern Mountain, rain falls on the Northern Mountain."

The first part of what Yun-men says is highly transcendental. How can Buddhas who lived ages ago have any intercourse with the round wooden pillar outside the temple? But in To My Sister Wordsworth says the same thing:

Love, now a universal birth,
From heart to heart is stealing,
From earth to man, from man to earth:
—It is the hour of feeling.

The third line says that love flows in two directions. Man loves the earth; that is easy to believe, not so true as it looks. The Earth loves man; this is true, and absolutely true, but how few believe it! Wordsworth speaks of human beings and Nature, Yun-men of Buddhas and a post, but they both had some kind of animistic experience, expressed by the Englishman in 1798 in a Neoplatonic way, by the Chinese a thousand years before in a Mahayana Buddhist fashion. And Wordsworth, while he generalises, also particularizes. Love is "now" born in every thing animate or inanimate. "Now" is the first mild day of March; "the hour of feeling" is this day of early spring. Yun-men also, in his own way, particularises. His second statement is one of scientific fact; the rising of the clouds over the mountain is inevitably followed by the falling of rain on this. A is not A; A is B. But A also is A, A is not B. He combines para-logic with logic. In haiku also we see this kind of thing, but implicitly, as in the following, by Ryōta:

Sato no hi wo fukumite ame no wakaba kana

The rain on the young leaves
Is charged with
The lights of the village.

Transcendentally speaking, the lights of the village in the evening, and the raindrops on the leaves are one thing, but we do not "realize" this, that is, make it real, make it true, until we "see" that the lights are reflected in the raindrops; the two are now blended, interfused.

Sometimes, in the midst of its unnaturalness—for zazen, lectures, chanting, bowings and so on are highly artificial—Zen admits the superiority of the fact, the material, the non-human, over the ideal, the spiritual, the human, as in this from *Zenrinkushū*:

> Yuima feels disinclined to open his mouth:
> A cicada is singing on the bough.

This is Wordsworth's "Let Nature be your teacher," not Christ or Buddha or Vimalakirti or Yun-men.

The relation between Zen and haiku is difficult to make out exactly. Many Chinese poets such as Hakurakuten (Po Chu-i) of the T'ang dynasty, and Sotōba (Su Tung-p'o) of the Sung, were more or less deeply interested in Zen, or influenced by it, for Zen was even more concrete, more simple, and in this sense more poetical than the earlier Taoism. Waka, however, was not influenced (at all?) by Zen, for the aim of waka was beauty and emotion, whereas the object of both Zen and haiku is significance, "the depth and not the tumult of the soul." Sometimes it seems as if we can glimpse a direct connection between haiku and Zen, for example the following lines from the *Zenrinkushū*:

> I know not from what temple
> The wind brings the sound of the bell.

This reminds us of Bashō's famous verse:

Hana no kumo kane wa Ueno ka Asakusa ka

> A cloud of cherry blossoms.
> The bell!—is it from Ueno?
> From Asakusa?

This was written in the first year of Genroku, 1688. The *Zenrinkushū* was published the year before, 1687. It might seem as if this collection of lines and phrases from the sutras, the Chinese Zen writings, epigrammatic sayings and so on, could not have influenced Bashō. However, Eichō, the Zen priest who collected these quotations, lived from 1426 to 1504, and the manuscript must have been circulating in Buddhist quarters for a hundred and fifty years before Bashō composed his haiku. Another example from the same book:

A broken mirror will not again reflect,
A fallen leaf hardly returns to the branch.

This is very similar to Moritake's verse:

Rakka eda ni kaeru to mireba kochō kana

Fallen petals
Returned to the branch?
A butterfly!

Moritake lived from 1472 to 1549, and thus even he may have seen Eichō's manuscript. However, there is a difference between the Chinese lines and the haiku. The Chinese is interested in the general truth that what is done cannot be undone, and as such it is far from Zen. The haiku gazes at the particular leaf-or-butterfly with the generality, the vagueness and uncertainty of Nature subsumed into that particular doubt. In being the particular as general, and the general as particular, two as one, one as two, this poor verse may be said to have some poetry and some Zen in it.

We may compare an English haiku at this point, to bring out the importance of the brevity of experience and expression in poetry, which the Chinese and Japanese seem to have known by instinct. The following lines are from Coleridge's *This Lime-tree Bower*:

I watched
Some broad and sunny leaf, and loved to see
The shadow of the leaf and stem above
Dappling its sunshine!

It strikes us immediately that "I have watched" is superfluous and that "I have loved to see" is worse than unnecessary. We may revise it into the haiku three-line form:

Some broad and sunny leaf,
The shadow of the leaf above
Dappling its sunshine.

The repetition of "leaf" emphasizes the fact that there are two leaves involved; "sunny" and "sunshine" also are needed to bring out the sunshine and shadow upon the leaf, rather than the leaf itself.

It is usually taken for granted, and I have done so here up to the present, that haiku has been influenced by Zen, that Zen is to a large extent the origin of flower-arrangement, Nō, the Art of Tea, and so on. This idea is expressed perhaps in these lines from the *Zenrinkushū*:

If you drink up, at one gulp, the waters of the West River,
The pistils of the peonies of Loyang will come out newly.

If we have swallowed up all the water of the great river, if we have transcended all dichotomy, even once, the gorgeous flowers of the Capital attain an even greater, a new glory. This kind of thing is often experienced upon falling in love, which is, ideally speaking, a transcending of the duality of two human beings. But is not the reverse also true? A love of Nature accompanied by misanthropy is somehow odious, and perhaps not possible. When we really look at a flower (especially the flowers of weeds, rather than those of the mundane and worldly peony), we swallow more of the water of the South River than we suppose, much more anyway than mere rationality can admit. Indeed, Zen does not produce poetry and art and music. They produce Zen.

Zen, like all the values, of which it is perhaps the finer and volatile essence, is not the cause of anything, neither is it something to be attained or achieved. It is not a means to spiritual or physical health, to raising one's salary, or batting average. Neither is it a goal, an end, an ideal. When we really listen to the music of Bach we hear the sound and clapping of one hand, everything is Mu; and at the same time we hear the sound of two hands, the bowing and fingering. Music and poetry and art and courageous life are a fullness of living, and an attempt to attain the fullness first in order to live afterwards is putting the cart before the horse, an inversion of the natural order. The natural order, which is no order, we see in the following, by Clare:

> While in a quiet mood hedge-sparrows try
> An inward stir of shadowed melody.

The chirping of the sparrows, usually so restless and excitable, is subdued, a mere essay in sound, approaching silence, just as the light under the hedge is a kind of darkness. These two lines are Zen, but without Buddhism, without the transcendence of opposites, without egolessness, without zazen.

Coming now to the relation of Zen and senryū, we may note first of all the unintellectuality of both, and of haiku also. Thoreau writes in his *Journal*, 1842:

> The squeaking of the pump sounds as necessary as the music of the spheres.

If Thoreau had written "is" instead of "sounds," the sentence would have been philosophical, but "sounds" makes it poetry, makes it senryū, makes it Zen. The squeaking of the pump does not sound beautiful; it sounds necessary. The pump, especially when lacking oil, manifests its existence value, its innate humour, and in this imperfection rather than in their perfection we perceive the divinity of things. This humour is, of course, common to Zen and to senryū, and always latent in haiku. The music of the spheres and the squeaking of the pump—how different! And yet there is an equally extraordinary sameness in them.

The poverty of Zen and senryū (and haiku) is not a coincidence. Poverty is equally material and spiritual. "How hardly shall a rich man enter the kingdom of poetry or humour or Zen!" This word "rich" and the word "poor" in "Blessed are the poor!" are both physical and mental. An example of the physical is seen in another passage from Thoreau's *Journals*, 1850:

> Autumnal mornings, when the feet of countless sparrows are heard like raindrops on the roof by the boy who sleeps in the garret.

The boy is poor, and sleeps under the roof, and that is why he can hear the sparrow's feet. But also there is a spiritual poverty implied. He has no ambition, no aim in life, no morality, no view of life, no religion, no politics. And thus he hears "the feet (of the sparrow) that bringeth good tidings, that publisheth peace."

Last, a consideration that makes us feel that of the three, haiku and Zen and senryū, senryū is the greatest achievement of the Japanese people, is this. Zen is the transcendence of the dichotomy of relative, of opposites. But the transcendent, the Absolute is itself thus opposed to what is not transcended, to the relative, and we have only one more dichotomy. How can Zen escape this? By asserting that the absolute and the relative are the same things, that enlightenment is no different from illusion; that illusion, just as it is, with no change whatever, is enlightenment; *mayoi sunawachi satori, satori sunawachi mayoi.* Another, more abstract form of the same statement, is the difference is sameness, sameness is difference: *sabetsu soku byōdō, byōdō soku sabetsu.* Now these assertions are exceedingly difficult, indeed impossible to understand, and can hardly be illustrated metaphorically. In this case senryū does what Zen (the sect) only speaks of. In senryū we grasp (and senryū is the grasping) that rather than the good, the true, and the beautiful, the bad, the false, and the ugly are value, are divine, are human, are interesting. In 1812 when Issa was at Tōkaiji Temple he saw some hungry-looking chickens, so he bought some rice and scattered it among them. But the effect was unexpected, though not unnatural:

Komemaki mo tsumi zo yo tori ga ke-au zo yo

> Scattering rice—
> This also is a sin,
>> Fowls kicking each other.

Fifty years before, in the 3rd *Yanagidaru*, which was published in 1758, we find the following senryū:

Ryōri-nin hiyoi to hōtte kamiawase

> The cook
> Nonchalantly throws it away,
>> And makes them bite one another.

The callousness of the cook and the hunger and rapacity of the dogs are seen to be of absolute value; vice rather than virtue is interesting. And now we go back to Issa's verse and see that Issa's foolish pity of the greediness and fighting of the chickens and the unavailing regret of Issa—this folly and failure are what feed us. Issa's illusion is what endears him to us. Without this illusion Issa would be nothing. His weakness is his strength. Senryū teaches us that our hypocrisy, affectation, falsity, cowardice, incompetence, cruelty are what the universe intended to create from the beginning of the universe. As with the witches in *Macbeth*, foul is fair, fair is foul. A good lecture is a bad lecture; a bad article is a good article. Where there is most Zen there is least; where there is least Zen there is most.

Mushrooms and Humour

This was written in 1964 at the request of Gordon Wasson, who is perhaps best known as the author of Soma, Divine Mushroom of Immortality, *a book that aroused considerable attention in scholarly circles when it appeared in 1972. Wasson asked Blyth to provide some haiku on mushrooms for a paper he was going to deliver in Tokyo. The paper did not appear in print until nine years after Blyth's death, when it was published in* The Transactions of the Asiatic Society of Japan *(December 1973) under the title "Mushrooms and Japanese Culture," using translations Blyth had supplied. In the same issue of the* Transactions, *Wasson arranged for an article titled "Mushrooms in Japanese Verse," an edited version of the translations and comments Blyth had sent him, to be published. The version given here is from Blyth's original manuscript text, which includes much material that was omitted from the text published in the* Transactions.

HUMOUR, POETRY, AND THE LOVE OF NATURE ARE INSEPARABLE in fact though highly differentiated in the dictionary. Mushrooms are humourous, poetical and lovable things. Of course all things are so,

> For the dear God who loveth us,
> He made and loveth all. [*Rime of the Ancient Mariner*]

All things are equal, yes, but some are more equal than others, or shall we say it is easier to see their equality. So frogs and crows and hippopotamuses and cabbages and kings are obviously humourous, and so it is with mush-rooms.

We may go through Japanese literature chronologically, and see the development of the idea of them as poetico-humourous objects of interest, and make a somewhat odious comparison with the absence of this sort of thing in other literature of the world, even Chinese, of which Japanese used to be thought a kind of imitation.

There is but one verse concerning mushrooms in the *Manyōshū*, compiled in the latter half of the eighth century, but interestingly enough it already foreshadows the haiku attitude in its grasp of the importance of physical sensation, here the sense of smell, as the fundamental poetical experience. Anonymous, it is one of the miscellaneous verses of autumn in Volume 10.

> *Takamado no kono mine mo se ni kasa tatete*
> *Michi-sakari naru aki no ka no yosa*

> Sedge hats so thick
> On Takamado Hill
> It seems less spacious;
> The overflowing fragrance
> Of high autumn.

Takamado (given in some texts as Takamatsu, the "matsu" of which suggests *matsu-take*, the "pine mushroom") is a hill south of Mt. Kasuga, on the eastern edge of Nara, a popular place for outings. The sedge hats (*kasa*) refers, of course, to the caps of mushrooms.

Here the smell of the mushrooms is autumn, just as in the best of all odes, sleeping reaper, the winnower, the gleaner, the wine-presser are not four symbols of autumn, but Autumn itself, himself.[1]

In the *Shūi Wakashū*, third of the poetry collections compiled for the Imperial Court and completed about 1008, there are two verses concerning *matsutake*. However, their authors used the mushrooms only as material for punning. One of these, in Volume 7, is another play on words.

> *Ashibiki no yama shita mizu ni nure ni keri*
> *sono hi mazutake koromo aburamu*

The skirts
Of the mountain below
   Are wet.
I will make a fire
And dry my garments.

There is a pun on *mazu*, first of all, which was possibly at that time pro-
nounced *matsu*, and *take*, to light a fire, making *matsutake*. Drying (the
clothes) and broiling (the mushrooms) is another play on words.

The point to be borne in mind is that mushrooms are used as poetico-
humourous material, but there is no love of mushrooms for their own sake,
no looking into the life of things, without which the humour and the liter-
ary poetry are all in vain. But the "life" of things and their "humour," in the
deepest sense, are identical, and it is the deepening of the humour which
we have to follow.

We have to make a huge jump now of about five hundred years to haiku
and its treatment of mushrooms. In Shiki's *Bunrui Haiku Zenshū* ("A Com-
plete Collection of Haiku, Classified"), published in 1929, we find two hun-
dred and fifty verses concerning mushrooms and mushroom-gathering, but
these are far indeed from "complete," for omitted, for example, are all of
Kobayashi Issa's mushroom haiku, of which fifty-six are known. In a simi-
lar collection, *Haiku Taizen*, published the year before, there are eighty-five
haiku on mushrooms, many of which are not in Shiki's compilation. It is
clear that the actual number of verses on mushrooms must be far above
three hundred, perhaps five hundred. What is important, however, is not
the actual number, but the very fact that, in contrast with the literature of
other nations, including China, wherein there are few or no verses on this
subject, Japanese poetry is rich in such verses.

The following are from Shiki's *Bunrui Haiku Zenshū*, with his classifica-
tion headings:

IWATAKE ("ROCK MUSHROOM")[2]
Iwatake ya ama no hagoromo susu no chiri

   Iwatake
Seem the dusty skirts
   Of the heavenly raiment.

                                         (*Joryū*)

IKUCHI ("WILD BOAR'S MOUTH")[3]

Warabe sae suteshi chimata no ikuchi kana

> Even children throw away
> The *ikuchi*
>   At the forked ways.   (*Kansui*)

They are thrown away because so small and insignificant, but the children of the next verse are less sophisticated.

Takegari ya ikuchi mo chigo wa ureshi-gao

> Mushroom gathering:
> The children are pleased
>   Even with the *ikuchi*.   (*Rigō*)

Asajū ya tsuyu namerakani ikuchi-dake

> The weeds luxuriant,
> The dew so smooth
>   On the *ikuchi* mushrooms.   (*Chōmu*)

THE FIRST MUSHROOMS

Hatsutake ya hitotsu ni ekubo hitotsu zutsu

> The first mushrooms;
> On each one,
>   Its dimple.   (*Suikoku*)

Hatsutake wo kazoete mireba hashita kana

> The first mushrooms;
> Counting them,
>   They were an odd number.   (*Seibi*)

There was an indivisible number, like seventeen or twenty-three, and therefore it would be difficult to portion out the mushrooms.

Hatsutake ni yō nita ishi no ōsa kana

> The first mushrooms;
> What a lot of stones
>> That look just like them!   (*Kijū*)

Hatsutake no kaori ni furidasu kosame kana

> Coming down the mountain
> Through the drizzle
>> To the scent of the first mushrooms.   (*Chigetsu*)

BENITAKE ("ROUGE-COLORED MUSHROOMS")
Benitake wa sara ni utsuseru ryōri kana

> Rouge mushrooms
> Reflected in the plates
>> Of food.   (*Tokugen*)

Benitake ya utsukushii mono to mite sugiru

> Rouge mushrooms;
> Looking at their beauty,
>> And passing by.   (*Kitō*)

Benitake ya sode ni iri-hi no yama modori

> Rouge mushrooms;
> In the sleeve the setting sun,
>> Coming back from the hills.   (*Kiekō*)

NEZUMIDAKE ("RAT MUSHROOM")[4]

Three verses by Teitoku:

> To father and son
> How extraordinary!
> *Nezumidake.*

> Eaten with father
> How wonderful,
> *Nezumidake!*

> Eat squeaking!
> A marvelous hole
> For the rat only.

Nekoashi no zen de kabaya nezumidake

> Rat mushrooms;
> I would like to eat them
> At a cat's-foot table.   (*Shigeyori*)

A cat's-foot table is a low one with feet like a cat's paws.

YANAGIDAKE ("WILLOW MUSHROOM")

> I will mend
> My straw sandals
> With the capped willow-mushrooms.

"Capped" refers also to the umbrella-like hat he is wearing.

MATSUTAKE ("PINE MUSHROOM")

Matsutake ya matsu yori oku no taka no koe

Matsutake;
From the depths of the pine forest
    The voice of the hawk.   (*Koya*)

Hahaso ochite matsutake mienu nioi kana

    The oak tree falls on them,
And the scent rises
    Of unseen *matsutake.*   (*Gyoji*)

Matsutake ya shiranu ki no ha no hebari tsuku

    Matsutake;
And on it stuck
    The leaf of some unknown tree.   (*Bashō*)

Matsutake ya matsuba de yakan yama no naka

    Matsutake toasted
Over a pine-needle fire
    Among the hills.   (*Ginkō*)

Matsutake wa matsu no shizuku no sugata kamo

    The *matsutake*
Have the shape
    Of dripping from the pine tree.   (*Taimu*)

Matsutake wa yama wo deru ka ya ame agari

Coming down
From the hill of *matsutake*,
    The smell just after the rain.   (*Tōri*)

Matsutake ya matsuba wo kaburu hikigaeru

    Matsutake;
A toad
    With pine-needles on its head.   (*Habaku*)

Matsutake wo miyako no hitotsu banashi nari

    Matsutake
Are one of the topics
    Of the capital.   (*Zuiyū*)

    Matsutake,
And the hills round the Capital—
    After two years absence.

    The smell of *matsutake*
Entering into
    The deep mountains.

Yume de nashi matsutake ouru yama no hara

    It is no dream!
Matsutake are growing
    On the belly of the mountain.   (*Shigetaka*)

Matsutake ya yama yori wameku daidokoro

　Matsutake!
Even more than on the hills
　　The clamor in the kitchen!　　　　　　　　(*Kyoroku*)

　Matsutake;
Onto the tray falls
　　The earth of the mountain.

Matsutake ya hito ni toraruru hana no saki

　Matsutake;
Taken by someone else
　　Right in front of my nose.　　　　　　　　(*Kyorai*)

　The smell of *matsutake*
From the sleeves
　　Of the straw rain-coat.

　The *matsutake*
Will not wait until evening
　　But smell strongly.

In the evening they will be eaten, but they smell all day long.

Matsutake wo awatete toru ya kasa bakari

　The *matsutake*
Seem gathered hurriedly,
　　The caps only.　　　　　　　　　　　　(*Masahide*)

Matsutake ya matsu no meoto no hito-shizuku

> Matsutake,
> Drippings from the man and wife
> > Pine trees. *(Chōsen)*

Matsutake are often called pine-tree drips, and there are male pine trees.

ENOKIDAKE ("NETTLE-TREE MUSHROOM")

Kuchiki to na aboshi mesare so enokidake

> Don't deplore
> The decaying tree—
> > Look at the *enokidake*. *(Ransetsu)*

TENGUDAKE ("LONG-NOSED GOBLN MUSHROOM")

Geko-domo ga kowagaru beki zo tengudake

> Teetotalers
> Must be afraid of it,
> > The *tengudake*. *(Benseki)*

They see the violence of a drunken man and a *tengu*, a long-nosed ill-natured monster, reflected in this red mushroom.

SHIMEJI ("WET-GROUND MUSHROOM")

Shimeji-take, which is of various colours, grows in damp soil, *shimeji*; the stalk is short and stout. Here is a remarkable haiku by Sōin on the *Shimeji-take*:

Matsu ga ne ni chiyo no kage sasu shimeji kana

> The *shimeji*
> On the roots of the pine,
> > The shadow of a thousand ages. *(Sōin)*

HIRADAKE ("FLAT MUSHROOM")
    A monk
Who has come to the town
    To sell *hiradake*.

The *hiradake* looks like *matsutake* but is said to be poisonous sometimes.

MUSHROOM GATHERING
Niji kiete ato wo tasuneru kinoko kana

    The rainbow faded,
And after that, seeking
    Mushrooms.   (*Yūshō*)

Ureshisa ni rakuba wasururu kinoko kana

    I forgot falling off the horse
With the happiness
    Of finding mushrooms.   (*Ukei*)

Tori no fun tsukitemo hirou kinoko kana

    Though the droppings
Of a bird were on them,
    I gathered the mushrooms.   (*Koji*)

This has the prescript, "A mountain scene, a pure mind."

Yoi no ame matsu to chigirite kinoko kana

    The evening rain,
And the mushrooms
    It promised.   (*Kisei*)

Takegari ya ori-ori kasa wo matsu no tsuki

    Mushroom gathering;
Occasionally the moon of the pine trees
      Glints on them.   (*Sekijō*)

Takegari ya mikazuki hitotsu torinokoshi

    Mushroom gathering;
Only the crescent moon
      Left unplucked.   (*Sanrei*)

    Mushroom gathering;
Raising my head,
      The moon on the peak.   (*Buson*)

Buson is more impressed with the (Chinese) moon than the (Japanese) mushrooms.

Takegari ya kyō wa ki no ne ni korobu made

    Mushroom gathering;
Today let's go on till we fall over
      The roots of the trees.   (*Kasō*)

Modoru toki ibara no ōshi kinokogari

    Mushroom gathering;
On our way back,
      How many the briers!   (*Gacho*)

They were not noticed in the first excitement.

Ureshisa no yama wo tsukamu ya kinokogari

    Taking hold with the hand
Of the happiness of the mountain—
      Mushroom gathering!   (*Raisha*)

Takegari ya yoku karamichi ni fumimayoi

    Mushroom gathering;
From greediness
      We lost our way.   (*Jiraku*)

Uta-garuta arasōta te ya kinokogari

    Mushroom gathering;
Isn't this the skill
      Of the card-snatchers!   (*Rogen*)

Uta-garuta is a Japanese game of cards on each of which half a poem is written. While someone reads out the first half, the players must pick from the face-up cards the one card on which the second half appears. Hunting for mushrooms requires such a quickness of eye and hand.

Se no takai hito ni heta ari kinokogari

    Mushroom hunting;
Tall people
      Are no good at it.   (*Yayū*)

Ue wo minu me ni mo yoku ari kinokogari

    Mushroom hunting;
When you find one,
      You are made to find more!   (*Yayū*)

Mushroom hunting;
The one who is not good at it
　　Acts as if the leader.

You pine cones! You mushrooms!
The light of my hermitage—
　　How faint it is!

When we are poor, we become familiar with things. This is why the poor are blessed and the rich accursed.

The following, all by Kobayashi Issa (1763–1827), are from more than sixty-five about mushrooms found in various collections of his haiku.

In the pine tree field
As if made and put there,
　　Mushrooms!

Te no mae ni chō no ikizuku kinoko kana

Before my hand
Stretched out for the mushroom,
　　A butterfly breathing.

Kono hō ni kinoko ari toya abu no yobu

"Lots of mushrooms over here!"
Is that what the horsefly
　　Is saying?

Utsukushii ya ara utsukushii ya doku-kinoko

How beautiful,
Beautiful indeed,
　　The poisonous mushrooms!

Hatsutake ya mitsuketa mono wo tsukitaoshi

The first mushroom,
Pushing over
　　The chap who found it.

Hatsutake ya futari mitsukete konamijin

Two found it,—
And the first mushroom
　　Smashed into smithereens!

Takegari no heta ya hitodaki kusa no hana

Mushroom hunting;
Someone not good at it,
　　With an armful of wild flowers.

Hatsutake ya fumi tsubushita wo tsugite miru

The first mushroom;
Treading on it by accident
　　And trying to put it together again.

Kai kinoko totta furi shite modori keri

Pretending
The mushrooms bought
    Had been gathered.

Enmaō warai kinoko wo chito maire

Try giving
King Emma
    Some "laughing mushrooms"!

The King of the Buddhist Hell always has a scowling face. The *warai* mushroom is said to produce laughter in those who eat it.

Mi ko-tachi yo akai kinoko ni bakasare na

Dear children,
Be not deceived
    By the red toadstools!

The theologians have never explained why God made these poisonous fungi for the "dear children."

Ōkinoko bajun mo toki wo etari keru

Horse dung also
Has its chance
    In the season of the great mushrooms!

Hito wo toru kinoko hatashite utsukushiki

The mushrooms that kill men
Are, sure enough,
    Beautiful.

This has a reference perhaps to beautiful women, but it may be applied to beautiful theories and beautiful religions (where women make a come-back in the form of Mariolatry), which kill all the poetry and love of truth that we like to think are natural to mankind.

Here are a few more haiku, not in Shiki's *Bunrui Haiku Zenshū*, which demonstrate Japanese feelings about mushrooms and mushroom gathering.

Hatsutake ya mada hi kazu henu aki no tsuyu

> Only a few days
> Of autumn dew,—
> > The first mushrooms!   (*Bashō*)

Such a small cause with a marvelous effect.

Kinoko-jiru ōkina kinoko ki ni keri

> On the mushroom broth,
> A large mushroom
> > Floating!

We eat with the eyes as well.

Yamabiko ya onna bakari no kinoko-gari

> Women only
> Gathering mushrooms—
> > How the hills echo!

Many of the above haiku are more poetical than humourous, and others are merely trivial. Issa understands mushrooms. Buson does not, neither does Shiki, though one of his verses is interesting.

Kinoko gari tori naite onna sabishi-gari

> Mushroom hunting:
> When a bird cries
> > The women feel lonely.

The point of the matter is the overlapping of the poetry, humour, and "life" of a thing. One of these only is not sufficient. A lack of humour spoils *Paradise Lost*. Insufficient poetry vitiates Buddhism, and Zen itself. Not being concerned with "life," makes all government and statecraft a farce. Who are the writers who have the three in more or less equal proportions? They are Thoreau, Hakurakuten [Po Chu-i], Shakespeare, and the haiku writers.

Coming now to senryū, whose flourishing time was between 1765 and 1775, that is, about eighty years after the age of Bashō, the balance among humour poetry and "life" is quite different. Whereas haiku put "life" first, poetry second, and humour third, senryū made humour its first consideration, then "life," that of beings, and last, poetry. In a way senryū is more difficult to write, since poetry and even "life" can be swindled, but not humour, which is the real thing, or nothing whatever. Senryū deals with mushrooms as means not as ends in themselves. The humour is that of human beings not of a natural phenomenon. And senryū also aim at the "life" of human beings, which is most clearly discerned in the foibles, the mistakes, the pretence, the weakness, of mankind.

Mushroom references are frequent in senryū, verses having the same seventeen-syllable length as haiku but differing from them, as I have said, in being about not the nature of things but the nature of man, humourous, often satirical, usually anonymous. Because they hinge so much on puns and allusions unfamiliar to non-Japanese (and to many Japanese as well), however, translations of them may have little meaning without explanations. To illustrate:

Nigemo senu no wo awate kinoko-gari

> Mushroom hunting;
> They don't run away,
> But everyone's in such a hurry!

We see the universal greediness of human beings even in such an apparently innocent occupation.

Kinoko-gari wa momiji-gari yori shotai jimi

Mushroom hunting
Is far more domestic
      Than tinted-leaves hunting.

Excursions for viewing scarlet maple leaves have been common in Japan from ancient times, but for men only, or for men together with geisha. In Edo times, on the way back, the men usually stopped in at the Yoshiwara pleasure quarters. Mushroom hunting, on the other hand, was done chiefly by women, accompanied by their children.

Nippon e miyage kikurage ni-san-byō

A present to Japan
Two or three bales
      Of *kikurage.*

Kikurage are so called because they are shaped like the human ear, for which these mushrooms are a symbol. From the Japanese fighting of 1592–98 in Korea, the noses and ears of the Chinese and Koreans killed were brought to Japan as trophies of victory instead of the customary heads. They were buried in the grounds of the Hōkō-ji, Kyoto, in a mound called Mimizuka (Ear Mound).

Shishitake wa gejo botan kara dekiru kae

"*Shishitake*
Must grow from peonies,"
      Surmises the maid-servant.

Shishitake is a local name for *kōtake*, "skin or fur mushrooms," and the *shishi* in this name is written with a character meaning "beast" or "deer." *Shishi*, written with a different character, is also the word for "lion." In art, the lion is connected with peonies, as the tiger with bamboos, and the *uguisu* with plum blossoms.

Waraitake kuwasete mitai kunikarō

It would be nice to make
The *kunikarō*
Eat *waraitake*!

Waraitake are psychogenic mushrooms, the eating of which causes a kind
of intoxication and laughter, and hence their name, "laughing mushrooms."
The *kunikarō* was the feudal lord's intendant while he was living on his pro-
vincial estate, distinguished from the *karō* who headed the Lord's house-
hold in Edo where he was compelled to live for certain periods under the
Tokugawa policy of alternating residence to make conspiracy and rebellion
difficult. The Edo *karō* was thought to be rather easy-going, whereas the
country *karō* was inclined to be very strict and rigid.

As far as old senryū are concerned, *Yanagidaru*, published between 1765
and 1837, in a hundred and sixty volumes, contains an as yet uncounted
number of verses on mushrooms, a selection of which are given here. They
are classified according to species.

The following comes in the 1st Volume:

Matsu ni ke de ogo to mukimi wo kakimawashi

With the *matsutake*
The *ogo* and the *mukimi*
Are ransacked.

Ogo, "sea-hair," is a kind of sea-weed, like hair, between one and two feet
long, green-black in colour. *Mukimi* is shucked shellfish.

The following is in the 3rd Volume:

Matsutake wo nigitte sagami nebari nari

Clutching the *matsutake*,
The Sagami maid
Does not let go of it.

This is an example, relatively mild, of the erotic element in senryū, which
was not confined, of course, to mushroom references. It was from Sagami,

the province now known as Kanagawa prefecture, that most Edo maid-servants came, and in senryū the noun *sagami* always signifies a highly sexed woman. The next verse expresses this:

Matsutake wo mite mo sagami wa hazumu nari

> When the Sagami
> Only looks at the *matsutake,*
> She breathes deeply.

Dōkyō no tsuka kara deta sa-matsutake

> The early *matsutake*
> Come out of the grave
> Of Dōkyō.

Dōkyō, who died in 772, was an intriguer of the first rank, who had a great influence over the ex-empress Kōken, a fervent Buddhist. During her reign the Great Buddha of Nara was cast. She was induced to ascend the throne again at the age of forty-eight by Dōkyō who then aimed at the throne, but the god Hachiman at Usa declared that a subject could not become an emperor. The next year the Emperor Kōnin ascended the throne and banished him. The senryū writer seems to think he must have been a very sexual man, even in his grave.

The two following verses from *Yanagidaru* also suggest this:

Dōkyō wa tsura-chū hana de sandai-te

> Dōkyō's face
> Was all nose, and by it
> He got into the Palace.

Mushi no sei ka to Dōkyō no haha anji

    His mother
Suspected
    What Dōkyō would become.

This means when she saw what a big nose he had, as a child.
    The following comes from the 3rd Volume:

Matsutake no motogusa wo wake nomi-gari

    Hunting for lice
At the root of the *matsutake,*
    Making one's way through the grasses.

Finally, here is a translation of a verse in Chinese by Murase Kōtei (1749–1818), Confucian scholar and painter, from his remarkable *Geien Nis-shō*, published in twelve volumes in 1819:

In the scent of them, men and women pass along the steep places,
Their clothes awry, their undergarments torn among the thorny briars.
Greedy, watchful eyes never leave the ground;
All day long in the mountains,—but who looks at them?

English Humour and Japanese Humour

This essay was published in the KBS Bulletin on Japanese Culture, *vol. 65, April–May 1964 (KBS: Kokusai Bunka Shinkōkai). I have omitted Japanese translations of some of the passages from English literature quoted here; presumably, they were added by the editors of the* Bulletin.

IF WE MAKE A CHRONOLOGICAL COMPARISON BETWEEN ENGLISH and Japanese humour, nothing seems to correspond, except perhaps the sudden emergence of wit in both countries in the 18th century. Japanese humour begins with the *Manyōshū, Kojiki,* and the *Fudoki,* but English humour does not begin with the contemporary *Beowulf,* but six or seven hundred years later with Chaucer, if we omit the "belly laughs" of the scenes of the Nativity and Noah's Ark and so on in the Mystery Plays. However, if we make the comparison between the different kinds of humour, we may read the story of the little tiny god Sukuna-Bikona-no Mikoto, whose meeting with Okuni-nushi no Mikoto is described so vividly in the *Kojiki,* and compare his anger, "insignificantly fierce," with the dignity and awesomeness of the Lilliput king, when he drew his sword; "it was almost five inches long!"

Humour in general may be divided into satire and humour. What distinguishes the two is the degree of cruelty, or rather, the degree of destructiveness. Japanese humour is lacking in satire proper, though we may call senryū satirical verse. Japanese literature has no Juvenal, no Swift, no Pope.

This comes from a national dislike of violence. Though or because Japanese people are easily excited, they admire above all things self-control, in art as well as in action. Sadism must be aesthetic; even *seppuku* is to be done elegantly; death-agony itself must dance. Though escapism is or was common, by suicide or shaving one's head, misanthropy is lacking; there is no Timon of Athens, not even a Robinson Crusoe. Again personal attacks are not to be found, partly perhaps from fear of the (physical) consequences. No Japanese would write, like Dryden, of his opponents:

> The rest to some faint meaning make pretence,
> But Shadwell never deviates into sense.

We find something approaching the spirit of satire in the *Pillow Book* of Sei Shōnagon, and the *Tsurezuregusa*. Sei Shōnagon tells us in Section xxiv and elsewhere that a lover should not leave too abruptly, but should tell her how much he regrets the dawn and longs for the approach of night. This is different from the cynicism of Swift in *A Description of the Morning*, 1709:

> Now hardly here and there a hackney-coach
> Appearing, show'd the ruddy morn's approach.
> Now Betty from her master's bed had flown,
> And softly stole to discompose her own.

Kenkō's opinion of women is not very different from Swift's; Section 190 begins:

> No man should have what is called a wife.

It continues:

> Whatever kind of woman she may be, if he wants to see her from morning to night, his heart will weary of her and he will come to hate her.

In section 107 he writes:

> Women all have jaundiced minds, are profoundly egotistic, exceedingly greedy, and have no idea of right and wrong. They change their minds

according to their fancy. They won't answer when asked the simplest question in easy words, but, without being asked at all, they talk a lot of nonsense after what seems to be careful preparation.

Compare this to Swift's *The Furniture of a Woman's Mind*:

> Never to hold her tongue a minute,
> While all she prates has nothing in it.

Humour, as opposed to satire, is in its best form a laughing *with* others rather than laughing *at them*. Just as the danger of satire is an excess of cruelty, the danger of humour is sentimentality. Japanese literature, however, is seldom excessively cruel or sentimental (Kabuki falls into both). Also, it excels in parody, riddles, puns, and word-play in general. This is partly due of course, as in Chinese, to the large number of homonyms, but this again may well be due to the pleasure of calling different things by the same names, thus emphasizing their similarity and ultimate identity. An English example is the following untranslatable epitaph:

> Here lies John Bun,
> He was killed with a gun,
> His name was not Bun, but Wood,
> But Wood would not rhyme with gun, but Bun would.

In the same way the following Japanese riddle cannot be translated:

一文菓子ナアニ　　歩行自慢ととく　　心はなんのうまかろ

ichibu kashi naani　　*hokō jiman to toku*　　*kokoro wa nanno uma* *karō*

> What is "a penny sweet?"
> It is a man proud of his walking, because,
> "Why should I borrow a horse?"

(*Nanno uma karō* has the same pronunciation as "How can it be nice?")
　　Light verse, which corresponds in Japanese literature to *kyōka*, is more

difficult to write than serious verse, because if it fails it is worse than nothing; tragic verse that does not succeed may become melodrama, or intentionally comic. In the *Manyōshū* there are already jesting verses:

我を思う　人を思わぬ　むくいにや　わが思う人
の我を思わぬ

Ware wo omou hito wo omowanu mukui niya
Waga omou hito no ware wo omowanu

    I don't love him
Who loves me,
    And—is it nemesis?—
He whom I love
Doesn't love me!

But the *kyōka* of the 18th century are far more complicated and ingenious. Just as what drama needs most is a good story, and the novel a dramatic quality, so *kyōka* and senryū need poetry, and waka and haiku need (some kind of) humour.

Omitting the faint humour of haiku and coming now to senryū, we have to parallel the psychological penetration, the humanity, the concreteness and particularity of these verses to lines of prose in English literature. Fielding says in *Jonathan Wild*, 1743, that one of the beliefs of Wild was that

The heart is the proper seat of hatred, and the countenance of affection and friendship.

In *Pride and Prejudice*, Mr. Bennet says of Mr. Collins:

There is a mixture of servility and self-importance in his letter, which promises well. I am impatient to see him.

Dr. Johnson said:

Men do not suspect faults which they do not commit.
It is commonly a weak man that marries for love.

The seventeenth century Selden is reported to have said:

> Though a clergyman have no faults of his own, yet the faults of the whole tribe shall be laid upon him, so that he shall be sure not to lack.

Senryū is merciless, but not cruel; it brings out what all men conspire to hide; Carlyle said, "Love not pleasure; love God." This is what senryū does. It loves the truth, not general principles, or art, or goodness, or beauty, but the particular faults of particular people, the false humility of the proud, the real pride of the beggar, all the snobbishness and hypocrisy and cruelty and self-seeking and sentimentality that make up what Zen kindly calls the Buddha-nature.

Ningen no yowasa hakaba e nigete-yuku

The weaknesses of men;
    They escape from them.—
To the grave-yard!

Even the enlightened monk dresses up when he goes out:

Rōsō mo kesa kitaru hanami kana

An old priest also
    Puts on his surplice
When he goes flower-viewing.

Virtue makes women weak; vice makes men weak:

Asagaeri mata tōfu ka to iwazu kui

Coming home in the morning,
    Eating, without saying,
"What! Bean-curd again?"

Even a courtesan, who must be proud, thinks of money first, herself next, and then her customer, if she falls in love, she becomes humble, doesn't think of money at all, and of her customer's happiness only:

Horarete mite wa jorō mo tada no hito

> When she loves,
> A courtesan also
> Is an ordinary woman.

"An ordinary woman" means "an ordinary woman in love," which means "an extraordinary woman."

Sometimes we try to make people tell the truth, and this cruelty has painful consequences to ourselves also:

Koroshi takarau na to yome wo ibiru nari

> "I suppose you want to kill me!"
> Says the mother-in-law,
> To tease her.

If she says "No," it is clearly untrue. If she says "Yes," it is too terrible (to be untrue).

There is nothing like senryū in English literature, so to preserve the balance, by leaning both ways, we may add that there is nothing in Japanese literature like the infinitely attractive grossness of Mrs. Gamp or the Wife of Bath: there is no nonsense verse like that of Lear and Carroll. Indeed, there is nothing really which overlaps in the two literatures, and that is why Japanese should be the first foreign language in England as English is (for other and less worthy reasons) in Japan.

NOTES

INTRODUCTION

1. R. H. Blyth, *History of Haiku* (Tokyo: Hokuseido Press, 1964), 2:347.
2. R. H. Blyth, *Japanese Life and Character in Senryū* (Tokyo: Hokuseido Press, 1960), iii.
3. Suzuki Daisetz, *The Complete Works of Suzuki Daisetz*, 40 vols (Tokyo: Iwanami shoten, 2002), vol. 35, 223.
4. Suzuki Daisetz, "Reginald Horace Blyth (1898–1964)," *Eastern Buddhist* 1, no. 1 (September 1965): 133–35.
5. Lawrence Durrell, *The Durrell-Miller Letters, 1935–80*, ed. Ian S. MacNiven (New York: New Directions Publishing, 1988), 364.
6. From my personal scrapbook of the essays and reviews Blyth wrote for periodicals, including reviews of Blyth by others; exact date of publication is missing.
7. David Schneider, *Crowded by Beauty: The Life and Zen of Poet Philip Whalen* (Berkeley: University of California Press, 2015), 3.
8. This and subsequent reviews by Donald Richie in *The Japan Times*, 1961.
9. Frederick Franck, *Zen and Zen Classics: Selections from R. H. Blyth* (New York: Vintage Books, 1978), xii.
10. Oka Kuniomi, "A Biography of Reginald Horace Blyth—Through his Books," *Kurume University Journal* (Vol. 20, March 1972), 44.
11. R. H. Blyth, *Zen in English Literature and Oriental Classics* (Tokyo: Hokuseido Press, 1942), 396.
12. R. H. Blyth, *A Survey of English Literature, from the Beginnings to Modern Times* (Tokyo: Hokuseido Press, 1957), 313.
13. R. H. Blyth, *A Chronological Anthology of Nature in English Literature* (Tokyo: Kairyudo, 1949), Preface.
14. W. H. Auden, *The Dyer's Hand* (New York: Vintage Books, 1960), 42.
15. Kuniomi, "A Biography of Reginald Horace Blyth," 46.
16. Shinki Masanosuke, ed., *Kaisō no Buraisu* [Blyth Remembered] (Tokyo: Kaisō no Buraisu Kankōkai Jimushō, 1984), 63.

17. Ibid.

18. Kuniomi, "A Biography of Reginald Horace Blyth," 47.

19. Nippon Hōsō Kyōkai, Japan's public broadcasting company.

20. Yoshimura Ikuyo, *R. H. Buraisu no Shōgai* (Tokyo: Dōhō-sha Shuppan, 1996), 76.

21. Kuniomi, "A Biography of Reginald Horace Blyth," 51.

22. Morodome Yutaka, "R. H. Buraisu no shi ni tsuite" [Regarding R. H. Blyth's Poetry], in *Kaisō no Buraisu*, 56–61.

23. R. H. Blyth, "Natura Resurgens," *Essays and Studies, Articles from Studies in English Literature* VI–VIII (1926–1928).

24. Insoo met a tragic end. Captured by North Korean forces when they occupied Seoul in the opening years of the Korean War, he was compelled to make propaganda broadcasts in English to Allied troops. When South Korean troops retook the city, he was arrested and executed as a traitor.

25. Shinki Masanosuke's chronology in *Kaisō no Buraisu* has Blyth leaving Korea in 1935, a year later, but the entry stamps in Blyth's passport prove 1934 to be correct.

26. Masanosuke, *Kaisō no Buraisu*, 147.

27. *Essays in Zen Buddhism* was published in three volumes between 1927 and 1934; it is not known which of these Blyth was reading.

28. "Zen wo tsujite: ichi eigirisujin no bukkyō-kan," *Zaike Bukkyō* [Lay Buddhism], Oct. 1962, 26–34.

29. Arai Yoshio, *R. H. Buraisu no ningen-zō* (Tokyo: Hokuseido, 2006), 142.

30. Quotes and other details on Japanese civilian internment camps from U.S. Department of State cables: http://mansell.com/pow_resources/camplists /fukuoka/fuk_01_fukuoka/fukuoka_01/CIC/HyogoCIC.html.

31. Robert Aiken, "Remembering Blyth Sensei," in *Original Dwelling Place: Zen Buddhist Essays* (Berkeley, CA: Counterpoint Press, 1996), 23–24.

32. Suzuki Daisetz, *The Complete Works of Suzuki Daisetz*, vol. 35, 223.

33. Adrian Pinnington, "R. H. Blyth, 1898–1964," in *Britain and Japan: Biographical Portraits*, ed. Ian Nish (Folkestone, UK: Japan Library, 1994). This narrative is based largely on William P. Woodard's account in *The Allied Occupation of Japan, 1945–1952* (Leiden, Netherlands: E. J. Brill, 1972).

34. R. H. Blyth, *The Genius of Haiku* (Tokyo: Hokuseido Press, 1995), 8.

35. Elizabeth Gray Vining, *Windows for the Crown Prince: Four Remarkable Years at the Japanese Court as Tutor to the Crown Prince of Japan* (New York: Lippincott, 1952), 54.

36. Yoshimura Ikuyo (p. 142) cites Yanagi's acknowledgment of the debt to them in his magazine *Kōgei*, #117, 1947.

37. Pinnington, "R. H. Blyth, 1898–1964," 258.

38. William P. Woodard, *The Allied Occupation of Japan 1945–1952 and Japanese Religions* (E. J. Brill-Leiden, 1972), 320.

39. Letter from Harold Henderson to the haiku poet James W. Hackett, dated December 25, 1964. The letter was accessed online at https://hacketthaiku.com, May 30, 2019.

40. "In Memory of Reginald Blyth," Eibungaku Kaihō, 12.14, 1964.

41. Blyth, *Japanese Life and Character in Senryū*, 4.

42. Among Blyth's posthumous papers are a large number of notebooks containing material he intended to use in these projected works.

43. Frederick Franck, *Zen and Zen Classics*, xvi.

44. In *Raise High the Roof Beam, Carpenters and Seymour: An Introduction* (New York: Bantam Books, 1968).

LETTERS TO DORA LORD AND PARENTS

1. "Hyogo Civilian Internment Camps," copy of cable received July 8, 1942, from The Special Dept. of State, The War Dept. (PMG), mansell.com, http://mansell.com/pow_resources/camplists/fukuoka/fuk_01_fukuoka/fukuoka_01/CIC/HyogoCIC.html.

2. Jinsen: the Japanese name for the Korean port city of Incheon.

3. Adam Gowans, *The Hundred Best Poems (Lyrical) in the English Language* (New York: Thomas Y. Crowell, 1903).

4. Probably a performance conducted by the Australian composer Henry Wood, with the English soprano Florence Easton (1882–1955).

5. The word *madder* may have been mistranscribed; I no longer have the original letter to check.

6. *Wertphilosophie*, meaning "philosophy of value." A religious philosophy associated with Max Scheler (1874–1928) that stresses the necessity of religious experience.

7. The number is presumably that of Haydn's early and later piano trios.

8. HMV is His Master's Voice, the popular name of the large Gramophone Company recording label in the United Kingdom.

9. Dim. for *diminuendo*, meaning "gradually decreasing volume."

10. Li Insoo, a gifted young Korean boy, nicknamed Jimmy, whose education Blyth and Anna were financing. He accompanied Anna to England when she returned there in 1934 and was educated at London University. He returned to Korea in 1946 and became a professor at Seoul University. When North Korean forces occupied Seoul in 1947, he was taken into custody and forced to make English-language propaganda broadcasts to American troops. When South Korean troops later retook Seoul, they arrested him, and he was subsequently executed for collaborating with the enemy.

11. The pianist Vladimir de Pachmann (1848–1933) was noted for performing the works of Chopin.

12. Presumably a picture of the area of West Yorkshire and East Lancashire where the Brontë sisters lived and wrote their famous novels.

13. Bach's 48 Preludes and Fugues, making up *The Well-Tempered Clavier*, a collection of two sets of preludes and fugues in all twenty-four major and minor keys.

14. Anna worked at the Bank of England.

15. Harriet Cohen (1895–1967) was an English pianist and noted interpreter of the music of Bach.

16. The International Bible Students Association, an alliance of various nonconformist groups promoting a return to the original Christian teachings.

17. Léon Jean Goossens (1897–1988).

18. Oblomov is the central character of the nineteenth-century Russian novel of that name by Ivan Goncharov. Often regarded as the incarnation of the superfluous man, Oblomov is young and generous but seems incapable of making important decisions or undertaking any significant actions.

19. By Donald Tovey (Oxford, UK: Oxford University Press, 1934).

20. A fast instrumental passage made up of notes of equal length.

21. *Viva Villa!* was a popular Hollywood film starring Wallace Beery. It was released in April 1934 in the United States and on September 24, 1934, in the United Kingdom.

22. *From the Hymn of Empedocles*, a poem by Matthew Arnold.

23. *Foundations of Music* was a radio program of classical music the BBC aired during the 1930s.

24. *The Masterpieces of Chikamatsu* appeared in 1926 and the *Nō Plays of Japan* in 1922.

25. This means he could spend 400 yen and buy a normal-sized piano or a 15/16 size with a slightly smaller keyboard.

26. The correct title is *Life of Jesus* (*Vie de Jésus*) by Ernest Renan.

27. Both of the Eugene O'Neill plays premiered in 1933.

28. The eighteenth-century composer Johann Gottlieb Graun (1703–1771).

29. Carlo Alfredo Piatti's *Cello Method Books* are popular tutors that take the student through the early stages of playing technique.

30. A handful of Cycill (the name also appears as Cecyll) Geraldine Tomrley's letters to Blyth exist, all dating from the early 1960s. Most of them contain reports to Blyth about his mother, Hetty, whom Cycill visited from time to time in Brighton. Cycill was a student at the Slade School of Art, London, when Blyth was at London University during his second trip home before the war. Her letters show that she and Blyth had been close, and there may be Blyth letters from the prewar period as well. Online sources show that Cycill was a well-known writer on design and home furnishing in the forties and fifties.

She received an MBC Member of the Order of the British Empire in 1967 for her work as a "Staff Officer, Grade III" at the Design Centre of the Council of Industrial Design. The return address on her letters to Blyth in the 1960s was Twickenham, Middlesex.

31. Fusan is the Korean port of Pusan.

32. Percy Bysshe Shelley's "To a Skylark."

33. *Mumonkan* (Chin. *Wu-men kuan*) is an important Zen koan collection, which Blyth probably began reading during his koan study at the Myōshin-ji Betsu-in in Keijō. A handwritten booklet dating from this time is extant containing his English translation of the work. His published translation, volume 4 of the *Zen and Zen Classics* series, appeared posthumously in 1966.

34. The "bungalow business" refers to his mother Hetty's bungalow at Rottingdean; there were discussions about her making a will leaving it to her son.

35. I have been unable to identify Miss MacGregor. She was apparently a member of the foreign community, perhaps church-related, who had come to aid Japan in its rebuilding efforts.

36. Kenneth Reed Dyke (1897–1980), a former advertising executive who served as head of CIE (the "Civil Information and Education" section of GHQ) until April 1952. He was charged with guiding Japan's education and communication systems away from militaristic ideas and promoting free expression of opinions in the press and on radio. SCAP (Supreme Commander for the Allied Powers) was the acronym used to refer to General MacArthur and to General Headquarters (GHQ) during the Allied Occupation.

37. L.C.C., or London County Council, apparently refers to what was at the time called London County Council School of Photo-Engraving and Lithography.

38. Fujii Masako, Fujii Akio's widow.

39. "That man is little to be envied whose patriotism would not gain force upon the plan of Marathon, or whose piety would not grow warmer among the ruins of Iona." (Samuel Johnson)

40. This 1944 edition, *The Sutra of Wei-lang (Hui Neng)*, a translation of the *Platform Sutra*, was republished in 1944 by Luzac in London. The original edition, which Blyth in fact also owned, was titled *Sutra Spoken by the Sixth Patriarch, Wei-lang, on the High Seat of the Gem of Law*, published in Shanghai in 1930.

41. See previous note to Letter #57.

LETTERS TO ROBERT AITKEN

1. Colonel Frank Blake. Robert Aitken wrote in a letter to me (July 25, 1967): "Col. and Mrs. Frank Blake [were] friends of my parents, who helped me to get in touch with Blyth again after we were separated by the end of the war."

2. Probably Mortimer E. Watson, who was also an inmate at the Futatabi camp in Kobe.

3. Beth Blake, the wife of Colonel Frank Blake, worked for the U.S. Red Cross while in Japan.

4. William Gordanier and Roy Henning had been interned with Blyth and Aitken in the Futatabi camp.

5. The Civil Information and Educational Section of General MacArthur's SCAP command had among its responsibilities control of the Japanese press, keeping civil order, and promoting Japanese understanding of the occupation.

6. The English poet Edmund Blunden, who taught at Tokyo University in the 1920s, returned in November 1947 to serve as cultural advisor with the UK Liaison Mission and remained until 1950.

7. This was published as *Haiku, Volume One, Eastern Culture*, the first of the four-volume *Haiku*.

8. *Eastern Culture* later appeared as the first volume of the four-volume *Haiku*, and *Haiku, the Flower of Eastern Culture* apparently became the other three volumes.

9. Mrs. Blake worked with Blyth to help save Yanagi Sōetsu's Mingei Museum. Mrs. Sasaki was Ruth Fuller Sasaki, who later moved to Japan and resided in a subtemple of Daitoku-ji in Kyoto.

10. *Mumonkan Kōwa* by Jimbo Nyoten (1942).

11. The senryū book and the first haiku book both appeared in 1949; *Will O' the Mill* on November 15, 1948; *A Shortened Version of a Week on the Concord and Merrimack Rivers* in April 1951; and *A Short History of English Literature* in 1953.

12. Moiliili is an area in Honolulu near the University of Hawaii at Manoa with a large population of Japanese origin. Aitken, who lived in the area, served from 1948 to 1952 as executive secretary of the Moiliili and Wahiawa (Hawaii) Community Associations.

13. The lines in Emerson's poem "Xenophanes": "As God and devil; bring them to the mind, / They dull its edge with their monotony."

14. "The Prisoner of Chillon."

15. The baby was Robert Aitken's son, Thomas L. Aitken.

16. Hisamatsu Sen'ichi (1894–1976) was professor and head of the department of Japanese literature at Tokyo University; Nambara Shigeru (1889–1974) was the president of the university from 1945 to 1951..

17. R. H. Blyth, "Ikkyū's Dōka," *The Young East* 2, no. 2 and 3, no. 90 (1952): n.p.

18. Futatabi: the camp in the hills north of Kobe where Blyth and Aitken spent the final year of their incarceration.

19. A compendium of eighteen classic Chinese Zen texts, published in 1929–30.

20. This must be Aitken's first wife, Mary, indicating the divorce was not yet final.

21. He was using a single-sheet, blue airmail letter.
22. The so-called Suzuki–Hu Shih controversy began with Suzuki's article "Zen: A Reply to Hu Shih," which was published in April 1953 in *Philosophy East and West*.
23. Perkins had opened a branch store in Kyoto. Like Perkins, Orientalia was a bookseller specializing in Asian books.
24. Dr. Ditmer Graeffe gave a lecture on July 1, 1954, at the International Christian University in Tokyo. The title was "Zen and the Spirit of Western Music."
25. After working at Perkins Oriental Bookstore in South Pasadena, Aitken was about to take on a teaching job at the Happy Valley School (Besant Hill School) in Ojai, California, where he worked 1955–57. Rosalind Edith Rajagopal (née Rosalind Edith Williams; 1903–1996) was a long-time director of the school, which she cofounded in 1946 with the Indian philosopher Jiddu Krishnamurti. Aitken was actually hired by Anne Hopkins, his future wife and the assistant headmistress serving in Mrs. Rajagopal's absence.
26. A reference to Mihoko Okamura (now Mihoko Bekku), who served as Suzuki's secretary until his death in 1965.
27. Richard DeMartino (1922–2013) was a student of Daisetz Suzuki, whom he met after the war while serving as a historical consultant to the defense panel of the International Military Tribunal for the Far East. He later taught at Temple University in Philadelphia.
28. Probably Arthur Christy's *The Orient and American Transcendentalism* (Columbia University Press), first published in 1932.
29. The philosopher Fung Yu-lan (1895–1990; also romanized as Feng), best known in the West for his two-volume *History of Chinese Philosophy*, devoted himself to reconciling traditional Chinese thought with methods and concerns of Western philosophy until the communist government took power; he then engaged in reinterpreting his earlier work from the Marxist point of view. The "supplement" may refer to Fung's *The Spirit of Chinese Philosophy*, published in 1947.
30. Reference to the proverb "The falling out of faithful friends is the renewing of love."
31. Yanagi Sōetsu, a student of Daisetz Suzuki, is best known as the founder of the Japanese Mingei movement. Blyth is referring to his collected works, *Yanagi Sōetsu Senshū*, published in ten volumes between 1954 and 1955. Volume 6 is titled *Cha to Bi* [Tea and Beauty].
32. *Haibun* (literally, "haiku writing") is a literary form consisting of a mixture of haiku and poetic prose.
33. The writer Kamo Chōmei (Kamo no Chōmei, 1153–1216), best known for the *Hōjō-ki* (A Ten-foot Square Hut, 1212).

34. *Hannya Shingyō,* or the *Heart Sutra.* Blyth wrote an essay on Hakuin's commentary and includes parts of his translation in *Twenty-five Zen Essays,* Volume 5 of the *Zen and Zen Classics* series.

35. Blyth is probably referring to Oda Tokunō's one-volume *Bukkyō Daijiten;* it had been republished in 1954.

36. *Mumon Oshō Goroku,* the collected sayings of the Zen priest Mumon Ekai (Wu-men Hui-hai), the author of the *Mumonkan.* Mumon's sayings appeared in separate book form in both China and Japan, although examples are quite rare. Blyth probably read about this work in Jimbo Nyoten's *Zengaku jiten (Zen Dictionary,* 1944) but was unable to find a copy.

37. A reference to Hisamatsu Shin'ichi's *Zen to Bijutsu,* which appeared in 1958 and was later translated into English as *Zen and Fine Arts,* Kodansha, 1971.

38. Kenneth Yasuda's *The Japanese Haiku* was first published in 1957.

39. The pamphlet is probably *Zen Training: A Personal Account,* Aitken's first published writing on Zen. It was self-published, copyright 1960, under the imprint of Old Island Books, the bookshop that he and Anne had opened in Honolulu.

40. Nancy Ross Wilson was an American novelist who compiled an anthology titled *The World of Zen* (1960), passages excerpted from books by Blyth, D. T. Suzuki, Alan Watts, and others.

41. Philip Kapleau, who was at this time studying Zen in Japan, later taught Zen in the United States; he is known for his book *The Three Pillars of Zen* (1966).

42. Blyth quotes loosely from Alfred Lord Tennyson's "Break, Break, Break."

43. Probably a dig at the American artist and poet Paul Reps, who in addition to haiku-inspired poetry and *haiga*-like ink drawings, had published a book titled *Zen Flesh, Zen Bones* in 1957.

44. Kobayashi Akiko, Blyth's secretary.

45. In *Taking the Path of Zen* (p. 122), Aitken describes Pauline Offner as a Zen student who began her practice in Honolulu and later went to Japan to study under Nakagawa Sōen. "Mr. S" presumably refers to Nyogen Senzaki.

46. Probably Charles Gooding, who later served as president of the Los Angeles Bosatsu-kai, founded by Nyogen Senzaki.

47. One of these rōshis is Nakagawa Sōen, 1907–84; the other is probably Yasutani Hakuun, 1875–1973, the teacher under whom Aitken was now studying.

48. Probably *A Buddhist Reader,* published in 1961 by the Young Buddhist Association of Honolulu.

49. Alan Watts (1915–73), a British-American best known as an interpreter and a popularizer of Asian philosophies.

50. The Anglo-Irish novelist Joyce Cary (1888–1957) was best known for *The Horse's Mouth,* published in 1944.

51. Yuanwu, *The Blue Cliff Records: The Hekigan-roku*, trans. and ed. R. D. M. Shaw (London: M. Joseph, 1961). Heinrich Dumoulin's (S.J.) *A History of Zen Buddhism* appeared in 1963.

52. Ummon is the Japanese reading of the Chinese Zen teacher Yun-men's name. Mumon is the Japanese reading of the teacher Wu-men, author of the *Mumonkan* (*Wu-men kuan*) collection of koans.

53. "Cheap-valleyish" is a literal reading of the name Yasutani, who was Aitken's Zen teacher at the time.

54. Gordon Wasson (1898–1986) was an ethnomycologist, whose book *Soma: Divine Mushroom of Immortality* (1968) was later to receive wide acclaim. His lecture was published as "Mushrooms and Japanese Culture," *Transactions of the Asiatic Society of Japan* 11 (December 1973): 5–25. The mushroom haiku Blyth translated (and commented on) for him was published as "Mushrooms in Japanese Verse" and appeared in the same issue (pp. 93–106).

55. Aitken had sent Blyth a new translation of the *Platform Sutra*, probably the one by Wing-tsit Chan, which appeared in 1963. When living in Korea, Blyth had bought the previous, and first, English translation of the sutra, *Sutra Spoken by the Sixth Patriarch, Wei Lang, on the High Seat of the Gem of Law*, trans. Wong Mou-lam (Shanghai: Yu Ching Press, 1930).

56. "The Zen Language" in *The Emerging World*, ed. J.N.S.V. Committee (New York: Asia Publishing House, 1964) 203–19.

57. Baso (Chin. Ma-tsu); the koan is found in the *Blue Cliff Record*, Case 73.

58. During Blyth's final illness, when his doctors suggested a change of locale might help, Aitken had made preliminary plans for him to move to Hawaii.

LETTERS TO DAISETZ SUZUKI

1. Blyth had published a translation of Ikkyū's *dōka* (literally "poems of the Way"). The page number refers to *Zen Essays*, the seventh book in the *Zen and Zen Classics* series.

2. Sengai Gibon (1750–1837), a Zen priest known for humorous Zen paintings and inscriptions. Dr. Suzuki introduced him to the West and would later write a book on him, *Sengai, The Zen Master* (London: Faber, 1971).

3. *Agyo* is a Zen technical term for the comments a person gives to a koan or Zen saying. The *Hekiganroku* contains many of these comments.

4. Engo (Chin., Yuan-wu) wrote the commentaries in the *Hekiganroku*.

5. Suzuki's essay "The Zen Language" appeared in a volume titled *The Emerging World* (New York: Asian Publishing House, 1964), 203–19.

6. Blyth's translation of this text, with a preface by Dr. Suzuki, appeared in 1966, after his death.

7. A medal awarded by the Japanese government.

8. Inoue Noboru, who I believe was a student of Blyth's at Gakushūin, assisted him during his final years, especially with the publishing of the final volumes of the *Zen and Zen Classics* series.
9. Mihoko Okamura, Daisetz Suzuki's secretary.

LETTER TO ALAN WATTS

1. *Mayoi:* "illusion," as opposed to enlightenment.

R. L. STEVENSON'S *WILL O' THE MILL*

1. Hermann Hesse, *Siddhartha.*
2. Alan Watts, *The Meaning of Happiness* (first published in 1940).

A SHORTENED VERSION OF *A WEEK ON THE CONCORD AND MERRIMACK RIVERS*

1. In a letter to Mr. Harrison Blake (May 1848) he wrote, "You will perceive that I am as often talking to myself, perhaps, as speaking to you."

R. L. STEVENSON: *FABLES*

1. The date is mistaken; Jones's translation was completed and published in 1789.

A WANDERER IN JAPAN

1. Blunden wrote: "Is it Japan, is it Ireland? Is it sometime in the past years, or in those which perhaps are to come? Am I far from the world's eye in Flanders, or away in the cherry-avenues of some Japanese countryside?"

THE POSITION OF HAIKU AND SENRYŪ IN WORLD LITERATURE

1. Apparently a rephrasing of Blake's "Everything to be imagined is an image of truth."

BUDDHISM AND HAIKU

1. The Japanese cuckoo.

BUDDHISM IN SENRYŪ

1. *Kyōun-shū* is a collection of Ikkyū's Chinese poetry; many *dōka*, waka with a Buddhist flavor, are attributed to him as well.

THE WAY OF SENRYŪ

1. Fujisawa Chikao (1893–1962) taught Japanese political thought and philosophy in Tokyo in both the pre- and postwar periods. English translations of two of his books appeared in the late 1950s. The word "Sumeracracy," which he coined, describes a dialectical synthesis of democracy and autocracy; it has been called an existentialist interpretation of Shinto.

BUDDHISM AND HUMOUR

1. *Monto* are followers of the Shin sect; *Hokke*, followers of the Nichiren sect.

WHAT IS POETRY?

1. *Furu ike ya* ("The old pond"), the first part of Bashō's most famous haiku, followed by *kawazu tobikomu mizu no oto* ("A frog jumps in—The sound of the water").

THE ZENRINKUSHŪ

1. *Engaku (Perfect Enlightenment) Sutra, Brahmajala (Brahma's Net) Sutra. Tōshisen* and *Sōshisen* are Japanese collections of T'ang and Sung dynasty poetry; the *Santai-shi (San-t'ai shih)* is a Chinese collection of Chinese poetry avidly studied by Japanese Zen priests. The *Chen-tao ke* (Jap. *Shōdō-ka*) and *Hsinhsin ming* (Jap. *Shinjin-mei*) are verses by T'ang dynasty Zen monks.
2. "Without faith it is impossible to please God," Hebrews 11:6.

MUSHROOMS AND HUMOUR

1. Allusions to Keats's ode "To Autumn"; references appear in the second stanza to "a half-reap'd furrow," "the winnowing wind," "a gleaner," and "a cyder-press."
2. The *iwatake*, despite its name, is an edible lichen gathered at considerable risk on the face of cliffs and does not belong to the fungal world except by popular usage in the past and here by poetic license.
3. *Ikuchi* or *iguchi* is the general name of a group of species of small mushrooms.
4. *Nezumidake* take their name from their resemblance to the finely articulated extremities of the rat's feet.

BIBLIOGRAPHY

WORKS ABOUT R. H. BLYTH CITED IN THE INTRODUCTION

Aitken, Robert. "Remembering Blyth Sensei," in *Original Dwelling Place: Zen Buddhist Essays*. Washington, DC: Counterpoint Press, 1996.

Blyth, R. H. *The Genius of Haiku: Readings from R. H. Blyth*. Tokyo: Hokuseido Press, 1995.

Franck, Frederick. *Zen and Zen Classics: Selections from R. H. Blyth*. New York: Vintage Books, 1978.

Kuniyoshi Ueda. *Buraisu Sensei, Arigatou*. Tokyo: Sango-kan, 2010.

Oka Kuniomi. "A Biography of Reginald Horace Blyth—Through his Books." *Kurume University Journal* (Vol. 20, March 1972).

Pinnington, Adrian. "R. H. Blyth, 1898–1964," in *Britain and Japan: Biographical Portraits*, edited by Ian Nish, vol. 7. Folkestone, UK: Japan Library, 1994.

Shinki Masanosuke, ed. *Kaisō no Buraisu* [Blyth Remembered]. Tokyo: Kaisō no Buraisu Kankōkai Jimushō, 1984.

Suzuki Daisetz. *Suzuki Daisetz Zenshū (The Complete Works of Suzuki Daisetz Zenshū)*. 40 vols. Tokyo: Iwanami shoten, 1999–2003.

Woodward, William P. *The Allied Occupation of Japan, 1945–1952*. Leiden, Netherlands: E. J. Brill, 1972.

Yoshimura Ikuyo. *R. H. Buraisu no Shōgai*. Tokyo: Dōhō-sha Shuppan, 1996.

WORKS BY R. H. BLYTH

Blyth, R. H. *Buddhist Sermons on Christian Texts*. Tokyo: Kokudosha, 1952.

———. *Edo Satirical Verse Anthologies*. Tokyo: Hokuseido Press, 1961.

———. *Haiku*. 4 vols. Tokyo: Hokuseido Press, 1949–52. (Volumes were 1. *Eastern Culture* [1949]; 2. *Spring* [1950]; 3. *Summer–Autumn* [1952]; and 4. *Autumn–Winter* [1952].)

———. *A History of Haiku*. 2 vols. Tokyo: Hokuseido Press, 1963–4. (Volumes were 1. *From the Beginnings Up to Issa* [1963] and 2. *From Issa Up to the Present* [1964].)

———. *How to Read English Poetry*. Tokyo: Hokuseido Press, 1958.

———. *Humour in English Literature: A Chronological Anthology*. Tokyo: Hokuseido Press, 1959.

———. *Japanese Humour.* Tokyo: Japan Travel Bureau, 1957.

———. *Japanese Life and Character in Senryū.* Tokyo: Hokuseido Press, 1960.

———. *Oriental Humour.* Tokyo: Hokuseido Press, 1959.

———. *Senryū: Japanese Satirical Verses.* Tokyo: Hokuseido Press, 1949.

———. *Thoughts on Culture—Or, How to Be a Human Being.* Tokyo: Eibunsha, 1950.

———. *Zen and Zen Classics.* 5 vols. Tokyo: Hokuseido Press, 1960–70. (Out of a planned set of eight volumes, five were published: 1. *General Introduction, from the Upanishads to Huineng* [1960]; 2. *History of Zen (Seigen Branch)* [1964]; 3. *History of Zen cont'd (Nangaku Branch)* [1970, posthumous]; 4. *Mumonkan* [1966, posthumous]; and 5. *Twenty-Four Essays* [first published as vol. 7 in 1962; republished as vol. 5 in 1966].)

———. *Zen in English Literature and Oriental Classics.* Tokyo: Hokuseido Press, 1942. Reprint, New York: Dutton, 1960.

Blyth, R. H., and Yoshida Kishi. *Seikai no fūshishi senryū* [Senryū, Satirical Verses for the Whole World]. Tokyo: Nihon Shuppan-kyōdō, 1950.

Lee Eun and R. H. Blyth. *A First Book of Korean.* Tokyo: Hokuseido Press, 1950. Second revised edition, Tokyo: Hokuseido Press, 1962.

STUDENT TEXTBOOKS

Blyth, R. H. *An Anthology of English Poetry.* Tokyo: Nan'un-do, 1952.

———. *An Anthology of Nineteenth Century Prose.* Tokyo: Hokuseido Press, 1950.

———. *A Chronological Anthology of Nature in English Literature.* Tokyo: Kairyudo, 1949.

———. *A Chronological Anthology of Religion in English Literature.* Tokyo: Bunkyo Shoin, 1951.

———. *Dorothy Wordsworth's Journals.* Tokyo: Hokuseido Press, 1952.

———. *Easy Poems, Book 1 and 2.* Tokyo: Hokuseido Press, 1959.

———. *English Through Questions and Answers.* Tokyo: Hokuseido Press, 1951.

———. *More English Through Questions and Answers.* Tokyo: Hokuseido Press, 1960.

———. *The New Vista English Readers, Senior I.* Tokyo: Sanseido, 1948.

———. *An Outline of English Literature.* Tokyo: Ginryu Shobo, 1949.

———. *The Poems of Emerson: A Selection.* Tokyo: Kenkyusha, 1949.

———. *R. L. Stevenson, Fables.* Tokyo: Nan'un-do, 1953.

———. *R. L. Stevenson: Will O' the Mill.* Tokyo: Hokuseido Press, 1948.

———. *Selections from Thoreau's Journals.* Tokyo: Daigakusyorin, 1949.

———. *A Short History of English Literature.* Tokyo: Nan'un-do, 1953.

———. *A Shortened Version of a Week on the Concord and Merrimack Rivers by Henry David Thoreau.* Tokyo: Hokuseido Press, 1951.

———. *A Survey of English Literature, from the Beginnings to Modern Times.* Tokyo: Hokuseido Press, 1957.

———. *William Hazlitt: An Anthology*. Tokyo: Kenkyusha, 1949.

Not included in this list are essays and translations that appeared in periodicals such as *Young East, Today's Japan* (later *Orient West*), and articles and interviews in Japanese newspapers (in Japanese), a number of which are found in this book.